Andrew Judge is an author and screenwriter from Liverpool who studied Business Management and Entrepreneurship at Liverpool John Moores University whose interest in data and finance has led him to research into football finance and the American Football scouting ecosystem. *The Boot Room* is his debut book lifting the curtain into footballs hidden boardrooms, exploring how football clubs operate within the transfer market. Andrew has written a number of screenplays and currently balances his passion of writing whilst being a civil servant.

To my family, friends and all those people who have supported me in this venture, thank you.

Andrew Judge

The Boot Room

AUSTIN MACAULEY PUBLISHERS
LONDON • CAMBRIDGE • NEW YORK • SHARJAH

Copyright © Andrew Judge 2024

The right of Andrew Judge to be identified as author of this work has been asserted by the author in accordance with sections 77 and 78 of the Copyright, Designs and Patents Act 1988.

All rights reserved. No part of this publication may be reproduced, stored in a retrieval system, or transmitted in any form or by any means, electronic, mechanical, photocopying, recording, or otherwise, without the prior permission of the publishers.

Any person who commits any unauthorised act in relation to this publication may be liable to criminal prosecution and civil claims for damages.

The story, the experiences, and the words are the author's alone.

A CIP catalogue record for this title is available from the British Library.

ISBN 9781035841059 (Paperback)
ISBN 9781035841066 (Hardback)
ISBN 9781035841073 (ePub e-book)

www.austinmacauley.co.uk

First Published 2024
Austin Macauley Publishers Ltd®
1 Canada Square
Canary Wharf
London
E14 5AA

Table of Contents

Characterisation of the Transfer Window	10
Chapter 1: Transfer Merry-Go-Round	21
Chapter 2: The Anatomy of a Football Transfer	48
Chapter 3: From Grassroots to Spreadsheets	74
Chapter 4: Moneyball VS Goliath	111
Chapter 5: Moneyball and Football's Broken Youth System	130
Chapter 6: 'The Architects' Directors of Football	143
Chapter 7: The Opening Gambit: Transfer Deadline Day	160
Chapter 8: "I've Got a Bad Feeling About This"	174
Chapter 9: Her Game Too A New Dawn in Women's Football	185
Chapter 10: Circumnavigating a Transfer Window	205
Chapter 11: Estate Agents 'Licensed to Thrill'	220
Chapter 12: Is Financial Fair Play Fair?	246
Chapter 13: Managing an Ever-Changing Situation	293
Chapter 14: Transfer Story and Quotes	315
Chapter 15: Fergie Time	322

Lifting the steel curtain on the dynamic and secret world of football transfers, evaluating the impact on football finance and the people working in football.

*Disclaimer: This book was written during the January transfer window 2023. All examples, Transfers and scouting analysis were up to date from this moment.

Characterisation of the Transfer Window

Every football fan can relate to the feeling. Spring showers fading into summer, the smell of fresh cut grass filling the air, in Europe, football at club level stops between May and August. The new season brings expectations for fans. For those whose teams have been successful, comes the hope that new levels of transfer recruitment can lead their teams up the football pyramid and possibly European football. On the opposite side of the spectrum, a poor season ending can be a relief, it gives the club months to prepare for a new campaign and fresh players to make a dreadful season disappear into long distant memories.

For clubs promoted to the leagues above, fans can dream of new ventures to historic grounds, relegated teams face the hardship of losing their star players and wondering how long, or even if their club may return to the big time. In the middle of all this is a ticking clock, silently ebbing away to transfer deadline day, the beating heart of a transfer window.

Football transfer windows can unite supporters from all backgrounds and be a blessing, bringing inclusivity to a sport that is seen as an escape for those in hardship. But with the recent growth of social media, fake transfer rumours created for commercial gains online, it is slowly growing into a cancer, providing ways for keyboard warriors to post, and spreading online hate on the deepest corners of the internet slowly manifesting its ways into the football grounds onto the terraces.

On a sporting occasion so big, workers take annual leave to witness the final 24 hours unfold on live TV. Thousands of words will be written, hundreds of pages swiped left or right on mobile devices to keep fans up to date, all holding onto the hope and desire for their club to come out of the window in better shape than they went in.

This book will peer under the steel curtain of the transfer window to bring a new perspective into the obsession which takes over work canteens, fills social media with thousands of posts, acknowledged as a cause for mental health illnesses, by seeking out and interviewing stakeholders from all corners of the footballing world. But first, starting with a look of where it all began.

The current guise of the transfer window was born out of a byproduct of the Bosman ruling, causing a seismic shock to the football world and removed the power which had been held by the football clubs regarding a player's contract, their right to seek out another club on the expiration of their current contract. Thus, giving the player a portion of control over their career and contracts. The tables turned in the mid-nineties when little known footballer, Jean-Marc Bosman, of RFC de Liege, took legal action against the Royal Belgium Football Association, it was a ruling that unequivocally changed the landscape of British and European football transfers forever.

After a five-year legal battle, the ruling decided that in December 1995, Bosman should have been allowed to move clubs on the expiration of his contract. Bosman had wanted to "transfer" across the French border to Dunkerque, but RFC Liege refused to release him. His legal team believed Bosman was no longer under legal contracted terms (his contract expired in 1995), Liege in their refusal to "release" him were in violation of EU freedom of movement legislation. Pushing the case all the way to the European Court of Justice who ruled in Bosman's favour.

This ruling meant players whose contracts had expired with their current team could move to any club they wanted. Power shifted to the player who could run down their contracts and leave their current club for no remuneration (transfer fee).

As a result, the transfer window became a way for the Football Associations and their respective clubs to protect their assets with transfer fees. In football, there was a fear of the growing power of players, for Associations. There was a desire to give the owners and directors their power back in their struggle over player movements.

Yet, talk of transfer windows in British football were not revelatory and had been on the table for some time. With the formation of the Premier League in 1992 and millions of pounds of television money pumping into the accounts of teams, big clubs had the urge to buy their way out of trouble after poor starts to the season.

Football clubs had been able to purchase players as late as the third Thursday in March, in a bid to buy their way to success. Those clubs with less spending power and forward-thinking managers argued reducing the trading period would create a level playing field. By the end of the nineties, UEFA were drawing up plans to standardise and limit transfer interactions across European football with the goal of creating parity across the leagues in terms of competitiveness. This would be in the form of a six-week window that would start in December and finish at the end of January. The Premier League joined by the Bundesliga were both vocal in their objections against the proposals.

Both these leagues wanted the best players to be always on the most marketable teams to help promote their respective products to the television audiences. But the ripples from the fallout of Jean-Marc Bosman's case was still being discussed by European lawyers. As players signed contracts with professional football teams, there was no writing in their contracts stipulating players couldn't have movement of jobs. The argument being that every worker in the European Union had the freedom to choose where and whom to work for.

In essence, a worker at McDonalds couldn't be stopped working for KFC if they offered more money. Hence, why workers can and do resign from their current posts. Football clubs argued the players signed contracts to a terminal point (end of contract) and the length of contract left should be their transfer value if a player wished to move.

With EU lawyers and players agents quickly studying the Treaty of Rome, FIFA drew up a compromise, plans for a biannual transfer window across the world of football. Cries of discontent from English clubs on the ideas were drowned out from the universal agreement across the continents.

The first season of the new biannual transfer window was set for the 2002/03 season, writers and clubs were both intrigued and scared for what the changes meant for their businesses. For clubs built on credit bloated cash flows, they needed transfers to sustain their business. For newspapers and magazines, they needed transfer stories to sell papers to sustain their circulation levels facing a long-term threat from the growing internet which I will discuss the impact later.

With any major change in business, there will always be people for and against a proposal. For every detractor, there are people willing to accept the change, evaluate it and turn it into a force for good. The biannual window brought a model shift in spending. Allowed managers more time to coach players, some argued that the level of football and sports science increased the skill level and watchability of football.

Detractors will cite the economic foundation of supply and demand. The supply of Premier League talent level of footballers is finite, meaning the number of Premier League talented players is small, but the demand, partly aided by the constant flow of television money dictates the demand curve is inelastic and has therefore inflated transfer fees.

A footballer can command such a price because economists theorise footballers' (goods) are inelastic, defining inelastic as a talented footballer with, pardon the pun, substitutes to their talents. Economists reading this argue that individual sports people are perfectly inelastic because there is only one Lionel Messi. (No substitutes) Which would justify why they have values far ahead of other players in their respective positions.

There is some irony to these equations, if we take Manchester United's new signing Anthony, signed on deadline day in the summer of 2022, for a princely sum for £86m on a rumoured £150,000 a week.

Breaking this down to a societal level, people are willing to pay more for me to teach a lecture on footballs transfer window or screenwriting, than they are to watch Anthony do his job at Old Trafford. Sadly, on the other scale, Anthony is likely to earn my entire life earnings in eight weeks. Here is why. Assume Old Trafford is sold out for every Premier League home game, 73,310 x 19 home games = 1,392,890 will see Anthony play live this season. This does not consider Champions League or Domestic cup competitions. Nor the millions of people watching their games around the world. That is the value of £9.28 per fan. 1,392,890 fans / £150,000 wage a week = £9.28 a game.

Assume I give a lecture to around 500 students over the next year (season) this would, on the current average wage per year in the UK (£38,131 UK ONS) = £76.26. That is eight times as much as Anthony.

Whilst the above is a tongue in cheek economic example by me, it sets up the reason footballers are paid their significant wages. It is the economic supply vs. demand as theorised by economists.

As an author, screenwriter and lecturer, an economist would argue that I am highly elastic, nicer way of saying easily replaceable. Premier League footballers are not easily replaced; therefore, footballers would be represented by a much steeper supply curve, despite there being more demand for authors (labour) exceeds that of Premier League footballers, the steepness of the supply curve (inelastic) would provide much sharper increases in wage if the demand curve is shifted. Hence, with more money in the game due to television rights deals, pushes the increase of the demand for players, equates to much higher wages. This is the reason Premier League footballers receive their huge salaries; their talents push them to the top and simple economic functions allow them to demand it on the open market where there is demand for them.

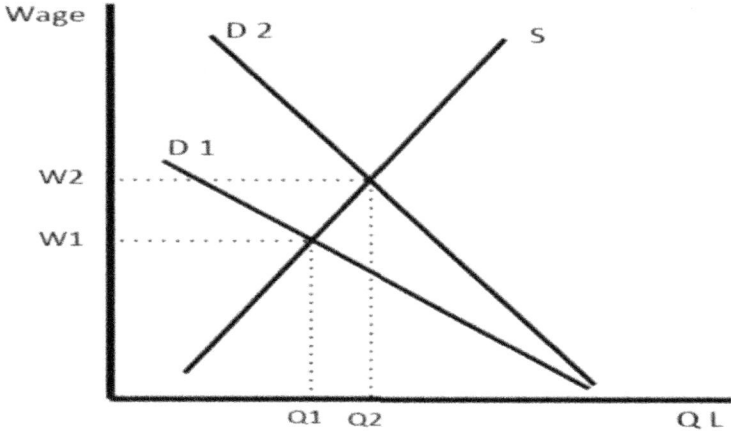

If we look at the above basic supply and demand curve, it illustrates how an increase in television money would expectedly cause Demand-Push inflation. The Demand curve is Pushed up to D2 from D1. Where the inelastic supply line S (Premier League footballer). Where the lines interject, is the wage increases which will come with new contract renewals and transfer fees paid after a bigger influx of cash into the football clubs. W1 represents the current wage of the footballer. W2 is the inflationary increase where the supply line interjects with the new Demand curve. This graph can also mirror the effect in the increase in transfer fees increasing in football as more revenue comes into football if you swap the axis from wages to transfer fee.

Some managers who were detractors to the transfer window starting up in 2002, spotted the economic hole in the plan for competitiveness. By having two windows with definitive end dates, essentially created this Hollywood ticking time bomb. There was a limited supply of players, excess demand of money and time was finite. The demand for players in these windows caused a Demand-Push inflation across the industry.

Fast forward to January 2023, the five-sub rule has seen the UK media's "big 6" accused of hoarding talent from teams below them and across Europe in the means to stop any competitive balance.

In the past, teams had been able to spend whenever and whatever they wanted. Keeping a market equilibrium of supply and demand. Now, all teams would be after the same player, thus creating a player market with the Demand (of players) Pushing (Inflating) the price. The windows demanded clubs rethink and created new roles within clubs whose remit would solely be on transfers, sporting directors, and Directors of Football, for managers, they could now focus on coaching their respective players.

The transfer window became a saleable commodity, with thousands invested in television and online to attract viewers in during the feverish months where the windows occurred. As the Hollywood saying goes. "Drama sells" and with transfer spending reaching levels where it overtakes countries Gross Domestic Product (GDP), the measure of the value added created through the production of goods and services in a country during a period, the transfer window became front- and back-page news.

In 2019, Premier League spending in the United Kingdom alone rose to historic levels of £1.4 billion pounds. This figure is taken from the summer transfer window which starts in June and ends around August. (In some cases, due to the football calendar, the window can creep into September.) For a comparison in 2019 the entire GDP of Kenya was $955m.

For even more context on the current level of spending in football, in the Covid-19 affected summer transfer window where football's financial credit bubble "burst" the spending only dropped to £1.31bn, in the Premier League based on 103 permanent signings for disclosed fees. This further dropped in the summer of 2021 to £1.04bn with clubs beginning to feel the pinch of the Covid-19 reduction in global finance.

Football clubs and managers such as Pep Guardiola have been criticised for their vast spending, their continued success at football clubs is used to defend their right to buy players. Managers cite football clubs are businesses and restricting a business from trading is in fact another violation of the Treaty of Rome, but also violates the Competition Act in the UK. One manager argued, if a player suffers an injury which puts him or her out for the year and cannot be replaced, the club essentially is punished by the constraints of the transfer window.

If a BP oil tanker broke down on the way to a petrol station, BP can freely go out and buy a new one immediately, allowing them to keep their supply flowing and their business competitive. Imagine stopping them from buying a new one and affecting their performance until a "transfer window" opened in January. Whilst the analogy to some may appear silly, you can understand the argument that all businesses registered with tax agencies should be treated equally based on EU and British law.

By having these restrictions, it is argued BP would be less competitive. For a football team in the Premier League, Everton lost star striker Dominic Calvert-Lewin in the first week of September 2021 a few days after the summer window shut. They could not buy a replacement until January. Everton, fourth in the league at the time, went onto win one game in thirteen and dropped all the way to 15th place. Whilst this can be debated either way, it is intrinsic discussion points like these that make the transfer window so watchable, and why we want to understand the behind-the-scenes access to transfer dealings. Football transfers are cyclical and find an interesting way to repeat themselves.

February 9th, 1979, the day English football's transfers became headline news. Before the days of social media or hashtags, the transfer fee which accompanied this move would certainly have "broken the internet". Trevor Francis was entrenched with Birmingham City, a club sliding towards relegation. League Champions Nottingham Forest seemed the perfect step up for the England International. The crossing of the Midland's divide wasn't the headline grabbing news. It was the transfer fee.

Before Trevor's move up the M1 towards Nottingham, only one transfer had previously crossed the threshold of half a million pounds when David Mills was sold from Middlesbrough to West Bromwich Albion a few months before. The jump to Trevor's Francis's million-pound move was even more outrageous at the time in football. Trevor was 24 years old, not even in his prime and Birmingham were adamant they would only sell for one million pounds. One pioneer of football was ready for such headlines, Nigel Clough, who had no problem stumping up the cash.

In today's world, this sort of transfer would be welcomed by the media, especially newspapers whose print product is in the final stages of its life cycle. They would have printed multiple editions, online articles, social media posts. But in 1979, the media were aghast by the transfer fee. Countless scathing headlines ridiculing the transfer, even making the first headline on evening news.

Francis made his Birmingham debut aged 16 and went on to score 119 goals in 280 league appearances without ever vying for a significant trophy. 'I want to be part of a successful team and unless I see signs that we are going somewhere I won't stay.' Having previously submitted six unsuccessful transfer requests, he had finally gotten his wish and was on the move.

To football followers today, the fee may seem nominal compared to some of the astronomical transfers submitted in today's game. Nigel Clough knew how to downplay the fee and possibly for any nerves Francis may have had by spinning the media quotes that the fee was a pound shorter than a million. Taxes and VAT ensured the fee was most definitely north of a million.

Back then, there were no agents, no meddling from club officials or agents. Transfers were made over the phone or face to face. Nigel Tassel explains in his book *Boot Sale* that Clough, Francis and Peter Taylor of Birmingham locked themselves away for four hours and thrashed out a deal. Today, deals and contracts can take days and even months of haggling before a deal is signed.

You would think the most expensive signing in football would be a major press event, red carpet, shirts and tie affair. But in a typical Brian Clough way, it was a downplayed low key affair. Clough himself turned up in a red leather jacket carrying a squash racket. Today, footballers normally bring either their family or as Harry Redknapp once said, 'an entourage which you can't fit in my office.' The club officials would be in suits and pose for the obligatory contract photo for the social media team.

Clough was impatient to get to the squash courts at Trent Bridge Cricket club and was eager to get on with the press conference with the eager clamouring journalists. Contrast to a suited Trevor Francis, accompanied by his wife Helen, stepping out from his Jaguar. Treated like film stars by the baying paparazzi. Clough was reluctant to give preferential treatment to Francis at Nottingham Forest. Days later, he was parachuted into a Midlands Youth game hosted in a local park. In Europe, ineligible to play, Clough had Francis on tea making duty during the Quarter Finals of the European Cup against Grasshoppers of Switzerland.

Tough acting managers today, with desires to put the club before players would have a mutiny on their hands if players were treated this way. Coming full circle to the summer of 2021, fresh off England's defeat in the Covid-19 2020 European Championship final in London, Jack Grealish was soon on the move as the first English player to be transferred for one hundred million pounds.

Having not long turned 25, one year older than Trevor Francis, Manchester City were champions of England, as where Nottingham Forest, Aston Villa had just managed to starve of relegation in the Covid-19 affected 2020 season thanks to the failure of "Hawk-eye", the goal line technology which failed to alert referee Michael Oliver that the ball had crossed the line. It left Sheffield United Manager Chris Wilder fuming 'I think the goalkeeper was in the Holte End when he caught it' in reference to the Aston Villa stadium. Orjan Nyland needed to unpick himself from the net and VAR deemed it couldn't get involved because no on-field decision had been made. Had Villa been relegated, Grealish's fee would have been severely reduced by their need to sell and shed high wages due to the loss of the Premier League's TV money from Aston Villa's income.

Aston Villa's victory meant they stayed in the Premier League at the expense of Bournemouth, but with the club at the time fighting relegation it had a scarily similar outline to the Trevor Francis transfer thirty years earlier. At his unveiling, Grealish arrived in an expensive sports car, Pep Guardiola in his laid-back attire, akin to Nigel Clough in 1979, Pep was dumbfounded by how much the British press were making of the record-breaking British transfer fee of £100 million pounds.

When asked how Grealish may cope with the pressures of the erroneous price tag. Pep shrugged, 'He's 25.' Pep, like Clough was a manager who knew how to take the pressures of players, turned a major event into a nonentity for the player. With the signing of Jack Grealish, BT Sport reported this transfer pushed Pep's spending at Manchester City to £918 million pounds. To those who critique his spending, Pep could point to the dynasty he built at the Manchester club, which includes a new academy, improvements to the city of Manchester and public engagements. Then there are the trophies, 4 x Premier League's, 1 FA Cup, 4 x EFL League Cup and 2 x Charity Shields. (As of January 2023)

How footballers are introduced in press conferences is not the only way the transfer window has changed in modern life. The way we view, receive and collect transfer information has changed technology as we know it. As the dawn of the Premier League was hustled in 1992, fans would get their taste of transfer gossip via newspapers, radio and teletext.

Social media highlights how quickly the world is evolving, it is obvious there is a need to explain teletext to potential younger readers. Teletext, or broadcast teletext, was a method for displaying text and rudimentary graphics on suitably equipped television sets and in the early 90s, was a favoured way for fans to get information on transfers. Those who use the free service will recall the stress of reading through the information before it ticked over onto the next page and missing out on the news and having to wait for it to come around again.

Sometimes this could take ten pages and up to fifteen minutes to cycle around. Missing out on the page of your team could be deeply frustrating for viewers. Many hours were spent waiting for the news to update. 'Player X is linked to Team Y' would change to 'Player X is having a medical at Team Y.' Now the news is played out via social media posts.

Before smartphones and social media, the days of spending summer holidays abroad searching out the local shop which sold British newspapers in the hope of a snippet of news from your team's transfer dealings. Fans can now get their transfer fix whilst sunbathing by the pool, sipping another beer as social media has overtaken print media as the quickest and best source of transfer information and in itself become a million-dollar business, with websites being set up to rake in clicks and likes in return for advertiser's cash.

Furthermore, with the growth in social media the way clubs use the transfer window to reach their global fanbases in the way they announce players in unique ways. Whilst players still hold press conferences to announce their arrival, clubs have tended to use short clips or graphics interchange format (GIFS) to show off their new players. Some have ranged from the funny; Burnley announcing the signing of Peter Crouch by having a toy robot walk around their training complex in reference to the striker's iconic goal celebration.

The more obscure announcement came from Villarreal using YouTube and Twitter with the help of a magician, some smoke and an empty box, conjuring up their new signing once the smoke cleared, Santi Cazorla. Burnley remain the best at promoting their new signings and for fans reading this, their account is well worth a view to see how the Lancashire club reveal their new players. Slightly more exciting than the old Ceefax.

Reveal videos have become more like mini movie trailers, Everton used a video which took fans virtually from their Finch Farm training ground in Halewood, Liverpool, to John Lennon Airport, aboard a plane in the air, landing in Spain, where a car is waiting for the camera to take the viewer to a hotel where their new signing Sandro Ramirez was waiting, in their new home kit. Quite the contrast from the twenty or so words in a newspaper from the early 2000s.

So here is to the stories within this book, that bring hope, optimism, and if your favourite player is being sold, then a few tears, this is a look behind the curtain of the ongoing mechanisms of the football transfer window to reveal hoe football transfers actually happen in football, what they mean to the clubs and the people who work in football, and what does all that finance lingo mean to fans?

Chapter 1
Transfer Merry-Go-Round

'The media writes the first version of history. How do you make sure it writes the correct version?'

Everybody wants to be the first to achieve something. How it helps build their legacy and footing in society. We all remember Neil Armstrong being the first man on the moon. But who was the first man on the second NASA mission? Charles Conrad was the third man on the moon, but his achievement seems lost to the second page of internet searches, no quiz questions about him, no national curriculum based on being one of the most successful astronauts in NASA's history. Now, like the Messi and Ronaldo debates, their followers would be able to discuss their careers and success online, in blogs, YouTube channels and podcasts.

Manchester United won the first Premier League, but how many people know Blackburn Rovers were the third Premier League winners in 1994. William Ralph "Dixie" Dean once scored sixty league goals in a season for Everton in 1927, a record yet to be broken. For younger fans who have grown up with video games, they would struggle to answer these questions. The transfer window is no longer alone in being read on the back pages of tabloid newspapers.

The growth in the media channels has allowed anyone with access to create and share transfer rumours which begs the question, how do you separate fact from fiction from online sources and today's news channels when journalists are reporting stories from unsolicited accounts?

Newspapers need stories to sell their papers and with newspaper circulations on the decline, they face challenges from their editors to meet their sales quotas. Media companies face the dilemma of their business's products being in decline and taken over by products they seem reluctant to replace. With printed news in decline, most journalists have gone onto social media to combat the issue of breaking the story first.

Back in the day, newspapers writing headline news would face the anxious wait to see if another newspaper would reveal the story first, or in an evening edition. In transfer news, most journalists would wait until the weekend edition to reveal their transfer scoop, but now, anyone can break the news in an instance on social media, crippling journalist's flexibility in getting the story out first, but also checking the validity of the "Source".

Journalists and fake In The Knows accounts (ITK) have more followers than newspaper circulations, David Ornstein, a well-respected transfer journalist, has over 1.7 million followers vs. Daily Mail, 850,000 print circulation. The business model of social media creates the need for content, posts, and stories to generate revenue for the account owners, so their accounts maintain top spots in online algorithms. It is now great business to create stories for clicks and anyone with access is now a "source" and more and more fake transfer news drips into reality as these ITK create fake rumours to make themselves money in a story for clicks cycle which the unknowing public buy into.

If a story is covered by "sources" it is difficult to dispute. Who is the source? What counts as one? Like all forms of industry, people have found a way to monetise the industry, and by using the word source, it protects their fake tweet as it cannot be exposed for its reliability, making the user money and to fans, believing their club is after a player when they are not.

Perhaps one of the most famous cases of ITK's spreading false information is that of Sean Cummins, a Liverpool fan who created an online alias of Duncan Jenkins. Launched on a popular Liverpool FC fan forum as a bit of fun to cope with the downtime of being a new father in-between feeding his child. By setting us this alias as a want to be journalist, it was different from other ITK's who pretend from the start to be an agent or know about stories. Duncan's backstory gave him a little credibility whilst also stopping people from trying to research him, because his origin story was out there in the message boards.

First, by commenting on matches and providing analysis his following grew. Sean used a stock image of a real person from Google, so people assumed the account was a real person. He also spotted someone else was posting the real Liverpool team hours before kick-off but was being ignored. Sean started researching this person. Realising the reliability of the source, "Duncan" began to copy the team news to further enhance his growing online profile.

As the January window approached, it became apparent the news was coming from a friend of a Liverpool player. As Brendan Rodgers took over from Liverpool legend Kenny Dalglish, Sean remembered seeing that Liverpool had scouted Joe Allan of Swansea a couple of months ago, now seeing Rodgers, the former Swansea boss, take over the reins at Liverpool, Sean knew managers normally dip into their former club's talent pool for players and remembered seeing the scouting news in the mainstream media.

The information was likely to be dependable because the media will have seen Liverpool's scouts and recruitment team at Swansea games and looked at the weakness in Liverpool's current team. Running with this thread, Duncan posted that Liverpool were interested in signing Allan from Swansea. When Allan joined Liverpool for £17m, Duncan's following online grew and Sean knew he had something going.

He saw another article which interviewed Rodgers and in it he gave a good scouting report of Fabio Borini, a player Rodgers had worked with at Chelsea and Swansea.

Another educated guess that pulled through when Rodgers signed him for £12m to give Liverpool's attack some versatility. Unbeknown to Sean, his posts had alerted other clubs to Borini's imminent move and caused them to bid for his services. This meant Liverpool were forced to spend £300,000 more than they wanted. It also meant the club became aware of the "journalist Duncan Jenkins" who was posting their transfer targets across the web before they had the deal done.

Sean also posted that Liverpool were interested in Gylfi Sigurdsson in the summer; this was also picked up by the local paper the Liverpool Echo. Whilst the transfer wasn't completed, for Liverpool fans, Duncan Jenkins was a journalist who was reliable with Liverpool transfer news and had correctly predicted Brendan Rodgers as their new manager and that Andre Villas-Boas was also in the running for the job.

Liverpool were keen to engage with their fans. They were accused of not being during Roy Hodgson's reign as manager, appointing Jen Chang to be the clubs Corporate Relations and Communications Director. He began to contact club's supporter groups, blogs, and journalists like Duncan Jenkins, asking for contact details, laying down his honey trap to out the mole he thought worked within Liverpool.

Sean sent one over, thinking he may be asked to come into a press conference and get more access for his social media page. During the Euro's, Sean's alias was asked to join Goal as a correspondent and documented in Alan Geron's book *The Transfer Market* he was often asked to be on Liverpool's foreign fan channels because they clamoured for information on transfers for the Merseyside club. Interestingly, Sean states this is where he felt he was taking fellow fans for a ride. Whilst unlike other ITK's, he hadn't set out to make money, or create lies, he was very reliable, but he felt the conversations weren't real and they were all behind an alias.

During his column on Goal, a real journalist revealed to him Chang's honey trap, he was angry at Duncan and was leaving no stone unturned to find him. To be fair to Sean, after hearing this, he wanted it all to stop, he loved his club and didn't want to fall out with them or cause them any harm in the transfer market.

He chose one final transfer story to go all in on, bet all his chips on the outsider in the hope it failed so he could escape this life that had spun out of control. Unfortunately, for Sean, things were about to turn sour. His gamble on Nuri Sahin joining Liverpool seemed to have "worked", he looked like he was close to Liverpool and the journalistic integrity of Duncan Jenkins hung in the balance. Sean closed the account as Sky Sports began reporting the deal with Arsenal was close.

But then other people, gutted they had lost their stream of transfer gossip, began opening fake or duplicate Duncan Jenkins accounts, hoping to cash in on Sean's creation. So, Sean reopened the account to wade off the fraudulent Duncan Jenkins ITK's he was surprised to see a Direct Message (DM) on Twitter from Jen Chang, not addressed to Duncan Jenkins, but to Sean. 'Back so soon after your sabbatical?'

With Chang knowing who was behind the Duncan Jenkins account, Sean wanted it to stop, but also intrigued to know how Chang had discovered him. They agreed to a cordiale meeting in Manchester for the following week to discuss the matter.

Alan Gernon detailed Sean mentions he was apprehensive, worried at what would happen. He describes Chang as very passive aggressive for their two-hour meeting. No humour. Chang grilled Sean and argued that Duncan Jenkins was costing the club money, using the Fabio Borini deal as the example and that he was reliant on a mole within the club. Despite Sean trying to explain that there was no mole and that his information was mere educated guess work.

Chang continued to use emotional blackmail to try and get Sean to reveal his "source". Claiming Sean was destroying Liverpool from within, hurting his beloved club. Admitting he had hired a private detective to find Sean. Unbeknown to Sean, Chang had not. It was another reverse psychology move to get Sean to fess up. Someone who knew Sean had "grassed" him up, revealing his real identity, all Chang had to do was Google Duncan Jenkins and some searches would have brought Chang all he needed to know.

But that was not the end. Chang made up a story that the private investigation fund had come from Liverpool's Community funds, which had been earmarked for handicapped children in Toxteth. On top of this, Chang stated that unless Sean goes home, pack it in and tweet out that Duncan Jenkins was a ruse and apologises for taking them all for a ride. If Sean didn't, Chang threatened Liverpool would withdraw his season ticket and ban him from Anfield for life.

If this wasn't enough, Chang claimed journalists were angry that "Duncan" was getting more exclusive's and were more than happy to run a smear campaign against Sean if he didn't comply by a deadline for Thursday 20:30pm, Chang would reveal Sean to Liverpool fans and whip them into a frenzy, so much that they would target his house and force Sean to move his young family to a new home and Chang even threatened Sean's parents' business.

As the deadline came and went, ironically, Nuri Sahrin signed for Liverpool. Sean began to tweet again as Duncan, only for Chang to DM Sean again, claiming he was renegading on their "agreement". Jen even spent the evening phoning Sean trying to contact him.

Sean was now fed up and angry at the situation that he wanted to come clean to a newspaper, but none were forthcoming. Sean took it upon himself to write a blog entry and come clean. He received an apology from the club, but Chang initially denied the claims of a meeting or the threats. As the blog entry gained traction with his followers, it wasn't long before people close to the club mentioned that Liverpool were aware of the situation and Ian Arye, Liverpool's then Chief Executive, wanted to talk to him.

A few weeks later, Sean met with Arye, by then the story had gone viral and was embarrassing for the club. At the meeting, Arye had a letter, which Sean claims "was a bit of a fudge" admitting some of the remarks made to Sean were out of order and an apology. Arye said Sean could do what he wanted with the letter. Sean contacted some journalists as this now proved his stories validity. Arye asked Sean what he wanted out of this whole affair. Sean admitted he just wanted some validity, that he was right with his stories and that he wasn't always making up the information.

Chang was eventually removed from his role by Liverpool following an investigation which included CCTV from the coffee shop which showed the meeting taking place and subsequent Twitter messages. It just goes to show how easy it is to not only dupe the public, but rumours being made up can have major impacts both on the transfer window and the clubs which operate within football.

Social Media has played a huge role in the way transfers are both conducted by clubs, but also how they are reported or sometimes misrepresented in the media. Taken as gospel by football fans and media outlets alike. As the final touches to this book was being put together in the final days of the January 2023 transfer window, well renown Twitch Streamer, Zealand, who has multiple YouTube and Twitch streams dedicated to football, and the game football manager, decided to make up a fake rumour, that was believable to see how far the story could go.

Posting on his Twitter account, 'Ismaila Sarr to Everton.' Everton were looking to replace Anthony Gordon, who they had just sold to Newcastle for £45m and had seen Arnaut Danjuma agree to sign for them, sign a contract, do social media interviews, only for his agent to withhold a piece of paperwork from Everton, before whisking him off to sign for Spurs. Unbeknown to Zealand, and the media, Everton were contacting Watford over a deal for Sarr. A loan deal with an obligation to buy if the Merseyside club stayed in the Premier League.

As Zealand pressed send, his knowledge of football from his streams made him a credible source to many levers in the transfer window ecosystem. Fans retweeted; betting markets crashed as money flooded into the "Ismaila Sarr next team market" by over 350% in two hours. I sat down with Zealand to discuss the transfer rumour and the impact the transfer window has on society.

'It was an experiment with the best intentions, for good purposes, wanting people to see how easy stories can be manipulated and taken out of context, so football fans could stop turning on one another. On Twitch, I made it clear I wanted it to be realistic, but not to hurt anybody, yet see how the media will pick it up, but also show the volatility of the betting markets. I wanted to show how many ITK's would fall for it.' It would catch them out and highlight to fans who had been taken in by people posing as ITK's for commercial ventures.

He used well renown ITK, Fabrizio Romano's style, copy and pasting one of his previous tweets for authenticity, he looked for a winger who had yet to move clubs, but one who was likely to move. Sarr was subject to a number of enquiries, both Aston Villa and Crystal Palace were allegedly lining up moves for the winger, and as Zealand discussed on Twitch. 'I just need to add another team to make it believable, with the world knowing Everton were sourcing the market for the replacement, Zealand lit the proverbial touch paper and pressed send.'

On his video later discussing the rumour breaking the internet, Zealand was quick to point out that in his tweet, there was no claim, or sources saying the deal is close, the transfer world did not read it properly and within six minutes, it had blown up the rumour mill. 'I wanted to test how quick the betting algorithm would change the odds because it had been posted online and retweeted by thousands of people fairly quickly.'

Sky Bet cut the odds of the deal, the silliness and simulation of the situation was hilarious, fan accounts picked it up and discussed it on Twitter spaces, despite Zealand stating seconds later that the tweet was fake. Miles Jacobson, Studio Director of Sports Interactive, who develops the football manager series Zealand documents on his platforms, was asked for his thoughts on the "proposed deal". Taken in, he replied to users saying that he did not see Watford signing off on the deal. Live on Twitch, Zealand had his head in hands watching this all unfold. 'I was literally telling the world it was fake, but it would not stop, no one stopped to check the source of the news for ages.'

Miles dug into the rumour, and discussed that after checking, it was likely the rumour mill was likely to be a lie. The transfer database, Transfermarkt, even linked Zealand as the source on their website, confirming to Zealand his experiment had worked. With the media now reporting the story was false, the fun really happened. Everton actually publicly announced they had failed in a move to sign the winger.

Now the media had rubbished the story, and looked even worse themselves when the truth came out, Sarr did not move in the end, but Zealand's experiment was important for fans to see social media is not always the best place to believe transfer news, the eight-minute YouTube video is well worth a watch and a welcome reminder of the power of social media.

'The transfer window becomes an added part of the show that is football. I look at it from an American point of view. We have American sports, and they have the Trade Deadline, where players can be traded between teams. There is no money traded, but the principles are the same, there is a hard deadline, and after this date, your team cannot be improved, you have to play with what you have. It creates the dynamic in the sports, economically, close to the deadline, the more economic pressure there is on the football clubs, or American franchises. Sport needs this dynamism; it is a show and a business product.'

We discuss the impact transfer deadline day has had on society and Zealand acknowledges it is going nowhere fast. 'The media love it because it will generate chatter. The hardest working ITK's like Fabrizio Romano has given everyone an insight the media had been unable to show, fans are getting transfer news instantly, now a player is judged before he has even signed or posed with a shirt. Fans are discussing, complaining and arguing over whether it was a good or bad deal.'

These debates were usually left until after the window shuts, where Jim White would do a mop up hour to discuss the deals and which ones had fallen through. "We would love society to suck less, it is human nature to complain and with regards to the transfer window it can bring just as many negatives as it does positives. We are seeing media change as a way of reporting news. It is changing towards the more interactive on the spot news. Fans do not want to see random debates, or sports channels always talking about, should player x join a "Big Six club" fans can see or have those debates themselves, at the pub, on fan channels or on Twitch streams."

I ask Zealand whether more fans will turn to fan channels and Twitch streamers for their football transfer rumours. "It is difficult to predict, transfer deadline day will always have an audience, because it has become an experience. We have fans outside the training grounds, for me, my job will always be a part of that bubble. I provide a stream for people to interact, talk about the world of football, it is organic, I understand my audience and give them what they want. But the media will not change the overall product they have, because the transfer window has been a boom to them, it is lucrative, but football has provided people like me with an opportunity."

"It is inevitable that streams are such a hit, I could see myself interacting more with transfers. Audiences can see the truth more, so speculation to fill the void has become a turn off for fans. But there is a need for transfer news. As I tweeted out about the fake rumour of Ismaila Sarr to Everton. Seeing the Everton fans take to the news and use it on their channels and spaces, because football has this emotional bond with fans."

I am keen to understand what it is like for a football fan on Deadline Day and ask Zealand how he feels on the day. "For me it is interactive, not just with the shows, but I have the sports news apps. SportsCenter, a number of platforms send out 'Push Notifications', so I receive the news as it happens, I then react to it. The good thing with these apps is it allows fans to sieve through false rumours. These apps need the news to be accurate because they are competing for viewership."

We discuss the game that Zealand produces most of his content on and one that has had a major impact on football and the transfer window. "It has become more than a game really, you have the core players who have made it their business, hundreds of thousands of fans buy it yearly."

It allows players to take over virtually any club in the world and be the manager and director of football. "Some real-life football managers play the game. Jose Mourinho and Will Still are the most common. But it opens doors for people. On one of my saves, I played as Floridsdorfer AC in the Austrian Football Second Division, and they invited me to one of their games. The manager later told me he played the game, not for any hints or tips, but for recreation and enjoyment. But it can help clubs in football, not all clubs have huge budgets for scouting, football manager gives the clubs and players access to a database of over 400,000 players, that is more than the population of Iceland, or the City of Liverpool. It becomes a massive asset to these clubs."

It makes the world of football even smaller, allowing clubs to fish for the same talent in the biggest of markets. "It also allows fans to form an opinion on a new signing and whether they will work within their team's system. Football managers developers have built their scouting into the game which has proved fairly accurate. Fans can now say they discovered player x first, or they knew about this seventeen-year-old wonderkid had potential due to the immersive experience the game allows its players."

It is the globalisation of football. The sport is at your fingertips, on our devices, fans can use the same scouting databases to find players, it does become harder to defend recruitment teams when a player is signed when they clearly do not fit a system, or signing a winger who does not create or score goals. "Football can be a healer, and there are people who watch my stream and play football manager because they cannot play the game on the field, in school, maybe it is their confidence, but the game and the sport gives them an avenue into football, and we should praise it for that."

The game has become more prominent recently with the success Will Still is having, currently on a fifteen-game unbeaten streak having taken over Ligue 1 club, Reims, despite not qualifying for a UEFA Pro Licence, Still has spoken about his love for the game and how it fuelled his desire to be a manager. Will Still is not a good manager because of the game, let's get this straight, he deserves massive credit for the job he is doing at Reims. If anything, it has brought more interest to the game, but as we discussed before, a number of clubs use the game as part of their scouting.

The game inspired Still to be a manager, but he has honed his skills across European football, starting as a youth coach at Preston. The game is changing people's perceptions, but whilst it allows users to buy and sell players, it will not change the desire for a transfer deadline day product. As Zealand prepares for his latest stream, he has recently used his following to raise significant money for a footballing charity. Perhaps the future growth of football transfer news is through fan channels and streaming, but most importantly, as Zealand stressed at the start of our interview, football can be a healer and entertainer, here is hoping there are more streamers like Zealand who use football as a power for good.

In contrast, due to the power of social media it's easy to see why it is manipulated when it comes to transfer rumours. As Newcastle United's takeover neared its prolonged completion in October 2021, ending Mike Ashley's fourteen-year tenure at the club. Instantly the new owners, Saudi Arabia's Public Investment Fund, due to Ashley's frugal spending in the past, had the facility and ambitious directors who planned to spend money in the club on transfers. But a club takeover is just one way the media can start transfer rumours surrounding a football club, there are several other ways.

Players wanting a move to a different club can play the game and leak information to the press stating they want to leave, or they would be interested to move to a new club. Kieran Trippier expressed the desire to return to the Premier League from Atletico Madrid for personal reasons. This alerted Newcastle to his availability, and they submitted a £12m bid in the January transfer window in a bid to avoid relegation the club was tumbling towards in January 2022.

Agents have also been known to contact fake ITK's and even newspapers to put their players in the news. Sometimes a football club will be in negotiations with another club and the player may not want to join this particular club, or the agent has the motivation to create a bidding war for their clients' services, as this would drive the price up for the buying club, creating an even bigger fee for the agent. Even players who aren't for sale are touted in the media in the hope the story perks up interest in the player.

Mino Raiola was well known for the way he orchestrates the media. Leading one journalist to say he was known as being the transfer circus ringmaster pulling all the strings. Whilst playing for Everton and under no transfer bid, meaning legally no club could contact Romelu Lukaku or Raiola, his agent, Lukaku claimed he had already decided on his new team and had agreed personal terms in the International Break of 2017. Despite no club contacting Everton or submitting a formal bid. Eventually in the summer of 2017, Lukaku joined Manchester United for £75m.

Football clubs are even known to push their players' availability in the media to drum up a sale or to create a bidding war to increase their transfer price of their player by letting other teams know a player they may be scouting is currently under a transfer offer. In the summer of 2022, Everton had a £32m bid rejected for Mykhailo Mudryk, the offer came out of the blue and the media were unaware of the bid, until Shakhtar Donetsk Director, Carlo Nicolini, made the bid public in the press.

Stating that Everton would need to bid £40m plus before they considered a deal, he even said Arsenal had made an enquiry in the hope a bidding war would start. It didn't, but after three months of intense negotiations, Arsenal believed they were closing in on the winger with an £80m bid under discussion, but their London rivals, Chelsea stole in and sealed the deal, signing Mudryk for £88m, despite the players public courting of Arsenal. It does need mentioning Nicolini's motive to drive up the transfer fee was unlike other examples, as Shakhtar donated over £20m of the transfer fee to the Ukrainian war effort, almost a year after the illegal Russian invasion.

Another way clubs engage with the media is when they are desperate to sell their players. In the aftermath of Covid-19 strangling the purse strings of European clubs, those who missed out on Europe faced a shortage of cash. This led to several Sporting Directors and Directors of Football putting several of their star players up for sale.

Rangers Managing Director, Stewart Robinson, told shareholders in December 2020 the club was in need to sell 'one or two' players in the summer of 2021 and it was something the board were really focused on. This was nearly six months before the Ibrox side claimed their first Scottish Premiership in a decade. Eight months before Ranger's failure to qualify for the Champions League cost them a guaranteed £30m for their club accounts.

The club posted a £15.9m loss in December 2020 and announced they needed £23m by the end of the current season, these were covered by loans from Chairman Douglas Park and Club Director John Bennet. This pushed the operating loss of the club since 2012 to the dizzying heights of £82.14m, alarming for a club who faced administration in 2012.

Ranger's went on to sell Nathan Patterson to Everton in January 2022 for £12m and George Edmundson for £788k with the aforementioned loans above and the Europa League Cup run of 2020/21 funding a portion of the deficit. A year later in November 2021, Stewart Robinson then told fans at the annual AGM that Rangers didn't need to sell players to balance the books, but the club posted a £16m net transfer profit after selling stars Calvin Bassey to Ajax and Joe Aribo to Southampton.

Transfer stories have also been known to be made up from journalists and ITK's. Sometimes drawn up from bedrooms or from office floors. Fan TV's and podcasts have also been known to peddle rumours to create traction for their employers or to increase their subscribers. UK newspapers published that Arsenal had bid £14m for goalkeeper Keylor Navas, only for then Arsenal manager Unai Emery, a few days later in a press conference to laugh at the rumour and denied Arsenal had made a bid and that they were interested. Subsequently backed up by Real Madrid themselves.

Perhaps a notable example of news outlets racing to break news before fact checking was Sky Sports reporting Aberdeen signing Yards Selzavon in January 2017. The issue being the player did not exist. Someone on Twitter had posted from an account using the official team's logo that had been picked up by a runner for the show and they used it live on air.

News outlets jumping the gun is not a new practice either, in 2001 Liverpool, then managed by Gerard Houllier, were reported to be on the brink of signing French footballer Didier Baptiste. The British press even managed scouting reports on the player. It was picked up by newspapers, including The Observer, News of the World and The Times who ran the story. Only problem, Didier Baptiste was a character for Sky One's television show Dream Team.

A similar story occurred in 2021 at the FA Cup final, where ITV News reporter Chris Skudder reporting and interviewing fans outside the ground, thought he had really met fans who had travelled over from Mexico for the game.

In fact, they were the cast and crew from the Emmy award-winning football show Ted Lasso, who told him to look out for a player called Dani Rojas, saying he was a 'brilliant footballer'. Little did the reporter know, the player did not exist, and they ran the interview. It can happen to even managers too. Who can forget the famous cousin of George Weah, once removed, Aly Dia.

Graeme Souness was the manager of Southampton in 1996 and allegedly signed Dia after a phone call from Weah. Dia came on to replace Matt Le Tissier after half an hour against Leeds in the Premier League. Only for suspicions to be raised by teammates over his ability quickly and in the dressing room at half-time. Souness eventually hauled Dia off after 54 minutes, before subsequently releasing Dia a few days later.

Whilst it can be fun to look back on some of the gaffes and blunders from the media in the transfer window, it is also important to acknowledge the cancerous nature of society that 'fake news' and 'stories for clicks' can have on a variety of people.

A simple tweet from a fan or a fake ITK might seem funny at the time. Be an exterior motive for the account to make money for the user, but a simple rumour or joke can have a serious impact on people's lives. A gamer posted a screenshot online from the computer game football manager, a realistic management simulator, where the simulator had fined Andros Townsend, then of Crystal Palace, for missing training.

His girlfriend saw the picture online and called Andros. With her mind racing, if her boyfriend wasn't at training and wasn't at home, where was he? Andros later joked about the event with his girlfriend and discussed the event on talkSPORT. But it isn't just the general public that have been guilty of disrupting players.

In 2019, Everton and manager Marco Silva were in the market for a goal scoring winger to partner Richarlison and Dominic Calvert-Lewin. They made an approach to Crystal Palace to speak to their marquee player Wilfred Zaha offering over £55m for the player in installments. Palace rejected, stating they wanted £80m for the player. Everton felt this was too steep for them and above their budget, Palace agreed with Everton amicably, there would be no further bids for the player.

Everton only had £30m available after spending £8m on Fabian Delph from Manchester City and £22m on Andre Gomes from Barcelona. With Everton now looking for alternatives, Sky Sports News reported Everton had made another offer of £60m which they claimed Palace had rejected. Palace released a statement saying they had not received a bid and that Zaha was not for sale in the transfer window and was an integral part of their future.

Sky Sports reported this but then doubled down on their report by stating the player was for sale, Palace were interested, and that Everton were preparing a final offer. Reporting this as £60m, plus two player exchange of Cenk Tosun and James McCarthy. Everton reaffirmed they had made no further bid. Internally at Everton, director of football told Everton's owners they could not afford Wilfred Zaha and that they were going to pursue other targets such as David Neres and Hirving Lozano for a fraction of the price.

Despite both Everton and Palaces putting out press releases saying that the deal was dead, and they had both agreed to go separate ways Sky maintained their 'sources' where saying Everton were interested in the deal and so was Zaha. The player, reading the reports and believing the deal was still in negotiation, put in a public transfer request to force through a move. A move that neither club was looking into, nor one Everton could afford.

Everton's pursuit of a creative winger would run the entire course of deadline day, with super-agent Kia Joorabchian, a confidant of Everton Owner Farhad Moshiri, recommending one of his clients, Alex Iwobi to him. On Deadline Day, Moshiri sanctioned a £28m pound move for Iwobi, despite Marcel Brands, or manager Marco Silva not having the player on their shortlist.

Iwobi signed up when he was on holiday. Wilfred Zaha never got his move to Everton. As of January 2023, he is still a Crystal Palace player, seeing out the final year of his contract.

Transfer markets are well oiled machines with a vast number of cogs and parts all interworked and reliant on one another. So is it possible for fans to work out for themselves whether rumours in the media are fake or whether the stories really have legs.

With Everton sacking manager Marco Silva in December of 2019 and the club now looking for its fourth permanent manager under his ownership (Not including David Unsworth's temporary role in November 2017) Moshiri wanted to sign Carlo Ancelotti, now a free agent after his sacking from Napoli. Moshiri made his desires clear to Jim White of talkSPORT that Ancelotti was his preferred target and was pursuing all channels to get the deal done.

In response to this interview, numerous publications mocked the rumour for being false and claiming a manager like Ancelotti would never come to Everton, making their own shortlists and published columns slating how long it was taking Everton to fill the vacancy and not having a plan ready after sacking Silva. In the interim period, Duncan Ferguson, took charge of three Premier League games and secured a much-needed victory over Chelsea, and combative draws against Manchester United and Arsenal to lift Everton up the table away from the relegation zone.

Slowly news corporations began to withdraw the stories as it became apparent Ancelotti was coming to Everton and he was interested in managing the team. Now Moshiri was heralded for being able to secure such a big name for Everton given their poor start to the season.

The subsequent 2020 summer transfer window with Ancelotti at the helm led to more false starts with the media. Speaking at a club event, Marcel Brands, Everton's Director of Football, stated he was working on five to six transfers from a shortlist of twenty players. This didn't stop the media from linking Everton with over seventy-five players for the forthcoming window.

As fans argued and fought over who was good enough for the club creating a toxic atmosphere within the fanbase and online where verbal abuse to users became rampant, none of Everton's actual targets were names that had appeared in the newspapers or online news forums.

Niels Nkounkou arrived from Marseille for £300k compensation after his contract had ended with the French club.

Robin Olsen was signed on loan with an option to buy from AS Roma to provide cover for England's number 1, Jordan Pickford.

Italian media began to circulate that combative midfielder Allan was number 1 on Everton's shortlist. Again, the British media mocked how a player who had just been in the Champions League would want to sign for Everton. Stories for Spurs Harry Winks were pushed across the columns and denials Everton were to sign Allan were printed. Everton signed Allan for £20m and quickly followed this up with Abdoulaye Doucoure for another £20m. Then raiding relegated Norwich City for versatile defence Ben Godfrey for £25m. But there was one final player Everton were looking to sign that would stun the media, the free transfer of James Rodriquez.

When he arrived on Merseyside holding up the royal blue jersey and face adorning Time Square in New York, with the club pulling off another wild transfer reveal, the media who had been outdone by the club again for the information, raced to report the deal. Despite Everton announcing the deal as a free transfer, the media began running figures that the deal was done for £12 million or that it was a two-year loan deal. Everton re-released the statement claiming it was a free transfer from Real Madrid and the player couldn't wait to link up with Carlo Ancelotti again.

The interesting thing with these transfers for Everton were that they weren't reported in the media before the deals were done, the media were in the dark all the time. When news began to break on them, the players linked were mocked with cries, "he'll never sign for a club like Everton." But all these players signed because Ancelotti wanted them, and they would transfer to play for him.

Could the problem lie with the business model of media publications? They know how transfer rumours drive people crazy, forming an addiction for fans to want more of them, fans want to debate, in person, social media, is this player good enough? But is it right to hide behind false stories or 'sources'?

Agents are well known to contact the media and plant the seeds "player x is for sale and these clubs are after him." So, is it wrong if the media publish it? If it is straight from the agent's mouth, they may not be telling the truth, but they are actively seeking a transfer for their player and they know the publicity might drive some traction.

Should the news publications verify the rumour? If they do so, they risk losing out on being first, by the time they contact the club, players, even if they get an answer, their media rivals have several ways to get the story out first online, and with every click and viewer gained, they steal a march on a very financial and dog eat dog industry.

Transfers are now being played out on Paid TV subscription programs, taking us beyond the curtains on the hidden aspects of football and giving viewers a deep dive into the side of transfers we don't see.

Amazon led the way with their 'All or Nothing' series following Manchester City and Spurs. Fans got to see how Manchester City's centurions were organised, from on the field with Pep Guardiola to the off-field transfers shortlisted and conducted by Txiki Begiristain during their record-breaking season. One episode in particular takes viewers on the journey to sign defender Aymeric Laporte from Athletic Bilbao for £58m. We see the club scouting him using data and scouting the player during a match before an internal meeting to decide whether to make a formal offer for the player.

Viewers for the first time get to see how the final parts of a transfer are conducted. Laporte and partner flew in on a private jet with his agent to have his medical conducted and to sign his contract. The calm nature of the approach to scouting and decisiveness of the deal giving viewers a different take to the window, which otherwise would have read, "Aymeric Laporte joins Manchester City from Athletic Bilbao for £58m." Not quite as exciting as seeing it unfurl live on TV from behind the scenes.

The next series focused on Spurs during the Covid-19 affected 2019/2020 season. Viewers were treated to the unfortunate sacking of Mauricio Pochettino and being replaced by José Mourinho mid-season. It also gave people a glimpse into the life of Daniel Levy, renowned for driving a hard bargain but loving a transfer deal and Technical Director, Steve Hitchen. Former manager Harry Redknapp, loves recalling many transfer tales about. Just don't call them 'Wheeler dealers' as Sky Sports' Rob Palmer found out when interviewing the manager during his time at Spurs.

With the January transfer window open, and Spurs having lost Harry Kane to injury, the documentary gave us a look at how Spurs conducted their business and the tribulations clubs face. Faced with Christian Eriksen's contract running down and clubs outside of England being able to sign him on a pre-contract for nothing, we see on screen Eriksen in a crunch talk with Levy and Mourinho. Levy laying the facts out there for everyone to see that he claimed he wanted to keep the player and would match any financial package (wages) another club put in front of Eriksen. Even when it became clear Eriksen desired a new challenge away from Spurs, we got to see how his fellow players reacted to the situation.

Whilst the players carried on with the business of football attitude, Levy and Hitchen quickly investigated getting the best deal for the club as the hours of the window ticked away. They negotiated a deal with Inter Milan which saw the Danish International move to the Italian club for £24m and quickly followed this up with signings of Gedson Fernandes, signed on an eighteen-month loan deal, £5m loan fee, with an option to purchase him for £42.5m.

It's the first time we have seen a football club internally discussing their budget, what they can and cannot afford. Hitchens describes how Spurs are fishing in a small pond with the likes of Chelsea, Liverpool and Manchester United and need methods to get ahead of the game. Mourinho is seen pouring through pages of scouting notes, using new techniques and data-led scouting such as expected goals and expected assists.

How he fits in with the squad that Mourinho is trying to mould on the fly, mere weeks after taking over the job. After selling Eriksen, all parties within

Spurs knew they needed a creative player to ease the burden on a strike force which was in the mix of a barren run. The television cameras thrust into Mourinho's face daily asking him why he isn't buying a striker.

Then we get to see what the journalist's couldn't, the reality was strikers like Harry Kane are not available in January, or if they are, clubs are forced to overpay for them. Spurs moved on to the highly recruited Dutch winger Steven Bergwijn, signing him from PSV for £27m. Amazon showed us Bergwijn being flown in and given a tour of the training complex.

But also, interestingly, a tour around a new-build house. One Spurs use to settle their new signings quickly. Make the transition easier from Europe to England with one less thing for the player to look for. Spurs believe the player would be much happier in a house, with a garden and normality, rather than being stuck in a high-rise hotel room with your bedroom also being your front room.

The fly on the wall documentary also gave insight to the outgoing and player fallouts. Danny Rose, England International and desperate to make Gareth Southgate's Euro 2020 squad is seen on the fringes of the first team. In a heated episode, Rose asks Mourinho for a chat, he calmly details how he feels he's been hard done, not being selected. Desperate to play, he pleads his case. Admits his performance against Liverpool, which Spurs lost, was not good enough, but highlights how playing one game in every four isn't easy for a player to build consistent form.

Rose details how he feels several of the players in the starting eleven also aren't playing well and their attitudes to training aren't good enough for the club. Rose claims that Mourinho playing the same players is unfair to him, as he is trying and training. Whilst Mourinho seems to take on board the comments, he challenges Rose and explains his thoughts are his opinion, to which Rose argues they are facts.

This confrontation is quickly followed by a meeting between Mourinho and Levy where they discuss the current ongoing January transfer window. For the first time, we see how a manager works alongside a chairman within the confines of the window. Levy describes the mechanism of the ongoing deals. With information on Rose. Spurs have three offers on the table. One from Milan, but this required them to shift (transfer) a full-back from their squad to another team, who were also trying to sell a player.

Levy breaks it down for Mourinho that he feels the two British offers, one from Bournemouth, which covered a portion of his wages, but had no loan fee involved. The alternative for Spurs, was a deal on the table from Newcastle, a club also in a relegation battle, but one that offered Rose the opportunity for first team football, but for Spurs, it also provided them with a loan fee which they could use towards the Gedson Fernandes deal they were working on.

From here, Rose approaches Levy and requests updates on the deals on the table. The first thing that would surprise most fans is how this is all done in the open air, in front of players eating and milling about in the canteen. Even as Levy discusses the Milan deal, which Rose preferred, was off the table unless other players left those clubs. Rose had found himself at the bottom of a transfer chain, at risk of being the last domino yet to fall. Desperate to move to Milan but needing several factors (dominos) to be bought before he got what he wanted.

Seeing Rose slowly understand the situation, and Levy's earlier comment to Mourinho "the player wants clubs up here (elite clubs) interested in him, whilst the reality is the only solid offers are clubs down here" (relegation battle) hit Rose in the middle of a canteen with all his teammates in earshot is gut wrenching to watch a human go through before us.

Rose just nodding, going through his options after realising his time at Spurs was ending abruptly. With the episode ending, we see Rose leave Spurs. On his way up North to Newcastle on a six-month loan, in pursuit of first team football and all parties happy with the outcome.

It isn't always plain sailing with transfers and in Amazon's other documentary, following Leeds United 'Take Us Home' in their attempt to gain promotion to the Premier League under the leadership of Marcelo Bielsa, entered the January window of 2019, looking for the final piece of the jigsaw to complete the tactic known as Bielsa ball.

Leeds' pursuit of James was well documented in the documentary. With Leeds United's director of football Victor Orta and club owner Andrea Radrizzani keen to keep Leeds momentum towards their promotion chase, they managed to secure a bid signing to replace their current embattled goalkeeper Bailey Peacock-Farrell with Real Madrid backup Kiko Casilla on a free transfer.

After solidifying their defence, Orta turned his attention to Daniel James, currently plying his trade for fellow championship side Swansea City. Orta is filmed walking with Managing Director Angus Kinnear at the club's Thorp Arch training ground and narrator Russell Crowe explaining James has been 'in fine form for the Welsh club this season, scoring goals and supplying numerous assists. He looks a perfect fit for [Marcelo] Bielsa's high-energy playing style.

Kinnear, when interviewed in the last week of January, excitedly describes how James's performances put him on the shortlist of Bielsa and Orta and reveals Leeds have held 'positive discussions' with the Wales international. Crowe explains 'confidence is high' Leeds will secure James and Orta claims they are 'in the last details' and is '80 percent' confident of signing James.

As the deal progresses and a fee is seemingly agreed, Swansea allow James to make the journey up North to Leeds where he arrives with his family. Orta starts to study his watch and is seen battering his phone with calls to his counterpart at Swansea for a sign off to begin signing the contract. Crowe narrates: "It's tight but everything is progressing as planned. As Angus attempts to tie up the loose ends of the deal, Dan James undergoes a medical at Thorp Arch."

The minutes of deadline day begin to dissolve away, in another bid to steal some more seconds, Leeds Team Manager Matt Grice asks James: "Going to get some kit printed up for training tomorrow at Elland Road. Any idea on numbers?"

James replies: "Twenty-one, mate, to be fair." As kit is hastily printed up, the club photographer is ordered to come over. Be ready for the club announcement on social media.

As the day edges on, James is seen both excited, but also exhausted by all the attention the transfer is set to bring. "I've been going crazy since I've been linked," James, lying on a medical table, says. "Swansea fans saying 'Stay', Leeds fans saying, 'Are you coming? When are you coming?'" With the medical passed with no problem, James and his father travel to Elland Road to sign the contract. Orta looks delighted at the progress that the move is making, meeting James and his family as if he has known them for years.

The documentary shows a timer ticking down, hours, minutes, seconds, 02:59:56 edging away. James posed with his name and number on a Leeds shirt before Crowe continues, "As the deal heads towards a conclusion, team manager Matt Grice begins the process of settling the new player into his home." Grice sits down with James discussing house viewings in anticipation of the deal going through, James seems happy, but daunted that this would be his first move away from his family.

00:59:53 To save more time, James signs his contract with the club's secretary, they shake hands and congratulate the deal, but Orta stops them, tapping his phone. Still waiting on confirmation. "But an unforeseen problem arises," Crowe adds. "Swansea's American owner, who is Stateside, and their chief executive, who is in Wales, cannot agree to the terms of James' proposed transfer to Elland Road."

Orta is filmed sending a WhatsApp message that reads, 'Any words from Swansea? We are all here waiting,' Crowe portentously adds: 'Neither are returning Leeds United's calls or text messages.'

For the first time we see James looking uncomfortable, living out a nightmare in front of the Amazon cameras. What started as a dream day, is slowly, by the second, turning into a circus, at no fault of James or Leeds. Orta reassures James, describing the matter as 'crazy' but promises they are 'near'. Orta utters 'no worries' as he leaves the room. The episode cuts to Leeds defender Luke Ayling in a post-recorded interview, describing how the players were messaging press officer James Mooney as the saga unfolded.

Orta is filmed growing increasingly irritated and appears to bang against a wall in frustration as the move falls through. Leeds cannot apply for a deal sheet. A form that allows a club a fifteen-minute extension to a transfer deal if all the paperwork is signed, allowing a football league Official to sign it off.

Kinnear is filmed having a conversation on the phone, laments that Swansea chairman Huw Jenkins was not returning his calls and that they have let his player down and why did they give permission for James to travel over 260 miles and five hours in the car, only to stall the deal and not return Leeds call.

As the Amazon clock ticks to midnight, a teary Orta comes out of his office, physically exhausted. Apologising to James and his family, ensuring he had done all he could to get the deal done. Seemingly heartbroken more for James than the fact he didn't get the deal done for Leeds. He waves the family off again on the return leg, another soul searching 260 miles and five hours into the morning.

In a cruel twist of fate, Swansea was due to play Leeds in the week after the January transfer deadline day. Despite not signing for Leeds, James signed for Manchester United in the Summer of 2019 for £16m. Ironically, on deadline day in the summer of 2021, Daniel James did sign for Leeds United for £26m. There were no setbacks this time.

Netflix have also dipped into the football documentary market with their critically acclaimed series 'Sunderland Till I Die' following the plight of Sunderland as a newly relegated club. Dropping from the Premier League into the Championship, ladened with a bloated squad on inflated wages and costs far outweighing their commercial income propped up by parachute payments, the club go through two managers and a vast overhaul of the playing squad.

The turmoil on the pitch with the club languishing near the relegation zone and trap door to League One led to deeper cuts off the field. Ellis Short the owner, was looking to sell and turned the club over to Stuart Donald, not long after relegation into League One was confirmed and Ellis personally wrote off tens of millions pound in liabilities to facilitate the takeover. Manager Chris Coleman, a few years removed from guiding Wales to Euro 2016's semi-final was sacked, and Sunderland were on the lookout for their 12th permanent manager in 10 years.

With the club in League One, Donald and his associate, Charlie Methven tried to lead the club on a revival and appointed Jack Ross to be their manager and pushed on with a policy of bringing through the club's youth players through their academy. Knowing with the current financial situation and Financial Fair Play (FFP) they couldn't spend their way out of the league, they needed to address a £35m deficit between the club's expenditure and the income, they focused on a youth movement and spending within their means and that also meant on players wages.

Enter Josh Maja, Sunderland's gem from their academy and star striker of the first two episodes of season two, who unfortunately for the player and the club, was to become one of the villains of the documentary structure. Just 19 at the time and entering the last year of his first professional contract at the club, the club were in a bind, with no club option added into the contract to extend the deal, Donald, with all the off-field issues and takeover to deal with, didn't extend or approach his agent and this meant as Maja hit form on the pitch, sending the club into the playoff races, the club faced a serious issue off it.

A player like Maja could sign for a club outside of England for free in January due to his contract expiring in less than six months. It also meant his transfer value in England decreased by every passing day. Donald was now metaphorically playing poker with all parties; they held all the cards and could see the hand he was trying to play.

Desperate to keep the striker but needing to balance the club's finances. With the opening episodes showing empty desks of the people who have been made redundant from the football club following consecutive relegations. The hidden cost of failure on the pitch is the cost to the people working behind the scenes.

Maja's rich vein of form had meant clubs from the Premier League and all over Europe were courting the player. Maja is rumoured to be earning less than £1000 pound a week. With the average League One professional wage £1300, Sunderland faced the issue of needing to show commitment to the player and give him the wage which reflected his talent which was attracting from the number of clubs scouts watching him, but also facing the fact they couldn't over stretch themselves.

It's easy to forget what it is like being 19, for some it is the freedom university can bring, others they are entering full-time employment following the completion of their A-Levels, all appear to be a 'Sliding Doors' moment that could affect their futures. For Josh Maja, a young man, probably still living at home and just enjoying doing a job he loved, now faced a million pound one. He left all negotiations to his agent.

Midway through episode two, Sunderland's recruitment team are seen discussing the young players out of contract, with it appearing the negotiations over Maja's contract to be stalling. Head of Football Operations Richard Hill 'significantly' increases Sunderland's transfer offer. He says he has spoken to Maja, and he was directed to talk to his agent who was overseeing the business of the contract.

Richard then mentions that the agent is not responding to calls or emails. Donald then tells us that these "players are from the clubs Premier League days" listening to what players earn and can make and it is difficult for them to detach they are no longer negotiating with a Premier League club.

Donald was keen to tie the deal down, but knew the agent had all the negotiating power. He faced the issue of continuing to negotiate post January in the hope he signs, even if he does not sign, promotion would take Donald back to the Championship first time of asking, the final option would be to protect the club's assets and sell him, so the business brings in transfer revenue.

On a radio show, Donald explains his frustration that the club have not put in an optional extension into his contract. Now the agent knows he can make Maja and himself more money by having him transfer clubs. On hearing that the agent is not responding to their final offer, Donald fires back to his team, "I'm not signing their agent, I'm signing their players."

Maja isn't going to sign a deal before January, Donald reluctantly looks to sell the player for the best price he can. With the hope of signing a replacement who can fire Sunderland to guaranteed promotion. Donald reluctantly sells Josh Maja to French Club Bordeaux for £1.35m.

Maja has since come out and told his version of the story, how Donald made him look greedy, but Maja explains he put his trust in his agent. That he was young, still is and his agent was experienced at looking after his best interests.

The program was enough for a lot of fans to believe this rhetoric on Maja and piled on with abuse on social media. Maja admits in hindsight that he could have dealt with the communication deadlock differently to get both sides talking. But this example highlights the dark side of football. Some agents will always look to move their players on, some will have the players interest at heart, others can see the pound signs and millions they can earn by moving a player.

The people left to pick up the pieces, the club, the players are not given the benefit of hindsight. But we watch it all play out on camera, not a fictional TV drama, a real-life shy football player, barely passed his GCSE, just wanting to enjoy his football and ignore the business side of football.

For Donald, having lost on one hand, he was now dealt another cruel blow. In a promotion race, needing a star striker, all clubs in the football league are aware of the £1.35m burning a hole in his pocket. Clubs outside of the Premier League are desperate to get there, but they are also in need of cash to maintain their businesses. With Sunderland now scouting and enquiring for strikers, the lack of forward planning or mitigating on behalf of Donald and his recruitment team meant, there was no player lined up to replace and now, every club had put an extra few hundred thousand pounds on the value of their strikers.

In episode 3, Donald homes in on Will Grigg of Wigan. With the dying embers of deadline day ebbing way, Donald becoming increasingly desperate, he is seen having a back and forth with Hill over a transfer fee. Wigan, sensing they are desperate, slowly upping the negotiation, Donald having already sold Maja, keeps returning, upping the offer. Hill advises him that the finances are not right, desperate decisions in Football are almost always bad ones.

Donald, who previously looked after National League Eastleigh, jumps in as the minutes tick away. Donald submits an offer to Wigan that would make Will Grigg a Sunderland player. The highest transfer fee paid by a third-tier club, costing the club a reported £3m pound after submitting a sixth transfer bid on deadline day. Sunderland faced a race against time to get the paperwork signed to meet the 11pm deadline. Contracts are signed just in time and Grigg is signed without a medical.

Sunderland didn't get promoted and in 2021, were still in League One, searching for another manager after the sacking of Lee Johnson, Maja has twice been loaned back to English clubs, Fulham and currently, Stoke who are in the Championship. Sunderland was eventually promoted, through the playoffs, into the Championship at the end of the year.

For Will Grigg, the move to Sunderland wasn't as successful as both parties would have wanted, with Grigg loaned out twice and currently playing for AFC Wimbledon in League Two.

Transfers are a merry-go-round that have a domino effect where fans can understand the window works as a cycle as a mechanism. As the examples above highlight, a player being bought needs to be replaced, the impact of a transfer has major impacts up and down the football pyramid.

Eden Hazard's transfer from Chelsea to Real Madrid inexplicably caused a La Liga arms race for talent. With an impending transfer ban incoming, Chelsea moved quickly to secure the signing of Christian Pulisic from Borussia Dortmund for £57m and followed it up by signing Mateo Kovačić for £40m. The money came from the impending sale of Eden Hazard.

Hazard moved to Real Madrid in the summer of 2019 for an initial £88m with clauses to make the deal potentially reach £124m. What followed was a reaction by Madrid's biggest rivals for the La Liga Title. Barcelona poached Antoine Griezmann from rivals Atlético Madrid for £108m, who in turn used the money to replace him with Portuguese wonderkid Joao Felix from Benfica for £114m.

One simple transfer caused two clubs to smash transfer records in response to Real Madrid purchase of Hazard. Over £340m signed off on just three players as club officials know the importance to keep all three clubs in the race for the title and Champions League race.

A more recent example of the transfer window being a cyclical mechanism for clubs is from the summer of 2021. One which may have gone under the radar and off the back pages of newspapers. Rui Silva, a goalkeeper playing for Granada was in the last six months of his contract and was one of the most sort after players on several club's shortlists due to his statistics putting him in the top 5 of performing goalkeepers in Europe.

But with football clubs tentatively spending money after 18 months of a frenzied selling period after Covid-19 caused the bubble in football finance to burst, more European clubs looked at free transfers to bolster their ranks in the interim period.

Real Betis beat a host of clubs to Silva's signature, which forced them to investigate alternatives. Firstly, Granada replaced Silva with Luís Maximiano from Sporting Lisbon for £4m. Sporting Lisbon, reached out to Everton and signed their highly rated youngster Joao Virginia on loan with an option to purchase for £3m. Everton, now in need of a backup, scoured the free agent market and looked at two possibilities, Sergio Romero a free agent after leaving Manchester United and Asmir Begovic from Bournemouth also available on a free as the South Coast club looked to reduce costs in the Championship.

Everton settled on Begovic and Romaro signed for Venezia to complete the transfer cycle in one window for these clubs. Had Rui Silva chosen another club, then the outcome of the window may have been different for these clubs. One tiny free transfer can have a rippling effect for several clubs and players. For fans clamouring for the news and reading the headlines, this is the hidden mechanism that is the driving force behind players changing clubs in a transfer window.

The way clubs spend money in the transfer windows continues to change with factors impacting clubs. For media publications desperate for a transfer scoop to boost sales, face a problem that a simple review of club accounts and understanding that transfers fees are spread out over the period of a player's contract would let journalists know whether the rumours they peddle have a chance of happening and what a football clubs actual transfer budget is due to FFP. A simple formula on the accounts could dispel nearly ninety percent of football transfer rumours.

It may also change the way football fans view transfer news. Will we continue to seek out information from social media accounts and newspapers if a simple review of accounts online would determine if what we are reading is false? Will people begin to unfollow journalists and ITK accounts when they realise they are being spun on a commercial lie that their clicks for like stories are making someone else money and wasting their time?

Only time will tell and as we saw with Sean Cummings pretending to be a journalist, the internet can be a cancerous place during transfer windows, whereas Sean was taking an educated guess with his endeavour, many ITK freely make up stories to boost their own profiles or profit from the stories. These fake stories put stress on players, some like Josh Maja are still teenagers just out of school. Others are veterans, whose partners read these stories and do not know where they may be living with their children. For clubs, radio stations like talkSPORT are filled with fans phoning in with anger at how they football clubs are run.

These clubs in question may never have been in for these players. Yet the anger is directed at the board of directors and the owners of the clubs. For the fans, chats can be full of fans abusing one another over fake stories. One set of fans will debate whether a rumoured player is good enough even before they sign, causing infighting between the terraces. On the other side are the fans of the selling player, who will argue that their player is "too big" for that club with rival fans in another way the transfer window has had a negative impact on society.

With teams now confided to the constraints of FFP and the revenues brought into the clubs, where a team finishes in the league is becoming more and more important. With teams transitioning towards Moneyball statistics for scouting and unearthing gems to bring the average age of their squads down. Keeping residual value and future sales potential high. A process sped up with Covid-19 bursting the football pyramids bubble in a similar vein to the US housing crash which led to the 2008 worldwide economic downturn.

Whilst the commercial world may not have learnt lessons, the early recovery in the transfer windows suggests football teams who had their fingers burnt may have learnt lessons. Albeit painful ones. Barcelona, who financed a lot of their previous transfers on debt and paid high wages to maintain their La Liga dynasty, fell foul to the global slowdown in transfers.

Stuck with several players on significant contracts struggling to get their wage bill down and consequently couldn't afford to keep Lionel Messi, who was allowed to leave on a free transfer. To think one of the greatest footballers to play the game would leave their club for nothing is unfathomable. Unfortunately for Barcelona, their win-now approach caught up with them and left them with little choice but to get Messi's wages off the books.

Chapter 2
The Anatomy of a Football Transfer

Black leather shoes pound the cobbled streets of Barcelona, as the sun recedes behind famous landmarks and locals come out from their siestas, there is no Jim White, perfect yellow tie, the ringmaster to the circus, nor is it the next installments of a Jason Bourne Movie, this is the hidden story of a football transfer. This is David Harrison, Everton's Head of Operations and Club Secretary, sprinting through the heart of Barcelona looking for a lawyer and a fax machine to complete a transfer. Now this would have been taking the transfer window to the next level, with Jim White shouting, "and we cross live to the streets of Barcelona, Everton's Dave Harrison is searching for a lawyer and a fax machine, as the deadline for deal is fast approaching" as a drome swoops in following his frantic search.

The reality was a simple sentence on a yellow ticker on the television, "Yerry Mina and Andre Gomes are close to signing for Everton, but it is a race against time." Not quite as dramatic as the reality of completing the transfer against the ticking clock of deadline day, but it does show the extreme lengths some key staff members are forced to go through to get these transfers over the line.

Football is a billion-pound industry and entrepreneurs have found a way to milk the system. Newspapers, media and social media feed off this addiction and desperation, helping create this fantasy bubble, showing the cancerous side to social media, virtual chat rooms where even journalists help stir the fans. So how does one separate fiction from reality?

The discourse and connection between fans and the football club boardrooms feel wider than ever. In the past transfer news came from teletext, now fans want to see the future, in some cases due to social media, they get the news before the manager does. Fans are desperate to get ahead of the game, try to be the one who can break news for the club. Fans get to know where the clubs do their business, the hotels where they hold players, and camp out to steal a photo of the new player. Even Sky Sports have fallen foul of transfer rumours. "Juan Riquelme has been spotted on County Road" was reported live on the airways following Everton fans joking the Argentine was in Liverpool. Ironically, he was on County Road a few years later, on the Villarreal team bus on their way to a Champions League game against Everton.

Harry Redknapp is synonymous with transfer deadline day, leaning out of his car window giving the incomings and outcomings of the clubs he was managing at the time, it is what the viewers of Sky Sports Deadline Day coverage wanted, a yearly tradition for several years.

Moving into his punditry position a few years later, Redknapp continued to give behind the scenes information on transfer stories from his days in charge of football clubs, the same stories change as they are told, the truth slightly changed for laughs and the audience, but supporters still lapped them up and coveted them. Muddying the waters between fact and fiction when someone so close to football talks transfers, so why do people alter the truth?

Matthew, a journalist in sport and specialising in football, reveals in the past newspapers waited for Sunday to reveal their transfer news. "Sunday's paper circulation is higher as fans would buy the platform to get an update on the previous days match. Now a Sunday news scoop can now be tweeted on Wednesday when a fan spots the player in the city."

Business is business, a journalist following on Twitter can be bigger than the circulation of a national newspaper, their stories are 'hot takes' encouraged to divide, force you to click on stories, bringing revenue and advertisement to the struggling print publications. "It's madness, but fans believe it, fall for it, argue over it and tweet out angry cries of just get it done!" The reality could be the player has no interest in joining the club.

The media have their own agenda, the "clubs that call themselves the big six, even though some of them are not big clubs, control the narrative and media, they have the fans who purchase the majority of the papers, bring in the views to the website from foreign means. Take the European Super League. Before the clubs across Europe announced their intentions to cartel themselves away into their own European League, the news had been leaked out before 2021. The clubs in this league wanted more money for themselves, profit and a chance to ring fence themselves at the top of the game."

As we have seen with Barcelona and the Covid-19 finance bubble, most of these clubs had spent heavily to procure the best players. As Covid-19 threatened revenue streams, it also threatened these clubs' stranglehold on world football, so the Super League was hastily drawn up behind the scenes by the select few.

Before the media and fan outcry, the Super League had been previously exposed, but the press largely ignored it. Dr Denise Barrett-Baxendale called out the early proposals for the Super League labelling the clubs as having 'Preposterous arrogance' that six clubs were undermining the competitive nature of English football, explaining Everton had refused to join or be part of the discussion. The 'Big Six' responded denying any of these talks were happening.

The media had the story but chose to side with these clubs. However, almost two years later, with Covid-19 impacting the game and fans still not back in the stadiums, the 'Big Six' went public with the other fourteen European clubs. This time, the media saw the instant fan backlash on social media, sensing they had picked the wrong side which threatened revenue streams, they spun the story to sell papers and condemn the 'Big Six', but crucially, the papers argued the Premier League should not expel them from the league, dock the club's points or enforce transfer bans. Why?

These clubs bring in the most revenue for the papers, the reporters are fans of these clubs, and the journalists support these teams, the Premier League had the power to expel them, and the fourteen other clubs could have voted to do this, but the newspapers campaigned for a 'softer punishment'.

The English Football League (EFL) were also up in arms. In the midst of clubs going out of business or administration, they had been trying to get more money from the Premier League in the trickle-down economics to keep their leagues afloat. So, you can imagine the anger from the EFL when the Premier League had been claiming there was no money when the 'Big Six' were looking for more money from themselves. After being 'soft' on their criticism of the 'Big Six', the newspapers turned the screw on other clubs.

Firstly, with Everton, twice falsely claiming they had broken FFP, demanding a points reduction, this led to Leeds United and Burnley seeking legal action, only for lawyers to indicate Everton had no case to answer, but their reaction to Birmingham, Bury and Derby, almost begging for these clubs to have points deductions due to the actions of the owner's poor running of the business. A stark direct contrast to the owners of the 'Big Six'. You can begin to understand why fans can become toxic in football, finance and how it is reported in the media.

Matthew, who is now a freelance journalist after working in the print media world, believes video games such as FIFA and football manager fuel the cancerous nature of the transfer window. More and more fans believe transfers can happen overnight, because in a game they have done it in seconds, some deals can be done quickly if there is no negotiation, but the legal paperwork takes hours. Fans are filled on forums saying that their player wouldn't leave their club for this club, when the reality is, the player will follow where the best money is. How long does it take to complete a transfer? Football Manager gives the player an immersive perspective, but even then, the situation is streamlined for the player when it comes to the detailed transfers.

The best example of how a transfer can evolve behind closed doors and away from the Sky Sports yellow ticker would be the example of David De Gea, Real Madrid, and a fax machine. With the sun setting on August 2015, as the dying embers of the summer transfer window edged to a close, reports were leaking through that Real Madrid had signed David De Gea from Manchester United. The clubs had been negotiating back and forth for months over the fee United would receive and add-ons. Eventually settling on £29.3m and goalkeeper Keylar Navas going the other direction.

To get to this point on deadline day, for this one transfer, despite the 'fans' cry of just get it done', there are a number of factors that need agreeing and legally checking before paperwork needs drawing up. Firstly, the transfer fee, Madrid's pursuit of De Gea had been publicly known for some time. Yet, Madrid had been playing the long game by testing the water by not meeting United's asking price until the very last moments of the window.

To save time, once clubs begin active negotiations, or ask the selling club permission, they can speak to the player's agent and begin sorting personal terms with the player. In this process, Madrid would finalise the agent's commission for the deal. This is likely to be a percentage of the deal, which to outsiders can appear to be a backwards step in negotiation, as the agent now would potentially have more reason to want the transfer fee to increase. To stop this, teams could offer the agent a one-off fee. But then the selling club would argue this hinders them from negotiating a bigger transfer fee as the agent now has more reason for wanting the deal to go through with the time running out.

The contract negotiation varies, depending on the player, league and agent. Neil Warnock once joked on radio, how agents can drag out negotiations on their players contracts for months, yet, if an opportunity arises on deadline day to move one of their clients, with the opportunity to make commission on the deal, it can be done in a matter of moments.

One new stumbling block for clubs is a player's image rights, agents argue that clubs now need to pay a fee to use their own player in advertising and publicity. Deals are made if the player is allowed to sell or market themselves to other products. With more video games seeking licences, this is another potential obstacle depending on the players media pull. A player signing in the English Football League Two would not discuss this matter in a transfer. Cristiano Ronaldo's image rights on the other hand, probably gives his agent, Jorge Mendes, a headache in contract negotiations.

Once this is agreed, the transfer then needs to be given international clearance and checked it does not break any immigration or Brexit rules. Once confirmed, the paperwork is then uploaded to FIFA's Transfer Matching System.

Which brings us to Real Madrid's approach of David De Gea, once Madrid made him their number one target from their shortlist, they seek an approach with United. This is asking United for permission to speak to De Gea over a potential transfer. United agree, Madrid begin discussing personal terms with De Gea's agent. United begin the process of replacing their number one. Madrid had a solution and offered their goalkeeper, Keylar Navas, to pacify United, speed up the process by saving United the need to sign a replacement so late in the window.

Both players would need to agree to the transfer and agree personal terms, in this instance, both players agreed terms quickly. Player part exchange deals can normally be tricky to finalise as one player could refuse to move and veto the entire deal. The club then needed to refinance the entire deal and now has a dissatisfied player on their hands.

As deadline day moved on, United finally agreed the overall transfer fee for the deal and allowed the deal to progress. Agents' fees were agreed at both ends; image rights were checked to ensure that their players' sponsors didn't conflict with the clubs' commercial deals. Another piece of red tape fans rarely sees. If the player has a deal with manufacturer Nike, but the new club wear Adidas, this could breach image rights with Nike and must be settled before paperwork can be signed.

Once signed off, the players will normally have a medical at the new clubs training facility, in some cases, the buying club has sent out their medical staff to international training camps when players have been on international duty, having no chance of flying to and from countries due to their international commitments. On rare occasions, clubs can elect not to have medicals done, but due to the nature and cost of transfers this is rarely recommended practice.

Then comes the logistical nightmare for club secretaries, with the ticking clock of deadline day looming, twenty separate pieces of information need to be sent to FIFA's Transfer Matching System. If these transfers are agreed early, with days or months spare, there is no hurry. But on deadline day, with Madrid's deal for De Gea ticking down with minutes to spare, there is no space for a mistake, or in this instance, a dodgy fax machine.

Some players need international clearance and work permits if they fail to qualify for Home Office legal status to work in the new country of employment. This also needs to be uploaded and agreed with the contract. Some clubs could be sweating on multiple deals right up to the last few seconds. Some even request an 'offer sheet' to gain fifteen more minutes to complete the deal and upload it.

With Jim White updating nail biting viewers, United fans protesting at selling a key player, Madrid fans already buying De Gea shirts, the clubs begin loading the paperwork into the fax machines to be sent to FIFA.

With the clock striking midnight, the window slams shut, no more deals or conversations can be had. Paperwork cannot be adjusted; FIFA reviews several transfers sent through in the final moments. Using a system to see if United's match with Madrid's. It didn't, a sheet was missing from United's copy, FIFA ruled the transfer incomplete.

The deal was off, Madrid was furious and accused United of foul play, United's gain of the clerical error was keeping one of Europe's best young goalkeepers and their future captain stayed at the club. All the summers hard work, agent fees, player negotiations, time, for nothing. Both players remained at their respective clubs.

Another interesting side note to transfers is how the fees clubs pay are misreported constantly in the media. Pundits use this misinformation to judge them, praise or even critique clubs for their spending. Daniel Geey, in his book, 'Done Deal' breaks down what transfer fees look like for accounting purposes for the buying and selling club. Using Gee's reporting, I will break down how

Everton's deal for Richarlison cost the Merseyside club and why it has been misreported.

Everton submitted a bid for Richarlison in the summer of 2017. The fee was set at £35m, which would rise to £50m if certain clauses were met. These being, Everton qualifying for the Champions League and winning the Premier League. If Everton didn't achieve these clauses, the deal would remain at £35m. (£7.5m each for each additional add-on.)

The media criticised the deal, chastising Everton for paying £50m for a player from Watford, arguing they had overpaid. Some citing it as the worst transfer of the summer. Geey breaks down how Everton would pay for this transfer. Essentially the deal is £15m up front, with the remaining amount spread over Richarlison's contract. From reviewing the deal, it is obvious that those reporting on the deal were unaware of the transfer deal itself, but also how transfers in football are conducted, with payments normally paid for in installments.

In the summer of 2017, Everton would pay Watford £15m. On the anniversary of the deal in 2018, another £5m would be sent to them. So forth on the second anniversary, another £5m. Another £5m on the third anniversary. Clubs would then likely have the remaining £5m paid on the fourth anniversary or the selling club could ask for it to be paid on the completion of 100 or 150 appearances for Everton. With Everton's current situation in 2022, no closer to Champions League football or a Premier League title, the fee looks to remain at £35m for a player who has been integral to Brazil's qualification for the World Cup in 2022 and their Olympic Gold medal at the 2020 games.

For Everton, Richarlison has over 60 goal contributions in the five years with Everton and was a mainstay in the Merseyside club's team and has attracted the interest of Barcelona in recent years with Everton turning down a transfer bid of £70m for their player. Before needing to sell him a year later for £60m to Spurs due to losses amounting from Covid-19 and mismanagement in the transfer market that saw the club splash the cash on ageing players on bigger wages with little future transfer value.

Geey breaks down the real financial cost of a player over their contract. Without knowing Richarlison's wage, I have used an example of a player signing a contract worth £110,000 a week. Assuming the transfer fee was the same at £35m, a simple accounting measure of £110,000 X 52 (number of weeks in a year) = £5,720,000m a year.

Now if this player's contract runs over five years and the player sees out the deal. This £5,720,000 is multiplied by 5.

£5,720,000 X 5 = £28,600,000
£28,600,000 + £35,000,000 = £63,000,000.

Assume the standard agent commission is between the average (3–5%) of the transfer fee. (£1.3m) and the player receives a nominal signing bonus/loyalty bonus, (£3m).

The potential total cost of signing a player for £35m and paying them £110,000 thousand pounds a week is potentially as high as £67.9m. Hidden costs a fan never sees, but signing players at any cost is a gamble to a football club. With the financial restrictions of FFP, it is easy to see why most Premier League clubs are scrambling to commercialise, needing money to come in to offset spending. It also helps fans see why all teams are now selling clubs. Clubs must sell their unwanted players to offset incoming wages and accrued transfer fees to help top up transfer budgets.

Geey also breaks down how transfer stories originate. Before they hit the press, the main example being a practice that is technically outlawed under FIFA regulations, tapping up of players under contract. In some cases, the players' agents are too brazen to do it, because FIFA seem to be reluctant to enforce their rules and have independent regulators investigate agents.

The Premier League outlaws the practice of a club contacting or approaching a player whose contract is due to expire until after the third Sunday of May of the same year, normally six weeks prior to the players contract expiring. "Any club which by itself, by any of its officials, by any of its players, by its agent, by any other person on its behalf or by any other means whatsoever makes an approach either directly or indirectly to a contract player… shall be in breach of these rules."

Geey provided a similar example of Ashley Cole and Chelsea. The Premier League came into information that in January 2005, Cole, his agent, had met Chelsea's Chief Executive and Manager Jose Mourinho. Chelsea was fined £300,000 and handed a suspended three-point deduction. Cole and Mourinho were both handed £75,000 fines.

But at the heart of all transfers is the players. It is ultimately up to them if, how and when they move. The nucleus of every transfer, their behaviour dictates the transfer move. Players can engineer their move away from their club in the form of a transfer request. John Stones reacted to a report from The Telegraph's Matt Law that Chelsea was interested in the defender.

Stones put in a subsequent transfer request which Everton rejected, causing the players form to drop, helping cause disruption in the Everton team. This led to six months of turmoil for both the player and club. With Roberto Martinez rejecting the request, the defender played in a League Cup game against his former club Barnsley.

Pundits accused him of jumping out of the way of a goal bound shot which caused Everton to fall behind. With no official bid from Chelsea, the unwanted press had unsettled the youngster. Fans had grown angry at the lack of loyalty shown by the player and booed him off the pitch at Oakwell. What followed next became ugly, when both the Everton team coach and a supporter's coach pulled up at a motorway service station that night. Fans confronted Stones about his future, demanding answers and loyalty to a club who had given the England International his Premier League chance.

Stones, who was with fellow Everton player Steven Naismith at the time, apparently let his emotions out in public after the footballer refused to answer the supporters' questions. Naismith, a senior figure in the dressing room, told the fans that Stones has been banned from speaking in public about his current situation. For the record, after the Barnsley game, manager Martinez again said on camera that the Chelsea target is not for sale.

An ugly situation for all parties, started from a journalist's tweet, feeding into a players transfer request. A year later, the Everton fan favourite had joined Manchester City for £47.5m, a year after his original request.

Players can also go on strike to force through a move. Robbie Savage discussed his move between Birmingham and Blackburn Rovers on BT Sport branding himself a disgrace. A source from Blackburn had leaked it to the press that the club were interested in Savage for the January transfer window and were ready to spend £4m on the combative midfielder.

The Lancashire club had offered him more money and Savage claimed the move meant he was closer to his family back in Wrexham, the AA route planner revealed Birmingham was two miles closer to his hometown than Blackburn, infuriating then Birmingham City owner David Sullivan.

Savage admitted in his autobiography that in his last game on New Year's Day in 2005 against Newcastle, he did not even try and in training prior to the move he had disrupted the training sessions. He was sold the next day.

Players can also perform well to gain transfers and improved contracts. The best examples being Leicester City's 2015/16 1000/1 title winning season, with Riyad Mahrez and N'Golo Kante. Players who were integral to Leicester's title charge and improved their transfer value during the season. Other key players such as Jamie Vardy and goalkeeper Kasper Schmeichel were awarded contracts for their performances.

Kante and Mahrez were the source of transfer interest from both Manchester City and Chelsea, teams who Leicester had usurped that year and had performed well and attracted the most interest. Bought for little amounts they made Leicester handy profits when they were sold respectively, Mahrez to Manchester City for £60m and Kante was sold to Chelsea for a little North of £30m.

Geey also demonstrates that players legally, according to the rules set by FIFA, negotiate the termination of their contract early. But it comes at a great cost to the player. If players wish to join another club whilst under contract, it would cost them millions. Their ability, contract length and proposed transfer fee all would need to be paid. The player could also be asked to pay the legal fees for the clubs whilst their legal teams discuss what the cost of the player is. The fee would have to be paid by the player; the new team cannot transfer money to the player to forward on as this would potentially be seen as tapping up.

Players can also use the media to engineer a move and create a story. The latest example being Harry Kane, on the eve of the delayed Euro 2020 tournament in 2021, he went on Gary Neville's podcast and officially valued himself at £100m, knowing that there was going to be interest in his services, he deliberately undermined his club's valuation of him. Giving Manchester City an insight to Spurs' hand at the negotiating table.

When this failed, and Manchester City refused to meet Spurs' £150m valuation of Kane, the saga continued long after England's Euro 2020 final defeat to Italy and into the last week of the window. To try and move things on prior to the Euro's, Kane, under the guidance of his agent, his brother, put in a transfer request. Spurs' chairman Daniel Levy refused to budge and rejected the request. Maintaining his stance that if City met the valuation, then Kane could leave. City couldn't afford Kane at that price and failed to submit another bid during the 2021 league campaign.

With City moving onto to purchase Erling Haaland a year later, the wonderkid, whose contract had a release clause of £63m if activated in the Spring of 2022. Kane, Captain of Spurs, now faces an awkward situation, he's not getting the move he desired, and publicly spoke out about Spurs not winning trophies or meeting his Champions League ambitions, not a good look for the club captain.

Players coming to the end of their current contract can let them expire, which drives transfer activity and can provide the column inches news outlets crave. If a player's contract runs out, the club is not entitled to any transfer fee. If the agent or the player informs the club, they will not be renewing their contract, it gives the club impetus to sell the player between 18–12 months of their contract running out, so they at least get some value for the player. An example being Ross Barkley, who with 12 months left of his deal was sold to Chelsea for £15m, or İlkay Gündogan joining Manchester City from Borussia Dortmund for £20m.

Harry Kane could have engineered his move if he and his brother had thought about putting a smart clause in his contract. They negotiated a nice wage increase for Kane, but without a release clause, one that could have been activated if a club in the Champions League offered £70m, then Spurs would have been legally obliged to accept them. Clubs hate these clauses, as they are easy for another team to find out about them, agents, players and the media publish them and give the buying clubs an upper hand when it comes to negotiations.

Another way Geey highlights how players become the catalyst of transfer rumours are if the club they play for are relegated. No player wants to have a relegation on their CV and very few will down tools to force a move via relegation. Players can have relegation clauses in their contract, one could lower their wage on dropping down the division, players driven by money will be straight onto their agents looking for a top division move. Secondly, players may have relegation transfer clauses which means other teams can purchase them for smaller amounts than normal.

Leeds United had a relegation clause in their talisman Raphinha's contract of £25m clause should Leeds be relegated in the 2021/22 season. With clubs like Barcelona circling, they risked missing out on £40m, as staying up meant this fee could be worth up to as much as £65m. The fee would be significant for Leeds in rebuilding and helping them with FFP measures.

Final option for players to drive the narrative is failing to settle. A player may prefer nicer weather, their family may not speak the language, moving to a new country away from their support bubble, a member of their family may be unwell. Players are human at the end of the day, facing the same struggles and issues as everyone else. With the example of Dimitri Payet returning to Marseille, after admitting his wife and children couldn't settle in the UK.

Back to the searing sun in Barcelona. Imagine with all the ways transfers can be instigated, you have spent months agreeing a fee, personal terms, juggling a player on international duty at the World Cup, David Harrison was not willing to allow the transfer of Yerry Mina and Andre Gomes from Barcelona to Everton fall through on deadline day. Ignoring the stares from the locals as he pounded the roads of the city centre in his suit, searching the local cafés for the agent who could sign off on the double deal.

Harrison made it in time, the paperwork was signed and submitted through a working fax machine. Just in time for Jim White to straighten his trademark yellow tie as he was counted back in from a commercial break, to announce that Everton had signed Yerry Mina and Andre Gomes on five-year deals. To viewers, we were none the wiser to one of the transfer windows hidden hero's, somewhere in Barcelona, in need of a cold drink and a pat on the back.

Contract negotiations themselves also bring with them hurdles that can instigate a transfer. Harry Redknapp joked that he signed an established striker and offered him £50,000 a week. The player's agent, his mum, then tried to negotiate a goal bonus on top of his contract to Harry's disgust, happy as always to recall the story to a crowd, "What do you think I am paying you £50,000 a week for? To miss them?" With the growth of data and social media able to clip footage in seconds, fans can see when players seemingly dip in form, or worse, stop producing numbers on the pitch.

Fans are asking for more accountability for players. Angry at players not putting in 100% shifts for their club, too easy to hide behind blaming the manager, downing tools, or underperforming and putting the club at risk of relegation. It is a dream, but fans are facing a cost-of-living crisis and the discord between players and their performance is never greater.

Watching football from the eighties, players always beat the first man at corners or free kicks. Now footballers publicly moan if they must do shooting drills. Variable pay deals would give the players the incentive to perform if the goal bonuses were reduced from their weekly wage, like the commission of car salesmen.

Fans want to see more of these types of deals. Players who are injury prone, pay as you play. Loyalty bonuses based on number of years served, not paid on a player transferring. Too many times, players are open to a move and give interviews where the state the club they are moving to is just a stepping stone for a future club.

Psychologically, they are already onto the next club. Loyalty bonuses would be paid every September, giving the players who have been offered them the incentive to stay. It works in the National Football League (NFL), the American football contracts award players for making the rosters and most contracts are incentive laden. A player can sign a five-year deal worth £10m. £10,000,000/260 (52 weeks x5) = £38,461 a week. But they only receive this if they are at the club for five years. No loyalty bonus paid on leaving. In some cases, players are only guaranteed half of this, due to a salary cap nature, players can be cut or traded based on performance.

Whilst this may be the extreme, it would certainly be a welcome move in the right direction for fans. Perhaps a softer approach would be meeting the proposal halfway, if a player is offered a £50,000 a week contract, they receive £35,000, topped up to £50,000 if they win. £42,500 if they draw. Players would hate it, but they would soon start to give the maximum to every game to ensure they got paid. Fans I have spoken to have argued the standard of football would increase, "we're tired of seeing a corner or free kick hit the first defender chest high, then players shrugging their shoulders, smacking chewing gum around their mouths as the opposition score another goal from a set piece."

Intricate clauses are also common in transfer deals. One transfer that got football fans talking, was the non-transfer of Luis Suarez from Liverpool to Arsenal in 2013. News broke that Arsenal had bid £40m and £1 for Suarez, to activate a clause in his contract that required Liverpool to accept bids over £40m for the player. When Liverpool rejected the bid and the media speculated over the reasoning for the pound in the offer.

Arsenal asked for the FA and the Professional Football Association (PFA) to get involved legally. As they believed Liverpool had failed to accept the clause in the player's contract which meant they were free to speak to Suarez. As the investigation took place, Liverpool owner John Henry tweeted, "What do you think they're smoking over at the Emirates."

Seemingly unaware that some sort of clause had been triggered. The PFA found that the clause was a 'good faith' clause rather than an automatic release clause. Explaining that any offer over £40m would need to be given to Suarez's agent to consider, it was not an actual release clause, more of a gentlemen's acknowledgement.

Arsenal argued that Liverpool had still fallen foul of legal rules and put the tweet forward as evidence, as a 'good faith' clause would mean that the parties are required to negotiate in good faith once a bid has been made. It does not mean Liverpool have to accept but make Suarez and his agent aware of the bid and interest of Arsenal.

The frustration that Liverpool and their owners faced was ironic, as the club is known for being shrewd in the transfer market, frequently taking advantage of contract clauses to build their squads and in recent years has been a significant reason they have been successful. Takumi Minamino, Christian Benteke and Joe Allan are just a few of the players Liverpool have successfully purchased from other clubs with release clauses. It is also a reason why Harry Kane's move failed in the summer of 2021. Spurs had agreed in good faith they would consider a transfer offer if one came in for the striker. Levy considered the offer and rejected it out of hand.

Football clubs when selling players can insert 'Buy Back Clauses' into any transfer deal. These can be exercised at any time during the player's contract at his new club or within an expiry date. Ensuring that the player will continually be linked with transfer moves until they do move, or the players contract ends. When Everton signed Barcelona prodigy Gerard Deulofeu for £5.4m, two years after a year-long loan, it was seen as such a coup by the club and new manager Roberto Martinez in 2015. Inside the deal, a clause had been included, Barcelona could buy back Deulofeu at any time for £10.8m.

With Everton changing managers frequently over a year-long period, Barcelona saw an opportunity to recall the player and make a potential profit as clubs enquired to Barcelona on his availability rather than Everton, as they would have to pay more to the Merseyside club. Barcelona activated the clause in summer 2018, but no bids materialised, and he spent a year struggling at the Camp Nou before being offloaded to the Premier League to Watford for £11.7m and an initial loan fee for £900k.

Loans with options to buy can create headaches for several different reasons, if a club manages to loan a player, but wishes to push the payment further down the line to the next transfer window and into next year's accounts, clubs can agree such a deal. Southampton did such a deal in 2014, signing Atlético Madrid centre-back, Toby Alderweireld, in a deal giving them an option to purchase him the following year for £6.8m. Atlético had a counter clause in the deal which meant they could reject the option by buying it out for £1.5m.

With his performances on the pitch growing his stature, Spurs came sniffing around the player and approached Atlético for a deal. Southampton missed the opportunity to trigger the clause in January to legally bind the deal. Spurs offered £11.5m before the summer transfer window and Atlético accepted, making £3m more for the player had they sold him to Southampton, who were £1.5m better off, but missed out on the player.

Which begs the question, should a club be allowed to tout a player that isn't theirs? Some will argue Spurs were savvy and knew about the deal and pounced, others will defend Southampton and claim that legally, Spurs shouldn't know about the clause, and how did they get the information, when they didn't enter the negotiations the year before? It could only have come from an agent or Atlético acting in bad faith to Southampton.

It isn't just the Premier League clubs who can manufacture stories in the transfer window. Reaching out to football league fans, Ray, a Peterborough fan, opens what it is like for a fan in the football league. "Transfers fill the football void during the long summers without games but seeing players (Erling Haaland) signing for Manchester City and getting £500k a week doesn't feel right. In four months, his wages will be bigger than some Championship's yearly wage bill. How do you compete with that?"

It takes some of the beauty out of football; it is no longer the working-class game. Clubs in the football league are scrapping for every penny to survive, and footballers only care about money now. Look at Everton, a team full of millionaires, half-hearted, not interested in the fans or the clubs' employees who will be made redundant if they are relegated. Then the players leave, rather than play in the Championship, they demand moves and more millions, quicker than rats from a sinking ship, it is never their fault.

When quizzed on Peterborough being in the Championship, Ray smiles. "I have been a Posh fan for fifty years. I take immense pride in their achievements, I know it will be tough, the lowest budget in the league, but we enjoy it." The club's director of football, Barry Fry, has worked well given their budget constraints. "He found players, Mo Eisa from non-league football, Ivan Toney, free transfer from Newcastle, turned him into a £5m. He build's his team always within a budget, we don't want to do a Derby, gamble the future of the club on promotion and nearly go bust."

Football clubs are the soul of towns, look at Bury, what happened with them going out of business. 'Unthinkable' Ray shaking his head. "Makes my blood run cold, sadly football clubs are just toys for billionaires. I am happy for my club to be 'The Loan Arrangers' in the transfer market, we may never reach the golden ticket of the Premier League, but the club will always have a connection to the fans."

But Ray's point highlights the issues clubs in the lower league face, unable to purchase players due to FFP and salary caps. They are forced to dip their toe into the loan markets, scouring the divisions above to use a young player for a year, just to make up their twenty-three-man squad. "You hope they can play, cause if not, you are stuck with them. The desire can be there, because they need games to get better, but some of these lads have never played a professional game before."

A problem all too well known for Peterborough owner, Darragh MacAnthony, who with DOF Fry, scour the Premier League for talent to keep them in a division, where every game is like David vs. Goliath for them. Engaging with fans on Twitter, MacAnthony used the platform to explain how Manchester United had demanded a £200k loan fee and 100% wages for a youngster with no first team experience. Unrealistic due to the salary cap, and the players wages likely to be more than some of the senior players.

"I understand his disappointment, Premier League clubs seem to live in their own little bubble," Ray concurs. "You wouldn't spend that money on a player who might not be able to hack it in the league. It is a double-edged sword for lower league clubs, you're always one bad financial move from disaster."

When discussing the future of the transfer windows with fans, it is interesting to get their views on whether the current system is working, or fair for all clubs. "The window should shut before the season starts, open it sooner and close it before a ball is kicked," sighs Ray. Teams are forced to wait until June before opening negotiations, tweaking the football calendar would give the agents and clubs two, possibly three more weeks to iron out the business they would lose by shutting it earlier.

Ray confers. "Teams could lose their star players and have no time to replace them, half a season without them could relegate clubs, look at Spurs, they nearly lost Harry Kane a few weeks into the season. They kept him and managed to put in a bid for the top four because of it."

Further to this point is, teams with bigger budgets can replace a player if they are injured in the first few weeks into the year. A club at the bottom of the league cannot replicate this, the aim should be to build a versatile squad, but this becomes a challenge if your best players are poached three to four weeks into the season. Even more so now with the five-sub rule. It is impossible to build a squad in the Premier League if you are outside the top six, Brighton is the latest club to have their players poached just as they seem they are about to mount a challenge on the stranglehold of the "top six. Football as a competitive sport sadly may be dead."

Changing the January window to loans only, with no clauses to buy would certainly change the footballing world, all the business would need to be done in the summer window, then clubs would need to maximise the summer window, any injuries would need to be covered by their squad and youth players. A way Premier League clubs could blood their youngsters and give them first team experience. It could also break the stranglehold of the teams with the bigger budgets up. More chances of clubs doing a Leicester in 2015.

This is backed up by the 2020/21 season, where Liverpool lost an unprecedented three first choice centre-backs to injury. Van Dijk tore his ACL, Joe Gomez suffered a non-contact knee injury on England duty and Joël Matip suffered ankle ligament damage, forcing Liverpool to play academy graduates Nat Phillips and Rhys Williams, who performed well given the circumstances. They got experience they would not normally get. For Phillips, he was put in the shop window and Liverpool put a £15m pound price tag on him in the Summer of 2022. For Liverpool, this is important to allow them to reinvest in new and better players.

This did not stop Liverpool from signing two centre-backs in desperation in January, however. Ozan Kabak signed from German Bundesliga Club, Schalke 04 on loan with an option to buy and Ben Davies signed from Preston for £1.67m. In his first training session, Davies suffered an injury which put him out for the year. Preston lost their starting centre-back and had no chance to sign a replacement.

"It would have impacted us, it is good in principle, but is it fair?" Geordie Becky argues, with her beloved Newcastle's long-drawn-out takeover was finally finalised in October 2021, their new owners, a Saudi Arabian consortium led by PCP Capital Partners, Reuben Brothers, and the Public Investment Fund (PIF), with Newcastle in the bottom three, sacking incumbent Manager Steve Bruce and replacing him for Eddie Howe, results did not immediately turn for the better. January 2022 was to be a pivotal one for Newcastle and their history. Get it right and they would have a chance to upset the apple cart of the so-called "big six", get it wrong and they would be the richest club in the world in the Championship.

Newcastle's 'panic buys' as the media called them, started with a loan for Aston Villa left back, Matt Targett, followed by the signing of Kieran Trippier for £13.5m. With star striker Callum Wilson injured, Newcastle activated the release clause of Chris Wood for £27m and followed it up with their best and marquee signing, Bruno Guimaràes for £38m. The signings, a change in tactics and philosophy led Newcastle from 19th to easy survival in the league.

The expected purchases were explored by Jim White on talkSPORT, "I cannot remember an occasion where a club tried to buy their way out of trouble." For the outside viewers, it would be fascinating, before January, rooted in the bottom three Newcastle looked dead and buried. Written off by journalists as dead and gone along with Norwich and Watford. Newcastle battled back and went on a run that saw them climb up the table, buoyed and galvanised by the new signings.

There is an argument to be made that without this transfer window, Newcastle would not have survived, how many clubs would be able to get billionaire owners and spend £90m to keep them up? It also can be said it helps move players who have six months left on their contracts and could begin to immediately look to sign pre-contracts with another team.

Ray is not sure on the loan only January philosophy. "It makes sense and works, but smaller clubs may need to sell a player to survive, denying them that could be fatal with the rise in costs of football operations." Taking the point further, if a club falls into administration they are denied a chance to sell players to pay creditors. "It would not stop loans to lower league clubs, so it is an interesting proposal."

Short term, supply-side inflation would cause panic buying which could see prices rise, yet, with the global supply of money drying up in football, then clubs need to sell players could see prices drop significantly, as more football clubs look to be smarter with money and wages. The bigger clubs would be against the move, recently campaigning for the use of five substitutes which would favour their squads over the other teams.

These teams would vehemently campaign to stop this happening and possibly even the biggest European clubs, those who opted to join the European Super League, would join in as this would threaten the dominance they currently have over the teams in their leagues. Marcel Brands, director of football at PSV, would possibly be open to it. At his time at Everton, he was very vocal against the January window, citing the inflated prices and panic buying. January should be about loaning out youth players and signing young players.

The January window can also be used to weaken some clubs, abusing the principle of competition. The previously mentioned example of Newcastle activating Chris Wood's release clause and taking the player from their relegation rivals Burnley at the time seemed to all but seal Burnley's fate.

In another case, Everton and Spurs tussled for the final UEFA Cup places in the 2010/11 season. Spurs approached Steven Pienarr, who was entering the final 12 months of his contract. Harry Redknapp saw the opportunity for a bargain and a chance to weaken an Everton team that was reliant on the Pienarr and Leighton Baines partnership with little finances to strengthen the team.

Everton turned the bid down, but Spurs came again in January, turning Pienarr's head and he rejected Everton's contract negotiations. With the fear of losing a player for nothing, they sold Pienarr for £3.24m. Spurs barely played him, finished 5th, Everton finished 7th and missed out on Europe. The following year Spurs loaned him back to Everton, before selling him to the Merseyside club for £5m.

Daniel Geey broaches the argument for transfer windows, presenting both cases in his book, laying out the argument for both. By having a defined transfer season (January and summer), it provides fairness to the competitions. Allowing teams to do transfers late into the season would favour certain teams one another. Manchester City or Liverpool being able to buy players in April or May would stop a team like Leicester from ever repeating their heroic title win, it would, as Geey puts it, distort the proper functioning of the whole season.

Teams with nothing to play may be inclined to sell players to other teams at inflated prices, but this could have major impacts on the title race, Champions League places and the fight to stay in the football divisions. It could also mean more clubs go into debt in the lower leagues. Owners could and properly would gamble by breaking FFP to survive and take a 12-point deduction the following year, if it meant they survived.

The integrity of the competition and sport must be protected. Allowing the teams to buy and sell players would change the sorting integrity of the competition. Games played after the transfers would be ultimately affected by these transfers and results would disrupt the level playing field teams have outside the window.

Also, as previously highlighted, players are easily unsettled, some seemingly already don't give a 100% each week. By having an open window all year, what would stop clubs talking to players before a big derby, or cup semi-final. Player turnover would be even greater, fan affection would be down, and international fans would follow players and not certain teams. The European leagues as a result would become weaker products.

The main arguments against the transfer window come from the legal challenges, is it right to stop someone from changing teams or jobs until two windows? Employees in any other industry have the freedom to move from one job to the next. Some argue the players' contracts and the value of the money they make is the trade-off. Given that more agents and players tend to demand, or engineer moves, many footballers do not make it to the end of their current contract. Economically, clubs argue having no window, or reverting to the old Premier League transfer window which closed on the last Thursday in March would bring transfer fees back under control.

By reducing the window, we would also lose the ITK's and by-products of fake accounts which have provided unique quirks. School boys can now pretend to be journalists and make money off people's desires to know transfer news. Perhaps in recent memory, Sam Gardiner created a fake online profile from his bedroom and had several clubs and journalists fooled that he was really in the know on football transfers.

A sixteen-year-old who just wanted his voice on Arsenal heard, frustrated at seeing them falling from grace on and off the pitch. Given a voice in Nigel Tassell's book, 'Boot Sale' his goal was to create a fake account to highlight how someone who appears to be in the media can create a narrative. He would post near identical tweets on his personal account and fake 'Dominic Jones' a fake football scout who had written for Goal! Magazine. He was quickly rumbled upon by an actual journalist who wrote for Goal.

Gardiner did not panic, he closed the account and set up another, Samuel Rhodes, coupled with a profile picture of a businessman from the thirteenth Google page, this time calling himself a freelance writer and had worked with the Financial Times and The Telegraph. Gardiner's alias account quickly reached 30,000 followers, whilst his personal account, posting identical tweets, hovered around 200. Gardiner had realised the likes of Arsenal and Chelsea had the type of player they were looking for. Arsène Wenger had an affection for flair players, when they needed a Tony Adams style centre-back or Patrick Viera Centre Midfielder, Chelsea on the other hand were always looking for the next Drogba.

Opinion and journalism are a fine line often crossed is the point Gardiner raised, because a so-called journalist tweets the information it is lapped up by people and the story spreads like wildfire. People lap it up and run with the story. His tweets would often go viral, predicting Mo Salah would sign for Liverpool five years before he did. (He went to Chelsea but after a spell in Roma eventually wound up at Anfield.) Al Jazeera ran with the story of one of Africa's and Egypt's most valuable players. Creating more substance to Gardiner's alias. By token of gratitude, the same tweet got the odd like and retweet from his personal account.

His personal best story came from Roberto di Matteo being sacked by Chelsea after a poor run of form. Gardiner noted he used his formula for the story. "Roman Abramovich did not have long-term confidence in the manager. He was used to changing managers every few years." He predicted the sacking the next day, based off articles he had seen a few weeks earlier, coupled with Chelsea's poor form and he waded in.

Gardiner was finally rumbled when The Telegraph put out a social media post claiming the account was fake and that Samuel Rhodes had never worked for them. But for Gardiner, his point was proven, a niche market within football could easily be manipulated and had been for years. A fake Twitter account and Google picture was all it took for people to buy into these stories.

Fans had become dissatisfied with the bias in print media, or the broadcasters and Sam had just proven how easy it was to manipulate the media's own mechanism. People still set up these accounts now, as their followers grow, they abuse the accounts to harvest revenue from advertisers.

Football fans are dissatisfied with the coverage from the big broadcasters, they are biased, happy to keep the current 'top six' on their perch, the future of transfer news and sports news could be podcasts, YouTube channels. All it takes is another brand to come in, Amazon have been tentatively dipping their toe into live games. Their coverage is paid for with their Amazon Prime account. For one amount, users get their Sport, next day delivery and television for one price.

Could the answer be to give more power to the fans to give them a voice? "Currently the big two broadcasters are unreliable, but with no alternative, we are, as fans, close to losing our game." Fans can watch live stream television shows, but why can't they watch every game from their own home?

Perhaps we can have more fan discussion, where we can enjoy talking about football, get rid of online hate and remove the keyboard warriors. Football should be a healer, not a divider. Gary Neville's online podcast, The Overlap could be one of the answers, fans have more of a voice and Gary provides access to stories most fans demand but have limited access to.

Fabrizio Romano, perhaps the most reliable ITK accounts on Twitter took this desire for access one step further on the summer deadline day in 2019, Romano did a feature for Bleacher Report which was showcased on YouTube, the ten-minute feature shows how he gets his inside information, there is no made-up story, he is seen walking and driving the cobbled streets of Milan. His arduous work to get the inside story displaying to people how he operates, provides readers with the comfort that his news is likely to be dependable and further shows up some of the fake stories that we see in the media, but also how hard he works to provide reliable information to his followers.

Opening his show, Romano is shown making and taking calls to his sources, entering hotels looking for football managers, agents, and sporting directors for transfer information, so he can update his followers on Twitter with. Romano runs through the deals he has broken in this window; from João Cancelo's move to Manchester City from Juventus, with Danilo going the opposite way in a swap deal plus £28m. Romelu Lukaku's move from Manchester United to Inter Milan, in his tweets he even lets fans know where the deal is up to, and that paperwork has been signed. He was also first on Alexis Sanchez's move from Manchester United to Inter Milan.

Romano gives specific details on transfers revealing that Rodri's move to Manchester City from Atlético Madrid was down to City activating his release clause in his contract for £62.6M, providing the information quicker than the clubs do for their club's fans. Romano also details Eden Hazard's protracted move from Chelsea to Real Madrid is complete. In response to this, Barcelona signed Antoine Griezmann from Atlético Madrid and he also broke the news that one of Europe's highest rated teenagers, Matthijs de Ligt was to join Serie A club Juventus from Ajax.

09:30—We travel around the quiet streets of Milan; in search of his transfer news, he directly phones an agent of Stefono Okaka of Watford and is told he could be on the move to Anderlecht in Belgium.

10:02—Romano takes a call with the agent to confirm the clubs are in talks.

10:30—He meets with a colleague and discusses a potential signing for Roma. They need a centre-back so they work out potential targets the club may pursue.

10:36—Romano receives a text to say Mario Mandžukić is not going to PSG. He will stay at Juventus who are expected to be busy today, on the move, he updates his Twitter feed.

10:50—He speculatively waits outside Juventus's offices for sporting director, Fabio Paratici when he is alerted to Roma targeting Chris Smalling, a centre-back from Manchester United. He immediately calls one of the agents working on the deal and is told the deal is on, professed and would have a £3m loan fee, with no option to buy. He immediately tweets his trademark message to his followers, here we go! Within minutes, Romano checks the traffic the tweet has created, thousands have seen it and interacted with the tweet by sharing it.

11:50—Into the town of Gallia, Romano scours the hotels for agents. looking for clarification on whether Angel Correa is going to get his move to Milan. His agent is due in the hotel and Romano waits for him to arrive. When he does, Romano gets an update of him regarding the ongoing deals he has for his players. Romano then investigates other hotels for AC Milan representatives, but there is no one there, so he moves on in search of more news.

14:00—Romano texts Neymar's lawyers over his rumoured move back to Barcelona from PSG, he asks if Barcelona have blocked the move. The lawyer confirms and hints, "we'll see, few days left."

Gianluca Di Marzio, another journalist tweets Neymar to Barcelona is on. Romano calls him to share his information, the deal is stalled but he is working on it.

15:00—Romano arrives at the Sheraton San Siro to finish his day, reporting for Sky Sports News, explains how if Neymar goes to Barcelona, then there will be a domino effect and Juventus will be prepared for bids. As the night wears on, Neymar stays put and there is no domino effect that causes anymore player movement from Juventus. For fans and aspiring ITK transfer accounts, it shows reporting on transfers can be done, Romano canvases hard to get his information and by presenting himself rather than a fake avatar, it makes him a credible source to follow for fans looking to get the insight into the transfer window.

Football fans are also finding their own ways of capitalising on the world of football, the growth in fan channels over the last few years has forced and, in some cases, led to the mainstream media losing some of its viewers. It gives the fans the option to choose what type of channel they watch, but also the topics. It also gives the listener content that the big television companies steer clear off, cheaper content and avoiding a top six bias.

Dan is a Crystal Palace fan, who on top of his day job, runs a daily podcast on Patreon, for a small monthly fee, currently £2 as I am writing this, offers fans of Crystal Palace a view and opinion they cannot get on the main channel. Called HLTCO in honour of former Palace footballer, David Hopkin who scored the goal in the 1997 Play Off final against Sheffield United to ensure Palace would be a Premier League team the next year and lead to the famous commentary from Rob Hawthorne, "Hopkin, Looking To Curl One."

Building up his viewers over the years and whilst tailoring his podcast on his beloved Palace, he is keen to interact on key topics in football, from his views on VAR (Video Assisted Referees), to former Referees refusing to admit their colleagues have got key decisions wrong to a top six bias. But where the podcast stands out is his ability to discuss a wide range of topics that are happening at the London club.

With the growth in his podcast, Dan has achieved what all fans, and television companies crave, and that is access to interviewing Steve Parish, Chairman and current owner of his beloved club. With more fan unrest in football than ever, his podcast style allows his viewers to have a once-a-year interview with the most influential figure within the club. In his most recent interview with Parish, Dan discussed the recent controversial World Cup in Qatar. Talking about Palace and his views on how the season has gone so far. Hearing an owner discuss their clubs' fortunes with a fan, how the season for him is going well, to plan, the impact on how the five substitutes impact clubs at the lower end of the Premier League spectrum and how they are using data with their director of football, Dougie Friedman to see if they can gain an advantage from this.

The interview allows Palace fans to have that bond with the board, to learn new things about the club and the aspirations about the future, talking about their club link with Botafogo the Brazilian club and how their scouting network can be tapped into to allow Palace a view on the wave of Brazilian talent that is coming through Palace scouts may have found this information difficult to get hold off.

They also have friendlies lined up against Napoli and Parish used this interview to explain to fans how the club are dealing with the Winter World Cup and ways the club are using these friendlies to feature the club against big opposition, all available to view on Palace TV Plus. Dan's platform allows both his and the club to grow, allowing the dialogue between fans and the board to get a message and direction of where the club are looking to go. Asking your Clubs chairman directly for an update on the proposed new stand at Selhurst Park. Why it is important for the process to be conducted properly with developers.

Parish was keen to emphasise the cost of redrawing plans, or changes to the size, or issues in the work could veto a project and prove costly to the club. Parish also described how the plan was to grow the fanbase, both corporate and regular match day fans. How the extra revenue could be used to help the club grow financially both on and off the field. This is where Dan steers the interview onto the transfer window, for his clubs January window and the future of Palace talisman Wilfred Zaha, who was entering the final six months of his contract, meaning a clubs outside of England could sign him on a free transfer, an outlier of the Bosman ruling in the 90s.

Parish sheds light on his desire to re-sign the player who is beloved on the terraces, how manager Patrick Vieria also wants the player to stay, but the decision is likely to come at the end of the season, meaning the risk of him leaving for nothing is always there. But Parish reiterates he wants what is best for his player, would love him to retire at Palace, but is also aware the player may want to move as he enters his thirties. Open and honest view gives viewers and fans clarity on a tense citation proving transparency to all Palace fans.

This type of interview is what makes the HTLCO podcast appealing in the current cost-of-living crisis, for a Palace fan who may be unable to afford the more expensive television channels or radio shows pushing all stories within football. It is what the big companies crave, but the trust between Dan and his podcast gives his viewers a peek under the curtain of the inner workings and progress at Crystal Palace. Dan is also branching out, discussing the key stories in football, giving an unbiased opinion on matters, but crucially giving fans their voice back.

Why the growth in fan channels can be explained by how sport can seemingly take over people's lives. Football becomes a rite of passage being a football fan, fans live for the transfers, it can bring out the best and worst in them. Some football clubs have more followers than religions, fans live and breathe the club, then when the season ends, the tap is turned off and fans have two months to find their fix of news. "It can be an unhealthy addiction" fans lose their routine, more likely to go to the match than a local pilgrim to a place of worship.

"For fans, the stadium is the place of worship," laughs Matthew, a fan I interview outside on deadline day. "Where fans come sometimes twice a week to celebrate or commiserate with each other based on their team's performance. Outside of football, we may never see these people, work with them, but on match day we share memories with them, tour the country and Europe with them, all following a football club. The transfer window is often a hot topic for us, we are starved of football over the summer, when most of us go on holidays, we still sneak looks online at who our clubs are linked with, who may be sold, the football season may end, but the need for news on our clubs doesn't. It is why fans are turning more towards fan channels with their subscription fees."

Chapter 3
From Grassroots to Spreadsheets

"Intelligence is the ability to adapt to change." Stephen Hawking

The days of standing in the mud and rain watching endless games of grassroots football are gone. The changing in the landscape of scouting players has had a seismic shift in how players are found and evaluated which has had a trickle-down effect into the game of football, data analytics and spreadsheets have become more important in becoming an integral part of the game. Many supporters may not have heard of the name Sam Green, but his work in football will certainly have influenced the way you watch the game, understand it, and possibly change the way your team recruits players. He is perhaps one of the biggest influencers on football without fans even realising.

Sam is one the pioneers behind data being used in analysis within football, slowly creeping into television footage for presenters and analysts to use as a rhetoric for describing what they had just seen play live in the match. Initially little icons would appear on the scoreboard on the television scoreboard. XG, (expected goals) chances created, it was not long before clubs with less spending power began to experiment using the data to find players in the transfer market, but this was not a new philosophy. It had been coined across the pound in two of America's biggest sports.

The scene in the major Hollywood film 'Moneyball' where Oakland Athletics' Billy Beane (General Manager) discusses with his scouts on replacing three of Oakland's best players in free agency on a fraction of the budget the rest of the teams have in the MLB. We see the scouts highlighting players the team cannot afford, giving us an insight to how professional sports teams reviewed players.

Everything regarding the players is debated, comments such as a player's confidence is described in several manners, from the players confidence being so big that he already has a presence in the room preceding them entering and giving off confidence to other players. Those teams try to replace players by paying big transfer fees for big name players who appear to have key attributes to be good footballers, but no discussion on how they play the game. Whilst the dialogue will have been dramatised for the big screen, conversations in these manners do occur in sporting war rooms when it comes to recruitment and a player's personality.

Trying to move on from an outdated mantra where good-looking players selected as it could help season ticket sales, a sign that their genes may have been better than someone who did not fit a social style. Football scouts when looking at youth players have been known to look at whether a younger player had hairs on their legs, a sign that they are hitting puberty and how much more their bodies may develop, if interested in the player the scout would enquire whether they have an older brother. Another way they could gauge whether the player had much more to grow, they could compare the player to their sibling.

Billy Beane is seen to push the new agenda to recreate an aggregate. If your player had 20 goal contributions last year, clubs should use metric data to find a player who had similar output and playing style. In football terms for an attacker, how many goal contributions do they achieve? How do they go about achieving these? In a high press, create on their own? How many chances do they create? Work rate, progression of the ball. For defenders, interceptions, positioning, football intelligence, positioning, ball recoveries. By using the metrics of Moneyball, Oakland Athletics and now many football clubs use these metrics to unearth the future gems before they become recognised major stars, under Billy Beane's Darwinian mantra, "adapt or die."

Michael Lewis detailed the scene in his book 'Moneyball' the now inspiration for how sports teams have changed the way they conduct their scouting methods, not all teams have jumped on board, some are significant Premier League teams, the ones who have been left behind in recent times. The example of how if Oakland Athletics act like the Yankees in here, you will lose on the field out there.

Football equivalent is Brighton Vs. Manchester United. United have been burning through millions to finish sixth in the Premier League, whereas Brighton, are known for their analytical approach to scouting with the signings of Yves Bissouma for £7m, later to be sold for £25m to Spurs, planning they beat several high-profile European clubs to the signing of Moisés Caicedo for £4.5m.

In true Moneyball style, they signed Joël Veltman for £900k from Ajax, as other Premier League clubs looked at his height, 5'10" and deemed him too small to be a centre-back. He has been a solid signing compared to Harry Maguire (£75m) of United's. Brighton have also been smart to utilise academies, even if it is not their own, snapping up former Chelsea youngster Tariq Lamptey and giving the Ghanian first team football which has seen his value soar to £30m in January 2022.

In the 2021/22 season, Brighton had a positive net spend of £3m in the transfer market. (Made a £3m profit from player trading.) Following on from two windows where they made a negative net spend, but ensured the players bought in the 2019/20 season, (£48m) were vital for the club to maintain and sustain their Premier League status. Their recruitment has seen them compete with those clubs who have significantly more spending power, close the gaps on the clubs in the European places, play attractive football, all while building for sustainability and beating United 4–0 towards the end of the season.

The changing face of the scouting network has been changed by the formation of data around football which seem to explode in the recent decade. More and more recruitment teams are using the data which has adorned football streaming services and are using this to build databases on footballers all over Europe, this allows Directors of Football to find players who are like-for-like versions of current players.

For the smarter clubs, gone are the days of managers picking players without real knowledge of what the player may bring to the club. Which is madness when you think that in one window, clubs spend more money on transfers than a country's GDP. It also makes you wonder if managers, whose job it is to coach the players, really understand the art of the game and coaching.

A further view to support the claim comes from Simon Jordan, journalist and former owner of Crystal Palace in his award-winning book, 'Careful What You Wish For' Jordan is discussing the potential transfer of striker Noel Whelan, who they earmarked to fire Palace back into the Premier League by signing him on loan from Middlesbrough. Manager Trevor Francis really wanted the player and completed the deal.

When Jordan asked Trevor what he thinks of the player, he responded by saying the player was very good looking. Not exactly the answer an owner is probably looking for but proves that scouting in the football league at the time relied more on what the manager thought, rather than could the player actually play and is eerily parallel to the scene from Moneyball.

Sam Green's model began to understand the game more, stripping back the layers to find a correlation between vital statistics and how a player performs. How many shots does it take before a striker scores? The 'if you want to win the lottery, you have to buy a ticket' methodology, a commentator discussing 'a striker's willingness to go for goal' but does this make a striker any good? It gives you a percentage chance to 'win the lottery' but does it mean you are more likely to score a goal? What is a good chance?

If shooting from distance, or from a narrow angle turns possession over to the other team, is it reasonable to equate this into number terms to find out how impactful a player really is for a football team?

There are still people who feel data analysts won the culture war on football scouting, changing the scouting process, it is evident some clubs, like the example dramatised in the film Moneyball, some still scoff at the idea. Sean Dyche on his Monday Night Football debut scoffed at the idea of 'Expected Goal' theory but is a believer in data in scouting methodology. For the purists wanting to stand on the sidelines at grass roots level and spot the next Wayne Rooney, ankle deep in mud on grassy commons, their argument that data analysts haven't worked in football before is a dying argument.

Grace, a data analyst working in football and has presented player data to lower league clubs, is keen to point out how the data can be interpreted, even by those who have never played the game before. "Technology caught up with the game and allowed people to understand it more. Some people are not fond of math or data analysing a sport they believe they already understand. Expected goals (or xG) and Expected Assists are words now whispered in and out of football clubs now. New indicators of how players are evaluated."

"Expected Goals puts a number on how inefficient it is to shoot from long range, so clubs have changed their approach. As a result, the number of shots from outside the box has declined to two thirds of what it was when the model was introduced, from roughly 4800 to 3200 per season. The metric is changing the way the game is played."

"Expected goals (or xG) measures the quality of a chance by calculating the likelihood that it will be scored from a particular position on the pitch during a particular phase of play. This value is based on several factors from before the shot was taken. xG is measured on a scale between zero and one, where zero represents a chance that is impossible to score, and one represents a chance that a player would be expected to score every single time."

"We see this in game after game. Team A has an xG of 3,1 and Team B has an xG of 2,73. Based on the quality of the chances, the likelihood of scoring was bigger for team A than it was with team B. This, however, does not mean that Team A should have won. Expected goals measure the quality of the chances and the likelihood of scoring. However, it does not predict the expected outcome of the game, which is a whole different metric. It is not as simple as saying that a player 'should have scored' a particular chance because the xG was high.

"Similarly, if the chance is missed, the player is not necessarily putting in a bad performance. Expected goal consists of varied factors. These include distance to the goal, angle, one-on-one, big chance, body part, type of assist, and pattern of play. Data is important as it allows the analysts to report to the coaches on trends within their team and what the team is lacking and how this can shape the transfer recruitment."

The data can be used to 'predict' what a player may achieve statistics wise after the player is signed. "Interpreting the data is always key, signing a player with XG of 0.5, extrapolating this over a 38-game season would expect to see the striker score around 19 goals a season. But, if the team signing the player are not great at creating chances on average, the striker is not going to score 19 goals as they will not get the chances to score."

Grace also is keen to point out goals are not always the best metric to scout a striker when using data. It goes back to whether the shot was expected to be scored.

A manager asked for our opinion on a player for his League 1 team. He had scored 20 goals the year before and the manager thought he could be the player to push his team into the Championship. What the data showed, and the manager had missed, is that eight of these goals were penalties. His team averaged one penalty a year. We highlighted to the manager that spending nearly £200k on this player for a League 1 team is significant and they were likely getting a player who would score 12 goals a season. Their current striker averages around the same output.

When Match Of The Day used Sam Green's model on the BBC highlight show to benefit the audio-visual media package to give fans more analysis to the match they are watching. If scouts look at it from a coaching or analyst point of view, what does the single match xG really tell us a lot about the long-term performance of a team? More on the impact of one game with several influences. "We as analysts build pictures for the team we work for and opponents for future game plans. In the transfer market, we usually work year-long with the scouts and the director of football to see what our strengths and weaknesses are, then use the data on players on our shortlist to narrow down those who we should sign."

We discuss the scene from Moneyball where the scout's rebel on the General Manager over the newfound metrics being used, Grace chuckles and smiles at the thought. "It happens more than you would believe, even today, but the managers and scouts who scoff are of the older generation. Most scouts haven't been professionals or even played the game, those who have are stuck in the era where scouts put emphasis on a players, height, weight and old-fashioned metrics, rather than what the player actually brings to a team, and this is what data can do, it paints the picture what a player actually does, how many chances does a winger create?"

It would seem there has been a general misunderstanding of what certain players bring to teams. Wingers in the past were judged on their pace, flair and assists. "A few issues with this theory, pace is great to have, but if the player has no end product, then a defence can game manage against this. What a scout would want to know is how the player creates chances? Crosses, set pieces, their positioning, progression of the ball up the field."

A winger who can take the ball from their own penalty area and move their team up the field is invaluable. Current teams focus on resetting, playing backwards rather than transitioning up the field. Players who play in teams where their strikers are not great at finishing were easily overlooked in the past, whereas the data can highlight they are good at creating chances and a better striker would have led them to have more assists.

"Two recent prime examples of players being bought incorrectly are Theo Walcott for Everton and Joelinton for Newcastle." Some managers prefer to bring in experienced players rather than coach younger players and this is exactly what Sam Allardyce did when identifying Theo Walcott with his Director of Football Steve Walsh.

"He looked only at his pace, ability to run 100m in less than 11 seconds. Reviewing data would have shown a player who didn't create chances, no longer a goal threat from his younger days and not great at progressing the ball or holding it up. Allardyce spent £20m and gave a huge contract to a deprecating player past his peak. The data would have shown Walcott to be worth around £5m and a fraction of the wage given. Not the players fault about the price and nor should the player not take the wage, but a bad decision by a manager who had Ademola Lookman and Nikola Vlašić, creative youngsters warming the bench."

Joelinton has turned from a bad transfer miss into a great coaching situation for Eddie Howe. When Newcastle, manager Steve Bruce and incumbent owner Mike Ashley splashed £40m on the Brazilian it raised a few eyebrows around scouting circles. Grace rolls back, recalling hearing the news. "Joelinton was a good target man for Hoffenheim, averaging eight goals a year, data wise he was around 0.25 in expected goals per game. Not someone you would spend £40m on. He was worth around £10–£15m given the Premier League tax. He was good at holding the ball up and distributing it off to wingers."

"When Eddie Howe took over in December 2021, he made a great coaching decision to move Joelinton into a pivot/number 10 position where his skills at linking up the play could be utilised. He finished the season as one of the first names on the team sheet looking like a player reborn, most managers who would have inherited him would have asked the board for a new player rather than study what Joelinton brings to the game and Eddie Howe deserves some credit for this."

Grace believes data is used by nearly all Premier League clubs use data, they just do a poor job of integrating analytics into their process and understanding what it is trying to show them. Those more successful clubs who cracked the code were unwilling to share the secrets or data, football clubs do not like giving each other an inch in competitive advantage. Liverpool is known for using data under Michael Edwards, one of the smart movers in the transfer market. Do not forget Liverpool were alleged by The Times to have hacked Manchester City's scouting database in June 2012, the clubs later settled the dispute to a tune of £1m paid to City. But it goes to show, data in transfers is not a new thing. More clubs are catching up to the curve.

Grace has one more piece of advice on data directing the transfer market in today's game. "Data is making clubs see a bigger picture when it comes to transfers, some will still make mistakes, but transfers can be unsuccessful for a variety of reasons. Data cannot see a player's desire, mental attributes to succeed. Is the player going to train to be the best, or the first off, the training field? Injuries can derail careers. Data has narrowed the transfer pool of players, more teams are fishing in the same pond looking for the big prize, some will still panic and end up making expensive mistakes or missing out to other teams."

Data has also seen youth recruitment thrive, with more deals being done for youngsters than ever before, as more pressure is being put on football clubs' academies to produce youngsters for the first team.

Squelching through the quagmire on the training fields at Bellefield, in West Derby, Liverpool, Everton's FC former training ground would have been hard for a purist to visualise how this warehouse, in the middle of one of Liverpool's most densely populated areas was to spearhead the future of one England's most successful football clubs? Tasked with designing a model that was to be copied throughout England, Tosh Farrell looked across the vast broken fields that had been Everton's training ground since 1946 following World War 2 with a vision and a plan.

Officially purchased by the club in 1965 and opened in the year England won the World Cup on 12 July 1966, used as a training base by the Brazilian National Team featuring Pele, Bellefield was to become the catalyst for Everton's academy model that has seen hundreds of professional footballers pass through the gates.

Tosh joined Everton part time in 1996 working in their coaching setup before stepping up in 2001 to become Everton's Head of International Football Development and Technical Director, fast forward over twenty years, the smile, enthusiasm, and dedication to the game still simmers as I sit down to talk about the impact the transfer window and evolution of data scouting has had on football academies. Fresh off coaching an afternoon game, Tosh has managed to squeeze time in between in his next training session and recalls his time at Everton.

"It started off in the grassroots, you must understand, it was inaugural, academies were only pipedreams back then. It was mainly the first team and the reserves, the term academy was very loose, all the staff were new to the club and the community program ran by Alan Johnson and Ted Sutton, seven further coaches were brought on. My background prior to this was as an FA coach in the St. Helens area, a role which I incorporated when I jumped on board at Everton. In this role we ran football camps, development centres and in the first year, Conor Coady was a player who came through those camps as an under 8, he later signed for Liverpool, but it is funny how the world turned seeing him come home at Everton. (Coady signed on loan with an option to turn the move permanent from Wolves in July 2022.)"

"We knew the camps worked and they were great at establishing players who have gone onto play for Preston and Wigan in the North-West, it was a good breeding ground, having finished my badges, I was ready to cut my teeth at Everton. I established good connections at schools and held soccer camps, working closely with Martin Waldron to align these 'silos' into one format to build an academy blueprint the club could use and monitor talent. It wasn't always easy to move it forward, it was trial and error, where there were competing ideas, but the passion to do the best for the players always came first."

The Everton Way, the culture Tosh created, became the pulling power in academy recruitment, years before David Moyes christened the club The People's Club. "It was bigger than that, it was a family, me and Martin laid a blueprint for the under 11's, but we had Colin Harvey as Reserve Team Manager, who would not want to play for Colin Harvey? He was instrumental and a huge pulling factor."

One third of Everton's Holy Trinity of Howard Kendall, Alan Ball and Colin Harvey from Everton's successful era of the 1960s. "We were the start of the pipeline, starting the flow of talent and building the network around the country, which grew onto the world. Just as many countries get their oil or gas, it starts miles away before flowing through pipeline networks to get to its targeted home, in this case, players into first team football."

"In my first intake we had players like Jose Baxter, Jack Rodwell, Callum McManaman and Adam Forshaw, this was just the start of what we were doing, we joke about it now, most of these young lads, were mad Reds (Liverpool fans), Bellefield was a sand-based warehouse, astroturf pitches and we were competing with the investment Liverpool had made in Kirkby, Blackburn made at Brockhall. But their facilities were multi million pound facilities."

"Before we purchased facilities at Netherton for the academy, ask yourself, why would you bring your child to a 'fridge warehouse' on the estate? The people we had at Everton, Bob Pendleton, God rest his soul, he would have the kettle on the go for the parents, a brew and a hello, chat to the parents as their children were coached, ask how they were? Were they happy? Bob was Everton through and through, he got Wayne Rooney to the club, he kept me and Martin on our toes, you need to do more of this, the kids are responding to that."

"Those two kids have fallen out and will not pass to each other. I used to run little competitions, one was 'crazy shooting'. If a player was struggling, we would make them win it and cheer them up, fun was always the most important aspect, no pressure on the kids. Making it a family-oriented feel was key, players could turn to Liverpool if they wanted, you called it the People's Club before, me, Bob and Martin would ensure we got to know the parents, their other children, what school they went to, given the youth intakes, we would know over 400 people by first name terms."

"For all the right reasons, it is your birthday today. Bob would go out of his way to wish someone a happy birthday, even their sister who had been dragged along to watch, we were keen to know how the kids were doing in school, we gained the trust in the parents, so they felt safe bringing their kids to the academy, nowadays, even in the youth groups, kids can be treated as commodities."

Youth team footballers now are traded just like their first team counterparts, other teams swoop in and purchase players before they are 17, before they can sign professional terms or have an agent represent them. At Tosh's Everton recently lost left back Thierry Small and attacking midfielder Emiliano Lawrence, both before they were 17. Both the jewels in Everton's intakes, but they will be sold for a profit by City for Financial Fair Play reasons when they are older. Those players who do make, need to move abroad, the Jadon Sancho effect (sold by City to Borussia Dortmund), sometimes, the parents can be misled to the pathway their children will be sent on.

Tosh is keen to emphasise "at Everton we built a philosophy of making them want to stay. Give them no reason to look elsewhere. I am proud at my time at Everton, we never lost one to a local academy. Parents and players at under-16 were loyal back to us. There is a reason why in my later days, loads of scouts would be keen on the next Everton player, lower league clubs would scour our released list for a player, because they knew they were getting a professional and loyal player."

"Players are open to moving academies now, and recruitment rules have allowed fluidity in youth recruitment. In Tosh's days, before agents and social media, players could be allowed to play, now football players are brands."

"Video games such as Football Manager and FIFA label children as young as 15 as wonderkids, players in academies are being unfairly labelled and for parents, seeing this, even a game, labelling their child as below average, could see this as a reason to move their child to another club. 'You must take away the reasons why a kid or a parent may want to leave. Nobody at Everton pushed the kids too hard, they grew naturally, the team of coaches and staff we had were amazing, Mike Dickinson, Bob Pendleton, it was not just me, Martin adding his direction, the graduates that we brought through were amazing when you look at the former Everton graduates in the football pyramid.'"

The numbers of graduates have come down at Everton's Finch Farm academy since Tosh and Martin moved on. "Football has changed in that time; scouting has moved on, it has changed significantly, the science behind the art of scouting has changed. We were ahead of the curve at the time, you could not take for granted the players physical make up. Some scouts would look at their older brother and go look at him, he's six feet at 16, I would look beyond that, also, you can't ask someone if they are their biological brother."

Chuckles Tosh, "with our games and challenges we got to see who had the edge, subtly teaching the players to scan, turn, look up. It was a marker if you looked at their parents or siblings. Footballers mature at different times; age groups are made of from school years. A child born in September would be playing against someone almost a year younger born in August, a scout or youth coach must factor this in. A player whose parents are athletes will always hold an advantage early on because of their genetic configuration."

"A Spanish player is likely to be built smaller, but be faster and more technical, because of the coaching they receive. They would struggle in the English system, because of the physicality, but keep them in the Spanish system, let them age and grow into the adult body and you have a gem of a player, therefore sometimes not moving your child from one academy to another is beneficial, they know what to expect and have their routines. Knowing all these little quirks gave us dynamite knowledge when recruiting youngsters."

"We live in a digital data driven world now, where players are easily put in spreadsheets to define their roles." Tosh understands this has helped football, but is keen to add, the eye test, physically standing on the muddy common and seeing a player for the first time is still integral to the world of football. "There is no point in signing someone if you haven't seen them. Now young players are sold for millions. Data cannot show you how a player reacts to a bad pass, their leadership, desire, hunger for the game. I could trust what I saw. If someone was six feet, but the player moves like he is running through treacle or his hips are not aligned properly, you would not pick him just because he was the tallest in the park."

"Nowadays, academy coaches are scouring athletic camps, looking for athletes they can chisel into footballers. The Premier League has become so fast, it is hard to succeed unless you are fast and technical. You must ask if you find a teenager at an athletics camp, is their heart really in football? I relished the days of standing in the rain on Buckley Hill or in Formby at the Craven Minor Leagues, in the howling wind and rain, those kids you knew loved the game, and that is what is important, ensuring you never lose the love for the game."

Money has certainly changed several aspects, some academy players are millionaires even before they make a first team appearance, because if you do not offer them the wage, another club will. "This is why the scouting will always start with eye tests or soccer camps. I recall recently being asked if a player I coached was two footed at 7 years old for Christ's sake! How many people are two footed aged 7, but this is what scouts are looking for now and missing the obvious."

Look at the Premier League and La Liga, Mohammed Salah and Lionel Messi are one footed (left), they are the best in Europe, would you really turn them away aged seven? "If you spot a child early enough, you can train them easily and it stops the brain from dominating the style of play. This is something Martin taught me. Nowadays, it has gone data processing scouting. Data is good and can highlight a player's strengths and weaknesses, but the over reliance on data has meant academies no longer have one intake at each level. Can I ask you why category A academies, some of the best in England, need four or five under 11's? That is possible fifty plus kids supplemented by summer camps, where is the quality individual coaching when you have that many players?"

It would seem the art of scouting has inverted itself where academies recruit too many players and rather than scout or coach them, "throw them against the wall and see which one's stick. Where is the data helping the process here. Looking at the raw numbers of first team graduates graduating to full-time professional in the Premier League is down from my time. Of course, the transfer market has not helped. Managers can now buy replacements, but do not forget, the homegrown rule, Brexit changes in points for work permits, these are there to help academies or the 'pathway' to the first team, but can I ask you, are we going backwards?"

It is a fair point Tosh raises, in looking at Everton, Under Tosh's intakes, "Everton had the likes of James Vaughan, Jose Baxter, Wayne Rooney, Victor Anichebe, Jack Rodwell, Adam Forshaw, Ross Barkley, Callum McManaman, just to name a few to hit the first team and make an impact in the Premier League, there are hundreds more who have appeared for Everton, but now forge a career within the football pyramid. Recently at Everton, Anthony Gordon and Anthony

Robinson are the only real players to force his way into first team action in the Premier League.

"Many have come close, made a first team appearance, but then been loaned out. It is not just Everton either, Liverpool have brought through Trent Alexander-Arnold and Curtis Jones, Manchester City have spent millions on their state-of-the-art academy, Phil Foden is the only one to make a dent on the current dynasty Pep Guardiola has built, many of their scholars are sold onto other teams.

"It is the survival of the fittest, take as many kids on as you can and let them battle it out, let the invisible hand guide you. But clubs are spending more money to sign players than some countries produce for their Gross Domestic Product. We should be coaching them up to be great, not relying on others."

The individual coaching of players has decreased which disappoints Tosh, "data has almost inverted the system to find a spreadsheet player and it is missing the personality, are you a good egg or bad egg? Some players come from difficult situations, take the current cost-of-living crisis, some of these kids are playing for their future meals. Look at the South American youth, Richarlison played football barefoot in the Brazilian Favelas, he had to fight for everything, data cannot show you a player's desire or willingness. Look at Messi, they are great because they train, some footballers now do the bare minimum. You must live it, research the game, train harder to make the games easier."

"This is why the family feeling worked at Everton, we were there for the players, but worked on the individual skill sets. We asked parents not to shout or coach from the side-line. We educated the parents that this can have a negative effect on the kid's mental health. But I understand why when there are fifty kids in one age group, parents move them on, it is too much, and academies are missing the personal touch and losing good kids as a result."

"Coaches must be able to explain to parents that their child is not quick enough to be a striker, but if I can make them a centre midfielder, players would leave Everton being able to play in multiple positions. Tosh cites Callum Connolly and Kieran Dowell as successes of this, we made them diversify, increasing their chances of being able to make the first team. The more you can do philosophy for the team, the team first oriented mindset and their parents understood we were doing it for their child's long-term benefit. I have heard stories now from coaches where a player has been moved from striker to centre-back and their parents removed them from the academy as a result."

"We once had a session, an open one, a week before Liverpool had theirs, during the games, I made sure every kid got on, give them minutes. Each one signed up for Everton, in some cases we had to turn some players away, not because they were not good, but because we had enough, and we wanted to give them the best coaching and time."

"We took on players that we felt were Everton players, does not matter who they support, they had passion, worked hard, loved football, good kids who loved being coached. Parents asked me, 'Is my kid the best at Everton?' I would always reply, no, they are in a team full of the best."

"I wanted healthy competition, competition breeds success. I invented the 'starburst competition' the sweet. There was only one winner a week, I borrowed the idea from Bill Shankly, over the course of the season, all the kids would win, but it made the training fun, the kids would try for it, how many goals tonight, free kicks, penalties. You make sure the players are always happy and developing."

Tosh jokes that they would sometimes move the boundaries to motivate them. If Jose Baxter was the best at scoring, Tosh and the coaches would make it so he would lose one, the next week Jose would come back more motivated and double his record. "I never wanted the youngsters to call me coach, call me Tosh, by enjoying the sessions the kids would listen, there was no need for authority, again, you wanted the players to enjoy coming to the sessions. Everyone was treated the same, the best in the class was made to run the same circuits as the rest."

Transfer windows started in the early 2000s and the impact on the academies certainly impacted the pathways, but for Everton, their lack of disposable transfer income ensured the academy succeeded. "We made our pound stretch further, we had to. When the transfer window evolved, it is ok to have champagne tastes, but there are always buyer concerns because it is hard to know the players mindset. The flood of money meant more clubs will spend on replacements rather than look to youth, but if they get it wrong, next week's TV money is the replacement."

"In the 2000s, the pathway to the first team stayed the same, we made sure we reported to David Moyes if we felt a player was ready. We brought good players through Rooney, Leon Osman, Tony Hibbert, Leighton Baines, Rodwell, Barkley, Adam Forshaw, local lads forming the spine of the decade's teams. The explosion in the window possibly helped us at Everton, we had the pathway, we needed to, but the lads could see it. Local lads are heralded and savoured at Everton and Liverpool. It is harder for them now, they are easy targets, one bad game and social media keyboard warriors are after them, mentally players crack, they love their club and with one bad pass, the boos can crush them. This is nationwide by the way."

At Everton now, the money came under Farhad Moshiri's stewardship and with managers changing regularly, the pathway to the first team has become convoluted, Everton signed Ademola Lookman form Charlton's academy, a young winger full of pace, skill, and trickery to change a game for Marco Silva, with Dominic Calvert-Lewin and Nickola Vlasic, all signed for a total of £10m, Everton had the hallmarks of the best young front three in the Premier League. Marco Silva was sacked and replaced by Sam Allardyce, who complained he needed more money to help him push Everton from 13th to 8th.

He campaigned and signed Theo Walcott aged 30 for £20m and Cenk Tosun, a striker also for £20m. Both players signed for huge wages, each left Everton for no return, Allardyce was sacked six months later. Later he claimed Everton lacked pace, skill, and goals. Allardyce already had it there in his squad, developed from his academy, as the famous song from The Beatles, also from Merseyside, "Money Can't Buy You Love."

Lookman now stars for Atalanta and is a regular in Europe, Vlasic has played in the Champions League, DCL, finally broke through at Everton under Carlo Ancelotti and after scoring 20 goals reserved and England call up to the Covid-19 delayed Euro 2020s finals in England. "Money can make you blind to the talent you already have in your club, again, more managers now want their players rather than coach the ones they have. We are losing good kids because of it."

There is one situation at Everton that impacted one of Tosh's graduates which disappointed Tosh, the summer Farhad Moshiri took over, Everton had Ross Barkley and Kieran Dowell as their two number tens, known for their creativity, both seen as the future. But loaded with money to burn and first time Director of Football Steve Walsh went out and purchased five number tens in one summer window, and just like that, Dowell's future at Everton was blocked and Barkley would soon move to Chelsea, fast forward to 2022, and Everton are still counting the costs of not trusting their academy and a lack of creativity in their first team.

"Ross Barkley was electric for Everton, it is easy to forget how good he was at Everton, yes, he never reached the heights he could have done at the club, but he would take over games aged 17, only Wayne Rooney did that at Everton. Ross suffered and came back from a severe triple leg break on England duty aged 15. It clearly impacted him, and he still made an enormous impact."

Tosh takes a breath, "without the injury which robbed Ross a year where we could have worked on his decision making, and he lost a year of first team football, what could have been, I think he would have been great."

Seeing Everton finally be able to spend money and their academy stall slightly is sad to see given the progress it was under Tosh and Martin, with Everton limping to 16th last season and having to sell their best player Richarlison to balance the books from the effects of Covid-19 and failed transfer expenditure. Perhaps with new Director of Football Kevin Thelwell being given more control on transfers and overhauling the academy, Everton may be able to turn this around.

The likes of Tom Cannon, Lewis Warrington, Isaac Price Stanley Mills, Reece Welch, goalkeeper Billy Crellin and fullbacks Ishe Samuels-Smith and Romain Quintyne provide the next players itching to make the first team, here's hoping they get the opportunity if the club is looking to build sustainability again if the club is to progress back up the Premier League. (Samuels-Smith was sold to Chelsea for £4m in the Summer of 2023)

Tosh is keen to point out that during his time with Everton, we had family days. Under 12's to under 16's would come in, we would set up five a side goals, areas for their parents, all players from the first team were invited to come and get involved. This still happens at Finch Farm today and category A academies have joined Everton in the initiative. Managers David Moyes and Walter Smith loved the idea, even during the jovial football games, Moyes would come to me and ask, "who is the next one, where is the next one, Tosh. They would watch the players."

One occasion brings out a wry smile in Tosh, "One year we did it, David came over to me and asked, Tosh, who could I have next week if I needed them. Jack Rodwell, I said, you can have him tomorrow if you need him. I was adamant he could do a job for David, aged 17, he was. David gave me a side glance; they had just dipped into the transfer market for future England International and Everton captain Phil Jagielka from Sheffield United for £5.5m. In 2007/08, it was a lot of money for Everton. David smiled and reviewed the practice, Moyes looked at Tosh, "are you that confident?"

"I said, yeah. Moyes came back, if you're that confident can I sack you if he doesn't make it to the first team?" Tosh took it in stride, "I will have a job for life here because he will not fail. He will not let you down, David." Rodwell was called up to the first team for pre-season and never played for the academy again. It was a crucial summer for David Moyes and Everton, one that helped him have five years of European football and never drop out of the top seven before he left to become the manager at Manchester United.

Everton and Moyes refreshed the team, selling squad players like Anderson Silva, Gary Naysmith, James Beattie, and James McFadden for a total of £15m and spent £30m on the following players: Yakubu, Leighton Baines, Phil Jagielka, Steven Pienaar, Tim Howard, Dan Gosling and loaned in Manuel Fernandes. Rodwell was established with these players on the pre-season tour. When they came back from America, assistant manager Alan Irvine sidled up to Tosh during a youth team training session, joking. "Erm… Just to let you know, your job is safe, Tosh."

Wry smiles all-round. "But that was the relationship with David and his team. In the beginning, Walter Smith and his assistant Archie Knox were the same. But with Moyes, we worked well together. I gave him the information he needed and required, I would never send a player up too early, and David knew it. He always had an eye on the younger lads, and it showed, the ones you have written about earlier, they came through our intakes and made their Everton debut for David. David had his way of making you feel valued, he joined in those youth days, he understood how much it meant even for the younger age groups."

Tosh recalls one session and cites it as a reason players continued to choose Everton over perhaps more lucrative offers. "In the early days of the family days, each manager found ways to help recruitment. Not many under-9's can say they have had a 1 vs 20 game against Paul Gascoigne, he ran round with glee, committing sliding tackles on them, recreating the Euro goal against Scotland, this was most nights, he loved giving back to the youth players. We did not need to have bonding nights with them as it was all done in house, at Bellefield, the players, staff, management all singing to the same hymn sheet."

"We had to be different, we didn't have the funds to compete with other academies, but at the time other academies didn't do this. Everything we did for one scholar we did for all. During the late training sessions, we made sure there were pre-booked cabs for the scholars to get them home, and called ahead for their parents to let them know if they were late. These were the days before mobiles, now scholars are on their mobiles from an early age reading what people think of them, taking it too heart. We wanted to emphasise that people make environments, not building and infrastructure. The staff were so helpful to the success of the project."

One thing Tosh was keen to continue was the development and the academy when on Wednesday, 10 October 2007, Everton moved to a new, state-of-the-art training facility at Finch Farm in Halewood and as he left Everton, more roles within the club began to match their European counterparts. Tosh explains there was no director of football at Everton during his time. Ray Hall, the academy manager, always supported the academy in pushing the new lads into the first team. Tosh has heard from contacts across football of Directors of Football purchasing under-18's and then telling academy coaches they must be played in the reserve teams over current players.

"It also does not help that the Under 21's and Under 18's play on a Saturday at the same time as the senior teams, how can the director of football see the players? Academies cannot have roadblocks, you see it now, when players leave, it is because there is no pathway for the player."

The Bundesliga is a great example where Borussia Dortmund and Bayern Munich are purchasing youth players from England and playing them in their first teams. There is no reason why as teenagers, they cannot be played in the Premier League. Tosh admits it is disappointing when any academy player leaves or does not make the grade, but discussing The Everton Way, he reveals why at the time, again, Everton were different. "Callum McManaman was one we should have kept at Everton in my opinion, when it was decided that he was to be released, we knew he would make it, he was a good kid and I reached out to Wigan, Davey Lowe the coach, to put his case across for them to pick him up. It was great to see him be integral to Wigan winning the FA Cup in 2013 under Roberto Martinez."

Now the technical directors are making these decisions without seeing the players, asking the managers to play certain players over others. McManaman was 5'4 at under 17 level, possibly deemed too small to impact the Premier League level, and didn't make an impact on big games. Tell that to Manchester City and Pep Guardiola as Wigan lifted the FA Cup.

England won the under-20 World Cup, and the spine was made up with graduates from Everton's academy, Callum Connolly, Jonjoe Kenny, Ademola Lookman, Kieran Dowell, England's best player at the time, Tom Davies did not feature because he had broken through and played a significant role for the first team, aged 19. Whilst these players have left Everton, (Davies is still there but his contract is expiring) it shows Everton were able to make five scholar's dreams a reality.

Tom Pearce was also at Everton around the squad, he recently helped Leeds win the Championship at left back. "When we build a prospectus for parents to read, this is in there, their children have a great chance of a professional career and an education if they go to Everton. We have a Wall of Honour for the graduates who play for the first team. They are on the wall next to the first team changing room."

Academies should be celebrated for bringing through talent into our game of football, even now given the constraints they face with the power of the transfer window, their job is to bring through professional footballers. Crystal Palace should also be celebrated. They have adopted a system where they bring education into the program, but more importantly, a program to look after their mental health, for players who make it, but have it available for those who do not.

Perhaps in the past, fans have been quick to question the success of first team graduates whilst looking at the overall picture of a player's development, clubs have shelled out millions on the levels of countries GDPs for players who are no better than the young lads in their academies, there is a reason why European clubs circle around the UK's academies release date.

They are getting good scholars, "I remember a coach from another team further down the football pyramid, called me and mentioned how professional our scholars were, they knew how to scan on the pitch, their technical ability to handle the pressure, create chances for themselves on the pitch, they were Everton players. Whilst it is never easy releasing a player, seeing another team praise your academy is always a nice feeling and it is why players stay connected with me today."

Even more so now, when we see players fail to deliver a set-piece over the first player, or not scanning around before receiving the ball, Tosh believes we have lost the talent and impetus at coaching level, "There are four or five academies who have lost coaches at the top level and the development of coaching pipelines has not carried on. Young coaches are not given the technical training side of it. With the explosion of tactics and false positions, 'quarterback of the midfield', do you mean a ball playing midfielder? A lot of coaches like to build formations and playing styles without trying to improve the players you have got."

This is further seen when managers are sacked, and new ones come in. How often do you hear a new manager make excuses that "these are not my players?" You are the manager of the football club, they are your players, you are employed to make them better. But too often they get to a transfer window, usually January, and overspend on players who are not as good as some of the academy players coming through. When a team is sliding towards relegation and the fans turn on the players who have seemingly stopped playing, an academy graduate who has come through is likely to show more loyalty and try harder than a professional thinking of their next contract.

Fast forward to today, Tosh has left the academy system, leaving Everton and setting up soccer camps in America, before coming back to the North-West, coaching in soccer camps and recently, dedicating time to the grassroots level in women's football. "Now I do one-to-one training with Category A Academy players as well. They come to me and are confused when I show them basic drills to help them technically, when to open their shape up, scan, weight distribution when receiving the ball, these were things we taught at under 10 level. Teams under the new academy structures and director of football are building teams, rather than trying to coach players, shoehorning players into positions they don't fit because of the imbalance."

"How can a Category A Academy not have a left back at under-21 level, none at under 18 level at the same time? This happens more than you think. Where was the recruitment and training at under 9, under 11 and under 13 level? Oh Tosh, a 16-year-old left the club, and he was a future England International, he refused to sign a contract. Why? There was no other left back in the academy blocking his pathway. Go back to give them a reason not to leave."

Perhaps this is where the power has shifted to the parents, Everton were not keen to take a new player on in case the parents of the current left back upped and left the next day. Tosh still strives to get his scholars into academies. "Even now, I strive to get my students trials, sell their talents to academies. I still have the same hunger and desire to see any kid succeed, it can be frustrating to see academies not take a chance on some players, only to see another club pounce on the player. Firstly, I am always happy to see the player succeed, but you look at the Premier League clubs who missed him and wonder why you missed him? It happens, of course it does, but it does not get easier to stomach when you see it happen."

Look at Erling Haaland, every Category A Academy had the chance to sign him, he was on trial at all the big clubs, scored loads of goals, but none took up the bait and allowed him to join Molde in Norway. "It doesn't surprise me with Erling Haaland, like the left back situation I mentioned, the academies would have been looking in different areas. Remember when we discussed competition breeds success?"

Haaland tearing it up for Manchester City is another example perhaps were coaches looked too much into a players physical make up, he looks too tall for his age, will he suffer muscle injuries? Or will parents pull their kids if we sign someone new, parents can be protective of their kids. It is easier to step into hindsight corner, but all clubs miss on prospects.

Rooney was another example, "data would have missed Rooney early on, he was quiet, shy, but when he went into training, he came alive, miles ahead of other scholars technically. Data and scouting by looking at height, weight Rooney would have slipped through the cracks. We stepped him up earlier because he could, at 14, he was in the under 21's with Colin Harvey. He looked after Wayne, simplified the game of football, you don't need this person hanging on in your life, do this, eat this pre-match meal, play for me and I will make you a footballer."

Former Everton player Kevin Campbell echoed this Rooney story recently, "We played a game for Everton's under 21's at Haig Avenue, Southport FC's ground, this kid comes out the tunnel with us. I thought he was the ball boy. I was recovering from an injury and another professional turned to me and said, 'Kev, watch this,' setting Wayne up on the halfway line to have a go at a crossbar challenge game, Wayne hit the bar three times in a row, Campbell turned open mouthed, Rooney went onto score and dominate the game. At first team training, Campbell recalled the story to manager David Moyes. Moyes was quick to answer, 'we know all about Wayne, he is in the first teams' squad when he turns 16.'"

In general, Tosh thinks all clubs could do more to provide first team pathways for scholars. Recently Manchester City and Chelsea signed all the best young players before they turned seventeen before selling them for millions a few years later. It is their model to circumnavigate FFP, but at the same time if clubs like Everton and Southampton are always losing their players to these clubs then the power of these 'big six' will never shift. In League One, as we have seen Fleetwood lose three academy players in a year for less than a million pounds. Barry Fry, director of football at Peterborough was only half joking when he said current academy graduate and first-team player Ronnie Edwards being sold in the future will fund a new stadium, he is letting the big clubs know he will not sell a Rolls Royce defender for cheap and to help keep the sharks away.

But having said all that we are losing sight of what is most important, the player. Mental health is something I try and look after for my players. Top-flight academies, as we discussed, oversubscribed players, throw them against the wall and see which one's stick. Releasing players aged 9, how is that fair on them? Their mental health, there are hundreds of clubs where they would be taken on. But aged 9, they are lost to the system, clubs are telling kids they are not good enough to be professional aged 9, that is immoral, we talk about blocking their pathway, football is blocking their own pathway, turning the pipeline off at source.

Perhaps we should have an education system like America. Where players released from academies could play for the best colleges and universities in North and South leagues. This way players get an education, still play and a football league club could pick them up or be affiliated with the universities. Too many kids will change sports and drive the number of scholars down, ten years in a program and then the Head of Coaching at Christmas tells scholars, decision time is coming around, time to prove yourselves. What has the kid been doing for the last ten years?

Tosh stresses, "they have been at every session, every game, parents have travelled the country with you, players forgoing holidays to represent your club. To then say that can destroy players. Football should be a healer, inclusive for everyone, children, an escape. Sport could solve the issues we have in crime across the country."

More young people now turn to crime because it is easy due to government cutbacks. Meatball Molly McCann and Paddy Pimblett, representing UFC in mixed martial arts, also championed this, setting up gyms and camps with former boxer Tony Bellew in campaigning for youths across England to put down knives and take up sports.

"We want kids to enjoy football, some kids go into academies too early, coming back from America I could see this, we neutralise the kid's talents because they are not learning from their mistakes, not being coached on technical ability as we used to do, telling a kid under the age of 15, they are not good enough before they develop is madness. Make them feel top of the world, coaches in the system now face immense pressure to bring through the next Rooney or Barkley, forgetting we are there to create them, a shoulder they can lean on and have fun with. The best players in the world are having fun."

"Rather than cast the net wide, we are fishing in the high seas with a broken net. I have stepped outside the club game, but I can still spot talent on the muddy fields, train them, and recommend them. I love it, seeing a young kid enjoy their sport and get into academies. This drives me when I hold sessions, remember to smile, and don't forget to bring some Starburst to training."

As the November rain hammers down outside, Tosh checks his watch. "I must go now, I have another session to coach, proper football weather this." With a quick goodbye, Tosh is off into the Winter rainstorm, a smile on his face and possibly a packet of Starburst's for a competition, off to find the next Wayne Rooney or Kiera Walsh, the players who could drop through the system Tosh is there to help them, and his passion for the game never wavers.

For a scout's impression of their current ever-changing role, Jaime Hoyland, Everton's former lead first team scout and he recently revealed what it is like for a first team scout at a Premier League club when speaking to the Under The Cosh podcast. Hoyland followed his father, Tommy Hoyland, who played for Sheffield United, into the game. After making over 400 appearances in the football league and Premier League, the former midfielder turned to coaching and scouting, being the assistant manager at Rochdale in 2002, before stepping up to be academy manager at Sheffield United.

Following his resignation in March 2013, he joined Everton three years later and works in their scouting department. Starting off in the Under 23's, before Marcel Brands moved him sideways to the first team scouting. "I have been lucky, travelled the world doing it. I have been to Brazil a couple of times, Chile, and Peru. All of Europe is looking at players, and brilliant it is."

"That (knowing of players) can be through agents and stuff like that. If there are tournaments on. Like when I went to Peru it was the South American Under-17 tournament. So you are just going there to see and there are some players you know about, but you are just having a look like that really. You are just doing reports. Massive reports all the time. Every player you do a bit on and then follow as they are coming through. To be honest it can be a lonely place. I noticed your guys the other week and I had been in Germany. I finished up doing 1,200 kilometres driving because I had been right up there and right down there."

Hoyland believes technology has made the world a lot smaller for scouts. "No one discovers anyone these days," the days of saying I found him playing in the park, Sunday League, are incorrect, players are already in academies. Another way scouts 'find' players are agents letting clubs know their player is available. A lot of the time, the world of football is a small place, and most scouts know in advance who the skilful players are.

"It is fitting for your club. Somebody who might be right for Man City might not be right for Everton or Liverpool or whatever. It is just fitting them then getting them done really."

Grace agrees with this and is one of the challenging reasons why she wants to get back in the game. "I would like to be able to get back into one club, you can have an identity then and lay down a plan. I have investigated setting up a company who provide football analytics, recruitment and strategic advice to clubs worldwide, and added an interesting note when looking at youth team development and scouting."

With scouts like Jaime roaming the world looking for both first team and academy players, there has been a model shift in youth players transferring from academies aged 16 and 17 before they sign professional terms. Even from some of the best academies historically, because there are higher wages at the likes of Manchester City, Chelsea and Manchester United, even if their pathway to the first team is blocked, younger players' parents are choosing the money over opportunity.

A new paradigm shift seems to be occurring, mid-tier Premier League teams and Bundesliga clubs are prepared to pay huge fees for youth players from the above Premier League elite Category One clubs. Simultaneously we are seeing the best young players at Premier League clubs turning down scholarships to join the select Premier League academies above.

From the players point of view, it makes sense, they will receive a huge contract, sign for a high-profile club at 16, receive the best coaching, accommodation and academics, if you make it at these clubs, you are guaranteed trophies, more money, if not, clubs like Southampton and Crystal Palace will likely purchase you and as a Premier League player and receive a pay-rise. From the club's point of view, they make a profit on an academy player who was brought up, scouted, and 'found' by another team lower down the Premier or football league.

But for these teams, you lose your best prospects for nothing and can only buy back the players deemed not good enough, while the ones who could transform their teams are sold at great profit or become legends at other clubs. How can you challenge them? Reduce the gap that FFP, the media and other influences keep widening? It is an ecosystem that is broken and leaking millions out of grass roots football. As Jaime Hoyland at Everton explained, all clubs are fishing in the same small pond. If clubs are not already finding these players, or new markets to recruit from, they may never compete.

For Grace, her analyses help clubs in the lower leagues who have limited transfer budgets find players currently not on their shortlists. Steer them away from taking uneducated punts on free agents that "look good" and focus on players that contribute on the pitch.

Grace has broken down how the scouting world of football has changed how future transfers are discussed. Before the player becomes a column in a newspaper, a well-run football team will have scouted the player in person multiple times in person. Also compiling reports and data on the players to build a better understanding on what the player would bring to their club.

"Data analysts are often met with raised eyebrows by some managers and recruitment teams up and down the leagues. We are not here to cause uproar; we have found a better way to understand the game we all love. Data has broken barriers in recruitment and managers can be scared because their eye for talent can be proven wrong by the data."

The days of managers saying, I like this striker's height, or physicality has gone, do they score goals? Create chances, their movement. Football Intelligence will be muttered up and down the country by pundits soon. It is amazing how many players pass sideways or backwards, without influencing the game. Grace is keen to point out, like Tosh Farrell also discussed, scouting and the 'eye test' will never leave scouting, but the data will narrow what can often be seen as a vast chasm between clubs' budgets and the players they can find is not that big.

"I presented a presentation to a club in League 1 recently, I stood there and talked through a player who is in the Premier League, plays for his hometown club and was once considered one of England's next bright prospects. After bursting into the first team at 17, the player's development stalled. I asked the coaching team for an evaluation, £10m to £15m was quoted, I came back with £1–£2m."

"After scoffs and the shaking of heads, I broke out the spreadsheets, the player doesn't score, create, assist, carry the ball or progress it, eighty percent of their passes are sideways and backwards. Still more shaking heads. I played a video scouting of the player, Premier League against Manchester City, after five minutes I paused it, highlighted how the player would mark himself out of the game. hide behind the City players rather than create space for their centre-backs."

"On one occasion, their centre-back received the ball from the goalkeeper and turned, the midfielder was open for a pass, but ran behind the City player. Marked themselves out of the game, repeatedly. Now the shaking heads become nods, players can be unfairly labelled, but this player is a League 1 player at one of the Premier Leagues most established clubs, kept too long because he is a local player, a reason the club are sliding down the league. It is not a knock on the player, but examples of how managers would be willing to spend mega money on players based on a false reputation."

Data has allowed scouts and coaches to understand which type of players can deal with the demands of a league. For example, in the Premier League, the most successful teams have players who are technical and are able to revive a fast pass and move it quickly in transitions. A player needs to be physically strong and have the pace and workmate to get around the pitch. Several talented players have "failed" in the Premier League because more than ever, the league demands that all eleven players are working together and even a player like Cristiano Ronaldo, recent adventure back at Manchester United was deemed a failure because he could not keep up with the demands, becoming a detriment to Erik Ten Hag's tactics and a distraction.

Football clubs have even taken the next step and hired or paid for people to redevelop their scouting systems, purchasing databases from data analysts who have never played a professional minute in the game. "There are a few high-profile cases in football, two clubs in the Championship have partnered with analytic agencies as this saves the clubs millions on budgets. These are run by talented people who crunch data to narrow down the player pools for these clubs and they have unearthed some gems for these clubs."

"Matt O'Reilly is a great example, released by Fulham in 2019 and out of the game for nearly a year, picked up by MK Dons, a Danish player of Premier

League quality tore up the league before Celtic came sniffing and purchased him for £1.5m in January 2021. Fast forward a year and big European clubs are circling and Celtic could expect to bring in up to £20m in transfer revenues. A two footed player who is creative and energetic, missed by the entire Championship and Premier League."

"Another example is Swansea City, they have a good recruitment team there, they plucked Dutch striker Joël Piroe from PSV for £1m, he scored 22 goals in his first season. Another player I like, currently in the National League is Portuguese Rúben Rodrigues, signed on a free transfer from Dutch team Den Bosch, he has scored 32 goals in two seasons. I would love to see him play in the system Steven Schumacher uses at Plymouth. If they are promoted to the Championship this season, he would be a great free transfer for the club."

Data analysts look at the entire transfer system when they work at clubs, Grace points out they would provide a full analysis on the club's finances, their contracts at the current clubs, who is value for money, which players should be sold or moved on, bring the wage bill to a sustainable level so the club makes money. "Clubs in lower league football rarely have money to spend, but when they do have money, it is important they spend it well. We would create scouting databases on players who could become available and fit in the system. Stability is important, the owners of the club need to be patient, we have seen clubs like Derby gamble to make the Premier League and their financial failure now sees them languish in League 1."

"Clubs should look at the England Youth set up, for coaches as well as players. These are the players who could give your club a year or two on loan, loans are vital to lower league clubs, but again, they must be the right ones. Pending free agents and academies should be scoured to see which players may fall through the cracks at Premier League academies. We would build reports based on a points scale, this is not uncommon, in my case it would be out of 10. 10 being the highest but is broken down into decimals based on the players traits, and is very data driven, in UK football, focused on the physical nature of the game."

"I would keep it realistic and not have a 'Sunderland Till I Die' moment where their scouts were recommending Zlatan Ibrahimović to the Championship club in a move that would never have happened. I know the Spanish divisions well, several players who stand out in the data but would not survive in the lower leagues of England."

Listening to Grace, you understand it is the passion and love for the game which motivates her. "When you do a job you love, you're not actually working are you? Scouts usually come to us to help sell their players once they are on the transfer list, highlighting which clubs may suit their players playing style, but it can still be frustrating, I was scouting a Las Palmas game last year, they have a great little creative player, Alberto Moleiro, he was 18 years old, in the final year of his contract, with a £3m pound buy-out. Barcelona was interested, but wanted a ready-made replacement, I am stunned no Premier League club jumped at the chance."

"I put him forward in a recruitment mission to an English Championship club, they had money to spend, and he would have a great player there, but they signed another two players instead. Moleiro signed a new deal and I believe the buy-out clause is now £27m. Football is full of sliding doors moments. In January 2023, Chelsea signed Enzo Fernandez for £120m. Six months after Benfica signed him from River Plate for £14m. After winning the World Cup with Argentina and one loss in 29 in Benfica, his value had made an unprecedented 857 percent return on their investment in Fernandez when Chelsea activated his release clause."

"Moving down the pyramids, in League 1 and 2, when I work with them, I encourage them to forward plan more, projects can vary, but the majority of players signed are on free transfers or brought through their recruitment teams. The talent levels do vary between the three divisions, but it needs to be built around whether the player can survive in the league. A spreadsheet cannot tell you that, but this is why we also watch the games. To see for ourselves how the player operates, it is why clubs feel safer with players who have experience in the league, but with our reports, we can see or label how far a player may be able to take a club."

Forward planning is another area that Grace feels clubs could do more. "I worked for a club in League One who have a small budget, I met them for a meeting in October, and queried what their plans for the summer was, they replied saying, oh that is a year away, we will see how this season goes, the cup runs which could change the budgets, their manager doesn't like loan deals, because, they are not our players, they will not care, or give 100 percent in the tight games. Even though four loan signings could save a club on average £520,000 a year, based on the average £2500 a week wage in League 1. I appreciate, not all parent clubs will loan their youth players out and pay their wages, but some will if you guarantee game time."

The transfer window is a busy period for analysts like Grace, but truthfully, her job is year around. "Players being signed should be on database which we have looked at for months in advance, we know them, forecasting the best youth loan deals, there is no quick win in football, during the window, you are not acting in isolation, there are four, five clubs bidding on a free transfer, some players sign for the manager, some for the money. Some of your players at the club request to leave because their girlfriend wants to go back South, or to London. It is an ever-evolving door, and we would have a long list per each position."

"Normally around 50 targets, minimum three per position. I am not a director of football so I do not sign or sell the players, I do recommend them to clubs or alert them when agents tell me their player is available, but I need to burst fans bubbles, if you looked at media rumours, for every 100 transfer rumours, only one or two would be correct."

Clubs in England are seeing value now in Ireland, MK Dons are great at this, they signed two players, Darragh Burns from St. Patrick's Athletic, for around £150k and Dawson Devoy, signed for £100k from Bohemian Football Club. Gavin Bazunu jumped to Manchester City a few years ago, good young shot stopper, commands his area and is great with his feet. Signed for Southampton for £10m. If they were to go down, he would be an heir apparent to Jordan Pickford, David De Gea, Alisson Becker or Hugo Lloris.

The money in the lower leagues is better than some of the European leagues, and I am trying to steer some of the clubs I work with to look into Europe, players would move for the money and the clubs would create new pipelines. Data can also be used to create SWOT analysis for their teams. It baffled me when I looked at the Premier League and saw Rafa Benitez repeatedly being poor at set-pieces, it is basic coaching that sometimes managers fail at. Teams that win trophies are always at the top from scoring from set-pieces and not conceding them.

Likewise, if you get a player on a database who could be the next great signing and will be great for the club, if the manager or owner sees a player score a goal, they are likely to drift towards this player. I use the example of Theo Walcott and Everton. Sam Allardyce wanted pace in his team when he had two of Europe's best young and fast talents, in Ademola Lookman and Nikola Vlašić.

Grace describes how data is now being used to reevaluate how we understand the game, Sam Greens, Expected Goals model may have begun the motion. A bad player signed by a Premier League club for north of £100,000 a week, is likely to stay there, haemorrhaging a cash flow problem and likely to spend their time out on loan. Even if you follow Chelsea's method and amortise the contract over seven or eight years, you are still paying the transfer fee in instalments.

Football players tend to peak at 26–28 years old when you look at the data and fitness levels from a sports science level. In the past, people assumed this was 30–32 years old. We are seeing more than ever; more clubs are looking at younger players. Given the salary cap that was in place in the football league meant teams became a little more protective over what they spend especially with what happened during Covid-19.

Owners want quick returns on investments, because they are businessmen and women who are driven by returns. It is no surprise the two best run clubs recently have been Brighton and Brentford, run by professional gamblers. They have navigated Covid-19 and come out better because they are smart at recruitment. It has been a long game but these clubs were both in the Championship in the last ten years.

A well-run structure and strategy can aid and work with club scouts, data is not here to remove or change scouts, it is here to make their job easier, a scout for a Premier League club in Brazil with no data is looking at games blind, seeing thousands of players. A data driven scouting system can reduce this to hundreds.

The data can see players who are particularly good at creating chances, "I love saying a player who crosses the ball cannot always score the goal. There are players who create several chances for smaller clubs, but if their strikers are not great at finishing, their real value is lost in the process, this is where chances created and expected assists can help find the diamond in the rough. For a number 6, defensive pivot or guard, the N'Golo Kanté's and Idrissa Gueye type of player, looking at their pressing numbers, how quick they recover the ball and break up play. The number of interceptions and tackles they make when attempting to recover the ball."

"A player's positioning is also key to both the eye test and data test. If a player is static or does not scan to see where they are on a pitch, if they are marked by the opposition, then they need to learn quickly how to make key runs. It is amazing to see how coaches who are trying to install philosophies at clubs may turn their nose up to data that can help them coach the players to do these things to help them be successful. This is a big point of the process; managers should not have control over signing players. Transfers are a collaborative process; the manager and recruitment team should meet weekly if the fixtures allow it."

"You would not have the club accountant making tactical decisions and why managers should be making business decisions can be baffling, they are professional in their fields of coaching, but they need to coach the teams to success. At Liverpool, Jurgen Klopp worked with Michael Edwards, over talent scouting, they worked together on creating the shortlist, then Edwards got to work on the business side of the game."

"Klopp and his coaches then go on and coach the players to the success they have had. Famously in scouting circles it is rumoured Klopp wanted Marco Reus and not Mohammad Sarah and it was Edwards who made the final decision. Edwards stayed in the background during Liverpool's success, allowing Klopp to be the John Lennon to Edwards Paul McCartney."

"Where Liverpool were successful was their success rate in the transfer market, ability to sell squads and youth players at inflated prices, but also Klopp remembering the key to being a manager is to coach the players. Some managers such as Rafael Benítez demand total control of a club, even overruling the medical department. The problem with this is when your team are worst at conceding from corners, poor defensive record and sitting back with little possession it is a recipe to get the manager sacked, which ultimately happened to Benítez in January 2022, when there was no one left to blame for the team's poor performance."

Grace confesses to me she would love to be a director of football one day. Expressing the love of a project and finding the right manager for a forward-thinking club with patience can climb the leagues. "The gap in money makes it hard, but I would work closely with the manager, listen to their thoughts and we would adopt a playing style and recruitment around this. I think it would be important for the manager to also set out the following principles for the players at the club."

- Character

When a player's talent is less than another player, or they have a bad game, effort can see a player past this poor form, effort for 90 minutes is better than the odd moment of skill. A team full of character is better than a team full of skill and egos. Managers need character, to coach and to get information across to players who have grown up in recent times, the old hairdryer treatment may not always work. But managers also need time, it is unfair and detrimental to keep sacking managers. Process and progress can be slow. Klopp and Guardiola took almost 24 months before it all clicked into place for them, and their academies began to send the likes of Phil Foden and Trent Alexander-Arnold into the first team.

- Work rate and Leadership

This can be said in the industry. First in, last out mentality. Having players who want to succeed and get better is key to successful teams. When you break down Sir Alex Ferguson's Manchester United teams, all the players wanted to get better, they wanted to be the best in the game. You cannot teach this, this comes down to the player, their desire, and their motivations. When scouting a player, this can come from contacts within the game, seeing how they react to adversity on the football pitch and how they inspire others to get better. Leaders can be like coaches on the football field and lead team talks. Despite Harry Kane being England Captain, it was the likes of Conor Coady and Jordan Henderson who were the ones leading team talks on England's run to the Euro's 2020 Final.

- Basic football instincts

How players react on the pitch, are they scanning, wanting the ball, and progressing the ball forward. Their vision, can they see a pass, script players open, when running into the box, expect the cross to come in and have the technique to finish off the chance once it comes in.

- Set Pieces

For any team or manager, set pieces are more important than ever. Since the Tiki Taka revolution of Pep Guardiola's Barcelona, from a data point of view, defending set-pieces have gotten worse. Despite players seemingly being able to rugby tackle opponents, teams are leaking goals from corners and free kicks at an alarming rate. Worse still, Premier League teams on a regular basis struggle to get the ball over the first man at the front post. In extreme cases, some players have even stated that some managers in their careers have refused to practise or plan for them as they have wrongly believed set-pieces have insignificant impact on the overall game.

Had Rafa Benítez practised them and planned them at Everton and their total have been half their amount Everton would have been 10th in the League when he was sacked, not staring down thirteen games with only one win in the League to show for it.

- Do not make mistakes!

Ok, this one may seem silly for data analysts to preach, but digging into the numbers, when you see most professional football games in the League and knockout football are decided by one goal, and relegations can be down to one point, every goal and point matters. When playing out from the back, or in your half, players making mistakes leading to goals can easily be avoidable. When getting into trouble on the field, coaches and managers should be coaching the players to clear their lines, rather than losing the ball or playing dangerous passes.

On average, mistakes cost Premier League teams between 6–8 goals a season. In points, this can be between 6 and 10 points. Enough to go from a European contender to mid-table purgatory. From title contender to finishing in the top 4. This is before we talk about real tactics or spending millions in the transfer window.

From the simple character examples described above, it gives an overview of the desired characteristic a team should look for and where a new director of football should look to collaborate with the manager on evaluating every player in their squad and what their performance brings returns on the pitch. I have developed a theory which can be implemented within all teams called the Pyramid of Wages theory that allows teams to understand and properly reward players to regulate a wage structure that fits with their on-field performance. This assumes the club has the highest earners of £100,000 a week.

The theory of squad building for sustainability should mean the bottom part of the pyramid is a mixture of academy players and squad players who play marginal minutes on the pitch, equating to around 10% of the minutes. Players 20–23 spend the least amount of time playing, therefore contributing the least amount to the team's success. Assuming no injuries, this would equate to 3 or four games a year. (Assumes no European football)

These players should be incentivised to push the first team players for their positions, and this is where the final three players in the squad are normally the jewels in the academies. Most managers and DOF's fall into the trap that young players may hamper their position in the league, but this is often argued with no substance.

These players are not starting, they are integrated, if planned properly, the players would be used with the other 10 senior players and the chances of the results dropping is minimal. There are several things that can influence a loss on the pitch and too much emphasis is put on a loss if there is a youth player on the pitch. Sometimes the youngsters, if they are from the local city, play with no fear, passion and desire which can lift the crowd to give the team a boost.

Sadly, this is hard to get across to managers who face the pressure of potentially losing their job after they lose three games in a row. If clubs want to think about sustainability and long-term building, these places are better taken by young, hungry players, than mid-career squad players who on average could be picking up £50,000 a week, sitting on the bench, blocking a pathway to the first team, not happy that they are not playing given their inflated contracted could sap the energy from the first team and cause rifts within the squad. £50,000 a week, is a cost of £2.6m a year.

For the final four players in the squad, this would equate to £10.4m a year in wages, a significant proportion could be saved to give younger players a chance. Furthermore, in a world where FFP and the Premier Leagues profit and sustainability rules where a club's accounts and profits are severely scrutinised, it is paramount that teams trade for sustainability and do not have an inverted pyramid of wages. where the pyramid is held up by the tip, rather than a solid foundation.

The middle layer of the pyramid is made up of the 18 players in the match day squad. Players from 18–7 should be on the next level of wages. (In this scenario, wages should consist of between £30,000 and £60,000) Players are aware they are an integral part of the squad, are Premier League quality, a mixture of former academy players, senior players, utility players capable of playing in several positions.

The top tear, the smallest one, should be the best, but also importantly, the consistent members of the squad, keen to reward performance, rather than the name on the back of the shirt. The six players should be, unless injured, the spine of the team and the ones who are key contributors to the results. The captain should be in this team, and an argument could be made that if they are a good one, who sets an example and 'first on the training ground and last off it' should be the highest earner.

With the pressure and responsibility of the club duties, other players would be managed by the captain, and knowing the players are not bigger than the club, or the captain ensures the mentality and egos of players are kept in check. These players should be on the pitch the most, it doesn't mean they deserve to be, they still need to work hard and deserve to be selected, but the theory gathers momentum that the wrong players are being rewarded financially, if your bench has your highest earners on it, it likely shows the players have been over rewarded and have shown little desire and effort to fight on the pitch, a recipe which will quickly drop a team down the standings.

Another real-life example is Manchester United, players such as Phil Jones are on such high wages, United cannot move them on in the transfer window, clubs have become much more financially aware post Covid-19 and will refuse to take these players at their inflated wages just because they played for United. Coupling this with the knowledge Paul Scholes revealed it was Lingard who was passing him information regarding the players' lack of effort under former manager Ralf Rangnick further highlights the issues over players who can disrupt and sap the energy from the team.

The salaries are not the players fault, so it is not an excuse to single them out, yet it highlights why all clubs need to be smarter with wages and rewarding players for what they contribute on the pitch and not past exploits.

More and more clubs are unwilling to take these players have an inflated concept of how much they are worth to a football club, these players would expect to be paid more for 'stepping down' to another club, perhaps where there talent actually suggests they are capable of performing, but these clubs are starting to look into financial cost controls, like the Pyramid of Wages to build sustainable football clubs, so when the sell a player for a profit, they open up a competition for a player below to step up into the opportunity.

Manchester City and Liverpool have been the most successful clubs over the last five years because of the way they trade and operate their transfer budgets and wage structures. Both clubs sell players, mostly because they have given academy players opportunities and then sell them for significant profits.

Something United and Arsenal have failed to do and have seen themselves no longer seen as Premier League title contenders.

Arsenal over rewarded Pierre-Emerick Aubameyang with a massive contract, smashing their wage budget and making him captain. Splitting a dressing room as one player was paid more than the rest, making him captain, then when his form temporally dropped, his place in the team was questioned and he sulked as he was no longer part of the first team.

Sitting on a bench earning over £250,000 a week, before bonus, which could earn up to £350,000. £1m a month that later hamstrung Arsenal in the transfer market so much they allowed the player to join Barcelona on a free transfer in January 2022, so they could get the remaining £6m off their wage bill and repair a dressing room spirit.

Liverpool have deployed this technique and have been unwilling to pay their biggest stars Mo Salah and Sadio Mané. Unwilling to break their wage structure for the agent's demands, despite the success the two players had brought the club. Grace explains why Liverpool made the tough stance. Clubs and scouts have had this theory that strikers reach their peaks age 28–30. But there is no science behind it. Now science and performance data prove most strikers peak between 25–27, when a player is demanding their first major contract, not the second most lucrative one.

Unless the player is the top 1% and trending upwards clubs are pumping millions into a diminishing asset with no residual value. Liverpool chose to sell Mané for £35m a year too early, rather than a year too late, using the money for a future to target players such as Jude Bellingham, whom Liverpool have scouted extensively.

For Salah, Liverpool found a compromise, rather than pay him the £500k his representatives were looking for, Liverpool did what clubs would be advised not to do, let a player get to 12 months left of this contract where it usually means they are sold, Liverpool made him the highest earner, rumoured to be £350,000 a week, but reduced the length, to three years, covering themselves if the players form drops. Liverpool believed that Salah could continue to give performances that would lead to more league titles in the future.

Grace believes the transfer ecosystem is starting to recover from Covid-19, but whilst some still spend significant money, more clubs are now selling to buy. More and more clubs are getting smarter, understanding scouting players and when to sell. Seeing clubs like Everton, Barcelona and Leicester need to sell before they can buy, shows any club can get it wrong, and how one bad transfer window can set a club back three years. (The three years FFP is calculated.)

The market will eventually recover, but with covid-19, there are European clubs who need money to replace lost revenue and sponsors. Valencia is a club who may lose their best two players José Gayà and Gonçalo Guedes because they need to find upwards of £30m to plug a hole in their accounts. (Guedes was sold in the summer 2022 window to Wolves in the Premier League for around £30m.)

Aston Villa have invested in their Academy in recent years to become a club that develops and then sells their talent at a premium price. Following the sale of academy graduate Jack Grealish to Manchester City, the club were afforded the opportunity to spend significant transfer outlays and could look in-house to their own academy players. Scouts called the recent Under-19 Euro Championship the 'Aston Villa' Championships due to the nature that Villa could form the spine of the England team.

Villa purchased youth players, Josh Feeney, England under 16 captain, joined from Fleetwood, potentially followed this Summer by Rory Wilson who could be moving from Rangers. These will join central midfielder Tim Iroegbunam and Aaron Ramsey, Carney Chukwuemka, a box-to-box midfielder recently sold to Chelsea, came through with Jacob Ramsay and Louie Barry who are ready for more first team football. Not forgetting Cameron Archer, a striker who had a positive loan spell.

Which questions their reasoning for signing free agent Boubacar Kamara, a defensive midfielder aged 22, who could be blocking their pathway to the first team. The value of the transfer for Kamara meant it was a no brainer, but for the youngsters listed above, it just highlights the further issue in football for young players. Even when breaking through the pathway can be shut just as you think you are getting close to making it into the first team.

Chapter 4
Moneyball VS Goliath

"Art of the unfair game."
15 October 2001, American League Division
New York Yankees VS Oakland Athletics
$114,457,768 VS $39,722,689

Bennett Miller's opening card to his 2011 film written by Aaron Sorkin has all the hallmarks of the usual Hollywood underdog story. The extraordinary reality is the game was not a Hollywood storyline of David vs. Goliath fiction. Despite a salary cap to keep the league competitive, Oakland's Owners Stephen Schott and Kenneth Hofmann were unable to get anywhere near the ceiling of the salary cap to utilise the MLB free agency to acquire better players. Forcing General Manager Billy Beane to think creatively when it came to competing with the free spending pinstripes of the New York Yankees.

After a heart-breaking loss in the best of five series, Beane faced an uphill task just to put a team on the field with the film detailing how the franchise soon lost three of its stalwarts. Johnny Damon signed with the Boston Red Sox to be their leadoff hitter. First Baseman Jason Giambi was signed by the same New York Yankees who had broken Beane's dream of winning The World Series. The final gutting loss came from losing pitcher Jason Isringhausen to the St. Louis Cardinals.

The contrast in finances forced Beane to think creatively and evaluate how every dollar spent brought something to the field. It was here where the concept of Moneyball was developed. The Moneyball concept is about finding value and marginal gains where other teams don't see it and understanding the percentages of how a small play can have a major impact on a team winning the game. In Oakland's case, Billy Beane wanted hitters 'who could get on base' over always searching for the big home run.

One of the pioneers of this concept in football was Brentford, owned by lifelong fan Matthew Benham who purchased the club in 2012. Benham graduated from the pristine quad lawns of Oxford University. He spent the next twelve years working his way up the ladder in the finance sector, gradually earning a promotion to become the Vice President of Bank of America.

He left the company in 2001 looking for a fresh start and joined Premier Bet, a gambling company who were forward-thinking in their modelling analytics way of thinking. He spent two years understanding and studying betting and how analysing data could inform potential gamblers. Benham took a leap of faith and resigned in 2003 to become a professional sports gambler, armed with statistics modelling to aid his decision making.

Benham used modelling to make millions from gambling, putting the finances to use and forming a new betting syndicate, Smartodds, built on analytics, knowledge of algorithms and data research. As the business grew Benham strengthened his business portfolio by purchasing Matchbook, a peer-to-peer betting exchange designed for smart bettors who want more value to their bets.

In 2006, Brentford were in a financial crisis and struggling to pay the operational bills to keep the club running. Benham loaned the fans £700k so they could finance the club through a fan ownership group. In the deal, Benham had the option to own the club if the fans decided against fan ownership, the group preferred Benham to own the club, as he had the finances to turn the club around as they dropped into League 2.

Benham wanted to change the culture of the football club and how it did business. Hiring Rasmus Ankersen, Co-director of football and Chairman of Danish football club, FC Midtjylland, a club Benham also owned. The pair transformed the way Brentford operated with the use of cutting edge analytics to form their decision making on and off the field. The effects saw them quickly promoted to the Championship in the 2013/14 season. The following season, Brentford finished 5th, the first time in 62 years Brentford managed a season in Britain's second tier without being relegated.

Anderson, whose career was ended prematurely by injury, had written numerous books on understanding talent and success, devised a plan to make the club stabilised financially and cement them as a Championship club. In 2015 season, Midtjylland vindicated their Moneyball methods by winning the Danish Superliga for the first time in their history and qualifying for the Europa League for the following season. They faced Manchester United and even managed to win the first leg.

At the same time, Brentford stabilised in the Championship finishing 9th in 2015 then followed it up by finishing 10th. Ankerson based his sporting philosophy from the 'Art of War' and centuries of military battles to form their decisions. For example, when the weaker force tried to act in the same tactics as the stronger force, they lost four out of the five battles. However, when using more unconventional strategies, the odds of winning the battle shifted to three wins out of five. A philosophy Ankerson wanted installed at Brentford, a winning, battling mentality.

Benham vowed the club would be sustainable and with Financial Fair Play constricting the clubs spending power in the lower leagues Brentford needed to find new ways to achieve their dreams of reaching the top tier in English football for the first time since 1946/47.

But Brentford's rise to the Premier League hit a number of roadblocks on the journey and some of the solutions Brentford used changed the way the game of football is managed financially. Most clubs aim for sustainability, build around their academies and promoting their youth players by blooding them in competitive matches.

However, Brentford were soon to see the salutary reminder of the Premier League wealth and a reality check if they believed their plan was going to be easy, the painful truth was that most clubs in the football league pyramid are feeder clubs to those in the Premier League.

In the 2016/17 season, Brentford lost starlet Ian Carlo Poveda for a nominal training fee to Manchester City, a midfielder star for England U16's after two years at Brentford's academy. Just a few months later, Brentford lost another high-profile academy player. Josh Bohui, a winger who had represented England U17's was signed by Manchester United for a compensation fee rumoured to be in the region between £30,000–£50,000 apiece.

It's not Brentford who have seen their academies pilfered for cheap prices. Fleetwood in the 2021/22 season lost two key pieces of their Youth sides they hoped to build their future teams around. First, in the Summer, Aston Villa signed England U16 captain Josh Feeney for a training fee due to his contract being up and this allows Premier League clubs to approach lower league academies. In the January transfer window, they were raided again, losing goalkeeper Billy Crellin. The 21-year-old came through the Academy at

Fleetwood, represented England up to the Under-20s level and even won the Under-17s World Cup in China whilst at the club signed for an undisclosed fee.

Youth players in England can't sign professional contracts until their 17th birthday, there was no way Brentford could protect their young stars as the bigger clubs circled and turned their heads with the dreams of the Premier Leagues and Tier One academies. Brentford couldn't protect their academy players between the ages of 8–16. Ankerson quickly realised Brentford weren't on a level playing field when it came to the value of their academy.

Speaking to Bleacher Report, "It's an unfair game. We can't just be on the same playing field as everyone else and do the same thing, because it costs us a lot of money, and the compensation for those players is not significant. It doesn't even cover the cost of developing those players."

To maintain a football league academy, Brentford received a subsidy of £500,000 a year from the Premier League, this is topped up by £1.5 million of their own budget each year. Ankerson and Brentford's Head of Football Operations, Robert Rowan, doubted whether an academy represented good value for the club in their long-term plan. Sadly, like most academies, 90% of the players don't make the grade and are released. The best players were poached by teams in the Premier League at little return for Brentford.

At the time of the Bleacher Report interview, Brentford's last youth player to feature regularly for the first team made his first team debut in 2005. Rowan, whose background in football featured posts at Stenhousemuir and Celtic, believed in a new way of thinking.

"After ten years of the academy model, that's £15m. This money could have been spent on first team players to get you to the Premier League." Rowan's theory alone raises the question of why more Championship clubs don't follow the model. Most Championship clubs use academies, but never have the money to spend on transfers and rely on selling players in the hope of being better suited to reinvest it in a winning team then being left open to the "foxes pilfering the hen house every year," elegantly put by Oakland Athletics General Manager Billy Beane in the Moneyball film.

Brentford bit the bullet and dissolved their academy completely. Forfeiting their £500,000 subsidy but saving £1.5m from their budget. Meaning £1m annual net saving that could be spent on player trading. Anderson took his Darwinian theory on adapting in football and moulded it into a David vs. Goliath struggle of the football league. Using analytics in their recruitment to find hidden players in the same way Billy Beane was forced to rebuild the Oakland Athletics from the ground up, for Benham and Ankerson, instead of players 'getting on base', they looked for players who created Expected Assists and Expected Goals.

Ankerson still saw the benefit in having younger players in the squad but needed a way to secure them for the first team. He drew up plans for Brentford to have a B-team. Deciding to use the £1m saved from the academy and invest in this method, in the hopes these youngsters would secure a move to Brentford because the players would play under 'professional contracts', being aged between 17–20 years old.

These players were released from other academies based in London and the Southern Counties, meaning they cost Brentford nothing, any future sales would be a direct income to the football club.

The cost of developing the players had already been sunk into the other clubs who had given up on the players. This allowed the Brentford coaches the chance to polish the players into first team players, soften the edges to players who may have been overlooked in the bigger academies. Brentford successfully turned their main weakness of being in London to their advantage. When scouting players in the lower leagues, they came up against the big London academies of Chelsea, Arsenal, Crystal Palace and West Ham United, fishing in the same pond for young talent was hard for the club.

Once the B-Team was formed of recently released players, the close vicinity of Heathrow became an advantage. Now a team made up from talented teenagers plucked from Manchester City, Brighton, Chelsea and Celtic, with a sprinkling of their former academy could now use their base to fly out and play the best academies in Europe. Ankerson, rather than see Premier League clubs as the enemy, saw them as 'collaboration partners' in the future of Brentford. Football clubs even trade with Brentford B-team through the transfer market, rather than releasing players on free, they negotiate smaller transfer fees or agree future sell on clauses if Brentford go on to sell the player. A win-win for both clubs.

Not assigned to a league like the other academies, they would invite other teams to play them and travel across the continent looking for the best teams to play to provide the best competition for the future players of Brentford. They have played against professional non-league teams and travelled to play against Bayern Munich under 19's at Bayern's esteemed £62 million pound academy. The team and the training laid on by the coaches is focused on developing all aspects of the players and how they could fit into the future Brentford team and formation.

In March 2017, Joe Hardy joined the B-Team from Manchester City's under 18's. Never going to feature for their billion-pound assembled first team, Hardy saw his career at a crossroads to purgatory, he jumped at the chance to join Brentford to chase his dream of becoming a professional. Hardy's performances for the B-Team attracted the attention of Liverpool who signed him for their Under 23 side in January 2020.

Soon after Liverpool's Under 23 manager Neil Critchley left the club to become the manager of Blackpool. then in League one. Hardy's progress stalled and he was released, but he became a first team player for Accrington Stanley and was further loaned out to Inverness Caledonian Thistle to continue his career.

The majority of Brentford's B-Team may have been rejected for the wrong reasons. Using a study from 2015 academy data, showed 45% of Premier League academy players were born from September to November, which would indicate these clubs wrongly preferred bigger and older players over younger players with perhaps different skill sets.

Due to the exposure to European academies and the mixture of games against professional teams, talents from Denmark and Finland have turned down Premier League Category one academies in Favour of Brentford as they see the B-Team as a step up from the level of the current offering of Under-23 football in England.

Another change from the current academy system is how the B-Team and Brentford's first team train together, with the younger players getting exposure to first team players and coaches to further enhance and motivate them.

In the 2016/2017 season, four players from the B-Team represented the first team, more than the homegrown players who had made their debuts in one season in over a decade for Brentford. Ankerson developed the strategy in line with the club's philosophy and integrated this into the club's strategy with the number of games they played in a week. Seeking an arduous three fixtures a week to prepare the players mentally and physically for life in the Championship where the first team faced the gruelling, Tuesday, Saturday, Tuesday fixtures in the grind to make the step up the footballing ladder to the Premier League.

Scouting for the B-Team meant a scouting shortlist containing 22 players. Two for each position, watching the academies of those clubs currently participating in the Champions League as these academies face the best of

Europe in competitions aligned with the grand showcase in their own European tournaments.

Brentford B-Team players are regularly given three-year contracts, with priority recruitment given where they believe a spot in the first team may come up soon. Ankerson states, "the poor are better at making talent than the rich, because they don't have a choice, they need to give opportunity to players." He cites Southampton as a prime example of a good academy, but would the generation of Gareth Bale and Adam Lallana have played regular football if the club had fallen into administration?

Southampton had to blood them in League One and use the business model to improve their assets and sell them on to survive. It allowed a culture to be built and a legacy of producing first team footballers which also produced Alex Oxlade-Chamberlain to be sold on for a £20m pound profit. The legacy from Southampton almost going out of business is that despite the number of managers who have led the club since their administration their academy has always been held in high regard.

A thought not lost on Ankerson. He believes a young player needs to play, learn, and adapt. Given 35 games at professional level they can develop and learn things they wouldn't be able to at under 23 level. Recently at clubs like Liverpool, Manchester United, Chelsea and Manchester City there was too much at stake to invest and play younger players.

However, managers now are seeing the academy can also be a means to finance future sales. Jurgen Klopp and Frank Lampard employed youth policies at Liverpool and Chelsea respectively, seeing both clubs have a healthy number of academy graduates in the first team. The reluctance to play youngsters can be down the managerial merry-go-round if results go against them. Managers parachuted in can be too short sighted to look to academies for their squad.

Whilst the richest clubs in the world haven't adopted Brentford's methods, other clubs have begun to take notice. Hearts have begun looking into forming a B-Team to help them compete with the likes of Celtic and Rangers in the long run. It would seem the fallout from Covid-19 has only made the need for change and innovation more important.

A recent example of the financial disparity in football was Aston Villa spent more on transfer fees than Brentford have in their entire 130-year history in 2021 but still finished three positions lower after spending £77m. Brentford's operations in the transfer market mimic those of the heaving floors of a stock exchange. Buying shares when they are low and selling them when they are high. Using data and analytics to help them find players (shares) whose products are about to rise.

A model shift in looking for young players with a determination to find undervalued talents in European markets where the player market is less inflated than England. Ankerson stresses signing players as they are about to enter their peaks rather than signing an ageing player on high wages who essentially is a declining asset potentially motivated by one last pay day. Young players tend to be hungry, energetic players, who want to prove themselves, open to learning and embrace the club's philosophy.

The players have residual value that can be reinvested into the squad or club infrastructure. In one Championship season, Brentford's average age for their starting XI was 24 years and 139 days. The second youngest in the Championship according to Optasports. A belief that signing a player aged 29, two years removed from a cruciate ligament injury, who two years ago may have made a difference, but now the gamble is whether they will get you promoted? Or have any residual value if they do not? A poor transfer decision can set a football club back years.

Ankerson cites the inflated prices of English footballers, heightened since Brexit. A young inexperienced English player in League 2 was being quoted as being worth £2m. More than the entire squad put together. Ankerson validates his point by using Tim Sparv as an example, a signing for FC Midtylland's from Greyther Fürth, a second-tier German team for under £300k. A player integral to the championship winning team for FC Midtylland.

Brentford also have a secret weapon on which they can rely. Smartodds, their owner Matthew Benham's company could provide statistical data and research on players which it currently gives its gamblers. Brentford go one step further by evaluating a player's personality, whether a foreign player can adopt to a new culture, or if a young player would be ok moving away from home and their family. Typically, twenty-five reports are compiled before a player joins the first team and 10 for the B-Team.

Like any good stock trader, Brentford aims to sell high. Scott Hogan, a striker bought for £750,000 from Rochdale in 2014 was sold to Aston Villa for a reported £15m. This hasn't deterred Brentford from selling significant players whilst building a team in the Championship. When understanding, there was little chance of promotion or being relegated and to use the time to blood new players the management would look to move players on and build again, like how Billy Beane is forced to build a new team every year for the Oakland Athletics.

Brentford also changed the way they coach their teams, when using data, they spotted how the game could be broken down to chunks. On average, the 90-minute game is shortened to 70 minutes of actual play when you take away the time lost to set-pieces and substitutions. They discovered how set-pieces play a significant role in deciding games over a full season. By not conceding from free kicks and corners and adding a few goals, they discovered at no cost, they could rise the league table. Something which Premier League clubs spend millions of pounds doing.

The management team discovered a variant of the 'Expected Goals' model which backed up Ankerson's theory, with football being such a low scoring sport—the average game has 2.5 goals (pre-Covid) compared to Basketball which has over 200 points or the NFL where they average 4.5 touchdowns per game. Roberto Martinez once stated in an interview as Everton manager, his teams never practised corners as they held little significance to the overall game.

He took over an Everton team who regularly finished in the Top 6 of the Premier League and were one of the best at scoring and not conceding from set-pieces. When he was sacked, Everton had finished in the bottom half of the league twice and were in the bottom five for scoring and conceding from set-pieces. This is despite the massive outlays in transfer expenditure to crack the top 4. Everton haven't finished in the top 6 since and have been sliding towards life outside the Premier League.

Using their gambling data, Brentford discovered favourites only win 65% of football games, whereas in basketball this ramps up to 80%. Premier League clubs spend tens of millions to try to climb up the table without considering the basics of football. For example, the merit payment for finishing 12th in the Premier League in 2019 was £17m for Everton. If they wanted to climb into 10th place, that year occupied by Burnley on 54 points, 5 points ahead of Everton, or two wins. It would net them an extra £4m as a merit payment. (Not including TV money)

Everton next season did finish 10th. But after a transfer outlay of £62m on players. Everton, it could be argued, used a negative transfer outlet to rise a measly two places in the league, at a cost of £58m. Whilst there are several caveats to this one example, it goes to show how teams thinking using the transfer window to climb the table is the only answer are doomed to fail.

Interestingly, Everton didn't sell any of their major players to look at balancing the books; it was all investment in five players. Initially, it looked to have worked with Everton second at Christmas and 4th in March, before injuries caught up with them and they collapsed to finish 10th under Carlo Ancelotti.

Transfer strategy is integral to the growth of the club and moving teams up the table, but it is important to look at what the players bring, hard work, an identity and contributions week to week. Coaching must also not be forgotten. A well-coached and disciplined team that eliminated mistakes and goals conceded at set pieces could have moved Everton two places up the table without the transfer outlay. Once the players got injured, Everton's squad players from the previous year hadn't improved and quickly started conceding soft goals that should have been coached out of them.

As Billy Beane coined the phrase, "your goal shouldn't be to buy superstars, your goal should be to buy wins." Essentially, smart players who fit a system and play well in a team. Not buying three superstars in the hope they take you up the league.

A theme that continues to feed through the way Brentford build their squads year on year. But also, managerial appointments. Anderson claims that managers can be sacked too early, modern players are let off the hook by poor performances because it is easier to sack the manager rather than the players, and the players know it.

In 2015 Brentford, despite finishing 5th, Mark Warburton was not offered a new contract amid claims he didn't really buy into the club's philosophy. Rather than sack him mid-season at a cost to the club, Anderson waited until his contract ran out so there was no severance cost. To back up Ankerson's claims, in 2015/16 season, a record 73 managers left their jobs within the 92 football league clubs in England's top four tears and the compensation the clubs pay is seldom good use of cash.

Ankerson believes the manager or head coach should focus on training and improving the players. With specific sessions held on set pieces, penalties and counter attacks. The manager can have a say in players to be scouted or bought in an agreed line with the director of football but should focus on their main job in managing the team in preparation for their next game. In some cases, a manager is distracted by responsibilities of running the day-to-day operations of a football club, finances, spending money, short-term and long-term strategy.

An example cited earlier would be Rafael Benítez after taking over at Everton, rather than focusing on tactics, coaching and the team. He spent time rejecting director of football Marcel Brands transfers and sacking the medical team giving the first team little notice. His win rate of 26% is one of Everton's worst in the Premier League era and he was sacked leaving the club in a relegation fight.

Ankerson likens Brentford's corporate operation to a clock. The head coach is responsible for the day-to-day coaching operation, the second hand ticking away, the Directors of Football and CEO's, (Ankerson) responsible for the minute hand (medium term strategy) focused on transfers and succession planning. The long-term strategy, Board level including the owner Benham, the hour hand, moving slowly in the background.

The minute details of Brentford research can often be overlooked at great cost. All of which cost nothing. Brentford understood on average, one third of goals scored or conceded comes from set pieces, as one coach mentioned to me, "a goal is a goal, to think a set-piece goal is not worth as much as a goal from open play is ridiculous and the person is stood in romance land and full of bullshit."

But this does happen in real life, earlier I mentioned Roberto Martinez, when as Everton manager famously stated in an interview his sides never focused on set-pieces and that he wanted his goals to be beautiful, full of possession build up. In the year, he won the FA Cup with Wigan (ironically the winner came from a corner) they were also relegated and had one of the worst records at defending set-pieces. A little focus and training could have kept them in the division, they are now struggling in the Championship, on their way to League One.

Fast forward onto his next job at Everton, their average league position in the final years of the David Moyes era was 6th, built on making no mistakes and well drilled at set pieces. Under Martinez, Everton's average league position dropped to 10th, conceding a league worst at set pieces, a team that was built around good experienced and talented players such as: Seamus Coleman, Leighton Baines, Phil Jagielka, John Stones, James McCarthy, Ross Barkley, Gerard Deulofeu, star striker Romelu Lukaku and USA Goalkeeper, Tim Howard, he was sacked after the heart-breaking last second loss to Manchester

United in the FA Cup semi-final, when the players later announced they ignored his tactics in the second half when they were one nil down.

Ankerson, probably watching this happen in 2015, points out that in football, where all clubs are businesses and revenue is king, clubs spend 10% of their time where 35% of the revenue comes from? You can imagine Ankerson shrugging his shoulders, this is what happens in football. Brentford were one of the first clubs to hire a set piece coach, a ball striking coach and even employed a throw-in coach. Ankerson believes it won't be long before football has as many special skill coaches as the NFL. Liverpool soon followed suit a few years later, now most Premier League teams have a coach dedicated to set-pieces.

When FC Midtjlland won the Danish league in 2015, almost half their goals came from set pieces and Midtjylland scored nine goals from long throws last season. The same year, Everton went from finishing top 6 and European competition to finishing 10th in Premier League purgatory.

Ankerson debates, "when you can't buy a striker for £10m, you've got to find other ways to get your goals. Also, if your centre-back scores four more goals a year, his transfer value increases. You have a strategy, implement it, spend time on it, then the team's value goes up."

Psychologists call it the end of historical illusion. Look at your player as an asset, build their portfolio like a trader would look at his stocks and shares. The feeling from coaches in American Football inside the game feel in terms of professionalism football is a long way behind other sports. Footballers are keen to do the bare minimum.

In a radio interview on talkSPORT, Gabriel Agbonlahor stated he and the Aston Villa players weren't keen on Managers Roy Keane training practices in having the whole team take part in shooting practice. Days later, with the team struggling in the Championship to score goals, Keane was sacked, but the players stayed on for the next manager and Villa kept sliding down the table.

The coaches believe players in the modern era don't want to train or do the basics. Citing the rise in players who struggle to get a free kick or corner over the first footballer or wall. They believe as wages in football have risen with numerous televisions deals the quality of the basic skill sets of footballers has fallen. Work rate on the pitch has become a second consideration for some.

Ankerson is hopeful this will change soon. As more analysis and television analysis is used to scout players and more clubs use it to build tactics. Eventually, clubs will stop paying inflated transfer fees or wages to certain players because scouts and Directors of Football will begin to stop desiring to buy certain players. Ankerson goes as far as believing that in the future, players will train more in the future using more training aids. Possibly including virtual reality, with technology tests being drawn up to simulate situations where a player could do one-on-one drills with an opponent in training before the game at the weekend.

One of the knocks on the 'Moneyball' approach in baseball and soon to be found with the Brentford experiment, is that by playing the percentages and extrapolating points per game across the season using the philosophy discussed above works to get teams further up their respective divisions or into the playoffs. But in the one-to-one match ups, the techniques are void and it comes down to the individuals in the team and their performance on the day. No computer or spreadsheet can help a football team in a playoff final or FA Cup Final.

History in sports seemed to support this with teams adopting the methods being deemed perennial bridesmaids. Oakland Athletics who defined the concept have yet to win the World Series and seem stuck in the purgatory of always chasing their dream of a world series. Struggling to navigate the playoffs.

In the Covid affected 2019/20 season on 5 August, Fulham defeated Brentford following a brace from their left back Joe Bryan on their way to achieving promotion via the playoffs, or more recently, Brighton's heart-breaking FA Cup semi-final loss to Manchester United on penalties.

This is where the lack of Sports psychologists who primarily collaborate with athletes, from amateur to elite-level. Their work is centred on how psychology influences sport and how it can improve performance. Their aim is to prepare sporting professionals for the demands of their job, such as competition and training that can't be managed through data.

What drives and motivates a sports person can impact their clubs greatly. Lionel Messi and Cristiano Ronaldo are generational talents whose individual personalities inspire their teammates to better themselves. But Messi and Ronaldo, at their given ages, are built like sportsmen in their twenties. Each has teams dedicated to their fitness regimes and foods they ingest. They are determined to train their bodies to the maximum even as they go past their peaks.

In comparison, some players break through with enormous potential and remain average or fail to achieve their potential. Some coaches believe some players are happy just to be footballers. For those in the Premier League, just competing there is enough for them and the knowledge their agent can get them a move quickly in the transfer market is robbing them of their ambition.

Brentford hope their new way of thinking will lead them to their promised land of the premier league (achieved in 2020/21 season), disrupt and invert the industry by winning in the unfair game. Brentford, using their Moneyball approach won promotion in 2020/21 season via the playoff final against Swansea, where their 2v0 victory courtesy of Ivan Toney and Emiliano Marcondes two of the hidden gems unearthed following deep analyses of the transfer market. To understand the size of the odds Brentford overcame on their mission, here are some of the significant standout statistics.

Since the takeover in 2012, Brentford have never been involved in a relation battle prior to their promotion to the Premier League. With a few games to go, a draw at Champions League chasing Spurs seemed to have secured their Premier League status with six games to go. During their rise to the Premier League, Brentford only dropped into the relegation zone once. Prior to their promotion to the Premier League, they had previously failed to win their last 9 playoff fixtures.

Despite losing Saïd Benrahma and Ollie Watkins, their two most influential players for £25m and £30m respectively, following the defeat to Fulham in 2020. They signed Ivan Toney for £5m and Charlie Goode for £1m to post a positive net spend of £49m. Brentford gained promotion and entered the big leagues under the management of Thomas Frank. This David now prepares to take on their version of Goliath and are ready for the challenges of the Premier League, to show you just how significant Brentford's rise has been, here is their transfer activity since promotion to the Championship.

Season	Transfer Incomings	Transfer Outgoings	Net Spend
2014–15	£3.42m	£5.04m	-£1.62m
2015–16	£22.95m	£9.36m	£13.59m
2016–17	£12.96m	£4.64m	£8.32m
2017–18	£13.66m	£5.49m	£8.17m
2018–19	£31.46m	£5.90m	£25.56m
2019–20	£36.63m	£31.21m	£5.42m

19 January 2022, Premier League. Total starting 11 cost. Manchester United Vs Brentford.

£226m Vs £12.8m

This chapter is dedicated to Robert Rowan, who sadly passed away on the 12th of November 2018, aged 28. His vision and arduous work helped build the foundation for Brentford's remarkable run to the Premier League.

* With the fallout from Brexit hitting football recruitment, Brentford in the summer of 2022 took the decision to start up its academy again after a review of football operations. Six years after the football media deemed their decision to close their academy as 'controversial' as it meant they withdrew from the elite player performance plan in 2016. As previously reviewed, this meant focusing on a B-Team of players between 17 and 21. The resulting change is down to the restrictions Brexit has put on European recruitment and their successful promotion to the Premier League through the Championship playoffs.

The Premier League are also looking into making it compulsory for their members to have academies. Brexit has also hit Brentford's recruitment policy of targeting Scandinavia youth almost impossible. Under Brexit, English clubs are no longer able to sign EU players under the age of 18 and are limited to bringing in three players between the ages of 18–21 from the continent in each transfer window.

Further down the football pyramid, Forest Green Rovers are also taking on their own David vs. Goliath fable. One that goes much further than their dealings in the transfer market, but with making the club sustainable both on and off the field. Approaching Nailsworth, Gloucestershire, nestled in the Southwest of England is The New Lawn, stadium and home of Forest Green Rovers since 2006. As the crisp Winter air begins to decide and give-away to a spring evening to a League 2 midweek game against Leyton Orient.

The stadium, powered by solar power, hums with activity as Rovers continue their current promotion push towards League 1. A capacity of 5141 (2000), seated the noise builds as you make your way through the concourse, past neon advertising hoardings and kiosks giving out food to queuing fans. "First time?" Smiles the young lady serving in the truck, as I admire the vegan dish in my hands. "We are changing the way people experience football."

That experience has earned them plaudits from the United Nations (UN) due to their desire for self-sustainability and being the world's first fully vegan, carbon neutral football club. The advertising hubs promoting dairy free products and prominent space is saved for Ecotricity, a renewable energy company owned by Rover's pioneer Dale Vince.

Vince founded Ecotricity in 1995, now aged 60, left school at 15. Taking a voyage of discovery, two fans I speak to recall his backstory, Vince, a man in a van on a road trip to change the world, albeit with a wind turbine attached to it. I found out from a third fan; this is not a local fable written in stone. Vince actually did this, and it helped inspire who he is today.

In 1996, he installed his first wind turbine overlooking the site that would become 'The New Lawn' where I am currently sitting as Rovers go close to opening the scoring. It wouldn't be until 2010, with the club facing relegation from a regional league and financial ruin. Vince, now a self-made millionaire, stepped in and began a formal association with the football club. He started the journey to lay the foundations to neutralise the club's carbon footprint and aim to make the club self-sustainable. Bringing his expertise, learnings in energy, transport and food to build a sustainable approach to building a green football club.

Given that Leagues 1 and 2 at the time of writing were operating under a salary cap based on a percentage of a club's income, the need for new thinking drove the club and Vince to think differently. Being sustainable economically in the transfer window meant a need for self-sufficiency in operating areas of the football club. First came a ban on meat, providing an early indicator of the direction the club was taking and one that proved financially fruitful for the club.

The meat and livestock industry are responsible for around 15% of the planet warming greenhouse gases released due to human activity. The move came in 2015, the substitution of beef burgers for vegetarian equivalents came first to upset a minority of fans. But the distaste didn't last long, fans came, tried it and loved it. The quirkiness of the change drew new fans in. Attendances quadrupled and food sales increased fivefold. The 'quirky' club had found a niche, one with a cathartic meaning with encouragement for fans to come and try it.

The increased following brought new money into the club, allowing the club to grow both on and off the field. The club no longer looking over their shoulder at none league football, are now looking up at League One, as Matthew Stevens opens the scoring on ten minutes for them. Currently the club sit atop League 2 with a points buffer on the teams below. Vince has long-term plans of having the club become a Championship mainstay.

Pivotal to the continual growth is the investment in the club's infrastructure. In January, the local council recently approved initial planning permission for a new 5000-seater stadium. 'The Eco Park' state-of-the-art timber construction designed by architects Zaha Hadid. Vince believes it will be the world's first and greenest stadium.

Fans have jumped on board even though it will mean leaving their current stadium. "Maintaining the atmosphere and what we stand for is crucial, it might seem trivial to Premier League fans, but this club is the heartbeat of this town" chimes in another fan. "It is a cultural thing. Human nature is to reject change. The owner had a vision for change, helping us see a new way of life, and change our mindset." Looking at the vegan food in my hands. "It's not bad, is it?" It is good, and in comparison, to food available at Premier League grounds, well worth the value for money.

Commercially the club continued to grow on and off the field. Advertising revenue is increasing, companies are reaching out to sponsor Forest Green. the club no longer needs to worry about the marketing or commercial sponsorship in the interim period. As Leyton Orient score deep into the second half, the home crowd is not deterred nor upset by away crowds chanting cheap jibes over the home crowd 'eating all the grass' as a rough patch appears in the penalty area near the goalkeeper.

Like their Moneyball approach to finances, other clubs have caught on to their greener methods. Chelsea have recently adopted a vegan menu at one of their kiosks and the club joined Tottenham Hotspurs on 19 September 2021 in what was marketed as the world's first net zero carbon elite football match. #GameZero wants to raise the threat of climate change and inspire simple changes to reduce carbon footprints.

For Rovers, the message is the same, albeit the climate message of survival and change is also driven commercially as it is what keeps the club afloat every year. Upgrades in the playing staff though shrewd transfers have also helped the journey along. Clubs in the lower echelons don't have the finances to purchase players and rely on player loans from clubs above them and free transfers to field an ever-changing team.

"It's hard to see so much squad turnover, but some players can stay for years and become cult-like to the club" chimes a fan behind me. One such move for Reece Brown, released from Birmingham City's academy in the Championship and dropping down two divisions. After two years of good football, he was back in the Championship, a much improved and rounded footballer. It's these kinds of signings that could help the club grow further. Like Brentford, rejected youth prospects could become another hidden gem.

It's not just in the transfer market where the club have looked for the hidden percentages. The club are using the vegan diet off the pitch in the hope it adds to the players performance on it. No player can eat or bring meat onto club premises to be consumed. The ethos is installed in players to remove the stigma that some footballers have adapted for waste, motivated by money, Joe Mills, club captain in 2019 stated, "if we are able to leave the planet in a better state than we come into it, then why shouldn't we?"

The fitness coaches and nutritionists buy into the methods. Highlighting the performance advantages of veganism with plant-based food being much easier to digest when you are playing sport and exercising leading to better performance and recovery in the body. The club does not enforce veganism on their players, and it does rule out some players potentially, but those who buy into the project means the club knows the player is all in and committed to playing for the club.

Progress off the field has seen Vince given special recognition by the UN and is now an ambassador for their sport for climate action initiative. Vince believes the change in philosophy can drive a better future for the country, but for those who come after us. Politicians cannot see the benefits it would bring, but the club is a living example of how it can. New jobs created, cleaner energy, investment in infrastructure and more fans through the turnstiles.

Vince has since watched one of football's founder members, Bolton Wanderers almost enter liquidation. Months after Bury FC were removed from the football league after entering administration. The Bolton scenario still draws head shakes when I pose the question. Vince saw how poor financial management could hurt his club, Bolton put in a loan bid for Rover's star striker and fan favourite Christian Doidge in the summer of 2018. The loan had an agreement to be made permanent for £1m in January 2019 when Bolton were in the Championship.

It would appear Bolton's Chairman at the time, Ken Anderson, knew Bolton could not afford or oblige to the fee when signing the contract. Not only did Rovers lose their star player, but the promised funds could have been used to strengthen the squad. With his contract running down, Rovers eventually sold him to Hibernian for £250k in the summer of 2019/20.

Rovers aim to be active in the transfer market, but don't want to become the next Bolton, or Bury. Taking players from other academies and sell them on for profit or using them for two years to build their careers and help keep the club stable in the interim, as they look to journey up the leagues to the Championship.

Driving away from the club after the game, a hard fought draw, with The New Lawn getting smaller in the rear-view mirror, it is hard not to smile and wonder how far this little ripple in the ocean can go. Hopefully, like Brentford, it's all the way.

Chapter 5
Moneyball and Football's Broken Youth System

As the chapter on Brentford and interview with former Youth Coach Tosh Farrell highlighted, the transfer window has, and is having a negative effect on the grassroots system and academies at several football clubs. As ludicrous amounts of money have flown into the game. More and more clubs are more willing to spend money than be patient and bring through "homegrown talent."

The reluctance to give managers time in the job and the ease at which players seem to stop giving one hundred percent, makes managers reluctant to gamble on youth players. Clubs near the top of the league in the title race and European places have tended to rely on senior players or use the transfer window to buy a proven talent in their pursuit of lofty ambitions. Managers argue that if they blood youngsters, it could cost them points. It is not the players who get sacked, it is them.

Arsene Wenger on youth players in 2017. "You pay for the education of young players with points. If I play a 20-year-old centre-back, he will cost me points during the season and I take the blame for that. A less talented 28-year-old would cost me fewer points, but more money. However, by 23/24, that youngster will have turned into some player."

Likewise, teams at the bottom, desperate to avoid relegation and the financial purgatory of the Championship, rely on experience to pull them out of trouble. Any youngster at these clubs is pushed further down the pecking order. Even when top-flight managers make changes in the domestic cup competitions, the media are quick to accuse them of disrespecting the competition.

Pep Guardiola in his post-match press conference following their cup-tie with Wycombe in 2021, where he was criticised for playing a youthful side against the League 1 club argued, "They should play every day in the Championship or League One. That would be the best for English football."

For lower league clubs, they face the opposite problem. The more they play their youngsters, the more they are likely to be pinched for minimal value in the transfer windows from the teams above them. A lower league manager I spoke to complained teams in the football league cannot climb the divisions because they cannot build a team around players before other clubs poach them. Or in some cases, if their academy works, they unearth a good youngster, they then lose them for a nominal fee as these clubs operate contracts on a two-yearly basis.

Similar to the earlier scenario highlighted with Josh Maja at Sunderland, Youth contracts tend to be two-to-three-year deals. Which means teams are always subjective to another club coming in for their best players. Secondly, if the player is under the age of 18, unable to sign a professional contract it leaves the lower league clubs with an issue.

A fitting example of the issue is what has happened to Fleetwood recently. Sitting in League One, which has to compete with Blackpool and the other Lancashire clubs for the young talent around the North West coast, had unearthed two gems in their academy. Josh Feeney a centre-back, captain of England under 16's. Merited a few places on the bench in league games towards the end of the 2021 season. Being highly thought of in the England set up and a feature at youth tournaments meant a number of clubs circled around his availability.

Even before he could make an impression in the first team, Aston Villa approached them with an offer for Feeney to join their academy. With his youth contract ending. Fleetwood were left with no choice but to accept the transfer.

The player most likely could have gone for a nominal trainee's fee at the expiry of his contract, was on his way to Aston Villa for a substantial six figure fee according to the press release. Sadly, for Fleetwood, had he been able to make a few appearances for the first team and been on a professional contract the figure could have been in the millions and not the thousands.

Another example is the recent transfer of Billy Crellin. England under-20 international Crellin has penned a two-and-a-half-year deal to keep him at Goodison Park until at least June 2024. The 21-year-old, who featured in England's Under-17 World Cup winning campaign in 2017, made his senior debut for League One side Fleetwood in October 2018. Should have been a staple of Fleetwood's building blocks for the future with Feeney commanding the back four in front of him.

Instead, Crellin played 16 matches during a promotion-winning season loan with then-League Two Bolton Wanderers last term enjoying a good learning curve whilst out on loan. He had a shorter temporary spell in the National League with Chorley, where he played nine matches, in 2019/20, and the previous campaign spent time with FC United of Manchester in National League North.

Another nominal fee was secured for his services. But for a goalkeeper with such promises the fee secured may help Fleetwood in the interim, or even pay for their academy for two years. But the reality is, what are the chances Fleetwood brings through to players like that in the future? Like Brentford before them, seeing their best youngsters plucked from their academies.

Simon Jordan of talkSPORT has an interesting take on the situation. Stating that clubs like Fleetwood have a £500k subsidy each year dangled like a carrot in front of them to help finance their academies. The downside to this subsidy is it leaves them open to losing their youth players for nominal fees as they run their contracts down before they sign professional deals.

The subsidy in question is a part of the Elite Player Performance Plan, a long-term strategy designed to advance Premier League Youth development. Introduced in 2012 following years of consultation. With England struggling at major tournaments and the lack of young English players breaking through, the development of young English players was at a crossroads. With the homegrown talent rule in place the price of English players shot up overnight. Teams were required to have a certain number of homegrown players in their first team squads.

UEFA justified the rule, to encourage youth development and encourage competitive balance to the football divisions. By bringing through more Youth, it would save, in theory millions of pounds for the clubs, therefore making them more sustainable. The practical and where you could argue the rule had flaws, is Spanish born Cesc Fàbregas qualified as homegrown, because Arsenal signed him as a youngster, going through their academy, so he was English homegrown. Across London, England International Eric Dier, was not included as Homegrown and required Spurs to register him as one of their seventeen senior player slots for the upcoming season. This is despite Dier spending two years on loan, in England, at Everton's academy. Yet, this did not meet the criteria. Incidentally, Fàbregas spent less time in Arsenal's academy.

The fallout meant a third-choice midfielder was being priced out of a move both nationally and internationally. Youngsters were being kept, but not played at Premier League clubs so they could comply with the new rule. This compounded the problem rather than provided a solution, so EPPP was born with a long-term strategy with the aim of developing more and better homegrown players.

The EPPP works across three phases: foundation level focusing on under-9 to under-11. Then onto Youth Development under 12 to under 16, then onto professional development, under 17 to under 23. Built on four pillars to provide the foundation for the program.

Games Program. The Premier League provided up to 10,000 matches, 212 festivals and tournaments to football clubs across all age groups. These come in the following: Premier League 2, Professional Development League 2, Premier League Cup and Premier League International Cup and the under-18 Premier League and Development League 2, these competitions are set to bridge the gap between youth football and the rigours of professional football on the domestic and international level.

Education. Looking after the players is also at the forefront of the plan. The Premier League aims to provide world-class education via inspirational and innovative teaching. Developing rounding people through teaching and ensuring they pursue an education, focusing on supporting the technical, physical, mental, lifestyle and welfare development of all academy players.

Coaching. The scheme has launched an apprenticeship scheme, Elite Coach Apprenticeship Scheme, to develop and accelerate the development of coaches to the scheme. Giving them access to clubs and schemes to help grow their skills and enter employment.

Another area they have looked at to help developing youth is the launching of the Bio-Banding program, tournaments organised each season with the aim to match players to their biological age. Rather than pitching players based on their age in the school year, (September–August) they are focused on the actual calendar period they are born. Children born in August would play against children in the year below them at school, as biologically their bodies will be closer in their maturity.

Categorisation. The clubs who take part in the scheme and receive the subsidy, have their academies audited each season to ensure they meet the Premier Leagues standards. Given a category status 1–4. (1 being the most elite.) With ten factors determining the grading, from productivity, training facilities, coaching, education, and welfare provisions.

The higher a club's category the more funding will be available to it and the EFPP will see more Premier League and FA invest more central income in youth development programs. But here lies the issue for clubs like Fleetwood, unable due to cost, to achieve a higher category in academy, receives less funding than Premier League clubs and still loses its players to Premier League clubs for a fraction they could be worth in a further year or two.

An argument for signing a youth player and receiving compensation is covered when they receive a professional contract or have been offered one by their current club. When another club signs them at the expiry of their contract, the new club signing the player is entitled to pay them a fee/compensation. But even then, this method is flawed and the compensation, if needing a tribunal, rarely matches the player's potential fee.

Most cases do not need an FA tribunal. Some teams can reach a compromise on price. But the new 'buying' team holds all the cards. They know depending on appearances and other factors the players cost at a tribunal is most likely never to go over £3m for a Premier League academy. So, they are likely to bid under or around this mark, if the club losing the academy player disagrees it goes to tribunal where they are hopeful to get to this figure.

In January 2022, Liverpool put in a transfer bid for Fulham's starlet Fabio Carvalho, whose professional contract had less than six months to run. Meaning clubs outside of England could sign him on a pre-agreement for July. Fulham would have received between £200–£300k. If he reached July and left on a 'free' transfer to a British club, they would have gone to a tribunal and potentially received between £3m–£5m.

Liverpool, knowing this, opened negotiations with Fulham in January, but played the long game with submitting their opening proposal. Putting in a bid lower than £3m, knowing and testing the patience of Fulham who could lose him for much less. Fulham faced another dilemma, a key player in Marco Silva's promotion push which would see them gain £100m extra in revenue, had a decision, they could take the £3m Liverpool offered, wait and take the risk they may get more at tribunal, but this would open the door to a European club signing him for £300k.

Fulham decided to gamble, they rejected Liverpool's offer and asked them to rebid, closer to the £5m they believed they would get at tribunal as Carvalho. On deadline day, Liverpool came back with an improved offer, Fulham accepted but time ran out to get the deal registered. Despite a deal sheet being submitted to give them fifteen more minutes to complete the deal, they ran out of time. The deal will go to a tribunal unless another British club bids more for Carvalho, or a European club signs a pre-agreement with the player.

Another example where a club has been short changed is Crystal Palace, Simon Jordan was making those comments on talkSPORT because he had it happen to him personally whilst he was owner of Crystal Palace. John Bostock broke through into Crystal Palace's first team aged 16. Pictured on the back of all the papers in his school uniform, doing keep ups whilst holding his backpack.

Despite the odd appearance in the first team, it didn't deter Barcelona from bidding £1.5m for his services. Swiftly rejected by Jordan as it fell well below his evaluation for the youngster. Not forgetting, only a few years earlier Jordan witnessed an 18-year-old Wayne Rooney be sold for £27m. As his contract ended, he signed for cross London rivals Tottenham Hotspur. Jordan and Spurs couldn't agree on a fee, so a tribunal was held. The fee was set at paltry £650k.

Those who argue that football clubs should make their academy players sign pro contracts or longer deals miss the point that Financial Fair Play and other red tape factors impact the transfer world. By doing this, the clubs with the smaller budgets would be impacted as their costs would increase to unsustainable levels, this would further compound and increase the imbalance with clubs in the premier league. Clubs in Leagues 1 and 2 are under salary caps and would not be able to loan these players or sign them in the future as their wage demands would outweigh how far their budgets could stretch.

Some academy players have agents who are demanding their players get Championship level wages even before they make the first team, based on the fact they have come through a category one academy. Which brings us to the curious case of Thierry Small.

Making his debut for Everton in the dying moments of their FA Cup fourth round home tie to Sheffield Wednesday in 2021 and the tie over at three nil, Manager Carlo Ancelotti brought two academy players on for their first team debuts. Replacing global superstar James Rodriquez, Small played the final five minutes and touched the ball just once. A great moment for Small and for the club, as another two graduates appeared to continue Everton's fine trend of producing talent.

But following his debut and subsequent occasional appearances on the first team substitute bench, contract talks hit the rocks in March. Everton claimed Small's representatives demanded Small be named a first team player and have his locker moved in their Finch Farm training base from the Under 18's to the first team, guaranteed game time. On top of breaking Everton's academy wage structure. They wanted Small to be paid significantly more than current first team star Anthony Gordon, who had himself had recently broken through. Gordon had several appearances for Everton, but also had experience in the Championship for Preston.

Despite being the jewel in Everton's academy, director of football Marcel Brands offered him a new deal with a significant pay-rise and a first team locker. Not the amount Small's team wanted, nor the first team appearances Small wanted, but he had a pathway. Brands' problem was that Everton had Lucas Digne, French international, recently recalled to the World Cup winning side in time for the delayed Euro 2020 tournament. Statistically one of Europe's best defenders, Brands was being asked to push Digne out of the door at the expense of a high potential seventeen-year-old who had played a grand total of five minutes in the dying embers of an FA Cup tie.

With a final improved offer rejected and Small entering the final month of his academy deal, Southampton reached out to Small and offered him terms, which included a pathway to the first team. Everton countered, sending Niels Nkounkou out on loan, providing Small the first team pathway as he was now the reserve left back to the first team. Small rejected the contract and pre-signed a contract with Southampton, the final fee to be set at a tribunal.

The irony for both sides is neither got what they immediately wanted, Small signed for Southampton, but they also signed Tino Livramento, Kyle Walker-Peters (who could play both full backs positions) and twenty-three-year-old Romain Perraud to play left back ahead of Small.

Small ended up where he was at Everton, in the under 23's, with more players in front of him than he had at Merseyside. In the 2022 season, he was restricted to a few early domestic cup games. For Everton, left with one first choice left back, Digne fell out with new Manager Rafa Benitez in December, Small would have been playing first team football had he stayed on Merseyside.

Everton lost a player whose potential was estimated at £20m, were forced to sell Lucas Digne and replace him in January 2022 with Ukrainian international Vitaliy Mykolenko for £21m. Small, at tribunal, at best will get Everton £5m, most likely £3m, would have been a first time regular had he stayed. Both Small and Everton looked to have lost in the short term, only the future will tell who was right, but this example provides an early look at a future chapter, the perils of advisors and are they really in the players' best interest.

In February 2023, Southampton had the same youth transfer situation happen to them. Their highly rated youngster, Jimmy-Jay Morgan was poached by Chelsea in a comparable way the club purchased Small from Everton. Morgan signed for Chelsea for an initial £3m with add-ons potentially taking the deal to £6m. Described as one of the best finishers in the youth ranks, his January switch comes as a blow to the club.

With more and more academy players leaving clubs seeking first team football before they have reached their teams under-21 squads, clubs are continually looking for ways to get their younger players experience, so they are ready for the rigours of first team football. With places in squads limited, and manager turnover at an all-time high, they prefer to have experience over youth, giving clubs like Everton a problem.

Manchester City lost Jadon Sancho to Borussia Dortmund for £7m after he found his pathway to the first team blocked, he took a plunge young English players rarely do and left for Europe in his late teens. The move was a success, no way into City's title winning sides, Sancho thrived for Dortmund and left the German club in the Summer of 2021 to come back to Manchester, signing for United for £75m.

A happier tale than Thierry Small's, but Pep Guardiola is adamant for City not to face the future. Playing more of his academy stars in the FA and League Cup. Which brings us back to where the chapter started. How can teams provide a pathway for their academy players, getting them first team football without jeopardising their current results in the league?

Guardiola favours the professional 'B-Team' option. Not to be confused with Brentford's B-Team, their 'under-23' team which goes around Europe playing the best academies, Guardiola's wish would be for them to be in the lower leagues of English football. In fact, a proposal for several Category One clubs to have 'B-Teams' was once muted and swiftly shelved by the English Football League. The compromise being these academies could field a team in the EFL Trophy, a trophy for teams in League 1 and 2. Premier League teams academies can partake but cannot field a Premier League player.

Whilst this gives certain Premier League academies a taste of professional football, there are several points that critics raise. Firstly, it only benefits certain Premier League academies. Doesn't help clubs in the Championship of the rest of the English Football League (EFL), only those few bigger clubs in the Premier League. Devalues a trophy that struggles to find a place and revenue from the other English competitions. There is an argument whether it has actually helped bring through more 'homegrown' talent amongst those clubs.

Clubs in the Premier League will still persist with the B-Team option to be able to satisfy their youth players and to give them a long-term advantage over other clubs. But this again is weighed towards favouring certain clubs over others. Wouldn't stop Premier League clubs pinching academy players from lower league opposition and they have the significant advantage of not needing to worry over results. The academy managers would be more than happy playing younger players knowing their jobs are safer, whereas a manager at an EFL club is fighting for his career, match by match, in a result-driven business.

With the EFL losing Bury to administration, Bolton almost following the same fate and with Derby facing a winding up order, only to be saved at the last minute after a sinister drawn-out takeover almost lost the EFL another club, to have potential B-Teams take their place would further devalue and harm EFL clubs in perhaps their biggest hour of need.

Thirdly, in the example of Thierry Small at Everton, a regular in these fixtures, he didn't see any value in them, appearing to emphasise the academy players the move is meant to help see it more as a hindrance rather than first-team football. Furthermore, even more so post Covid-19 football clubs in the EFL are on the brink of liquidation. Teetering on the edge of financial ruin, face the fact the Million-pound Premier League clubs now potentially take prize money away from clubs who are desperate for the money just to pay the next heating bill.

Perhaps with clubs struggling and the Premier League clubs finally agreeing to release more money into the EFL another solution could be having certain clubs link up with the Premier League academies and loan their best players. The Premier League teams would pay the wages at the promise the EFL club would play their players a certain number of games. Whilst this would help get players first-term experience and help the EFL clubs, now fixed with a salary cap, it does create a false economy.

If EFL clubs used this system, it would deny their academy players a place in the first team. Make them reliant on Premier League loans to field a team, therefore, should they be promoted to the Championship, the growth will have been built on a bubble that could burst at any second. Finally, regardless of the

EFL clubs results, the team that benefits the most is the Premier League, their youth player gets first team football.

Whilst several of the current England team enjoyed spells in the lower leagues and even the National League on their way to being first team regulars, not all players enjoy the loans. Going from Premier League academies where everything is done for them, from washing kit and boots to top quality gyms, in the EFL, it becomes a culture shock to them, and some players struggle, and loans can actually damage their rate of growth.

A more drastic solution is the current trend seeking European Loans for academies best talents. Players such as William Saliba of Arsenal have enjoyed two years in Europe in the hope of breaking into Mikel Arteta's resurgent team. Arteta sensing the player needed consistent game time loaned out his £16m signing three years in a row to the French Ligue 1.

Chelsea have used this method to great effect which has led the club into criticism. In 2016, the club had thirty-eight players out on loan. Their method of procuring young talent rather than sending them out on loans continued year on year. In summer 2021, Chelsea sold England under 21 international Timo Livramento for £5m to Southampton and Marc Guéhi to Crystal Palace for £21m, two good talents from their academy which allowed Chelsea to reinvest the money in signing Romelu Lukaku and comply with Financial Fair Play measures.

Chelsea have been collecting talent and selling fringe players to continue to fund their yearly charge for the Premier League. Other clubs criticise them for hoarding talent, some will argue Chelsea have recruited and coached their academy well, but the large majority don't make the grade for Chelsea. For every Mason Mount or Reece James, there is a Lucas Piazon, Jamal Blackmon and Lewis Baker. Players who had great potential, whose careers seemed to be derailed by continual loans.

A vicious cycle and loop that looks likely to have been stopped following FIFA's announcement of new loan regulations starting from July 2022, clubs will be restricted to eight international loan signings, and eight players sent on loan abroad. World football's governing body intends to drop this to seven players for the 2023/24 season and then six for the 2024/25 campaign. Designed to prevent clubs from hoarding players, as Chelsea have been accused of. But it could also impact clubs looking to send their academy players out on loan.

At the time of writing, Chelsea have twenty-one players out on loan, eight at foreign clubs. With Chelsea under UK government sanctions from the fallout of Russia's illegal war with Ukraine and a bloated squad, there could be a firesale in the summer to bring their squad into line. Whether they will be able to spend the money raised is another question, but for some teams, Chelsea may be forced to sell and given their academies success rate, there will be several suitors eyeing up their players.

With the possibility of teams not being able to overuse the European leagues, it will push more players on loan into the EFL. Perhaps reignite more discussions over the B-Teams, as there is a belief that League 1 and 2 isn't good enough for talent progression. Perhaps more academies will follow Brentford's method and take their academies on the road to playing the best youth teams across Europe.

With rumours of the European Super League happening, will it be long before Premier League clubs explore having a European Youth League or search out teams in the German and French Leagues to affiliate themselves to send their best youth players to gain more experience. What is easy to see is that any decision can have a major impact and create a huge ripple effect through the football league.

In response to clubs hoarding youth players and continually loaning them out, FIFA announced a new set of stringent rules which will restrict and curb clubs from farming out their youth talent from 1st July 2022. The aim is to force parent clubs to play their 'homegrown' players more.

Clubs will only be able to sign a maximum of eight international loan signings in the 2022–23 season, while a further eight players can be loaned out across borders. It will drop to seven for the 2023–24 season and six indefinitely from the 2024–25 campaign. The change of regulations will not apply to players aged 21 and younger, though.

A FIFA statement said: "The introduction of a new regulatory framework for player loans is another important step in the context of the wider reform of the transfer system, the process of which began in 2017. Initially planned to start in July 2020, the implementation of the new rules had to be delayed as a consequence of the COVID-19 pandemic. The discussions with the different stakeholder groups have laid the foundations for this new framework and ensured that the new rules are firmly anchored on the following core objectives:

- Developing young players.
- Promoting competitive balance.
- Preventing the hoarding of players."

Detractors will say it does not stop teams continually loaning out their youth year after year with no real pathway created for the first team as the rule does not apply to players under the age of 21. It does however stop teams conducting two-year loans, where the obligation to buy is pushed further down the line for FFP accountancy reasons. Clubs would be forced to sell players to finance the deal.

In essence, football clubs will have to be more selective on where they send players on loan. Two Premier League club may feel the effects. Manchester City and Chelsea. Premier League champions City loaned out 14 players outside of England in 2021–22, while Chelsea sent eight out.

Another principle that was introduced to help British academies produce English talent was the homegrown talent rule. These rules initially introduced into English football in 2015 by then FA chairman Greg Dyke dictated clubs must include a certain number of homegrown players in their 25-man Premier League squad. The rule stipulated for a player to be considered homegrown, they must have played for an FA-affiliated club for at least three years before turning 21.

Importantly, clubs realised players did not have to be English, meaning a Spanish player bought aged 16 is classed as homegrown after two years, so according to the rules, for Arsenal, Cesc Fàbregas, born in Arenys de Mar, Spain, was classed as a 'homegrown' player.

Other examples including Paul Pogba and Hector Bellerin would all count as 'homegrown' and help their clubs register more foreign players in their Premier League squads, whilst the rule had good intentions, the rule could be manipulated and was. It created a rush on Premier League clubs to go out and sign European talents between the ages of 16–18 and by the time they were 21, these players would fall within the parameters of the rule.

Another rule implemented to improve the development of the English Youth system was implemented following Brexit. English clubs will no longer be able to sign players under 18 from EU clubs (and vice versa) using the Intra-EU transfer exemption. This means clubs will be unable to bolster their academies here with talented young players from abroad. During the transition period of leaving the EU, Premier League clubs rushed to get transfers of Youth players before the deadline.

Both these examples highlight how even government policy or legislation meant to help the game in a positive way can be manoeuvred around and given a chance, Premier League clubs will take advantage of situations in an ever-changing world which impacts their transfer policy. These examples actually saw a rise in the cost of British youth players, and some argued that it restricted British youth players in the last few years.

Now in 2022, with the rule fully in force, Premier League clubs are now canvassing the Premier League to help change the rules back because they fear they will end up paying inflated prices for players or missing out on the best talent altogether because they cannot compete for their signature until they are 18. With Premier League clubs hoovering up the young talent and selling them a few years later to circumnavigate FFP and Premier League rules, it does not come as a surprise when clubs like Chelsea and Manchester City are leading the complaints and canvassing for the rule change. Perhaps this shows the rule is working and puts greater emphasis on them to coach their own players.

Chapter 6
'The Architects' Directors of Football

"Rome was not built in a day."

As the transfer market has adapted over the years and progressed following the Bosman ruling, football clubs began to change the way they conducted business. Investing in scouts and recruitment teams, European clubs also identified specific rules for their club's transfer business, thus the role of director of football or Technical Director was developed. Their key role is to oversee their football club's recruitment and academy development, this means the manager is free to coach and develop the players.

A successful Director Of Football is tasked with hiring the manager at the club and understanding the tactics that the managers wish to deploy and buy players that fit this model. This chapter will look at the personnel who work behind the scenes to sculpt the teams we see on the pitches.

Earlier we looked at how the communication between football clubs and fans was at an all-time low, yet some sporting directors are finding ways to cross the purgatory of no-mans-land and interact and discuss the transfer process with the fanbase, to give them the truth instead of the tabloid tales padded with agendas and ambiguity. Kristjaan Speakman is now the Sporting Director of Sunderland in the Championship.

Having started his coaching career at Derby County as their Under 18's manager, it was not long before he moved across the Midlands to Birmingham City to become their academy director, responsible for bringing through talents such as Jude Bellingham, Jack Butland, Demarai Gray and Charlee Adams are just a few of the plethora of players Speakman has helped forge professional careers for, after leaving to take up the sporting director role at Sunderland, he revolutionised their transfer strategy with data-led scouting coming to the fore, he has set a goal and course for Sunderland to return to the Premier League and following the two-year anniversary of his appointment, he sat down with Sunderland AFC Unfiltered podcast to give the club's fans an update on the progress of the club and their activity in the 2023, January transfer window.

"It's been a really intense period, where the adrenaline flows through you, you get in a mode of working, which is not necessarily healthy, but you are doing your best, but it is what is required."

When questioned on his fourth transfer window and why business goes to the wire, Speakman is practical in his response, "There is a window and a deadline, it is used as a negotiating tactic, you do see more activity towards the back end of the window, we've tried to stay away from it, a reason for having a well-structured plan, an understanding of what you want to do. In January, you do not have a cohort of out-of-contract players floating around in the market place that has a knock-on effect to transfers to trade with. When looking to acquire a high-quality player in January, you need to find a club for one of your players."

Reflecting on the January business for Sunderland, Speakman explains the emotion so soon after can make it hard to review. "We are happy with the business we conducted, but also frustrated, the unexpected injury to Ross Stewart hurt us." (Sunderland's main striker and Ellis Simms having his loan from Everton cut short, ultimately left them short of attacking options.) Speakman is pressed on the fans' surprised the club failed to bring in another striker.

"Look, ultimately that is frustrating for us, but I will supply some context, we had a plan and vision coming into the window, we had a number of seven figure bids on players which adhered to our long-term strategy of the club, then we moved to get Joffey. (Joe Gelhardt on loan from Leeds United) It was one of the most competitive loan deals I've ever seen, and I am very proud of my team, we then need and looked for a third striker, but moments into a game, Ross Stewart gets injured and at half-time I am on the phone to reorganise our shortlist. Unfortunately, none of the players on our list of our striker's profiles fitted with what we needed."

Speakman is then quizzed on the fans desire for more news on Ellis Simms. "Well, look, we were constantly monitoring Ellis's situation and Everton's current situation is well documented, Everton were looking for a striker, which would have allowed Sunderland to re-sign the player on loan. Me and all the coaching staff have been adamant that we want the correct players for the club, the correct mentality, best for our formation and players' character... We've been clear we are not going to sign a player for the sake of signing a player, they need to be the right player."

Speakman also gives us an insight on how the sporting director deals on a personal level for the injured Ross Stewart, (likely out for the season). "I was there for him after the match and we talked in my office the next day, he was gutted for now, for the season, for the team, he is an important player for us, and we want to get him back as quickly as possible and have laid out a plan for him."

Highlighting how a good sporting director will still work with players during their rehabilitation progress, by being there for a player, the Director can use this situation when they next renegotiate a contract. In Stewart's case, his contract ends in 2023, given Sunderland may be promoted, or may strive for it next year, his contract renewal is integral to Sunderland's long-term plan.

"We don't want to go into games with one out and out number nine, but we felt the levels of players that were available, they did not fit our style, free agency and the names that will be banded around are likely not on our radar."

He is questioned on whether finances led to no signing. "Certainly not, we've had bids in their players that we felt appropriate, but selling clubs did not move."

On his new signings Speakman details with excitement. "They have all settled in well with the squad, echoes with the current dressing room cohesion we have… they need to get up to speed quickly with the matchday squad so they can contribute."

Fans will know the most about Joe Gelhardt, from Leeds. "When you are discussing the high number of options available to your club, there are few occasions when everyone is saying we must get this player. The fans base and their response helped, the players could see what it is like to play for Sunderland during the bidding war for Joe. Pierre Ekwah (21-year-old midfielder from West Ham) signed a four-year deal. We had been tracking him for some time, just been unable to crack West Ham's first team, but he is progressive in how he plays, the data highlights this, a box-to-box midfielder."

"A physical player that we feel we can enhance with our program. Joe Anderson, captain of Everton's Under-21 side. He has a lovely ability to control the ball, a left sided centre-back, a good enhancement to the group, we need to provide the transition to the first team we can provide, he is an extraordinarily strong character, and the core values of the club. Isaac Lihadji, a really explosive, quick dynamic player, more of a straight-line runner, someone who will excite the ground and can change the tempo of games, it shouldn't be understated how much goes into a deal that brings a player like Isaac into Sunderland. We want to sign players early, if they are from overseas, it helps them adapt and get up to speed with Sunderland, the way we play and the club."

The recruitment under Speakman is a far cry from the scattergun approach that I highlighted earlier with Stewart Donald's leadership at Sunderland, a longer-term project, with proper scouting, no last-minute panic buys similar to the signing of Will Grigg or having Zlatan Ibrahimovic on their scouting shortlist. It provides the insight fans would want, details that the strategy is based on long-term pillars to build the foundations for not only promotion, but one which will make Sunderland sustainable.

Sporting Directors or Directors of Football are often seen as the most important personr not included in the match day operation, because they are charged with managing the entire football-related operation of the business. When they are allowed to do their jobs, success and a strategy follows, when interfered with, issues can quickly arise. As was the case of Marcel Brands and Everton. Brands was nicknamed the architect for his role in developing PSV Eindhoven back into a force in the Eredivisie with his emphasis on developing youth and smart purchases.

After a career as a centre midfielder starting out at FC Den Bosch, Brands stepped in as General Manager of RKC Waalwijk, a municipality South of the river Bergse Maas. A club Brands knew well after two stints here as a player. With the club languishing down the division and tight purse strings, it allowed Brands to cut his teeth and use a model he would later replicate at PSV Eindhoven.

He appointed Martin Jol as manager and the club saw a turnaround in their fortunes in the eight years that he was there. The club knew it would not be long before a bigger club came calling and they did. AZ Alkmarr approached Brands and he was off to Alkmarr, located in a province of North Holland. In 2005, Brands took over the reins and hired Louis Van Gaal, known for his tactical approach.

Brands went about overhauling the scouting network and developed the academy so it would follow the same formation played by the first team. In the 2007/08 season, the club narrowly survived relegation. The following season Brands revamped the squad. Letting eleven players leave, which brought in around £2.5m in transfer revenue. Brands promoted goalkeeper Jordy Deckers and central Midfielder Toni Kolehmainen from their youth academy.

Moving quick to secure centre-back Ragnar Klavan on loan from Heracles Almelo, then signed Right Back Gill Swerts on a free transfer, Brands completed his defensive overhaul by spending £500k centre-back on Niklas Moisander from FC Zwolle. Attack was now the focus to make Alkmarr more potent, with winger Nick van der Velden signed from FC Dordrecht for £550k and Australian playmaker Brett Holman for £2.8m signed from NEC Nijmegen.

AZ Alkmarr lost their first game of the season. Subsequently going onto lose their second game, barely making an impact on proceedings, seeing a player sent off and losing the game 4–0. Third game of the season, AZ were set to play PSV Eindhoven. Given their previous season's brush with relegation, a loss to PSV could have meant an end to the Brands era at AZ. Certainly in the Premier League, both Brands and Manager, Louis Van Gaal, would have been sacked given the demands of the Premier Leagues on club executives to have an immediate impact.

AZ went onto win the game in a backs to the wall manner, what then happened has gone down in Eredivisie folklore. AZ Alkmarr went on a 38-game unbeaten run which saw them win the Eredivisie title with four games to spare, only the second time in their history. The following summer, brands implemented a new transfer strategy, focusing on players under the age of 25, allowing AZ to maximise any profit on their transfer business. Enjoying their first foray into Europe for over thirty years.

With Louis Van Gaal's success at AZ, he suddenly became hot property again, and it was not long before Bayern Munich came calling and left Brands needing another manager. In stepped Dutchman Ronald Koeman, who guided the side into Europe and a solid top-5 position in 2009. Before the curtain had come down on the season, clubs began circling Brands to be their DOF and it was not long before PSV who AZ pipped to the title in 2008 came calling.

Brands took over the reins and appointed Fred Rutten as coach. In his first two seasons, PSV finished third place twice. With Rutten as coach, PSV beat Feyenoord 10–0 in a home game on 24 October 2010. Feyenoord's heaviest defeat in their club history. However, off the field, the club experienced liquidity problems, needing to secure its future through loans and property sales. It was a necessity that key players Ibrahim Afellay and Balázs Dzsudzsák were sold. Director of Football Marcel Brands spent €25 million to improve the squad.

But the 2011–12 season proved difficult, the team dropped out of the title race early again, which led to Rutten's dismissal. Brands appointed a manager who shared a similar philosophy in football, Phillip Cocu, with PSV facing increasing pressure to remain in the European competitions due to the Premier League and Bundesliga dominance, Brands and Cocu put heavy emphasis on changing the philosophy with increasing their academy spending and hiring former PSV player Ruud van Nistelrooy to coach in their youth ranks and use as tool to recruit the best youngsters to play for one of the Netherlands best strikers.

Under their guidance, PSV won the Eredivisie title another two times. solidifying them as a top force in the European leagues and ensuring PSV have continued to play in a European competition every year since 1974; only Barcelona (since 1959) and Anderlecht (since 1964) have a longer streak in play. The fact Brands and Cocu kept PSV competitive during this reign was down to their scouting network and philosophy. Promote from the academy and buy low (young with potential) and sell high, PSV had a positive net spend of €56.59m.

It was no surprise to anyone when the Premier League came calling and Marcel Brands signed on to become Everton's Director of Football. Replacing incumbent Steve Walsh who had made a number of high-profile mistakes and after spending €290m in two years at Everton, with only Jordan Pickford ever justifying the price paid for him.

Everton was crippled by a wage bill that had risen to 110% of turnover. (For every pound coming into the business in revenue, Everton were spending £1.10 in business costs) and sliding down the table. Brands was left with a team devoid of talent, an academy that was once the leading producer of footballers, no longer bringing players through and an ageing squad.

It was here that Marcel Brands highlighted how the Director of Footballers work. Brands was questioned on the size of Everton's squad, Everton had over 35 first team players when Brands took over. Brands was quick to add a successful club should be operating with around 23–25 players. He gave an example of a club operating in a 4–3–3 system.

Brands believed a club should have three goalkeepers. Their first choice should be in their prime and be backed up by a senior professional, still good enough to be number 1, but mostly utilised in the cup games, then there should be a younger prospect (19–21 years old) who is likely to be pushing your number 1 in a few years' time.

In a team's defence, the team should have four fullbacks. (Two left, two right) To offer balance and coverage for a season, with both players sharing similar characteristics, important so that an injury to one full-back does not change the way the entire team operates. Then the team should have four centre-backs.

Ideally, two right-footed centre-backs and two left-footed centre-backs to offer balance and open the pitch up, having a left-footed centre-back opens the pitch and stops the left centre-back from needing to play across themselves and leave more of a risk of turning the ball over.

Brands broke down the midfield options, two defensive midfielders who should be mobile, quick and their main aim is to break up the opponents attacks and spring your team out from an aggressive press. The next two players, filling the number 8 role, commonly known as the box-box midfielder, need to be quick, agile and be able to mix key defensive statistics, but also be creative enough to create and score goals. The final two players would be the number 10s, the players tasked with unlocking the opponents defence, needing to both be able to score and assist their team in goal contributions.

Onto the forwards, Brands valued versatility, two centre forwards who are capable of scoring between 15–20 goals a season would hold the line and be provided by wingers. Four players who ideally would need to be able to offer ten goal contributions to a team, but also be able to defend and honour defensive duties to protect their full backs from being overloaded. One of these players would also be able to play centrally to cover for any injuries to the centre forward.

Brands was keen in promoting academy players, identifying teams should have three to four academy players around the first team who can step in during injuries and fatigue. Brands also brought up the challenge Premier League clubs face with promoting youth. At PSV and AZ, it was expected from fans that academy players provided the backbone of the team's match day squad.

Something that Everton had previously been well known for. It was a task that Brands knew he needed to restart at Everton but would face an arduous task as recruitment rules had been relaxed and more than ever academy graduates could move between clubs easier before they signed professional deals when they were 17 years old. Brands also indicated that several Premier League clubs send their young players on several loans.

Perhaps too many, citing the lack of quality academy coaches in developing players. In the European leagues, it is not uncommon to have 19-year-olds on the bench in big matches. In the Premier League, how many 19-years-olds have played significant roles for Manchester City and Liverpool in their dominant last five years. Two, Phil Foden and Trent Alexander-Arnold, this may be about to change as even these clubs are feeling the pinch from FFP rules.

Brands also discussed a DOF forward planning strategy to team building. Discussing the eleven roles' players can play on the pitch, Brands was keen to point out that a club should have a minimum of three players, per each position on the pitch, that they feel comfortable enough purchasing, if something where to happen to one of the first team players. (Sold, injured, retired) These players should be a mixture of experienced professionals, cheaper, but good enough to fill out your squad. Young players, cheaper, but with high potential and players aged around 24–25, in their prime and likely to have residual value for the club to maximise.

Whilst constructing your first team and having that priority list of players ready to go should it be needed. Brands was keen to point out the importance of building and maintaining a scouting database. From youth scouting across the major youth tournaments, to soccer camps and allegiances in emerging nations, it was important to always keep the plates spinning to ensure the club had a regular updated database on players coming through, scouting reports on hundreds of players, matching the club's style of play, vision and their progression.

In Brands' first season at Everton, the club finished 8th under Marco Silva, progress on what had been barren and poor few years for the Merseyside club. The next season, Everton hit a rut of poor form, Marco Silva's reluctance to address key defensive issues, combined with from several players had stopped caring and after another capitulation, Everton's owner sacked Silva and replaced him with Carlo Ancelotti. Several key first team players expressed their sadness at the sacking of Silva, Brands included, but the results on the pitch and the players attitudes made the decision for them.

During the Covid-19 impact season, Everton were within touching distance of the European places before the entire country locked down. Restarting the season with the Merseyside Derby in June, Everton were good value for a point against Liverpool, then picked up consecutive wins against Norwich and Leicester City. Everton were a point away from the Europa League, when they went on an unprecedented 7 game run without a win.

Failing to beat Southampton, Aston Villa and Bournemouth at home and Sheffield United away, four teams who were battling relegation which ultimately saw Everton limp home to 12th place, leaving Ancelotti blasting his players for a lack of motivation for not wanting European football and a lack of leadership in the squad.

Brands was tasked with rebuilding a midfield, seeking a defensive midfielder who could break up opponents attacks and a box-to-box number eight who could add some muscle to the Everton team. Brands would undertake what would be his most pivotal transfer window in his position as Everton Director of Football.

Struggling to shift players post Covid, only Morgan Schneiderlin and former prospect Kieran Dowell brought in money for a club that would be desperate for cash flow as Covid-19 robbed several revenue streams from all clubs. Failing to move on players who were Everton's top earners and now squad players, proved to be a huge hole in the Dutchman's transfer plans at the club. On paper, signing Allan and Abdoulaye Doucouré for £40m combined seemed like good business, but adding two more players to Everton's highest earners and the significant expenditure with little residual value highlighted Everton's short-term strategy.

Better and younger players were available, but Brands and Ancelotti gambled on proven players. Ben Godfrey was added for £25m, a young player, who could play all four positions at the back and even Allan's role in midfield. But the crowning piece to Brands summer plans was the free transfer of James Rodriguez to the club, a player of Champions League quality and was seen as the missing piece. However, loaning out Moise Kean, who had struggled to adapt to English football and life, meant Everton were short up front.

Everton raced out to a great start to the season and Ancelotti had the club second at Christmas, a return to Champions League football seemed possible, Europa League would have been a consolation prize for this position. With injuries to Allan, Abdoulaye Doucouré and Everton's lack of a second striker saw their lack of pace, coupled with their lack of leadership saw the Merseyside club collapse and finish a disappointing 10th in the League. The collapse should have been the perfect indicator for the club's relegation battle the following year, but everyone at the club seemed focused on the short term.

Everton and Brands had shifted away from a policy which had served both parties so well in the past and would come back to haunt them when looking at players such as Sven Botman, a left-footed player who could have been signed for £6m and Ibrahim Sangare, a midfielder who could have been signed for £8m were both overlooked for the likes of Andre Gomes at a cost of £20m and Ben Godfrey for £25m. Overall Brands spent around £288m on incomings at Everton. (NetSpend was £166m per Transfermarkt) Brands looked at Sangare and Botman and dismissed them for not being technical enough or Premier League ready, both players would have fitted at Everton, and now, would have been worth a combined £70m in the summer of 2022.

This switch in focus from young and upcoming players was not the only issue Brands faced at Everton. Unlike at PSV and AZ Alkmarr, Brands had called all the transfer shots and as most Director of Footballers, selected the manager. But the summer of 2021 highlighted, behind the scenes at Everton, there was a power struggle at boardroom level which could have lasting consequences to the Merseyside clubs stay in the top flight.

Brands had no say in the appointment of Carlo Ancelotti or Marco Silva, he would also have no say in the appointment of one of the most controversial and catastrophic decisions in Everton's history. The appointment of Rafael Benítez, a manager who had been Liverpool's manager and was idolised by their fan base. Brands highlighted Brighton manager Graham Potter as his logical choice, a young up-and-coming manager, who worked well with the DOF model. Club Chairman Bill Kenwright wanted former manager Roberto Martínez, or former player Mikel Arteta, owner Farhad Moshiri wanted a well renowned "name for a manager."

From day one, Benítez is alleged to have rejected Brands' transfer plans, which included right backs Denzel Dumfries and Nathan Patterson. Left back Vitalii Mykolenko, and midfielders, Matheus Nunes and Luis Díaz. Sacking most of the medical staff, Everton went on to have over sixty-six injuries during the Premier League season and tore up the deals in place for the players.

After a dismal first half of the season, and Brands steering a rudderless ship, he became the public fall guy for Benítez's failings, a drubbing in the Merseyside Derby led to fans to arguing with Brands in the stands with Brands replying with, "It is not me who is picking the team, is it only the players." It was out in the open, Brands had no power at the club.

Unthinkable for a DOF at any club, Benítez had been trying for total power and had gotten it. Ironically, signing two of Brands' key targets, Nathan Patterson and Vitalii Mykolenko in the January window after taking control of club transfers. To further add insult to injury, no pun intended, Liverpool splashed the cash on Luis Diaz, who immediately went into their first team on their way to a Champions League final berth.

Brands is not completely blameless in what happened at Everton, but he was hardly dealt a fair hand. From Steve Walsh's scattergun approach that left

Everton with an unbalanced, ageing and expensive squad, to a Chairman, Owner and Manager who all interfered with his role, Brands needed the players he signed to be all successes, unfortunately for Brands, they were not. With a board of directors vacant of a strategy, scattergun approach to recruitment and a revolving door at the manager position, Everton's decline is real and one the board need to act upon if they are to starve off relegation.

After rejoining PSV months after his sacking at Everton, Brands lifted the lid on his time at Everton, claiming (Everton's) owners are 'easy to influence' which made his job as director of football "exceedingly difficult." Speaking to ESPN—via Sport Witness—on his first official day back at PSV as chief executive, Brands said: "I wouldn't have missed it for the world. It is a wonderful country for football, a wonderful club, but very difficult to manage. Especially because the owners are very involved, which makes them easy to influence. That makes it exceedingly difficult sometimes."

"More English clubs suffer from that, but I wouldn't have missed the experience I gained there for anything. Let's put it this way; of course, we did good things. Only that was also the frustration. You do not get the grip that is needed to really change things. We have taken steps internally, in the youth academy and with the transfers from the first year. But then you see the impatience, and you fall back after having made steps by simple things. That is a real shame because it is a beautiful club with beautiful fans."

Looking into Brands' claim of interference at face value, his first summer, 2017, saw Everton bring in the following players permanently, Richarlison, Lucas Digne, Yerry Mina and Bernard were all permanent signings for a total of £87m. Everton spent £10m on loan fees in the same window. We could deem this a success as Everton finished 8th, Richarlison, Bernard and Digne were later sold for profits, whilst Mina is one of Everton's better centre-backs, but keeping him fit has been the issue.

In the second season, six more players joined, only two players were successful and one of whom was not a Brands signing. Youngster Jarrad Branthwaite was signed from Carlisle for £1m and remains one of Everton's best youngsters. Alex Iwobi, signed by Farhad Moshiri for £35m struggled for the three years Brands was DOF, he was even told by Benitez that he had no future under him as manager and told to find a new club. Currently, in Winter 2022, only Manchester City's Kevin De Bruyne had created more chances than the Nigerian.

Brands failed to address Everton's need for a right back which left the team unbalanced for two years. The gamble on Moise Kean did not work, yes Everton made a profit, but they needed his potential on the pitch, twice missing out on Europe when they could have used a striker to finish off teams. Brands purchased five midfielders in his time at Everton and not one was successful, despite nearly £95m spent on them. Brands recommended against signing the fan favourite, preferring other younger targets, but the club signed off on the deal for £20m. Fabian Delph, a Brands signing, was signed for his leadership, but spent nearly all his Everton career moaning at his fellow players.

Jean-Philippe Gbamin was signed for £25m, but suffered two serious injuries that left him on the treatment table for over 24 months. He is now out on loan at his second club, still owned by Everton. Leading the club to replace Idrissa Gueye with Idrissa Gueye, who resigned for the club, three years after he was sold to Paris Saint-Germain.

The failures to move players out and recoup money in 2018 and 2019 windows ultimately did for Everton financially and meant the club sailed close, but did not break FFP rules, but more importantly, none of the signings from those windows made progress to Everton, after the success of the first window, this and the board of directors' decision to overrule him on Benitez's hire was the final nail in the coffin for Brands' time at Everton.

Furthermore, his time at the club highlighted how currently the media can be seen to make up stories, rather than reporting the truth. During his time, Brands sat down with the media and stated he had a shortlist of 35 players for Everton. Using the example of three players for every position. The media over the summer linked Everton to over 100 players. Clearly the large majority were made up to direct traffic to online sources. Eventually, the players Everton did sign in that summer, none of whom appeared in print or digital media until Everton had lodged formal bids.

Given the struggles Brands faced at a board level and with managers, I have dived into what the role of a director of football entails and the success you can have if they are allowed to operate. Directors of Footballs like Marcel Brands are tasked with finding the means to stretch their clubs transfer budgets further, creating the flexibility for them to dip into the transfer market to continually improve their squads within the confines of FFP.

The director of football is to oversee the sporting side of the Club including the six departments: First Team, Academy, Player Recruitment, Analysis,

Performance and Medical. Whilst Brands faced trials and tribulations off the pitch at Everton, before the impact of Covid-19, across the park at Stanley Park, there was a change in the wind.

Liverpool's former DOF Michael Edwards had a sharp vision with manager Jürgen Klopp on which players they needed to play the German's style of play and which players did not fit the plan, they found new clubs for them creating more wiggle room for them to bring in new players. Whilst there have been several bargain buys and good scouting to find these players, it is perhaps Edwards' ability to sell players that he should be most heralded, recouping £270m in net transfer spend Liverpool were able to redistribute.

Since joining Liverpool as their DOF in 2016, Edwards conducted the following moves to build the team that could rival Liverpool's team from the 80s for success. Harry Wilson, a product of Liverpool's academy, only made two appearances for Liverpool's first team, both in the domestic competitions. Wilson went on loan five times in the football league, earning short spells at Crewe, Hull, Derby, Cardiff and Bournemouth. After much transfer speculation, Liverpool rejected a £12m bid from Burnley in 2020, before agreeing to sell him to Fulham a year later for the same price.

Marko Grujic was the first signing of the Jürgen Klopp era, joining the Merseyside club in the January window for a little over £5m from Red Star Belgrade. The player spent little time in the first team, he was shipped out on loan to Cardiff City, Hertha Berlin and Porto. Grujic made an impression on loan and saw Porto more than happy to sign him for £10.5m. A healthy profit for Liverpool for a player who had little impact in the Premier League.

Taiwo Awoniyi never actually played for Liverpool after arriving in 2015 for £400,000, due to his inability to secure a UK work permit. Spending his entire time out on loan. His loan with Bundesliga side Union Berlin which helped secure the club Europa Conference Football for the 2021/22 season. The club decided to purchase him for £6.5m, a hefty return on investment for a player who would have struggled to make an appearance for Liverpool. After a successful second season in Berlin, Awoniyi signed for Nottingham Forest in the summer of 2022 for £17.5m. Liverpool received a further £1.5m due to their sell-on clause Michael Edwards inserted in the deal.

Kamil Grabara was signed to play in Liverpool's youth system from Ruch Chorzow for £250,000 in 2016, impressing in the ranks, he found his pathway to the first team blocked and never made a first team appearance. The goalkeeper was loaned out to AGF and Huddersfield before being shipped off to FC Copenhagen in 2021 for £3m.

Another signing for Liverpool's youth teams was Herbie Kane, who joined from his boyhood club Bristol City in 2013 aged 15. Working his way through the academy ranks, he only made two minor League Cup appearances and then moved to Barnsley for £1.25m in 2020.

A similar theme occurs with this period with Liverpool poaching talent from other academies before selling them on for significant gains. None more so than Rhian Brewster. Plucked from Chelsea's academy aged 14 and touted as one of England's diamonds to build a national team around. He scored 11 goals from 22 appearances when out on loan in the Championship at Swansea in the 2019/20 season. Despite only making four appearances for Liverpool and claiming a Champions League medal for sitting on the bench in their 2018 Champions League Final, Sheffield United agreed to pay a club record total £23.5m to secure his transfer.

Ki-Jana Hoever was also plucked from the famed Ajax academy for just £90,000 in 2018, making a competitive debut in a domestic cup game defeat to Wolves in January 2019. However made a further three first team appearances for Klopp, but never quite broke into the first team, this did not stop Wolves splashing £13.5m on the teenager in 2020.

Ovie Ejaria joined Liverpool's academy from Arsenal in 2014 but managed to make eight first-team appearances in the 2016/17 season. Further first-team football came via loans at Sunderland, Rangers, and Reading, where Ejaria later joined on a permanent transfer for £3m in 2020.

Danny Ings came to Liverpool as a free agent following the expiry of his contract in 2015. Liverpool was later ordered to pay £8m for the striker at a tribunal. Unfortunately for Ings, he endured a torrid time with injuries at Liverpool, he resurrected his career with his boyhood club Southampton in 2018–19 and sealed a permanent deal with the club for £20m following the successful loan, averaging a goal a game over the two years. Ryan Kent came through Liverpool's academy and enjoyed making his debut in 2016, which unfortunately was his last appearance for the club. Enjoying a successful spell on loan at Rangers under former Liverpool Under 18's boss Steven Gerrard, the move became permanent in 2018/19 when the Scottish club purchased him for £7.5m.

Another signing initially for Liverpool's academy was Dominic Solanke. Joining the club following the expiration of his Chelsea contract in 2017 a compensation fee of £3m was paid to the London club. Despite struggling to perform at Premier League level and scoring one goal in 27 appearances, Bournemouth were convinced to sign him for £19m for his services in 2019. Initially failing to kick on at the club, he found his form in the Championship with him scoring 50 goals over two seasons.

Another transfer out of left field Edwards was able to maximise was the transfer of Danny Ward from Wrexham in 2012 for £100,000 in January 2012. The goalkeeper made three appearances in five and a half years on Merseyside. He fell down the squad pecking order to become fourth choice following the signing of Alisson Becker. Despite the minimal first team appearances, Edwards negotiated a deal with fellow Premier League club Leicester City in 2018 for £12.5m. As of 2022, Ward had made one Premier League appearance and a total of ten for the first team. In comparison, he made 12 appearances for Wales at the same time.

Perhaps Edwards' best piece of business was the sale of Philippe Coutinho to Barcelona in 2018. The deal makes up the largest percentage of the £270m Edwards has managed to recoup to be reinvested in Liverpool's first team. Ironically, Coutinho is a player neither Klopp nor Edwards wanted to sell, they failed in engaging the player to sign a new deal with the Merseyside club.

Had they succeeded, Liverpool would not have been able to assemble the team which went on to win the Premier League, FA Cup, League Cup, Champions League, and Club World Cup, all in a four-year period. Coutinho was originally signed from Inter Milan for £8.5m in 2013. Eventually being sold for £142m, despite never living up to the price tag at Camp Nou, Liverpool Signed Alisson Becker and Virgil van Dijk with the money raised.

Liverpool signed Mamadou Sakho from Paris Saint-Germain for £18m in 2013 and initially had success and held down a first team place. Despite the early success, Sakho fell down the pecking order under Klopp and suffered several disciplinary issues before being sold to Crystal Palace for £26m in 2017, an £8m pound profit for a player Liverpool no longer intended to use.

One of the players easily forgotten by Liverpool fans is Kevin Stewart, following his release from Tottenham in 2014, the box-to-box midfielder made 20 appearances for the club. He struggled to fit in with Klopp's style of play and was sold to Hull City for £8m. The same price Liverpool paid Hull to sign full-back Andrew Robertson in the same transfer window.

Lastly, Andrew Wisdom, successfully came through Liverpool's Melwood academy and scored on his Liverpool debut in the Europa League 5–3 win away at Swiss club Young Boys in 2012. Following multiple loan spells, he eventually joined Derby in a permanent deal accruing £4.5m in the Summer of 2017.

Edwards manoeuvring around the transfer marker allowed Liverpool to spend more on players than they would normally have been able to under FFP, giving them the edge in the transfer market over clubs around them in the Premier League. In his first window, he made Liverpool a profit and signed the following key players; Sadio Mané joined from Southampton for a deal that would eventually reach £38m, Georginio Wijnaldum signed for £25m from Newcastle who had just been relegated.

The best value came from the free transfer of Joel Matip and the promotion from the academy of Trent Alexander-Arnold. Edwards then made a further £10m the following year, whilst managing to improve his squad with stalwart signings in Virgil van Dijk for £75m, Mohamed Salah for £35m, Alex Oxlade-Chamberlain again for £35m, then full-back Andy Robertson for £8m. This transfer splurge was funded partly from Philippe Coutinho's move to Barcelona.

The signings guaranteed Liverpool Champions League football, but they still fell short of Manchester City in the title race, which led Edwards and Liverpool in the 2018/19 season to splash out a further £180m on Goalkeeper Alisson £60m, Centre Midfielder Fabinho £45m, energetic midfielder Naby Keïta signed from German club RB Leipzig, followed by Swiss winger Xherdan Shaqiri for £12m where a few of the headline signings. The following year Edwards sold squad players for a net gain of £30m and Liverpool went onto win the Premier League and Champions league in the following two seasons.

Edwards final transfer windows saw Liverpool splash a further £80m on key players, Diogo Jota signed from Premier League club Wolves for £42m and back up left back Konstantinos Tsimikas signed for £11m from Greek Club Olympiacos, before further spending £20m on midfield pass master Thiago from Bayern Munich.

When Edwards leaves Liverpool in the Summer, he will do so as Liverpool's most successful DOF, Manager Jürgen Klopp will go down in in the Liverpool FC Scouse folklore as one of their best managers, detractors are quick to single out that Liverpool and Manchester City's recent dominance of English football are a result of the clubs spending over a billion pounds in transfer expenditure. This in part is true, both clubs have far outstripped others in terms of spending, but where Edwards does not get credit is how he was able to turn squad players into vital transfer funds by selling them well above their actual talent levels.

Without this Liverpool would not have been able to spend the money they did and win the Premier League and Champions League. Thus, showing the juxtaposition between Edwards and Marcel Brands, Edwards had a vision, plan and was able to increase his spending by moving on squad players, Brands, albeit hindered by players on bigger wages, was not, and the clubs were chartered on different paths for the next five years.

Chapter 7
The Opening Gambit: Transfer Deadline Day

"The following takes place between 8am and 11pm."

No, Jack Bauer is not returning to save the world; it is the fast-paced nature of transfer deadline day returning following two slower years as the global shortage of money post Covid-19 hit football hard. It was not always the polished article we see from our television sets and subscription fees. But its incarnation story may surprise you. As Alan Myers, a journalist who has held several roles working for Sky Sports details, it was a fortuitous incident that had nothing to do with a transfer of a player.

Alan is a veteran of several transfer windows in his role at Sky Sports, having previously worked for Everton; he had built up several dependable contacts within the Merseyside club. He received information from a source that Everton were close to signing Louis Saha from Manchester United in the Summer of 2008 on a free transfer. Alan and Sky Sports thought it would be a good idea if he could break the news live on TV in front of Everton's Halewood training ground Finch Farm.

Going over his script one more time, looking at his television crew testing the cameras, just before the red light indicating he is on air flicks, his phone rings, its Sky Sports. "It was the central team, Manchester City had just been purchased by Sheikh Mansour, forming the City Football Group, I was the only Sky Sports camera within reach of Manchester City's training ground, they wanted me to break the story live on air, which given the irony of deadline day, I was leaving the breaking news of Everton signing Louis Saha on a free transfer from Manchester United, we left behind the camera crew and decamped up the M62 within minutes, normal for life as a Sky Sports News reporter."

What does the transfer window mean to Alan, a fan of football as well as being an instrumental part of reporting on it? "I don't do the reporting much now, outside Finch Farm, Brockhall and Melwood. It is an immense privilege to be able to report on the transfer window. Every fan wants to see the inside of transfer deadline day, the inner workings from the football side. It is not as secretive or as glamorous as most fans think, when you're there from six in the morning until midnight in the pouring rain, waiting for Jim White to come to you, fighting off the frostbiting wind, it can be hard work." He chuckles.

"The day the transfer window became the spectacle that it is today came from my reporting at the Etihad. It was not pre-planned. As we made our way towards Manchester, I was briefing myself on the takeover, what it would mean for City, the Billions of pounds they could now spend. The shift in power towards Manchester City away from Manchester United had begun. I was living it, just as much as the fans, the transfer window."

Manchester City fans had turned Manchester into a carnival, streets became blocked as fans flocked to where Alan had managed to perch himself. "The feeling of joy and celebration among the fans is what I remember the most, as I was trying to break the story, fans would be dancing and singing behind me. You felt something was happening. There was no deadline day in those times, no theatre as it is today. That day was incredible. For the kids, they had swings and roundabouts, then we got the tip that Brazilian Striker Robinho was joining City for £40m from Real Madrid, it was a statement, City fans had believed Bulgarian striker Dimitar Berbatov was going them, only for Sky Sports to work out Sir Alex Ferguson had jumped in and signed him for £35m from Spurs."

"Our cameras were showing live pictures of Sir Alex leading him into Old Trafford. As the evening wore on, it looked as if the Robinho deal was going to fall through. (Famously in his press conference, Robinho said he was happy at signing for Chelsea, before being hastily corrected) Fans still joyful at the takeover had left, a vast calmness had descended, and it was just me and the cameraman, it was quite surreal."

"Then, at around 11pm, I broke the news that the deal was back on, and the crowd reappeared out of nowhere, and were dancing behind me again. It was the first time we realised how alive and together this new signing and era was changing football reporting." At around midnight, City's press officer came out, called me over and opened the small window by the office and she whispered. "It is done! You can announce it now."

I gave the nod to the camera operator; Jim White dropped a segment and came to me. I announced it live on Sky Sports the deal had just been done and it had beat the deadline. The fans cheered, sung City songs. While I was finishing the feed, a City fan kissed me on the cheek live on air and it was hilarious. It was the birth of transfer deadline day as we know it. One thing that stood out to me that day was two old gentlemen, they stayed the entire day. As we were tidying up, they were still there. Around one o'clock in the morning I went across and asked them if they were, ok?

"Yeah, is that it? I remember saying, yeah, that is it, the window is shut now. They thanked me and walked off into the night. Fans from the 60s era," marvelling at what the transfer window had become. The days of Trevor Francis in his Jaguar and Brian Clough and his squash racket press conferences had gone.

"After every reporting session, we would debrief back at Sky Sports HQ, it was here we discussed the Manchester City breaking news story. We discussed how we could structure the news breaking into how transfer deadline day is reported today and made it possible to invent the spectacle we have seen over our TV screens the last decade."

A spectacle which has seen football fans redefine the colour yellow. Sky Sports media production has a clock, slowly ticking down when the transfer window opens, to its female presenters asked to wear yellow dresses and then the highlight of the day. Jim White and his yellow tie would come on and ramp up the pressure as the final hours and transfer madness would kick in.

Darren, a Spurs fan who regularly takes annual leave for transfer deadline day explains why. "It is the day which your team's season hinges on, Spurs were always at it. When Harry Redknapp was Manager, he and Daniel Levy loved a deal. I would be there, whatever the weather in the morning, watching Harry give Sky an update from his car window, into the dying embers of the night when Jim White would come on. Either to gives us the positive news we had signed someone, or to break our hearts if Levy could not get a deal done. Jim White could even make a tooth extraction be exciting, he is like the character from 'The Greatest Showman', the circus ringleader who keeps us all in check during the media frenzy."

Back to Alan and his reflection. "From my perspective, I have also been a Director at Blackburn Rovers, so I know how clubs operate in the transfer window, so I have always tried to be fair when breaking a story. I have seen it from either side of the fence. I have been the Club Secretary, waiting in the office for players to arrive, trying to avoid reporters like me." Alan chuckles. "I have worked on the deals to sign players so I understand the pressure clubs can be under and I have seen deals collapse for a number of reasons."

It is this reason why Alan is the perfect person to talk to regarding the transfer window, why fans love interacting with him on social media, but it is also his love for the game of football and recalling why he loves working in football. "Anecdotally, we had accidentally created this phenomenon. As you said, the colour yellow, people taking annual leave to camp outside grounds with us. Most football clubs bought into it; it brought fans into the game. Training grounds were not really the places where fans came, for obvious reasons. Crowd control could be an issue, but the ability for fans to know when you were about to go live was incredible."

As soon as a Sky Sports presenter would say, "we are coming back from a break and we will go live to Alan Myers, I would be presenting a live segment, then the crowds would appear from nowhere. It was amazing how quickly fans could mobilise before you started reporting. It shows the interest and desire, what it means to fans. They want to know more about their team and how it operates."

The transfer window can boil over into uncharted waters and have an adverse effect on those who work in the game. "Deadline Day used to make the clubs nervous for a number of reasons, there was a feeling fans would not understand the ecosystem or the finances of the football club and how clubs purchase players. When you go to the match as a fan, like I do, we get lost in the emotion of the sport. If we had people who would break down the transfer dealings to fans, it could mediate or temper expectations. But then you lose the passion and the spontaneous."

The fan involvement made people money. But it changed the way we reported, privacy became an issue. The days of a club secretary opening a side window and talking to you are gone. Fans could break the news before you do, be whipped into a fever pitch and you would not be able to broadcast your segment. Also, if a player fails a medical and there are thousands of fans outside printing shirts, it can be heart-breaking for the player whose dream move has collapsed.

"At Everton, we had a situation when they signed John Stones. I was outside Finch Farm and the media had linked Everton with around two hundred players. I think I reported one hundred and ninety-nine of them. But given their budget, you knew they were not going to spend big. As the time moved on, fans were drifting away disappointed, venting their frustration at the board, not knowing the reality of the club's financial constraints. But we knew Everton were trying for a player. Then this black car pulls up, which is not unusual, but this tall young lad stepped out. It was John Stones, I asked the club, who is this? A lad from Barnsley, he is a good one, Alan, going to cost around £1m."

"So, I immediately called in and requested Sky come to me. I had to fight for the segment, amongst the bigger Deadline Day deals to break the news. I presented the scoop, and the red light went off, I removed my earpiece and the next minute, my phone rang. It was Wigan's Press Officer. 'Why are you saying John Stones is signing for Everton, he is signing for us. He is on his way here.'"

"After telling him, sorry, but the lad has just walked past me on his way into Finch Farm, they were unaware that David Moyes had gotten involved and talked to the player, he was integral to the deal falling Everton's way. Roberto Martinez, of all people (Everton's future manager in a years' time) was fuming he had missed out on the future England International. I remember checking my phone on the way home and seeing Everton fans contacting me with the 'is that the best you could do for us?' You know, he turned out to be a £50m player for Everton and a very good player for Manchester City, integral to them winning several Premier Leagues. Not bad for a quiet night reporting in Halewood."

"It goes the other way too. A team can give you information, but if you report that Player X is signing for Everton, the deal can be hi-jacked, another club scouting him, could be alerted and make a move, offer more. You just never know how a transfer is going to develop. Roberto Martinez once told me when I had returned to work for Everton, this time in a club communication role. On the eve of the 2013/14 summer, I was camped in his office, or in the canteen just next door. Waiting for news, to see how we could direct news or stop news from getting out. But Roberto had the philosophy, you can only judge a transfer window once it is over, are we better than when it started? You may not know the day after deadline day, but have you fixed problems that were around before the day started?"

It can be fascinating and even heart-breaking for fans when they see a club get it so wrong when buying players or deals falling through and it is no different for Alan, when he first worked for Everton in the early 1990s, back before the two-window transfer market we have now, Alan recalls Everton's attempts to sign Norwegian Striker Tore André Flo and a defender on the last Thursday in March (the original transfer deadline day), when the deals fell through incidentally, Everton manager Joe Royle resigned with the stress. Now the way the transfer window is set up it really causes drama, "back in those days, it was a little more relaxed, but now, if you don't sign someone in January, you know your fate is sealed and you are done until the end of the season."

Discussing the two-window system with Alan, he jokes that he much prefers the summer window. "The weather in January can be quite difficult, especially in Lancashire, one January deadline day in particular, in the snow and hail at Burnley, I was fighting to keep warm in the storm. The clubs are extremely helpful, they feed us, keep us warm and give us cups of Coffee. Sky ensures you have food and facilities where needed. You know with a definitive time and date transfer deadline day is over. It never fails to amaze me, given all Summer to conclude deals, how many deals are made on the last day, or the final minutes?"

"There is a lot of brinkmanship; clubs rightly use it as their bargaining power. Fans need to understand, you live and die by those decisions in football clubs, they cannot turn around and say, oh well, that did not work out, or well, we tried. You are responsible for these deals, one of the biggest criticisms people ask me is why clubs like Everton take so long in announcing deals? The truth is they don't, I have seen several clubs take the same amount of time."

"For a fan reading this, deals can be done and agreed, there are still hurdles to jump through to get it rubber stamped. Medicals, agents, paperwork, the selling club, and the being club need to upload the paperwork into the transfer system for UEFA to sign it off. Then there is the registration with the Premier League and FA."

One example of this happened when me and Alan discussed the transfer window in the Summer of 2022. With Everton chasing attacking reinforcements, the club had reached out and approached Ajax for a season long loan with a view to make the deal permanent for £15m the following year for Mohammed Kudas. Ajax had agreed, the player was keen and given permission to speak with Everton Officials. Around 90% of the deal was done. Then Manchester United approached Ajax to sign their Brazilian winger Antony, for £86m late in the window.

The deal caught Ajax off guard, a huge fee for their key player, but with one week to go and several of their key targets to replace him off the market, it now meant they could not let Kudus go. This is the transfer domino effect I wrote about in an earlier chapter that some fans do not get to see. Even well renown transfer insider Fabrizio Romano was caught out. Declaring the Kudus to

Everton deal as done, when the transfer was being drawn out, he doubled down to fans, tweeting, "wait and see." For me and Alan, in the middle of this interview, a combination of checking sources and talking about the domino effect, we knew the deal hung in the balance for Everton.

Fans were bombarding me with, "why does it take so long, Alan?" The truth is, the ecosystem of the transfer window swung against them, we knew the deal was on a knife point. But the fans, fuelled by Romano's unlikely error, took their anger out on the club's board.

If the fans took a breath and sat there, putting two and two together, they would have realised Kudus would be going nowhere unless Ajax found another player. They did not and Kudus remained at Ajax. Football clubs can only announce deals legally once it is done; no one wants another David De Gea fax machine situation.

Transfer Insiders will always 'cheat' and say a deal is done once terms are agreed, because the agent has told them it is almost done. But the final twenty per cent of the deal is the most important. This then adds more pressure from the fans on clubs, and you can be blamed for deals falling through that were never on the table.

"As a fan, put yourself in the players' situation, you want the best outcome for yourself. I had to tell an agent to leave my office because I did not like what he was saying or proposing. Everyone is trying to get the best deal for themselves. It is easy for fans to say, just pay the extra £4m, it is easy when it is not your money, fans mention it like you are in a supermarket buying a premium brand of bread instead of your usual one. Deals are getting more complicated due to marketing and image rights of players."

"When I left Everton in 2001, and came back in 2013, so much had changed in terms of players and transfer deals. On my first day in 2013, I had a meeting with four senior players, each had a briefcase, full of legal documents on what we (Everton) could use the player for in marketing promotions for the club. In 2001, the only thing I worried about with the players was whether Gazza (Paul Gascoigne) had 'borrowed' the window wipers off my car again. Players trained and went home. Players are entrepreneurs now; they are models and brands. This is all included in transfers now. I have great sympathy for people at football clubs now; they very rarely get any credit now for their challenging work. Anyone can sit there with hindsight and critique."

Communication and education with fans are paramount to all Premier League clubs, but the amount of information the club can pass to fans is limited. Clubs would love to involve fans more in transfers, but like all clubs, fans leak information from club sources, which damages the middle ground between fans and the board of directors at football clubs. "At Everton, when I was Head of Communications, I wanted to and did engage more with the fans, it was brilliant. The first season we almost pipped Arsenal for a Champions League place, then the following year's Europa League adventure when Everton topped the group stage league dubbed 'the Champions' League group, those memories with the fans I cherish most."

"But we would still get, 'why do clubs undisclosed transfer fees?' Truth is, there are several reasons, many things can impact it down the line, add-ons. The selling club can request it and have it written into the transfer. As a reporter it is difficult in reporting this to fans, when you are trained to deliver a sensational line. Your contacts are crucial as a reporter, your information is only as good as the news you receive. I will always be honest, report the facts and be accurate. Agents and reporters stay away from, as reporters can be used to spin the soap opera into gear. Fans accuse reporters of helping the betting companies, but we do not, we have no interest in the companies and they have algorithms that explore rumours and react to the market."

Nige Tassel debunked this myth fans have when interviewing a Sky Bet Trading Director and how their job is impacted by the transfer window in his book 'Boot Sale'. Firstly, Sky Bet and Sky Sports are two different companies. Although the confusion happens due to Sky Bet sponsoring the adverts in-between Sky Sports big sporting events, and Sky used to own them, the branding remained in the sale, they are a Sky brand, but the licence is paid for by the company who own Sky Bet.

Sky Bet have run a trading account on transfer deadline day for over a decade now. What started between betting on four or five players has turned into hundreds of players globally, as punters can request their odds, prop bets have become more popular and punters can bet on how many times Jim White could say, "this just in, or breaking news." Sky Bet do not get their news or information from Sky Reporters.

Their trading floor is reactionary, built on algorithms and monitoring competitors trading odds, when a punter lumps a significant amount on a player joining a club, the odds would naturally shorten. If a Transfer Insider such as

Fabrizio Romano or David Ornstein tweet the news, the odds on the move are likely to crash, too quickly for fans to make a move. Transfer Deadline Day poses its own threat to the bookmaker, as the unpredictability can mean transfers even catch them out.

Sky Bet even monitor where the bets are being placed, for example, if a player living in the Midlands is rumoured to be joining a new club and there is a flood of bets from this area, one can assume, people close to the player have got wind of the transfer and have lumped on. Betting companies can also build a profile on their punters. If a punter is reliable on their Arsenal bets, when they bet on future Arsenal transfer news, the odds would reduce, as there could be substance to their gamble, or they could have a source close to the club.

Tassel spends a whole chapter digging into how Sky Bet deals with the transfer window, highlighting how they have an entire team full of analysts reviewing trading patterns and working out whether the rumours are true in the transfer window. They spend just as much time as journalists do when trying to clarify a story.

"Transfer Deadline Day is an interesting day, that is one way to describe it, I was at Everton the day Peter Odemwingie turned up at QPR to try and force through a move from West Brom," remembers Alan. Details would later show, QPR's management team had led him on, suggesting the deal was further along and asked him to come to their facility to put pressure on West Brom, they did not budge, the excruciating interview between Odemwingie in his car, and the Sky Reporter will go down in folklore.

Natalie Sawyer, who was presenting for Sky Sports at the time, recalls feeling sorry for the player and wishing she could tell him to go home as it was obvious to everyone, but Odemwingie the deal was not going to go through. Alan reveals that the reporter's message each other through the day, so they can keep up-to-date, and the situation plays out behind the scenes as well. One can only wonder what the group chats would have looked like. What did unfold was, other reporters saw their segments dropped, for Alan and Everton, in the middle of signing three players late in the window, it briefly paused the entire conversation with a player so they could watch it unfold on Sky Sports live.

Alan reveals incidents like this are common, with deals falling through every window, but not as dramatic as Odemwingie's. We only got to see Dan James's failed move to Leeds because of the Amazon's All or Nothing documentary, at the time all fans got to see was the Sky Sports Yellow ticker, Dan James—

Swansea—Leeds deal fell through. We got to see it play out from the comfort of our own homes, and you can see the personal toil it takes on players. In the Summer window, five months before Odemwingie gave his interview, Alan and Everton had their own issue.

"I was on holiday on transfer deadline day, I was there in the morning, at Finch Farm, we had four lined up, striker Romelu Lukaku was set to join from Chelsea, for at the time, a record fee for Everton, Gerard Deulofeu, a winger from Barcelona was due to sign on loan, after Everton beat a number of sides in Europe to his signature, and the midfield pair of James McCarthy and Gareth Barry were also scheduled to sign. I spoke to the Chief Executive around 4pm and they told me it was all on. I remember in the airport tweeting out 'Busy, Busy, Busy.' All the Everton fans were delighted and interacting with me, then as I was boarding my flight, the Chief Executive told me there are issues with two of the deals. Just as the flight's gate was closing and mobile phones needed to be switched off."

"There had been some late clauses or negotiation on the McCarthy and Barry deals. Unknown to Alan, both players were sitting in their cars, in a garage in Halewood, waiting for the green light to drive around the corner to Finch Farm. Waving out of their cars to each other and talking. When I landed in Dubai, it was the morning and I dreaded turning my phone back on. With one eye closed, I recall looking through the hundreds of notifications and was delighted they were happy ones from Everton fans. Vastly unaware of how close the McCarthy and Barry deals where to being off."

"It is interesting to see the parallel between the Odemwingie situation and Everton's. Everton protected the players and had a place to hide the players away from the vast crowd, whereas QPR used the player tuning up as a bargaining chip."

"There is a vast amount of information regarding transfers out there and you want to report the correct facts, some are just completely made up. You must understand, the people who participate in these transfers are not always in control," warns Alan.

"At Blackburn, around 5pm on a deadline day, we had done a deal to sell a player, fee agreed, player was ok to leave, Manager was happy, paperwork ready, all set to do the deal. I had left the compound and as I was leaving Brockhall, the player was turning around, driving back past me, the deal was off. The owners had decided not to sell them. Now we must call the buying team's manager and tell him the player was not for sale. His plans on deadline day had gone up in smoke through no fault of his own. When you see this confusion as a fan, you forget an owner can change their mind at the last minute. It is easy to forget there is a player and their mental health to consider."

Odemwingie was a player who had been told their dream move is on, then just like that it is gone. As a fan reading this, how would you feel if your deal fell through, knowing people were laughing at your predicament, and sadly the player had no fault in the deal collapsing.

Players are people like everyone else and with the madness that ensues; it is easy to forget the thousands of people working behind the scenes trying to do the deals, as Alan and his fellow reporters are trying to keep us updated. It is this unpredictability that fans love, but it is also easy for us fans to forget the human element of the transfer window.

"Getting the news is key. Contacts are important, not all reporters get Harry Redknapp rolling his car window down to talk to you, and there is no two ways about it. Clubs want to keep the information airtight for reasons. Some contacts may tell you the story because they want to get it first. The first challenge as a reporter is to confirm the substance of the information, I always insist on having two separate sources before I report. It is never about being first; it is being accurate that counts. We have a responsibility to get it right. If I had a pound for being told every transfer rumour that was not true, I think I could be a millionaire." Alan chuckles.

"It is the responsibility of the reporter to present the facts. If you don't cover your bases, you run the risk of escalating or receiving criticism. Also, when you get the news, it could be correct, and then an hour later it is incorrect. There are a few occasions when people have tried to give me false information, and then a second source denies it. Your contacts need to be good, dependable and be trustworthy."

Remember Peter Crouch is on his way to Stoke in a helicopter, the reality, he is sneaking in a cheeky McDonalds before his medical, waiting for the green light to travel to the training ground, it is easy to see how stories can be manipulated. Sadly, fans are easily taken in by the false information.

Alan has now moved onto regional reporting with all North-West clubs regarding all football news and his days of standing outside training grounds may be over. But the days of reporting on the game we all love is still there, the good news for Alan, he will be like us fans, hopefully on the sofa in the warmth, not in the driving sleet of January outside Burnley waiting for a live segment.

On the future of Deadline Day reporting, Alan believes the current aim to get the information out fast and accurately will never change. We have moved onto digital formats, but it would be hard to not see reporters outside grounds. There have been two major incidents that have seen the window change from a reporting angle.

Crystal Palace fans, once angry at their owners, let off fireworks which flew towards the Sky Sports reporter, who took emergency refuge inside the training ground. Then came the incident which now sees all Sky Reporters safely inside training grounds and not outside the gates, when Alan Irwin was surrounded by a boisterous crowd outside Everton's Finch Farm, he was approached and had someone wave a dildo in his face.

Clubs do not want to see unsightly scenes outside their grounds either, the vast crowds that danced around Alan in 2008, may be in a previous chapter of the transfer window history, to be written about, but never seen again, but there still will be fans there, on annual leave, possible having the BBQ's cooking we have seen in the past. "There is no better privilege as a reporter than to break the news of a transfer and see the fans delight and happiness, knowing you have made someone's day, you can, as a reporter, forget how much sports mean to fans." With that, Alan's phone rings, diving back to the fast-paced nature of the world of football, with a quick thank you and goodbye.

The attacks, or stunts on reporters, are serious incidents, one person's second of fame highlighted how vulnerable the Sky Reporters were and should act as a reminder of what journalists go through to provide us as fans with the information we crave and keep us updated, they are the heroes who report in the shadows and the rain, whilst we are at homes, in the warmth, with a cup of tea, the reporters are not there to be assaulted or made fun off in their line of work, they are there reporting for us fans.

In 2021, we saw a renaissance of deadline day following the worldwide lockdowns the public had faced during Covid-19. Reporters were back on the road, players and millions of pounds were traded. Betting companies even ran books on the strangest props to be seen on the day. Fans with a new signings' name on their shirt. Or a tattoo of their name on their body. A Peter Odemwingie sighting. Harry Redknapp, and a car door. But the strangest thing to happen on deadline day on this occasion was the interview of David James.

Whilst delivering his analysis on the transfer window, pictured behind him was a painting of Clark Kent, I'm not sure even the bravest of bookmakers had thought of this scenario. But it was a reminder of the spontaneity of the transfer window that fans have craved and missed during Covid-19, it was not always like this, for some fans, back in the good old days, it was reading the newspapers or waiting for Ceefax to tick over.

For those fans, young enough to be reading this and not have the privilege of reading or knowing what the teletext pages was. This is how the 2021 summer window would have looked back in the good old days. Now, where is Jim White, the yellow tie and the "Breaking News!"

2021 transfer deadline day unfolded. (Teletext style)
08:02 Moise Kean—Everton—>Juventus—Two-Year Loan with an obligation to buy. £30m overall.
09:00 Nikola Vlasic—CSKA Moscow—>West Ham—£30m
09:03 Dujan Sterling—Chelsea—>Blackpool—Loan
09:30 Christiano Ronaldo—Juventus—>Manchester United £12.9m
09:35 Jordan Henderson—New Contract signed.
11:30 Marc Cucurella—Getafe—>Brighton—£16.2m
11:31 Maxwell Cornet—Lyon—>Burnley—£12.85m
13:55 Connor Roberts—Swansea—>Burnley—£2.5m
15:01 Dominic Revan—Aston Villa—>Northampton Town—Loan
15:30 Troy Deeney—Watford—>Birmingham—free transfer
16:01 Santiago Munoz—Santos Laguna—Newcastle—Loan
16:02 Ainsley Maitland-Niles Move is declared off, after Arsenal block a move to Everton.
16:15 Daniel Jones—Manchester United—>Leeds—£30m
16:35 Reiss Nelson—Arsenal—>Feyenoord—Loan
17:00 Dennis Praet—Leicester—Torino—Loan
17:30 Abdallah Sima—Slavia Prague—>Brighton—£7m
18:00 Ademola Lookman—RB Leipzig—>Leicester—Loan
18:02 Rhys Williams—Liverpool—>Swansea—Loan
18:30 Emerson Royal—Barcelona—>Spurs—£25.73m
18:40 Ethan Ampadu—Chelsea—>Venezia—Loan
19:30 Andre Gray—Watford—>QPR—Loan
20:35 Alex Kral—Sparta Moscow—>West Ham—Loan

20:36 Niels Nkounkou—Everton—>Standard Liege—Loan
21:50 Odsonne Edouard—Celtic—>Crystal Palace—£14m
22:00 ONE HOUR WARNING!
22:30 Hector Bellerin—Arsenal—Real Betis—Loan
22:48 Serge Aurier—Spurs—Cancelled Contract
22:50 Takehiro Tomiyasu—>Bologna—>Arsenal—£19.8m
23:00 Saloman Rondon—>Everton—free transfer
23:00 Saul Niquez—>Athletico Madrid—Chelsea—Loan with an option to Purchase.

Chapter 8
"I've Got a Bad Feeling About This"

January 2003 was considered English football's very first transfer window, where all the drama was about to start. The new rules brought in by UEFA were expected to see an explosion in panic buying. What we got instead was panic selling. With comments such as Arsene Wenger saying the window was unfair still ringing in our ears. Michel Platini believed a January window is damaging and Harry Redknapp likened it to 'gang warfare'.

Just off the M621 slip road lies Elland Road, a historic ground once graced by Don Revie, who led Leeds United to their most successful ever spell. It was about to become centre stage to a nightmare for the Yorkshire club. Leeds had gambled big time with their financial future on continual Champions League qualification and lost big time. Despite reaching the Champions League less than two years earlier, the financial bubble of Leeds's balance sheet had burst, debts were rising quicker than cash could come through the turnstiles.

The newly introduced January transfer window essentially trapped Leeds, with a limited time to raise funds, teams could essentially wait towards the end of the window to force Leeds into selling their players on the cheap. Once then Chairman Peter Ridsdale officially announced the club's dire financial situation. It was as if the starter's gun had been fired. "Should we have spent so heavily in the past, probably not, but we lived the dream, we enjoyed the dream!" Leeds were in trouble of going insolvent.

Six months earlier Leeds had already begun selling off their star assets. Robbie Keane was sold to Spurs for £7m. Rio Ferdinand, their best player was jettisoned off to Manchester United for £30m. But as the Winter dark nights gave way to January rain showers the dark clouds had settled over Elland Road. As clubs in the Premier League began to jostle in the transfer window, Leeds were ready to shift a substantial proportion of their team just to survive the season financially.

Lee Bowyer was first to leave the club. Linked to Liverpool in the Summer of 2002 for £9m, with six months of his contract left, he signed for West Ham for £330k. Robbie Fowler joined Manchester City for £6m and Jonathan Woodgate signed for Newcastle for £9m in the fire sale. Leeds under manager Peter Reid, performed a miracle and survived. But the damage was done, and the club were relegated the following year.

Leeds were caught up in another transfer nightmare in January of 2020. With Leeds chasing promotion to the Premier League, Jean-Kevin Augustin was hot a commodity in football and his name adorned numerous newspaper and internet columns. Leeds thought they had uncovered a coup by stealing a march of several Premier League clubs when the signed him from German club RB Leipzig on a loan deal with an obligation to purchase him for £18m if they were promoted to the Premier League.

In March 2020, Covid-19 was spreading across the world at a rapid pace and the UK was heading into lockdown. The Championship season got suspended. The two months' pause pushed the EFL past the June 30th deadline written in the contract to make the deal permanent, three weeks later, Leeds were promoted to the Premier League for the first time in 16 years.

Leeds refused to pay the obligated £18m to Leipzig as they claimed the Covid pandemic had nullified the deal with Leeds not being promoted before the original deadline in the contract. Leipzig challenged this, claiming before the pandemic and lockdown Leeds were well on their way to promotion before the league was suspended. When the League resumed, Leeds didn't include Augustin in their squads, assuming the deal had been nullified. Once promotion had been secured. They sent Augustin back and refused to pay the £18m.

Leipzig appealed to FIFA to sanction the transfer. Leipzig refused to play him as their lawyers argued he wasn't their player, and this would cause ramifications with their legal case. Augustin was stuck in a footballing purgatory. Neither club is willing to play or pay him as this would be seen as the club claiming ownership of him.

In 2021, Augustin signed for French Club FC Nantes in a bid to get his stalled career back on track on a free transfer. His case was brought before the Court of Arbitration for Sport (CAS) in February/March 2022 where it was ruled Leeds's would need to pay Leipzig the £18m as it was deemed the Covid-19 pandemic was not a reason for the transfer to be concluded with Leeds well clear of the fellow promotion chasers.

Bad moments in the transfer marker can even occur with the most strident of negotiators. Daniel Levy had one of Europe's most sought footballers in 2013, Gareth Bale. A miraculous story is the growth of Bale as a footballer. Signed from Southampton to ease the South Coast club's administration burden, Spurs pounced and signed the left back for £13m in July 2007. His start to his Spurs career didn't exactly go to plan with the player enduring a 24-game winless run in the first team. Finally tasting victory in a 5v0 victory over Burnley. A switch in position from left back into a left-winger transformed Bale from a transfer bust into a world-class footballer.

It was not long before Europe's elite clubs game circle around Bale and it wasn't long before Spurs owner Joe Lewis and Chairman Daniel Levy had agreed an £85m deal for the Welshman's transfer to the La Liga giants. Spurs now had the funds to refresh their squad and went into the market with glee. The problem they faced was every club knew they had money burning a hole in their pocket.

Prices and negotiations overnight saw inflation in the markets as clubs new Spurs had already sold Bale and played their hand. Spurs went out and signed 'The Magnificent Seven' according to the media. Garth Crooks likened it to 'Spurs have replaced Elvis with the Beatles' a seamless transition into a new decade. So now, nearly a decade on from the spurge, how successful were they?

PAULINHO—£17m—CORINTHIANS

Compared to Frank Lampard due to his goal scoring exploits. He played 67 games and scored 10 goals. Moved to Chinese side Guangzhou FC in 2015 for £12.5m.

CHRISTIAN ERIKSON—£11m—AJAX

Spurs most successful signing. Spent six and a half years at the club, with 69 goals in 305 appearances. The Danish international was named Spurs player of the year in 2013–14 and 2016–17. Made Premier League's PFA Team Of The Year 2017–18.

As discussed earlier, with his contract running down, Spurs sold Erikson onto Inter Milan in January 2020 for £24m, as documented in Amazon's documentary, 'All or Nothing'. Helped Inter win the Serie A title in 2020/21. Made a miraculous comeback to club football with Brentford in January 2022, after suffering a near fatal cardiac arrest in the middle of one of Denmark's delayed Euro 2020 group stage games. His goal contributions helped keep the London club in the Premier League as they had fallen into a rut of form prior to his signing.

ROBERTO SOLDADO—£26m—VALENCIA

One of the most prolific strikers in La Liga, struggled to adapt to the pace and physicality of the Premier League, managing 7 goals in 52 games, before resigning with Valencia in 2015 for £14.4m.

NACER CHADLI—£7m—FC TWENTE

Spent three years at Spurs, two with West Brom, having 15 goals and 7 assists over 73 games.

ETIENE CAPOUE—£9.3m—Toulouse

Showed flashes of quality, but never the consistency Spurs needed in the 24 appearances for the club. Sold to Watford in July 2015 for £6.3m. He later joined Villarreal in 2021 and was Man of The Match in their Europa League final victory in their victory over Manchester United.

VLAD CHIRICHES—£8.5m—STEAUA BUKAREST

Played 43 games for Spurs over two seasons, before being sold to Napoli for £4.5m in the 2015/16 season.

ERIK LAMELA—£25.8m—AS ROMA

Argentine winger scored 37 goals in 255 games for Spurs. The longest serving member of 'The Magnificent Seven' was sold in 2021, in a cash (£22.5m + player exchange) to bring in Bryan Gil to the football club.

Gareth Bale went on to win multiple La Liga titles and Champions Leagues with Real Madrid, despite never winning over the local media or fans, there aren't many Real Madrid legends who can match what Bale achieved with the club.

Spurs are not the only Premier League team to have been caught out recently with spending big and missing out in the transfer market. Everton, before their disastrous 2021/22 season, were mainstays in the Premier League top 7, normalised as the 'best of the rest', money had always been hard to come by for the Merseyside club since the 'Mersey Millionaire' days of Sir John Moores.

Famous for turning down Manchester City's current owners, with current Chairman and previous owner Bill Kenwright, 'wary' of the background of where the consortium's money had been established, finally sold his majority share in Everton to Farhad Moshiri, formally a shareholder at Arsenal.

Everton were undertaking a transition in the 2017/18 season, the David Moyes squad built on hard work and leadership was slowly being dismantled, piece by piece and manager by manager. John Stones was sold to Manchester City for £50m the previous year and replaced by Ashley Williams for £15m. Everton had sought to hire a director of football to handle transfers, but instead hired Leicester Chief Scout Steve Walsh to handle operations. Signings happened quickly with Manchester United outcast, Morgan Schneiderlin signed for £20m and Yannick Bolasie purchased from Crystal Palace for £27m.

The investment in the squad was not enough to entice Romelu Lukaku to stay with the club. In March, on international duty, he declared to the media that he and his agent Mini Raiola, had agreed a deal with his new club for next year. Despite no club contact with Everton or transfer bid made, Lukaku and his agent has basically sold himself and left Everton to agree to the fee later in the Summer.

Fast forward to the Summer, Steve Walsh was seen trailblazing around Europe to sign new players, with the John Stones and Lukaku (£75m) money burning a hole in his pocket, with the knowledge he needed a 20 goal a year striker. With their position weakened with teams knowing Everton were flush for cash and desperate to replace a 20 goal a year striker. Wayne Rooney had come the opposite way on a free transfer, as a Centre Attacking Midfielder (CAM), his lack of pace forcing him further back into midfield.

Steve Walsh returned from Italy with no players. New Manager Ronald Koeman had asked for Cuco Martina, a free agent formerly of Southampton to be signed, despite Everton having academy graduate Jonjoe Kenny deputising for the injured club captain Seamus Coleman, who had been injured on international duty, but was due back in a few months.

What happened next was a prelude of seven years of financial madness at the club. Walsh went on a spending spree. First signing Ajax captain, Davy Klassen for his £24m release clause, another (CAM), Jordan Pickford was signed for £25m from Sunderland, one year after breaking into the first team from Sunderland's Academy of Light. Sandro Ramirez (CAM) had his release clause activated from Malaga and signed for £5.4m.

Henry Onyekuru had his release clause activated and signed for £7.2m from Belgium club Has Eupen. Everton were desperate to replace John Stones after missing out on Ronald Koeman's number one target, Virgil van Dijk, who had signed for Liverpool, splashed £25m on Michael Keane from Burnley. In Everton's Europa League playoff game against Hadjuk Split, Walsh watched their CAM, Nikola Vlasic slip in between Everton's defence and cause them nightmares all night. Learning that the player had a £9.75m release clause, he signed him too, days after Everton had knocked them out of the Europa League.

With the transfer window entering its last week, Everton still had no striker, leaving teenager Dominic Calvert-Lewin as the only first team option, with a handful of first team appearances to his name. Walsh publicly went after Swansea playmaker Gylfi Sigurdsson in the dying stages of the window. Having repeated bids turned down, before agreeing a £45m deal to bring the Icelandic International to Everton. Their 5th CAM signed in the window. Everton signed no striker in the summer window.

Walsh also failed to agree a new contract with Ross Barkley and agreed to sell him to Chelsea on transfer deadline day, with the attacking midfielder (Everton's 7th), normally clubs have two or three, for £35m. Barkley and Chelsea pulled out of the deal, citing his knee injury at the time. The truth lies more in more tactical thinking by the London club. With Barkley out until November. Chelsea pulled out of the deal. Knowing they could come back for Barkley in January and get him for less money.

The circus continued at Everton, Henry Onyekuru could not get a work permit and was loaned out to gather enough points to help his work permit application. He suffered a serious knee injury just two international games before he would qualify for one. He never played for Everton. Walsh had sold Everton winger Gerard Deulofeu for £10.8m, after Barcelona activated their buy-back clause in the player, then signed no replacement once Onyekuru was loaned out.

Everton started the season playing 3–5–2, with the clubs only striker, Dominic Calvert-Lewin playing right wing back. Manager Ronald Koeman was sacked in October, on the back of Everton losing 5V2 to Arsenal. Ross Barkley was eventually sold for £15m in January.

Farhad Moshiri claimed he wanted his club to sign Borussia Dortmund star striker Pierre-Emerick Aubameyang for £50m to talkSPORT, claiming Everton had the money to do so. Despite this, new manager Sam Allardyce and Walsh went out and signed Cenk Tosun from Besiktas for £27m and Theo Walcott from Arsenal for £20m, because the manager wanted to add pace to the Everton team, despite Walcott's goal contributions at Arsenal had dropped at an alarming rate and Tosun had been clocked at 17mph in his sprints vs. Aubameyang who had been timed at 22mph.

Fast forward to 2023, the spending splurge and subsequent reluctance to sell players, left Everton with a bloated squad, bursting wage bill, for every pound in revenue, they had one pound, twenty worth of costs and teetering on the brink of FFP and relegation. Only Michael Keane and Jordan Pickford are left from the splurge, with Pickford being the only success from the entire operation.

To make matters worse. Wayne Rooney left Everton for the second time in his career. During the international break, he signed for DC United on a free transfer. Leaving Allardyce to find out via the press that his captain had jumped ship and agreed a deal with the MLS club. Rooney later cleared up some of the rumours that he had quit Everton by sitting down with Toffee TV. "I had several huge offers in the summer I joined Everton, China, Middle East, MLS franchises, but I wanted to come to Everton."

With Everton away at Swansea, rumours of a transfer to the MLS heated up, Rooney approached Sam Allardyce and demanded answers. Allardyce was unaware and told Rooney as much. At Swansea, Rooney approached Everton owner, Farhad Moshiri, in the car park, he too, denied he knew of the deal that had been brokered, yet claimed, director of football, Steve Walsh, had sourced out MLS teams to remove Rooney as he had fallen out of Allardyce's team sheets. With his DOF football beginning the negotiations, it would appear Rooney saw the writing on the wall and made the next move before Walsh made it for him.

Walsh and Allardyce were sacked in the summer of 2018 for the failures. A net transfer loss of around £70m was declared, the wage bill meant Everton's turnover was drowned out by the wage bill costs. Accounts posted in 2022, showed Everton posting significant losses between 2018, 2019, 2020, 2021 and with the impact of Covid-19 affecting all clubs with lost gate receipts, Everton were close to breaking the Premier Leagues sustainability rules.

Liverpool in direct contrast had purchased wisely during Everton's turbulent time, but even one of the most successful transfer regimes under Michael Edwards and Jurgen Klopp nearly fell afoul of transfer rules and regulations.

Before Liverpool became the European conquering juggernaut, there were a few false starts in their program. Fans witnessed some below-par performances and the club limped its way into fourth place. Some fans believed the club was going backwards and were calling for Klopp to be replaced when he took the team on a lap of honour to the famous Kop stand after a draw with West Brom. Initially, the fans hated the action, ridiculed for celebrating a point against a team who were battling relegation. But Klopp maintains it was to install a relationship with the fans and apologise for the result.

Let the players know that this is who they played for and even after you play badly, home, or away you go to them. It was perhaps at this moment that the disconnect the club had had under previous managers had ended.

With owners Fenway sports affording Klopp time, he installed a formation in the first team right through the club to the academy. A never say die attitude and slowly began to integrate players into his favoured 433 pressing formation. Klopp also worked closely with Edwards to identify targets who would fit this system and be able to get crosses quickly into the box. Building a quick picture of his squad of who was good enough and who wasn't. Those who fell below the standard quickly moved on, to ensure Liverpool always remained well above FFP measures.

The foundations for their Premier League Title and Champions League win were well underway. Liverpool moved quickly to sign Joel Matip from Schalke on a free transfer. Klopp using his experience of the Bundesliga to find a Champions League centre-back for free. Followed this up with Gini Winjnaldum for £25m from Newcastle and Sadio Mane from Southampton for £37m.

To have a positive net spend, Liverpool sold Philippe Coutinho to Barcelona for £121m, Mamadou Sakho for £25m and Lucas Leiva for £5m. The net spend would help with future splurges in the transfer windows, but with each player coming in, one went out, meaning Liverpool's wage budget stayed the same. Edwards worked with the commercial team to further grow Liverpool's sponsorships, meaning their commercial revenues grew at the same time.

But amongst these successes it was their approach for Virgil Van Dijk that caused headlines and controversy for the football club. Yahoo Sports reported Klopp had face to face meetings with the Dutch International and there were rumoured WhatsApp messages between the defender and Liverpool officials. Personal terms were agreed with the players' representatives. Meaning the contact was illegal under the current transfer rules. Clubs can only talk to players once there is agreement between the two clubs.

Liverpool hadn't spoken to or agreed on a fee with Southampton but were already breathing news outlets that they had won the race to sign Van Dijk, Southampton's captain over the likes of Chelsea and Manchester City. They assumed the player would force the issue, hand in a transfer request and Southampton would be forced to sell, perhaps at a cheaper price.

Except Southampton did not budge, or wish to sell the player, rejecting his transfer request once the player admitted he had accepted personal terms with Liverpool. Van Dijk gave a press interview over his desire to play for Liverpool and posted a picture on a private jet with the aero plane emoji looking upset.

It was at this point, with the issue being publicly drawn out, Southampton reported Liverpool to the Premier League over the tapping up of the player. Stating they 'needed to take a stand' against clubs who were tapping up their players. Liverpool immediately apologised and withdrew from the transfer in June. The Premier League acknowledged the complaint and confirmed Liverpool had broken the rules. But despite the admittance of guilt, Liverpool pulling out of the transfer deal was enough for the Premier League not to dish out fines, points deductions or a transfer ban.

In the next summer, Liverpool went onto sign Van Dijk for £75m, Mo Salah for £38m and Andrew Robertson for £8m. The signing of goalkeeper Allison and Alex Oxlade-Chamberlain followed for £50m and £35m respectively, with the promotion of Trent Alexander-Arnold from the academy Liverpool went onto their current successful run. A transfer ban from tapping up Van Dijk could have stopped this pivotal window from happening.

As with the decline of Everton, at the time of writing, their Premier League status was hanging in the balance with ten games to go. One club who gambled to get into the Premier League at the same time, Derby, were perhaps weeks from liquidation.

Spring 2022, Derby County had early in the season been deducted a further nine points after admitting to breaches of the EFL's profitability and sustainability rules over the £81m sale of Pride Park to their former owner Mel Morris, taking their total deductions this season to 21 points. Morris had gambled on Derby winning promotion under Frank Lampard's stewardship but fell at the final hurdle in the playoff final.

The debts that had been collated had no way to be paid. In a desperate move to keep cash flowing into the business, Morris sold the stadium to himself. But this sought of financing had been outlawed by the EFL's FFP and profit and sustainability rules. Despite the 21-point reduction and transfer ban, Manager Wayne Rooney had pulled Derby within 6 points of safety with 6 games to go. Despite administrators being called in and struggling to find a new buyer for the club.

Sky Sport were told, "The club has amassed almost £30m of debt with HMRC, owes a further £20m to the US investment firm MSD via various loans secured on the stadium, and a further £10m is owed to other football creditors." With no assets to sell and a Derby team built on free transfers and academy players, the job Rooney was doing should be heralded. Instead, news columns were full of several more millions being owed to non-secured creditors, though they are likely to receive much less than the full amount.

Derby received an initial stay of execution when HMRC refused to issue a winding up order. But the Covid pandemic complicated matters and with no crowd to bring in income, their debts rose to unfavourable levels. The uphill task Derby's administrators face is the ever-growing tax bill any potential buyer would face if they wished to purchase the club. On top of not owning the stadium, they currently call home.

On a sporting matter, Derby also face two legal matters with Wycombe Wanderers and Middlesbrough, Wycombe are unhappy that they were relegated when Derby had been found guilty and in breach of the rules. Middlesbrough are arguing Derby cost them a place in the playoffs and denying them a chance of £100m Premier League dream.

These are to be addressed in front of an independent hearing and could help to decide Derby's fate, with the club sending in papers to the EFL to show they have the funding required to meet their running costs until the end of the year.

Yet, the Guardian reported there is a further issue should Derby survive but be relegated to League One. "Under EFL rules, any buyer must pay football creditors—such as Arsenal, whom Derby owe for Krystian Bielik—100% of what they are owed and unsecured creditors—such as small businesses—at least 25% of what they are owed, or the club would face a 15-point penalty next season." As reported in the Guardian online in January 2022.

The real loser in all this is the fans. Derby fans who cherish the club, their life, the jobs of those who are employed by the club, are the last to get the information. Poor and greedy transfer business could rob fans and the city of another football club, like Bury before them, the fans are the ones who are left to pick up the pieces. The owners, Directors of Football, the players. They move onto the next club.

Chapter 9
Her Game Too
A New Dawn in Women's Football

"Equality is the soul of liberty; there is, in fact, no liberty without it."

"They think it is all over. It has only just begun." Gabby Logan on the momentum in women's football with England's Euro 2022 victory on home soil.

If I asked you which footballer has represented England the most times at international level? Most people, fans and pub quizzes would respond with the following, Peter Shilton (125), Wayne Rooney (120), but what if I told you that you would be wrong? That this unconscious bias from years of sports reporting focusing on the men's games meant millions of English football fans were unaware that our most decorated players are in fact: Rachel Yankey (129), Alex Scott (140), Karen Carney (144), Queen of the Jungle, Jill Scott (161) and Fara Williams (172) are England's most capped players.

This is just one hurdle female footballers must overcome during their professional careers and for most of our current Lionesses, their start in football is even more unconventional even before we discuss the transfer window.

Whilst the men's game has millions of pounds poured into grassroots football and category A academies, the women's game has lagged for several years.

Let's not forget, the FA banned women from playing football in 1921, the inbuilt misogyny between men and women in sport was further entrenched by the ban for many, many years and continued long after the ban had been 'lifted' around 1970. No wonder it can feel women's football in Britain is 50 years behind the men's game. But there is hope, the number of girls in England playing football in England has increased by 100,000 since 2017, before the crest of the wave of the England Lionesses success in the Euro's win in 2022 is considered. But to learn for the future of the women's game and understand the impact money and transfers have on it, we need to review the past.

Karen Carney who recently hung up her boots after the World Cup in 2019 and moved into the commentary analysis side of the game. Her path to the top, from the cobbled streets of Solihull to the highs of playing for Chelsea were not always paved with an easy route to success. Opening up to Joe Cole and comedian Tom Davis on JOE's YouTube channel opened up on her career struggles.

Before winning the fifteen major honours in her career and representing England across four World Cups, four European Championships, Carney's career started within Birmingham City's academy. Making her first team debut aged just 14, earning FA National Young Player of the Year honours in 2005 and 2006 respectively.

Earmarked as one of England's emerging talents at her age level, it was not long before Arsenal, the most established English Women's team at the time, signed her on a permanent contract in July 2006. When you consider Pele played at Four World Cups, you understand the longevity of maintaining her career despite the lack of resources and opportunities open to Carney at the time.

Despite being one of the youngest members of the squad, Carney played an integral role in Arsenal's squad which won four major honours during the 2006/07 season. Making twenty-one appearances over the season in the Women's First Division, scoring over 10 goals. She added another three goals in all competitions and overall played 36 appearances in a season where Arsenal won the Women's Premier League (now Women's Super League), Women's FA CUP, FA Women's League Cup, and the Women's UEFA Women's Cup. Detailing her career on the podcast, she discussed how at 16 years old she moved to Loughborough to continue her education, this allowed her to continue her sporting journey and continue her education.

When at Arsenal, she was only allowed by the college to be released for games on Sunday's. "I did Monday-Friday training, went home to Birmingham to see my parents on Saturday and played for Arsenal on the Sundays, then went back to Loughborough to continue my studies. I was never with the team, but because I was in the England Senior team with some of the senior Arsenal players, they looked after me. But players back then would fly in for one game, that was the norm, somehow Manager Vic Akers was able to get us to play together."

As a young seventeen-year-old woman, pressure on being an England International then being thrust into the first-team at Arsenal, Carney also had to juggle the pressure in knowing she still need both a job, and an education to maintain a career after the game, in comparison, a 17 year old professional in the men's game, would have been earning £5000 a week, been full-time, with access to state-of-the-art academy facilities with no pressure on young shoulders.

Undeterred, this spurred Carney on for the next season, despite calling herself shy, and earning the nickname, mute, due to her quiet nature. Carney would score 17 goals in 34 appearances, despite the lack of trophies, Carney found the extra gear and became a starter full-time, pushing more established professionals down the pecking order. Carney's biggest issue she found was "where did I sit in the dressing room with all these legends?"

Carney would wait for everyone to sit down and then would sit in the corner, or in some cases, on the floor if there was no room. Hidden under the towels falling off the physio tables at Boreham Woods ground, a long way from the Emirates stadium, or any Premier League ground for that matter. Carney describes how even Arsenal's quadruple winning team had to wash and look after their own kit, Akers, was also the Arsenal men's teams kit manager and could not do double duties.

Despite this, Carney found this helped ground her as a professional, Akers would talk about how it would force the players to respect the badge and ensure their own kit was pristine. Carney would joke with fellow England International Rachel Yankey, "God, I hope we don't get fouled this week, we've got white shorts. Ice white shorts and we have to get the grass stains out." But having to sustain this kit, I became more professional and understood the size of the club. It also helped deal with the 'egos' in the dressing rooms, as with all the talent Arsenal had, it meant all players were the same.

Emotions ran high in the dressing room, Carney is quick to point out in the Women's game, just like the men's, you needed to have a different side to yourself on the pitch, a stark contrast to her personality off the pitch, because you are there to entertain and be a Gladiator in the arena. If you didn't, there are others willing to take their place. But Carney is keen to point out the players must back it up on the pitch, giving 100% at every game. To emphasise this, in Carney's final season with Arsenal, she made 13 Premier League appearances and scored eight goals.

In all competitions, Carney made 21 appearances and scored 12 goals, representing England made sure the new growth in women's football grew her profile at the time. In America, the professional game had taken off, the

American Draft for their new professional teams to select their star international players, Carney was considered a top pick. (A Draft system is where teams, under a ticking clock, each take a turn to pick players, the best players would be high picks. Starting from 1 and filtering down to the number of American franchises.)

The new professional league in the USA saw several high-profile coaches poached by the franchises and one, Emma Hayes, now of Chelsea's Women's Dynasty, was a coach of Arsenal at the time and had her eye on her former starlet. "The draft was madness, my degree was going to finish in the Summer, my contract with Arsenal was up, and Emma told me she wanted to take me to America and draft me. I had just finished university, I was in debt, with no money, despite being an England International, the draft was six months away, I went for several jobs as a receptionist in Birmingham. My parents gave me six months. Play for Arsenal and England, do your best to get drafted, but if you don't, go and get a job. I had to do my own training sessions, at the park in the pouring rain, no coaches. Dogs would nick my cones, pee on my bottles, I did everything to stay fit so I could be drafted."

Nowadays, a young professional would have an agent who would produce highlights, or tapes of a player and send it around the respected franchises. It was another hurdle Carney would need to overcome, just to maintain a playing career as a professional, another came a few days before the draft.

"Emma Hayes rang up and told me she couldn't draft me." Her confidant, her former coach and one of the main admirers in America now told her that she may not be guaranteed to be drafted. Carney was away on tour with England with fellow England stars Kelly Smith and Alex Scott, both who were also expected to be drafted, and had held conversation with the franchise already.

Emma told me she was going to draft Kelly, and the way the draft system works is that you can only have five international players and the other teams would have the opportunity to pick Carney, or other players. But the higher a player is selected, the more money they could earn, still not enough to have a full-time career, but more in line with the average yearly wage in the UK at the time. Carney recalls how in the moment, when it looked like her dream was crashing down all around her, she wanted to send an abusive text to Emma, "thanking her for nothing and leading me on." But I stopped and thanked her for the opportunity. Little did Carney know the next hurdle she would face would lead to an open door by none other than Emma Hayes.

As fate would have it Boston selected Kelly just before Hayes's Chicago Red Stars outfit were due to pick. In the middle of the night, Carney received a call, to little fanfare as most of the elite USA men's drafts are held, Hayes was calling to select Carney, in the 3rd round of the WPS International Draft, 19th overall, aged 21, she was Chicago's 3rd pick of the draft. The draft was seven teams, seven draft slots, over four rounds.

Only 28 internationals would be selected. But now the daunting part, having to move to Chicago where she knew no one, to live on her own for the first time, but more importantly, would Arsenal let her go? The Chicago Red Stars made Carney their first official signing. Carney and Kelly Smith would be the only English players selected, with Alex Scott missing out, showing how hard it was even for the most elite female talents at the time. Carney was off to Chicago to live with her mum, but also to rejoin her coach, Emma Hayes.

To fit in with the American league posed another emotional hurdle for all the women, Carney details how for the first time, she needed to bulk up, to be able to deal with the physicality of the league. Something which was alien to her. "For a young female athlete at the time and in general, this can make women feel bad about their appearance, even more so due to social media describing women's bodies and what is perceived to look like." The women can hide this on the pitch in the pantheon theatre of entertainment, but off it, players can lose themselves when they are not playing.

On the pitch, Carney started seventeen games for Chicago, scoring two goals and assisting another, the team finished in sixth place in the league. The following season, Carney started twenty-one games as Chicago finished sixth for the second consecutive year. With Carney settling in the USA, she was to face yet another obstacle in her career. Aged 25, her franchise folded and ceased to exist. Carney was faced with another crossroads. She packed her bags and returned to the UK to play for her childhood club, Birmingham City, back at a semi-professional club, Carney's influence helped take the club to a second-place finish.

The following season, Carney helped the Midlands club to finish second again, but scored the winning goal and was the Player of the match in the 2012 FA Women's Cup Final. The following year, the international calendar clash with the English league meant Carney only played six matches in the league where the club finished fourth in the league. Attacking the next year with vigour, it was to be her best for Birmingham City, Carney was an integral player during the 2014 season.

Scoring 6 goals to make Carney their top goal scorer and tied for top in the league. In the last game of the 2014 FA WSL season, Carney missed a decisive penalty in Birmingham City's 2–2 draw with Notts County that would have ensured they would win the league title. The dropped points meant Birmingham City finished in third place.

The following season, international duties meant Carney could only appear in 11 matches, scoring 3 goals, helping keep Birmingham in the top division. Carney would also help England compete in the 2015 Women's World Cup, helping the underfunded side finish 3rd, after a heart-breaking own goal in the last minute against Japan, cost England a chance at Gold against the United States.

Carney's appearance at the World Cup and ability in the Women's Super League had not gone unnoticed and she left Birmingham on a free transfer to join Chelsea on a two-year contract, joining up with manager Emma Hayes again, describing the Brummie as 'World Class'. Quickly inserted into the team, Chelsea went onto finish 3rd, with Carney contributing three goals in her 16 appearances, on the opening day after scoring a key penalty, Hayes, who has always saw more than a player in Carney discussed the signing with the BBC.

"Karen Carney was at the heart and the core of everything, especially in the first half, and she looks like she's been playing at Chelsea for years. I thought she was instrumental in everything we did, whether she was on the left side, down the middle, or on the right."

In the same year that Birmingham made her the youngest player ever inducted in their Hall of Fame, she was named player of the year for Chelsea and shortlisted for England Women's Player of The Year. Hayes was quick to extend Carney's playing contract through to 2020, to ensure her playmaker would not leave on a free transfer, before the significant television money came, most player transfers in the Women's game would be transferred for free and with no agents negotiating deals for the players.

Another hurdle the women faced at the time was their season was often only seven or eight games long, depending on whether a team went bust during the season. More games in the domestic cups or European games were there if the teams won their respective matches, but there seems to be an urge to stop the women's calendar from clashing with the men's, possibly due to a fear that it would drive sponsors and money from the men's game.

In 2017, Carney's goal tally of seven ranked third in the league, as Chelsea went onto win the League, Chelsea and Carney would also go on to win the FA Cup. Carney would go onto captain Chelsea the following year, scoring a winning penalty in the Champions League, also winning a place in the Champions League team of the season.

Despite this success, another issue and hurdle raised its ugly head that women face in the professional game. On Instagram, Carney was subjected to sexist, death and abuse threats by a user after the match. The user was banned from the social media platform for threatening and abusive behaviour, but Carney declined to press charges as this was just another regular occurrence that several professionals had faced.

The 2018/19 season would mark the final season for Carney's career, just as the league became professional for the first time, too late for Carney to make a living from a professional career, but one she would not trade for the experiences gained from playing the sport she loved; overcoming enough obstacles that would make a jockey facing the famous obstacles of the famous Aintree Grand National blush. On 23 November 2014, Carney competed in her 100th senior international match in a 3–0 loss to Germany at Wembley Stadium in front of a then record 45,619 fans.

Carney is the youngest player to earn 100 caps for England. The match marked the first time a women's national team game had been played at Wembley. Carney remarks the game was her favourite moment in her career: "Getting my 100th cap for England was a real honour… It's every boy's dream to play at Wembley so for me being a girl and leading the national team out at one of the most iconic stadiums in the world is a moment I will never forget."

Carney would finish her career playing for England at the 2019 World Cup, where defeat to Sweden denied the Women another Bronze medal, but Carney came off the bench to mark her 141st and final appearance for the Lionesses. Carney also represented Great Britain at the 2012 London Olympics.

Carney has stepped into a career as a pundit, breaking down the game for viewers across several television providers. Breaking down the Women's Super League on Sky Sports with full-time analysis, a far cry from her playing days when only the Women's FA Cup game was the only game televised. In her final season, the women's top division was rebranded the Women's Super League and the television rights were picked up by BT Sports. Still a far cry from the amounts in the men's game, but it allowed clubs to turn professional, offering better wages. But several clubs still rented grounds of National League clubs, rather than invest in proper facilities.

Everton became the first WSL side to purposely build their own ground for their Women's team at Walton Hall Park, with some of their 'bigger games' played at the current home of the men's team Goodison Park. But even in this success for the women's game, the stadium has better facilities, but is still below the standard of the men's game. The women train at Finch Farm Training Ground just like the men, having access to the same gyms and recovery units as the men's game.

But the stadium has no undersoil heating, as does the men, so a cold snap is likely to mean most WSL games will fall foul to the weather. With the Lionesses success in winning the delayed Euro 2021 finals, Everton regularly sell out their Walton Hall Park capacity of 2200. Perhaps if they could and they do have the room, more seats and facilities could be added, with the possibility of a ground share with another local Regional Club could bring in revenue to pay for them.

Despite the Lionesses win and a push to grow the Women's game, the money and investment in the women's game still lags behind the men. When looking at adverts on television, No one is sponsoring the lionesses after their Euros win. The men's team continue to rake in multiple sponsorship deals, despite losing their Euro final and subsequent Quarter Final knock out to France in the World Cup. A missed opportunity for a few commercial companies, even if jumping on the bandwagon of the Lionesses' success, would have helped promote the game at a national level.

Despite the success, several of our Lionesses now play abroad, potentially for more money as opportunities for women after retiring will not always present themselves. The WSL rebranding and sponsorships saw an increase in the playing level and several stars came into the league, following the USA's World Cup win, Alex Morgan came to Tottenham Hotspur on loan, as she came back to the sport following the birth of her child. Currently international stars, Hanna Bennison—Everton, Sam Kerr—Chelsea, Vivianne Miedema—Arsenal, are just a few of the players playing in our highest division.

Before the Lionesses win, Barclays agreed to invest in excess of £15m over the three years from 2019–22 that included the title sponsorship of the Barclays FA Women's Super League. Sky Sports have now also joined coverage and the

BBC have picked up the rights to a portion of the women's games. The Premier League also announced a funding package to help the National League Level.

"The Premier League is today announcing increased financial support for FA Women's National League clubs to help the development of the women's game and improve facilities at the grounds clubs play at. This includes £3million of funding for a new strategy for The Football Association Women's National League, which will help support the development of the women's game at tiers 3 and 4."

"An additional £1.5m is being made available by the Premier League to clubs at the same level for stadium improvements that will make grounds more inclusive and enhance the playing and spectating experience in women's football. It follows the recent announcement that the Premier League is providing £1.75m per annum for the next three years for The FA's new network of Girls' Emerging Talent Centres, to help grow the existing talent program for women's football in England."

A review into WSL clubs in 2021 found that despite the investment and sponsorship, some teams still had major issues. Alleging that some players are earning less than the minimum wage and complained of delays in medical treatment for injured squad members, a lack of access to the training-ground gym, substandard practice pitches, a shortage of pre-match overnight hotel stays, lack of payments for non-contract players, inadequate changing facilities and travel arrangements before away fixtures. Players in some teams were still washing their own kit and were not receiving support around women's health and in specific women's products.

We have seen a gradual shift in focus in a number of WSL teams, more teams are incorporating their women's teams into their training grounds and opening up facilities for their women's teams. It is an encouraging start, but one which itself is beginning to lose traction in the shadows of the Lionesses win, but as we saw with Karen Carney's illustrious career, which was in this decade, further highlighting how one of our most decorated players struggled throughout her playing career just to continue to play at the top flight, showing the need for a pathway to be designed to make it easier for the women's game to progress starting from a grassroots level.

The recent funding has been pinpointed at this level and the FA will hopefully invest in coaches and regional areas to open up more access and camps aimed at young girls to attract them into the game. Even now, we are seeing the 'bigger, or more financially able' clubs are already cherry picking the best young players from the other development teams in what is becoming a plague for the smaller clubs as the gap is widening just like the men's game. Deterring teams from investing in the women's game because they see no return on their investment.

Perhaps then, we could learn from Carney's experience, could we develop a college or university system, where the top ten sporting colleges or university offer scholarships to young female athletes can be offered a free scholarship (degree), whilst having the access to accommodation, the best gyms and coaching. They could have a North and South division before competing for a National Championship.

Twelve institutions could have their own televised games which could be used to grow the women's game and bring prestige to the system. It would present a situation where Professional teams could still have their regional development academies to find the talent who slip through the cracks, or do not gain a scholarship into these universities. But it would give the women a chance to earn an education alongside the top-level coaching. Should their careers hit a wall, or injuries derail their careers, they would have the opportunity to switch careers more easily and not be burdened by debt.

With the Women's Super League now having a division 2, and the Regional Divisions below this, it would reduce the ability of having a Draft system or the competitive nature of the system. In the American system, the worst teams would have the first pick, but the issue here is you would need to, for competitive reasons and fairness, you would need to include both divisions. The best players in theory would start their careers in the Championship, where the facilities may not be the best and the level of coaching could hinder their development.

Of course, teams could opt out of the draft and run their own academies, it may not stop the more financially better off teams from purchasing the younger players, but it would give them some remuneration for any transfers. It would be an option that would address the current issue of competitive balance in the leagues that we see currently and perhaps allow the women to receive better coaching earlier and be fitter and more technical when they reach the professional ranks.

The potential need for this has become more apparent with the recent explosion in the women's transfer markets. In Britain, they fall in line with the men's game. Just as the press were aghast at the million-pound price tag of

Trevor Francis in his move from Birmingham City to Nottingham Forest, the first million-pound transfer for a woman is not too far away. Despite the effects of Covid-19, transfer spending in women's football almost doubled in 2020 and surpassed $1m in a year for the first time. While global figures in professional men's football—£4.14bn, down from £5.4bn in 2019—remained comparatively high, spending rose from £0.51m in 2019 to £0.88m ($1.2m) in the women's game.

When digging into the data, I found the following information, FIFA, as part of their global transfer market report, showed the number of transfers involving a fee also rose from 31 to 36, with the median figure just above £8,000. Free transfers involving out-of-contract players made up 87.6 per cent of moves, while a further 5.5 per cent were loan deals. A significant rise in transfer fees from the previous years. In 2019, Chelsea broke the women's transfer world record to land 2018 UEFA Player of the Year and 2018/19 Champions League top scorer Pernille Harder, a fee believed to be in the region of £250,000.

Normally, the only destination for a player like Harder would have been Lyon. WSL clubs sign players who blossom into world beaters (see Vivianne Miedema), but rarely did the English top-flight attract a player widely considered to presently be the best in the world—and on a three-year deal to boot. The WSL was changing the game and British football was now a force in the women's game.

It worked both ways too, agents are also becoming more influential in the women's game, with more and more money flowing into the game, more expertise is needed to ensure women receive a fair wage, unlike what we described before when a report found several players in the WSL earned below minimum wage.

The flow of money into the women's game has granted both clubs and the players access to players and markets that followed a domino effect in the transfer window. When Everton received a record fee of £100k when Lyon activated her release clause as Lyon sign Dutch midfielder starlet Damaris Egurrola in January 2021, it allowed the Merseyside club the funds to raid Swedish club FC Rosengård for their starlet, Hana Berrison, a Swedish International for their record transfer in 2021. This was before the Lionesses Euro triumph and following this, England holding midfielder, Kiera Walsh was snapped up by Barcelona for £400,000, making her the new most expensive transfer.

To put this into perspective in the men's game, FC Bayern Munich agreed to £300,000 to sign 13-year-old striker Mike Wisdom from Borussia Mönchengladbach for the forward to join their under-15 team in the early parts of 2022. Mönchengladbach Director Roland Virkus stated, "Such deals are anything but beneficial for German football, it is distasteful." It also showed the discrepancy between the men's and women's game. This was almost six months before Walsh moved to Barcelona, meaning men's teams, who also had women's teams, were investing more money in transferring youth players than they were funding their entire professional women's teams.

The money was there all the time, the clubs chose not to use it. Considering the opportunity that the women's game represents, it is interesting why a business does not invest itself into football, later in this book, I will look at Red Bull's impact on football finances, how they would wash a club of its history once taking it over, so why not the women's game, if there is little history already there?

Again, is it a choice, even the most ardent entrepreneur looking for another capitalist opportunity could have used the Lionesses triumph as a springboard, but also as an opportunity for them to take advantage and ride the crest of the wave created by their triumph.

There is also a discrepancy in remuneration, where female players earn a fraction of what their male counterparts do in the Premier League. The top players may earn between £60,000–£80,000, but the current average wage for a WSL player is closer to £25,000 (figures from Sporting Intelligence), less than the average UK wage of £38,131 according to the Office of National Statistics for 2021.

Those players lucky enough to be around the national team selection may be one of the lucky 30 players who receive/awarded a centralised contract to supplement their income often in the region of £30,000. This is also changing, with perhaps another reason why female footballers need proper representation by agents who are regulated. Wages are increasing, and footballers are now making million-pound decisions themselves and run the risk of being taken advantage of.

The FA could lead the way here, training the next batch of agents to focus on their clients and use the growing women's game as a way agents can help the game grow, but also protect the player's interest. Per Amanda Ezaza on Twitter, BK Häcken striker Pauline Hammarlund is close to signing a two-and-a-half-year contract with Fiorentina worth millions. The deal would make the Swedish International one of the highest paid players in Italy.

Brighton have taken up the initiative, releasing a new women's football strategy with a focus on six key areas; Player Pathway, Recruitment, Performance and Coaching, Medical Wellbeing and Marketing. Part of the vision to be a top 4 club in the WSL, alongside exploring options for a new home between now and 2024. The following strategy was unveiled by Michelle Walder, Director and Chair of the Women's Board.

From Brighton's official website, "It's been an absorbing process to be part of, involving lots of consultation with a wide range of stakeholders, both within the Club and externally and the next two years promise to be an exciting journey for all involved." Chief Executive and Deputy Chairman Paul Barber added, "The strategy document sets out our objectives and overall vision and we're looking forward to the opportunities it presents in the next two years. Having a team in the top four of the Women's Super League is an important part of the Club's overall vision. We have achieved a lot in the last few years with promotion to the WSL and the development of our new £8m training complex at the American Express Elite Football Performance Centre, and we're looking forward to the next chapter in the team's professionalism."

The strategy covers player recruitment and helping players prepare for dual careers. It also focuses on developing homegrown players who can compete in the WSL, increasing attendances and engaging with the Club's target audience. One of the main objectives is to explore options for a long-term home for the women's first team that is closer to Brighton and Hove.

Another is further strengthening the links between the women's and girls' sections and working collaboratively across the Club to integrate operations. Under the six pillars are five enablers covering facilities, operations and stakeholders, commercial, people and culture and budget.

Beverly Sawyers, Senior Vice President International Operational Excellence American Express, said, "Sponsorship of, and support for, the Brighton Women's team is a key aspect of our longstanding partnership with Brighton and Hove Albion, and one we are passionate about. We have been impressed seeing the development of women's and girls' football at the Club in recent years. The Club is now firmly established in the Women's Super League and have ambitions to be in the top four. We are delighted to support this strategy and look forward to seeing the continued growth and evolution in the coming years."

Kelly Simmons, The FA's Director of the Women's Professional Game, said, "Brighton have made so much progress in recent years on and off the pitch and this comprehensive strategy will build on the excellent foundations they already have in place for women's and girls' football. We're excited and intrigued to see how they will achieve their objectives and build a women's and girls' section they can be proud of, and which sets the standard for other clubs to try and emulate."

- The strategy covers player recruitment and helping players prepare for dual careers. It also focuses on developing homegrown players who can compete in the WSL, increasing attendances and engaging with the Club's target audience.
- One of the main objectives is to explore options for a long-term home for the women's first team (WFT) that is closer to Brighton and Hove.
- The other is further strengthening the links between the W&G sections and working collaboratively across the Club to integrate operations.
- Under the six pillars are five enablers covering facilities, operations and stakeholders, commercial, people and culture and budget.
- **PROCESS**
- The Club followed a robust process to develop the strategy, which included:
- Consulting 67 internal stakeholders.
- Consulting 22 external stakeholders including the FA and strategic partners.
- Analysing 74 data sources including performance and marketing statistics.
- Reviewing eight benchmarks including average.
- WSL budgets and retention targets.

"Sponsorship of, and support for, the Brighton Women's team is a key aspect of our longstanding partnership with Brighton and Hove Albion, and one we are passionate about. We have been impressed seeing the development of women's and girls' football at the Club in recent years. The Club is now firmly established in the Women's Super League and have ambitions to be in the top four. We are delighted to support this strategy and look forward to seeing the continued growth and evolution in the coming years."

- Beverly Sawyers, Senior Vice President, American Express

"Brighton have made so much progress in recent years on and off the pitch and this comprehensive strategy will build on the excellent foundations they already have in place for W&G football. We are excited and intrigued to see how they will achieve their objectives and build a W&G section they can be proud of, and which sets the standard for other clubs to try and emulate."

- Kelly Simmons, the FA's Director of the Women's Professional Game

YEAR 1 IMPLEMENTATION PLAN—PILLARS
(April 2022–June 2023)

- **Player Pathway:** Revamp the player pathway, providing flexible options to develop and stretch homegrown players ready to compete in the WSL.
- **Player Recruitment:** Strategically recruit players for the WFT to help achieve the top-four vision.
- Strategically recruit players for the WU21 and Girls' Academy to help achieve the top-four vision.
- **Performance and Coaching:** Develop a WSL team capable of achieving and retaining top-four status consistently.
- Improve technical and tactical intelligence throughout the pathway so that players are ready for the WFT.
- **Medical:** Ensure scheduling and loading are optimal for performance.
- Optimise performance.
- Long-term alignment, direction, and succession planning.
- **Wellbeing:** Further develop a high-performance culture.
- Help players transition into and remain at the Club.
- Help players best prepare for dual careers.
- **Marketing and Communications:** Develop marketing and communication strategies specific to the Club's target audience.
- Increase attendances.

YEAR 1 IMPLEMENTATION PLAN—ENABLERS
(April 2022–June 2023)

- **Facilities:** Explore options for a long-term home for the WFT that is closer to Brighton and Hove.
- Spot opportunities to align Club standards when using third-party venues.
- **Operations and Stakeholders:** Continue to spot opportunities for the W&G program to integrate within the Club and align operations.
- **Commercial:** Monitor the media value that the WFT create to help inform future commercial strategy.
- **People and Culture:** Align the women's strategy with the Club's top-ten ambitions.
- Ensure resources and responsibilities are appropriate to the increasing professionalisation of the women's game.
- **Budget:** Ensure the budget reflects the aims of the strategy.

This type of strategy is one fans in the Premier League have been craving for all clubs, a transparency to understand what the club is aiming to achieve, of course exterior events can impact these desires, and this is something fans need to understand when critiquing the club, if it fails to achieve an objective in a time period, or the management, players on the pitch fail to achieve the results. Brighton is leading the way in the women's game, the plan came before the Lionesses success, there is no reason all the clubs could not sign up to this level of transparency, or for the WSL to design Club Charters for their members to adhere to.

Another reason to look at the pathway and transfer market for female footballers is how one of the current Lionesses, Sandy MacIver, former Everton goalkeeper, now at Manchester City, had an unconventional way of becoming a professional, almost a decade after Karen Carney was forced across the Atlantic, MacIver had come through Manchester City's Youth teams, but felt the need to explore the USA college system for a scholarship to gain a qualification, but also to play NCAA Division One football for the US College Clemson Tigers, so she could maintain a potential career after her education.

In 2016, MacIver represented Clemson four times in her freshman year. In her sophomore campaign, MacIver took over as starter and played 17 times over the next three years before graduating as a senior with her degree. It was here and during her performances between the sticks earned Sandy MacIver the Golden Glove at the FIFA U20 Women's World Cup in 2018 putting her on Everton's radar. The Clemson University student helped Mo Marley's side win bronze in France, saving spot-kicks from Selma Bacha and Amelie Delabre as the Young Lionesses defeated the host nation on penalties in the third-place playoff.

She previously represented England at U17 and U19 level after catching the eye with her performances for Everton at the time. Sandy was first called up to the senior squad in August 2019, for the double-header against Belgium and Norway as then boss Phil Neville assessed some of his younger players with a view to the next EUROs on home soil in 2022. Sandy made her England senior team debut against Northern Ireland in February 2021 and was included in Sarina Wiegman's provisional EURO 2022 squad.

MacIver signed for Everton in January 2020, on a free transfer and was instantly installed as their first-choice goalkeeper. Producing a record-breaking display in Everton's 2020 FA Cup Final to Manchester City, where her saves earned her Player of The Match, it was a performance that made several clubs take note and scout MacIver's performances over the next year. On 2 July 2022, Manchester City announced the signing of MacIver on a three-year contract for an undisclosed fee.

Perhaps if we use MacIver's experience it would seem to suggest the option of the College and University system in the UK could work. It would provide the women with an opportunity to receive an education that is paid for, reducing the risk some athletes face when choosing sport over education at an early stage of their life. It would open the girls' opportunities to the best coaching and gyms, so they are better prepared for a professional career once they graduate. On top of this, the Lionesses would be able to have the springboard for future generations and close the fifty-year gap the FA opened in 1921.

Lucy Bronze is another player who benefited from a similar career progression path, using the American College system to play for the University of North Carolina Tar Heels. Before playing a significant role in England winning the delayed European Championship 2021 (played in 2022), Bronze was voted the best FIFA Women's Player in the World in 2020, Bronze is the only English player in history to win three successive Champions League titles, when she represented Lyon and living up to her mother's maiden name, Tough by name, Tough by nature, Lucia Roberta Tough Bronze has inspired and played down a pathway for future Lionesses. Her pathway was forged through the US college system before she moved back to the UK to star for Everton following her Youth Career at Sunderland.

Speaking to Forbes online, Bronze recalls her time with the Tar Heels, impressing Coach Anson Dorrance in summer Camps, Bronze earned herself a scholarship in 2009. Aged just 17, Bronze moved to North Carolina unaware of the legacy the Tar Heels had in college soccer claiming at the time, "I don't really understand the American system anyway so it's just another game for me." Now reflecting Bronze can see how the US College system became a significant reason in her development.

"I think it had probably one of the biggest influences at an important time in my career. When I was younger, in Europe in general, women's football wasn't really a huge spectacle. Whereas in America, obviously everything was amazing." Whilst times were changing in the UK, some female footballers were still washing their own kit at the biggest clubs in England and training at subpar facilities.

"Going out there and playing at college for a year was a dream come true and made me realise that's really what I wanted to do. Playing with the players there who went on to be so successful at such an early age, at 17, it had a huge influence on me as a player and a person. I think I've said it before—their mentality—learning that at 17 years old, I think that's what has helped me grow my mentality in an England environment."

Coaching at the time in England was not the greatest, whilst Hope Powell was innovative in the England set up and Mo Marley at Everton and Emma Hayes were seen as pioneers, women were still not always given access to the same facilities as their male counterparts. Her college coach, Dorrance, led dynamic, relentless and innovative training methods. Bronze, a freshman (first year student) would regularly go head-to-head with senior teammates such as future Olympic Gold Medallist and World Cup winner Tobin Heath.

In the Forbes article Bronze revealed why this was key for her, "it was like a one vs one tournament. Tobin was like the best player on the team. I was 17, the youngest player on the team. Tobin, I mean everyone knows what Tobin is like now, but this was over ten years ago."

"I was assessing myself against one of the best players in the world, already at such a young age. It was a good eye-opener to see the standard of what it takes to be at the top. Tobin, at the time had broken into the US team and was kind of the first player that I really played with who was that kind of world-class standard and I got to go head-to-head, literally head-to-head with her in training sessions. I realised that I need to work a lot harder and push myself if I want to compete against those kinds of players."

An investment in the UK game with top universities offering the same scholarship and opportunities to young coaches could offer similar platforms and opportunities for younger women to have the same success and pathway as Bronze who is not showing any signs of slowing down her success. Easily the most decorated female footballer that England has ever produced, Bronze has won everything in the English came, conquered Europe in France with Lyon, and is now onto Barcelona, pushing herself further outside of her comfort zone.

"I think it is the highest demand I've ever had to play for a team because all the players are so intelligent, that's what they've lived and breathed they're entire life. I've played in Lyon but a lot of it was made up of international players whereas the core of Barcelona is the best Spanish players, the Spanish way, the Barça way."

Perhaps the biggest thing to take away from her interview with Forbes is despite the investment in the Women's Super League in England the coaching and intensity could still be lacking. "I think even in such a short space of time that both Keira (Walsh) and I have been at Barça, even coming back to training here with England—I think Sarina (Wiegman, England Manager) mentioned it a little bit in training—we have a little bit of added intensity in defence."

"The Spanish girls are just so aggressive when they defend which makes them have to play quicker in training, so the tiki-taka comes, so I think me and Keira kind of had a look at each other and thought, 'okay we need to lift the intensity a bit in training' and it's kind of just clicked and happened and Sarina was like shouting, 'well done Lucy, well done Keira.' That was something where we were both kind of thinking, okay, this is what we do at Barça let's add this intensity to England and help push on and keep improving."

If we could create this pathway for the women's game here in England perhaps there will be more Lucy Bronze's representing England at the higher level, provide the coaching and the training and our Lionesses have proven they can beat the best and break down the barriers that have been holding back the women's game.

This is a choice that faces the English FA, it is now up to them to implement the changes in the women's game. The Lionesses Euro win in 2022 needs to be the catalyst, a change in the way everyone views women's football, go to the WSL games, representation on video games such as Football Manager and FIFA, just as the initiative set up recently, it's #HerGameToo.

Following England's success in the Women's Euro's this must be the spark that lights the fire and be the catalyst that brings more support, people and finances into the game to give them equal opportunity, not just in football, but in schools which puts the ball firmly in the governments court. For us fans, the impetus to go and watch their games, we need to take notice and be the future, not stay away and ignore problem, because then we are a part of the problem and for clubs to invest in long-term plans, to not tick a box, but actively go out and build infrastructures for women to succeed.

The FA should take control of women's grassroots football so the best up-and-coming coaches are training young women and they have the same access to gyms and opportunities as young men do. As Gabby Logan closed her segment at the Euro's, "they think it is all over, we've only just begun."

Chapter 10
Circumnavigating a Transfer Window

The media writes the first draft of history, so how do you stop them from getting it wrong?

The window itself resembles a Hollywood movie, the drama unfolding in real time as a ticking time bomb, building to a tantalising finale where football clubs chase a MacGuffin that holds the key to the whole movie. Speculation sells papers, rumours can give footballers stock market like values, values and slumps depending on the rumours. But for those people who work within football, it is just another day at the office, so what exactly does go on?

Whilst most of us are still asleep as the sun rises on deadline day, for others who work in football, deadline day is the most stressful day of their life. Which is why it was special for me to get an interview with a Club Secretary at a football league club, who has requested their name and current club be redacted for confidential reasons.

"Transfer deadline day, it is a roller coaster of emotions at a football club. It is important for a club to come out of the window in a better position than when you go into it. When I arrive, the January weather is biting hard at skin on my face, making me want to race to the coffee machine to warm up, our security guards at the training ground are already watching Sky Sports News, sneaking a look between their rounds, because football does not stop, we have a game in a few days, so the first team are due in. But this complicates matters, as the players we are looking at are also due to be training across the country. It is another hurdle we navigate in the transfer window, but one we prepare for in the football league.

"At seven o'clock, our sporting director calls a meeting, runs through the plan of action for the day. We are planning to get three players in, one out, and possibly a fourth to come in on loan, but we are up against it. To save time, three medicals are booked in advance yesterday, our manager is briefed on the targets, we're optimistic we can get the three players in, a centre-back, midfielder and striker, we're prepared for the long day, and I am asked to get the transfer sheets ready. (Offer sheets put in before the 11pm deadline allow the club extra time to complete the deal.)"

"Outside, our marketing team are waiting with bated breath to upload any photos and social media campaigns of any new player coming into the club on deadline day. At eight o'clock, the first team arrive for training. They're a no Sky Sports cameras this far down the pyramid, but we do get some fans bracing the icy winds for any transfer news. Our director has been working on this loan deal for a centre half for over six weeks now, at our level, most deals are free transfers and loans."

"Money is only raised from players trading up the football pyramid, but unusually, there are two teams lower down the pyramid who have rich owners and are splashing the cash, offering twice the wages we can, in some cases even our players can be heard saying they will drop out the football league for that kind of money. Four signings and one player out would mean I am busy, but I have seen eight players join on deadline day once, so the pressure is on, but I have had worse pressure before. I turn my phone off so there is no distraction, I have instructed my family to call the club desk in case of family emergencies."

"Just as the Director thanks us for our efforts, his mobile rings, it is a buying club, by the look of resignation on his face, it is not unexpected. We are ushered out to carry out our current plan. Behind the frosted glass, we can hear snippets, "buy-out clauses, not enough, happy if our evaluation is met, but a lunchtime deadline is set." It would be nice if we got lunch on deadline day."

"Our first potential deal arrives at half 9, a centre-back, on loan from a Championship club, six months until the end of the year. Good move for both parties, he gets a shot at first team football to aid his development and the loaning club will get a player ready for the Championship. He has turned up, driven by his dad, not the sort of helicopters or private jets of the Premier League. I begin to sort the transfer documentation and contracts out as he is taken for his medical by our physio."

"He is the beating heart of our club and does his best to calm any fears the player has before conducting the medical in our physio's room. We can do a lot of the medical in the training ground, but we can also hire other machines, or bring in specialists if we need them. In an extreme case, if a player cannot get to our ground, we can hire a local private facility for the player, but you always want to be in control of the situation."

"This kid is our top target, and he was given extended time in the pre-season by their new manager. We knew he was always going to be available, but we've been made to wait since the Summer. As the player emerges from his medical, smile on his face, the Director gives us the nod to go through the signing of documents with the player. You can tell players are happy and nervous, sometimes you need to have little sticky notes to show them where to sign. Contracts are signed and the green light is given by the loaning club. I can proceed to upload documents to make it official to the football league, the player is given his new shirt, and our social media team go to work on their promotion."

"Then transfer games can get interesting, as we think we can pause for breath and celebrate the done deal, our deal for the striker has hit a snag, the loaning club from the Premier League have included him in an under 23 squad and they are travelling further up North. It will be a dash down a motorway to get him here after the match. A quick Google Map shows they would need to somehow average 80mph plus to get him here after the match. Our director is calm, this would have been the icing on the cake, so the plan is still good. A midfielder and another striker are still on."

"Paper comes through our email box, we use a specific one for transfers, a Premier League club from London has sent through transfer documents for a player who is currently our third-choice striker option. It is a power play; they know our number two option may be out and they think this could force our hand. I glanced through the financials to brief our director, 6-month loan, we pay 100% wages and a loan fee. The club thinks we are desperate."

"I take the paperwork, tiptoe towards our directors' office, past our physio belting out 70s classics from his office, I update him on the paperwork for the centre-back, but also on the paperwork for the mystery striker. From our Director's point of view, he is just as confused as anyone. "I'll look into it." He gets onto the phone with our Chief Scout to see if he has been speaking to the Premier League club."

"He updates me on two fronts, the striker we want from the Championship is on his way, currently waiting in a service station on the motorway, the midfielder has been taken out of training as we negotiate clauses with his parent club. The concern is, a bid has come in for our star midfielder, below our valuation, but our chairman and owner must be informed."

"We sold a player in the Summer, so the clubs finances are ok, but at our level, an FA Cup or EFL football league Trophy run are vital, so any bid is considered, and the players agent wants his client to know, as the personal terms from the team a league below us is bigger than his current package. Our Director informs the coaching team to keep him training. The potential buyers have had all month to make an offer and they have come in low with their offer. It is frustrating, but this is life in football."

"Outside, a small cheer from our security staff as Sky Sports confirm our deal for the centre-back, just a one-word sentence. I always get amazed at where they get the information from so quickly. No media knew of the deal, so it must be from the League to Sky Sports."

"Midday comes and we have officially rejected the offer from the club for our star midfielder. News in football travels quickly and when the first team come in, they discuss it in the canteen. But news that we are tracking a striker from the Championship is also the talk of the training ground. He is a prolific striker who hasn't fired for his current club, we are excited that he could score 15 goals for us this season, he is on big wages, so we are covering only a portion of his wages. From Premier League to the Championship, then on loan onto League 1, you never know what they will make of the facilities here, will players settle."

"I have seen players' reactions when they join a new club and forcing smiles as they have uprooted their family for an umpteenth time. It is the hidden side to the game no one sees, but the stress is unbelievable for players, I have had to console a young player once when his dream moved collapsed, the club itself will move onto plan B, there is nowhere the player can move, in this instance the player had failed a medical and we could not take the risk, for the player, the entire football league will find out his move failed due to a medical, and this will be discussed with every negotiation for a new contract or transfer."

"I feel for the striker in our current starting 11, he himself is a newer recruit from the Summer, watching Sky Sports News as there are rumours of a new striker on his way. The contract issue which was holding the deal up is solved, an option to purchase has been added in the deal and the striker has now left the McDonalds in the service station and on his way here, our physio is in his element, he is onto the 80s now, belting out his entire back catalogue, the younger lads, the Noughties generation are confused by a record-breaking single, or it could by our physio 'intentionally' murdering the lyrics."

"When the striker arrives, the fans instantly recognise him, this one will not be a secret, our Director meets him with a hug, this is a big deal, another Championship club have made a last-minute bid. The player would prefer it here. It is close to his current home, so we are happy to proceed with the deal and medical. The deal for the second striker from the Premier League academy is off."

"He is playing tonight for the under 23's, and the club have accepted an offer from another League One club in the Northwest, close to them so they can monitor his progress easier. The unseen side of this deals collapse is our director and manager now have to tell one of our youngsters his loan move is off to a League 2 club. He is desperate for game time, but with little options for him, it will be another six months on the bench unless something else comes unexpectedly."

"Our physio has finished the medical with a quick thumbs up to our Director, he has given me the green light to send the paperwork before the other club has time to come back. As the paperwork hits the fax machine, the dulcet tones of 'another one bites the dust' echoes from the physio room. We submit the paperwork, and the social media team are handing over the new shirt, the number still hot off the press. They have just uploaded our first signings video to social media, now they are onto take two."

"A second offer comes in for our midfielder and he asks for a meeting with the Director, our club captain comes back into the office with a takeaway for all the club staff. We love him and he is part of the furniture here. His presence is key, and he has a meeting with our midfielder to talk through the deal and what the players options are. The deal must be progressing as our recruitment team have arrived and are now going through a presentation of options with the Chairman dialled in, to top things off the Premier League club who sent through the paperwork are now calling me for the Director, their new deal has now increased the loan fee. They must know the other striker is definitely off."

"There goes the takeaway. The second offer for our midfielder is rejected after a meeting with the manager, for him the pressure is now on, the deal would mean only promotion would equal the transfer fee offered and he may now have a player who is upset at his move."

"As we move onto around half 4, there are still complications in the deal for the young midfielder, he is due to fly off for international duty and he now needs clearance to arrive late for the training camp. The loaning club are now stipulating they want guaranteed playing time, our manager is now discussing whether the deal is still good for the club and whether there are alternatives. According to the Championship club loaning him out, another club in our division have submitted an offer. Our director asks me how quick I can prep new paperwork, both for an incoming player and a player going out."

"He jumps on the phone, he believes he knows the club who have submitted an offer for our target, he offers them the youngster we tried to loan to League 2 four hours earlier. Juggling two phones, muting one, then another, to complete a sentence, our accountant is on the other, we are seeing if we can cover some of the wages of our player as he goes on loan to sweeten the deal."

"A third phone is needed. I am asked to call the League to let them know we are sending a player on loan, but the deal may be difficult because the player must travel across the country for the medical. Then I phone the club of our intended target and ask can the player travel up for a medical? They come back with another team that are interested and has offered more."

My director waves to me to keep them talking, as we discuss paperwork changes, I see our director make a fist pump, he has just agreed to loan our youngster to our divisional rival. Just as the Championship director proclaims, "I am wasting my time talking to him as their player is already on the move."

"Imagine my smile when he rings back five minutes later, when he learns our director has outsmarted him, the deal is on, the player is on his way, but it will be a late one. I don't need asking, the deal sheet, contract and transfer paperwork is already being printed, and we already have their copy so there is no delay there. A top tip for future secretaries out there, get their copy first. No David De Gea fax machine issues here."

"With the sun setting, even our brave fans have gone home, we go down to skeleton staff at this time, the director, me, the manager, recruitment team and the security team. It is now a waiting game. If we get this midfielder, it will have been a good window. I send over the loan deal to our League 1 rivals for our youngster's loan. He is on his way there, happy to get additional game time, with his pathway blocked here. Jim White's arrival on television signifying it is crunch time. Nervous conversation becomes muted whispers. Even our security staff go quiet and do double rounds. In these times, Google Earth comes out again so we can track the players progress on the roads. Our physio is a veteran, he has got a medical bag packed in case we need to do this medical in the service station."

"As Jim White gives the hour to go signal, there is no chatter now, the player arrives, again with his parents, they want to document the entire deal, not realising there are things we need to tie up quickly, the contract issues and the medical are done simultaneously, even the physio is no longer singing, he is working through the final creaks in the deal and the muscles."

"The security team are now valuable, keeping the family's company in the canteen so we can do the finer details. The medical is done, and I begin to upload paperwork, we are granted the 15-minute extension for the football league and the deal will be completed as long as I send the document in time."

"I click a timer on my phone to count down from 15 minutes just for an emergency measure. All electrical devices except my computer are shut down, in case there is a shortage, with one backup in the director's office. There is not even time for the marketing team to do any social media, after another check on the signatures and the detailed breakdown, I hit the send button and our transfer window is over."

"At 11:12, the night for us is over, the adrenaline slowly ebbs away from the shakes, and we have a debrief over a cup of tea. When the transfer window goes well for your club, it brings optimism which channels through the club, it humanises the job and the sport. Transfer Deadline Day is stressful, but I wouldn't change it for the world."

Often overlooked during the transfer window is the impact on the main protagonists themselves, the player and the impact it has on their lives, but also how the quirks of transfer deals have on the players careers. One of these quirks that affected the players career was in the case of Wolves' recent transfer of striker Francisco Trincao, they are reportedly going to pay £5m not to sign the player. According to BBC Sport, the Portuguese forward's loan deal included a fee in case Wolves decided against using the option to buy in his contract. The Premier League club will now have to pay up as Trincao returns to Barcelona, although they will reportedly receive 20 percent of his transfer fee if he is then subsequently sold.

The reports also suggest the 22-year-old could join Sporting Lisbon for £15.5m, which would see Wolves receive around £3m due to the clause that Wolves receive a percentage of the next transfer fee. Trincao was a regular for Wolves last season, scoring three goals in 30 games. He was reunited at the club with Pedro Neto after the pair played youth football together in Portugal for Vianense and Braga.

The Portuguese national side have taken notice of the young winger, who has made seven senior appearances since 2020 as well as 53 for their various youth sides. The decision not to sign Trincao is an interesting one from Wolves given the speculation over several of their key players' futures and use of the Portuguese super-agent Jorge Mendes.

Sometimes the deals within the transfer window can be much easier and less time-consuming. Crystal Palace were forced to sell their captain, Fitz Hall, after the £3m release clause in his contract was activated by Wigan. In this instance, a club cannot stop a player from leaving, it does not mean the player will leave, but if the club steps up, then the club is powerless to stop it.

A release clause provides clarity for a player of they have an option for a transfer built into their contract, this is agreed with their current club during contract renewals, it removes a club's power to bargain or haggle over a price but can sometimes be seen as a compromise for the player to not be stopped from moving on as was the case with Harry Kane and his gentlemen agreement with Daniel Levy.

Simon Jordan's autobiography 'Be Careful What You Wish For' provides the perfect insight for football fans on the ongoing struggle to keep clubs afloat in the aftermath of the worldwide economic crisis in 2008, but also, what it is like for Premier League owners to negotiate player transfers. Jordan gives viewers a peek behind the curtain at the reality of being on the receiving end of a transfer fee that is unlikely to appear in the national print media.

After suffering several heart aches with the Elite Player Performance Program seeing several of his highest performing youngsters leave for minimal returns to other clubs, he faced losing starlet Wayne Routledge, who had one year left on his contract, for a minimal fee, and as deadline day ticked on. Daniel Levy of Spurs came calling at 7pm four hours before the window closed. Jordan and his team at Palace offered Routledge a new and much improved deal, only to be told by the player's agent, Paul Stretford he would not be signing a new deal.

Levy offered Jordan a paltry sum of £1m for the England under 21 players. Jordan rejected the deal out of hand, despite Levy calling back a number of times in the next few hours, upping the bid by a few thousand each time, famously so Jordan was to retort, "Levy spent more money on his phone bill than he was upping the offer for Routledge." At 11pm, with time running out, "the fiftieth time of rejecting Levy's insulting offers, the fee had only increased to £1.25m,"

Jordan pointed out that even if he wanted to do the deal, there would be no time for the medical, as the player had not travelled across London for the deal to progress, as no permission had been given to Spurs to talk contracts with the player either.

Routledge and Stretford were actually 500 yards away from Tottenham's offices, deal agreed. Once Jordan found this out, he hung up a final time and told assistant manager Bob Dowie to call Routledge and tell him not to be late for training in the morning.

From the players perspective, the furore around transfer deadline day is whipped into a production value for people to watch and take annual leave for, doesn't seem to be as over-the-top as it was a few years back. Peter Crouch describes what it is like to move clubs on deadline day. What it means to be the player on the end of a Sky Sports News segment. One set of fans clamouring to the training ground to hopefully catch a glimpse of their new striker, the other set of fans, Tottenham's screaming at television sets to just get the deal done.

Inside the £10m move, Peter had very little say on the matter, speaking on That Peter Crouch podcast, "I went from Tottenham to Stoke. I was happy at Spurs, but I had a conversation with Daniel Levy on the day. I was happy and settled, had no idea I was moving. Then a bid came in from Stoke. Harry [Redknapp] wanted to bring in Adebayor and the situation was 'see you later' basically. Levy and Redknapp were keen to move me on given the price and Adebayor could be coming in."

"I said, 'well I'm happy here, I'll see you in the morning.' So, I went home, and had lots of missed calls. The deal progressed anyway, the clubs negotiated the fee and terms. My agent became involved with Stoke who offered terms. Then I went halfway (between London and Stoke), my mum had a friend in Birmingham, so I stayed there in the middle, just in case. With the clock ticking down, Sky Sports went into overdrive. Tipped off by someone at Spurs that the deal may happen. 'It got to eight or nine o'clock and I realised it was going to happen, so I made the trip up to Stoke.'"

"Crouch, having had a long day, decided to take a detour and stop in a service station with his father. He decided to look for some food, confident his agent was completing all the paperwork on the finer details of the contract. Crouch took a seat and took in Sky Sports reporting on the big screen, the yellow ticker adorning his name. 'They said I was in a helicopter on his way to Stoke. I was in a motorway service station eating McDonalds.' You couldn't be further from the truth, a reality Peter found hilarious. Completing his move soon after, his agent gives him the green light to approach the ground, clear to avoid another Peter Odemwinge situation."

Peter Crouch's transfer further highlights the significant changes a footballer's career can change overnight. He began the day settled in London, at a club chasing European aspirations. Children and wife Abbey settled in schools and life in London, only for the club and manager who he had sacrificed so much for (Redknapp had signed him three times previously) basically chased him out of the club because a situation developed out of the blue. He ended the day at a team in a relegation fight, 150 miles from his family, unsure of what was to come next.

Footballers are by no means perfect, but the strain transfer window can put on them and their family is tremendous. Negated if the business would be done earlier, during the school holidays, now their children are forced to start new schools after terms have started and in some instances, the player may not want to go, or have any plans for a new house, schools. Had these moves started earlier in the window, players would be able to stomach it more, but further champions having one window in the summer as a better value for the players welfare, or one where transfers are loans and not permanent ones which favour the clubs more.

Fast forward a few years, Crouch and his wife Abbey Clancy were partying at the Isle of Wight festival when they bumped into Sean Dyche in the summer of 2018. Recently released from Stoke and unsure of his next move, Crouch was busy weighing up options and a potential media career when a chance meeting with the Burnley manager opened one final door.

Crouch recalls the chance meeting on his podcast, detailing how Abbey mentioned Peter was out of contract and that Dyche should sign him. Dyche jokingly broached the subject, dangling the carrot in front of Crouch and asking would he sign if the opportunity arose? Crouch agreed he would and as chance would have it, a few weeks later, Crouch was signing on a free transfer and beginning a chapter of his career in Lancashire.

As Peter Crouch's story partying on the Isle of Wight in 2018 showed, certain players still have little control over their careers, and towards the end of their playing days. This is not a new scenario for players, not all can control whether they are sold or not as we saw earlier with Alex Iwobi, enjoying a holiday, happy to be playing for Arsenal and living in London. Iwobi got a phone call from his agent explaining he had sold him to Everton for £35m and Arsenal were packing up his locker. No need for a medical, no chance for Iwobi to think about it. Only weeks earlier, Arsenal manager, Unai Emery, had told Iwobi he liked him and wanted to make him an integral part of his squad the following season.

Footballers are not the only people involved in football that are affected daily by the transfer window. The pressures that are faced by the players during this time are also matched by the medical teams within each club. With a player's dream move depending on their medical results, sometimes million-pound decisions can come down to a professional's opinion on matters off the field that are just as important as they are on it.

Mick 'Baz' Rathbone is a veteran of football, he has worn the T-shirt and has the scars to prove it, despite the stress football and the transfer window can bring, Rathbone is back in the game, never stops smiling and is hungrier than ever to work in football. Highly academic and determined to become a doctor, football remained a pull, leaving school aged 16 he signed professional terms with Birmingham City F.C. Selected soon after for the England Youth Team, he went on to make his senior team debut aged 17. Rathbone finished his career in the lower leagues of English Football, but his second love of players' health shone through, and he retrained as a Chartered Physiotherapist.

Retiring as a player and working his way up the lower leagues before landing at Everton in 2002, aged 44, becoming head of the medical department. Spending eight successful years with the Premier League club, after leaving Everton, Rathbone documented his career in his extremely popular autobiography, The Smell of Football, Rathbone was tempted out of retirement and back into the game, currently the physio of Oldham and following the release of the much anticipated, "The Smell of Football 2," Rathbone is just as happy as ever to discuss football and how the transfer window has impacted his role in football.

"Specifically highlighting how the transfer window impacts a physio's ability to conduct medicals. Very stressful, especially on the last day. The chaotic nature of club recruitment and the transfer window is that a domino effect occurs that cannot always be foreseen. One player leaving your club, or another club can cause a domino effect within the market."

One player who looked sure of staying could be off. When this means a player could be coming in on deadline day, "I get a shout with a few hours to go that we need a medical! Of course, the clubs have things in place for these eventualities, MRI scanners booked, cardiac screens booked, blood tests booked, but even the best teams need time. For example, a blood test needs time to be analysed whilst time ticks away in the background. Of course, we do have background info on all the potential signings," some may bring alongside any existing medical records for the medical team to evaluate. "We can assume his heart is ok if he is currently playing at a high level as they are checked annually. We can look at his playing record and see he has been fit and playing regularly. Those things take a lot of pressure off medics."

But what about those players carrying injuries on deadline day? "Problems occur with last-minute signings if the player is currently injured, and time is running out. Then it becomes a judgement call. Some may call it a gamble! Undoubtedly many top players have been signed without full medical." Which seems ludicrous and a huge risk when clubs are spending millions of pounds on players, which can put the future of the clubs at risk.

Even the medicals can miss or not highlight some players underlying health issues, recently Brighton's Enock Mwepu, their record signing was forced to retire, aged just 24, after doctors identified a hereditary heart issue, which posed an extremely substantial risk of a potential fatal cardiac event if he didn't give up playing. Rathbone is keen to stress why medicals need to be thorough and notes a number of deals do collapse because a medical cannot be completed in time.

Rathbone has had to make the difficult decision to tell a player his dream move is off after failing a medical. Rathbone would never put the club before a player, but this respect is not always given back to physios. "When you fail a player on the medical, all hell breaks loose. On the three occasions I have done it, you end up being accused of being incompetent and not knowing what you are doing by the players selling club and representatives. It happened to me on each occasion."

"Tough time personally, but I made my mind up for the best of club who are paying my wages and the players' health, so I did not back down. On each occasion, time proved me right! Recently, at a lower level, something funny happened; I had reservations about a player's ankle, so he signed elsewhere, for a less affluent club. I then moved to the club he had just signed for. He walked over to me on day one, said there were no hard feelings, and it was business. We became really good mates but every time a new player signed, he would introduce them to me with the line, 'this is Baz, the physio, he just cost me 50k a year in wages!'"

Football can be a harsh business for all involved and recently more emphasis has been put on mental health for all those involved in the industry. Awareness is improving, but players still will not open up on the stress of the move in case it makes the buying club pull out of the deal. Rathbone reveals players do not open up during the medical.

"Twenty years ago, when I was first at Everton. It was assumed it was all fine. Today, there is more acknowledgement of the emotional stress and or strain of change of club, the environment the player may have been comfortable in and of course, some players will now be in a foreign country, unable to speak the language having a medical can be a daunting prospect. Then there is the pressure on the player to perform by fans and pundits when they discuss the players transfer fee, something the player has no control of. But clubs are slowly and rightly factoring players' mental health into the equation."

Having said that, physios have the uniqueness that they are sometimes closer to the players than the manager, working on the players through the season, tight nit bonds can be formed. The whole club mentality can change after a player is sold. "Absolutely depends on who? Why? How much is the transfer? At Everton, when Wazza (Wayne Rooney) went to Manchester United for £30m in 2004 I was gutted."

It was a what if moment for the club, a world-class player aged 18 leaving the club, a sliding door moment. "It was a good deal for the club and his opportunity to play at the very top." In some ways, it united a remarkably close dressing room. Following Rooney's departure, Everton Manager David Moyes signed Tim Cahill for £1.5m and Darren Bent for £300k from Ipswich many tipped the Merseyside club for relegation. What followed seemed like a miracle. Rathbone mentions how the move helped make the dressing room even closer and the club went onto finish 4th in the League and qualify for the Champions League. An accolade Moyes, his staff and players deserve credit for.

Staff can also be "glad if a player wanted to leave and had stopped trying so the club would be forced to sell him." It is easy during a transfer window for a player to have his head turned by another club or his agent. The effect on the dressing room can derail a season and take a toll on the staff inside the club as well. But Rathbone is keen to point out that it can also be positive feelings when a player leaves.

"Buzzing, if maybe a young player who was not going to get in the first team but deserved a good opportunity elsewhere to play and make a good career for himself." As Rathbone experienced with one of his failed medicals, football in the English pyramid can be a small place and no sooner has a player been sold, a physio could be on the move too, seeing the same players again.

Best to not hold any grudges. "The transfer window is an emotional rollercoaster for the staff too, even worse if you support the club, different emotions based on circumstances. If an injury prone player is sold, it can be a relief for all parties, the player gets a fresh start, the club may get a fee and the medical staff feel relieved in no longer needing to update the manager on the players progress through injury."

"During the window, a physio must juggle managing the first team and keep track of any transfer dealings, adapting to the situations that may befall them. 'It is never a major issue; pre-season tours happen in July and most transfers happen in August or on deadline day. Many times, we signed a player when I was in the USA pre-season with Everton. I was in Denver when we signed Louis Saha, I think. I made a simple call to Man Utd medical staff who provided the information I needed. They send medical records electronically and besides, we always got Doc and one other physio (Jimmy Comer) back at Finch Farm to do the formalities.'"

"It allows me to continue touring with the players and allow for a seamless transition for the manager and care for any first team player who picks up a niggling injury. Transfers and medicals differ up and down the football pyramid, as Rathbone has come back into the game and worked tirelessly around clubs, he has noted the difference stance some clubs make on transfers and medicals."

The facilities vary, at the top-flight, they are amazing. Medical staff can do blood tests and heart scans at training grounds now. Lower down, the facilities decrease generally in line with the club's overall budget and wealth. However, lower down the pyramid, often past the Championship there is no fee involved by the buying club. Contracts are worth much less, so medicals are less involved, they are considered time-consuming and costly. Medicals centre around current injury status and their latest playing record will be sufficient for some clubs and nothing further is needed before the business is concluded.

For a veteran like Rathbone, the pressure of medicals and the transfer window no longer phase him. The smile and passion for the game never waving, finding the time to do this interview whilst getting ready to patrol the touchline for Oldham in midweek, football finds a way to draw you in and never let you go, with the same passion he had when he signed professional terms for Birmingham all those years ago.

Football needs people like Mick 'Baz' Rathbone they remind us of the people who make our clubs we support special, we may not know them personally, but a physio, like Rathbone is cheered when he grabs his medical bag and sprints onto the pitch, staff like Rathbone, work behind the scenes, in the shadows to make our clubs work and be successful, they are part of the football family and just as important as the players on it.

Chapter 11
Estate Agents 'Licensed to Thrill'

"YOU CAN'T EXPECT LOYALTY FROM THOSE PEOPLE WHO WOULD DO ANYTHING FOR MONEY"—Author Unknown

You often hear the expression in life: "keep your friends close; keep your enemies closer." Wise words of Sun Tzu trickle through society, but the 'enemy of your enemy is your friend' could be more fitting for the relationships football clubs have with their players' agents. From the outside world the perception of their glamorous lifestyle, taking millions out of the game, is responsible for driving transfer prices up as this boosts their commission in an unregulated industry where they have made themselves king. There will always be a minority, possibly the highest profile, who are cancerous to the industry, but agents can help the game of football. But the game may need an independent body and tweaks to the system to protect the system.

Firstly, agents have given themselves the self-proclaimed titles of agents. It sounds more powerful and legal, a profession to make them sound more like Lawyers, but as you dig further into the industry, it is quite frightening how easy and quickly one can become one. FIFA recognise 'agents' as Intermediaries, a go between for the club and player to negotiate with on contracts and transfers. By FIFA's previous rules and laws, an Intermediary can only talk to clubs once a buying club agrees with a potential selling club to begin transfer negotiations. FIFA's new regulations has them retitled as agents and needing to pass an exam.

For every Mini Raiola, often painted as the pantomime villain of football for his constant brokering of deals and speaking to clubs whilst his players are under contract to unsettle them and make another lump sum from the commission of a sale. Raiola was rumoured to have made £40m commission from the Paul Pogba transfer from Juventus to Manchester United for £89m, considering the agent fees and legal costs, with Pogba leaving United for free in the Summer of 2022,

£130m for a player who has been criticised as being lazy and no desire for football seems a colossal mistake by United.

There are over 1800 agents registered and representing players in the Premier League and football league, not all agents are bad people looking out for themselves, some really do care about their players and the game of football.

But for all the good transfer deals, there are all the scars of those who have been misled and misguided at such a young age. Mohamed Ihattaren is a Dutch professional footballer currently on loan at Ajax from Juventus. One of Hollands expected wonderkids to lead their next generation, was represented by Raiola who looked after his deal from Dutch club PSV to Juventus for £1.71m in the Summer of 2021, where the players nightmare began.

Loaned straight out to Sampdoria to gain experience, the football quickly realised things were not that his agent had promised him that led him to consider retiring from football aged 19, following a diagnosis of depression following the passing of his father.

He never played a minute for Sampdoria, after a few training sessions, he requested to go back to Holland on personal grounds. The media painted him as a rebel, questioned his character, where these stories came from remain unclear, but the player is keen to reveal the truth, along with his personal loss of his father. "I left (Sampdoria) because of the conditions. I often found myself alone, abandoned in a hotel room. All kinds of agreements had not been respected. It was like I did not exist." Promises to the young player had not been kept. Some of them are vital for a player who has moved to a foreign country for the first time.

Ihattaren recently shared the truth behind the saga. Revealing the following details which show how important it is for fans to gather the full facts before casting judgement. "Nothing was organised, no help with a bank account, no medical insurance. What if I had broken my leg at Sampdoria? I did not get a salary." Alarm bells began to ring when Ihattaren found, "the coach didn't even know I was left-footed." Raiola managed several deals that Summer, but the club argue it is the agent who organises those minor details. Which is echoed by agents, they represent and look after the player, not the club.

"Raiola said he is worried for me, but he disappointed me." In January 2022, Ihattaren returned home to Holland with a loan deal to Ajax, with a new intermediary, Ali Dursun, to begin rebuilding a promising career. Ihattaren is one example of where players need to be careful in choosing their representation, it also shows how much modern footballers rely on other people to function and help them in the basic day-to-day lives, even more so now younger players are moving to new countries for the first time.

Agents are a new commodity to the world of football. In the foreword for Daniel Geey's insider's guide to the world of football transfers, Gianluca Vialli reveals when he signed his first professional contract for Cremonese, there was no agent, only advise from the AIC, the Italian version of the Professional Football Association, no involvement from Lawyers, banks or agencies.

A decade later in 1992, Vialli signed for Juventus, again no lawyer or agent, Sampdoria's president even negotiated the contract for Vialli. It was not until England's top division was rebranded the Premier League and money began to flow through the game that commercial deals filtered onto the negotiation table.

Vialli reveals this, in 1996, with his move to Chelsea on the cards he hired his first agent for what would be his final transfer. Players were now brands, commercial commodities for the clubs, transfer prices and salaries have risen to astronomical levels, given the rise in sponsorship deals it would be impossible for footballers to negotiate these deals, but worryingly, players seem to have completely come away from the discussions.

We saw this earlier with Josh Maja, when he stated his agents were looking after his deal and he didn't know where it was up to. Neither would players allow their club Presidents to negotiate their new contract like Vialli once did. The newer sub industries introduced to football has allowed better legal protection for players, more jobs created, the downside, more players are focused on making money out of the sport, in fashion, music, gaming, the desire and standard on the pitch looks like it is currently plateauing. Difficult for the match going fan if millionaire footballs don't give their all and their beloved club is relegated to the lower leagues or out of the football league.

Agents have a scarily similar start to football scouts when beginning their career. The search for established clients is particularly hard for new entrants into the world of football, where the established stars are already signed up with the bigger parties or agencies. They must start at the bottom, it is dog eat dog, where they need to hustle to build clientele and then keep their enemies closer to ensure they are not poached by another client.

To gain a licence with the FA they need £500 plus VAT, for their initial one-year registration. No professional qualifications are needed and what an agent legally cannot do involving a transfer is never discussed or shown to a budding candidate. If the candidate complies with FIFA's opinion that they must "have what's termed an impeccable reputation," Then there is the FA's test of good character, but that really is it, once applied and registered, you can really call yourself a football agent.

Before April 2015, agents needed to pass a rigorous exam, and the removal of this regulation has been staggering and has seen billions of pounds leave the game, agent fees rise and players moving clubs at an alarming rate. The pass rate fluctuated between 6% and 35% between 2008 and 2014. The recently reinstalled agent's exam in 2023 saw an alarming pass rate of 52% for the professional agents currently operating within the game.

Since 2015 there has been a leap of almost 300 per cent increase in the number of agents registered following the previous deregulation. Mohamed Ihattaren case study highlighted bad choices are being made on behalf of footballers and in some cases young players' talents may be getting exploited by players like they are companies on a stock exchange. Once they get to an age where the player's 'big move' has gone and agents are only getting money from player transfer, the agent moves onto another younger client.

Prior to 2015, in the UK there were between 500–600 agents registered according to research of Alan Gernon. By June 2018, according to the FA, this figure had skyrocketed to 1897. Those who had failed FIFA's regulatory exam were now given free access to the market. Players' family members were now also given the platform to represent their family.

Agents to get their five-year licence by their national association had to sit a 20-question multiple choice question exam, 14 correct answers where required to pass. Not an easy test either as Gernon presented a typical question from the exam.

1) The Greek player Angelo Patsouris, born on 1st March 1990, was registered with and trained by the Greek club FC Anthropos, a category 3 club, as from 1 January 2002. The football season in Greece runs from 1st July until 30th June of the following year. On 1st January 2004, the player signed a two-year scholarship agreement with FC Anthropos, according to which the club agreed to pay all expenses incurred through his football activity, plus an additional monthly amount of 80 Euros. During the following two years, Angelo signed a professional contract with FC Anthropos, valid until 31 December 2008.

On 1 January 2008, Angelo and FC Anthropos agreed to terminate their employment relationship and simultaneously signed an agreement that both parties had no further had no further financial obligations towards each other. On 2 January 2008, Angelo was registered as an amateur with the Belarus club FC Bensko, a category 2 club. On 1 January 2010, Angelo signed a professional contract with FC Bensko and was consequently registered with the Belarus Football Federation as a professional one day later. On 28 September 2011, FC Anthropos lodged a claim against FC Bensko in front of FIFA's Dispute Resolution Chamber, asking for training compensation. How much compensation is FC Anthropos entitled to receive from FC Bensko for the training of Angelo, if at all?

NB: Greece is a member of the European Union (EU), and Belarus is not a member of the EU.

a) 0 Euros
b) 110,000 Euros
c) 185,000 Euros

The answer to the question is C.

This is just one example of the questions the exam posed to applicants. Undertaking this exam would need candidates to understand, study a number of articles, laws, and by-laws before they even thought of approaching players for representation.

Over 2000 pages needed to be studied to give applicants the legal knowledge of the world of football, but also the local Football Associations they wished to operate in. Applicants were also required to have professional indemnity insurance and proof they had no criminal record. The exam was set up to trip up applicants who did not do the research into the regulatory provision which was the basis for most of the questions. Fifteen set by FIFA, with the applicant's local Football Association setting the rest.

FIFA later explained its decision to deregulate the industry was solely down to the fact, 25 to 30 percent of transfers completed and sent through their transfer system were completed by FIFA licensed agents. Rather than fix the issue and perhaps cancel the transfer of the 70 to 75 percent of transfers submitted, some in the industry admit FIFA simply gave up. Overnight, people with a mobile phone and £500 people could sign up and call themselves Intermediaries in less time than it would take to read this chapter.

Managers have also mentioned how since 2015, negotiations have changed, the language and tone of intermediaries is much more disrespectful, one manager stating they had gone from discussing a contract with lawyers, accountants and barristers to people with no legal knowledge and are not scared of using 'colourful and robust' language to get their way in negotiations.

The fallout from deregulation has seen a 300 percent increase in intermediaries and one manager explained the reasoning for the change in relationships. "They feast on one another, chasing or poaching each other's players. One player told me it was like the Wild West, if this agent does not get you this, I will. It is in the agents, not the players interest to keep moving, this is their source of income."

To support this theory, some agents, because there is no regulation, chose not to hide this. Denzel Dumfries agent, Rafaela Pimenta discussed with Sky Sports after his client had starred at the 2022 Winter World Cup in Qatar, "I hope his value doesn't increase—otherwise it will be difficult to transfer him to a Premier League club." The Dutchman was under contract for another three and a half years at Inter Milan. The irony being, his agent steered Dumfries away from the Premier League, when Everton had a deal agreed with his previous club PSV in Holland.

His agent stalled the deal, knowing his client would get more offers from clubs in Europe, offering more wages, when his client would star at the rearranged Euro 2020. Two things, an agent only receives an income when the player is sold, or signs a new deal, so this is why Pimenta wanted to transfer his client, and secondly, if his agent really 'wanted' his client to join the Premier League, why reject Everton's offer in 2021? Agents are supposed to have clients' interests first, right?

With his value increasing, clubs may look to younger alternatives, which means it would be three and a half years before Pimenta get his next pay day of Dumfries. The words, "difficult to transfer to the Premier League" Inter Milan may not want to sell their star player, and why is it bad for the current club to ask for the best price, for their best assets in their prime? It is this reason, why fans and clubs are asking for regulation to agents and their conduct, here is evidence in the open, said to the press, on television, where an agent is trying to sell a player, with apparent no permission from the selling club for less money.

There is a solution though that can be broached. If players paid their agents monthly, like a normal direct debit, there would be less money lost from the game which could be reinvested in grassroots football. Should clubs be paying millions for agents to facilitate one deal, where agents can legally drive up the price in a bidding war, so their 'fee' is bigger. If two club's cartel together and set a price of the transfer, they could be investigated for illegal trading. But deregulation has allowed agents to do this to football clubs. If agents were to receive a one percent retainer a month of all his clients, do agents make these comments?

Players select agents to work on their behalf, but most do not pay them at all. The work and uploading are done by club secretaries or directors of player personnel. The agent oversees the negotiations. If you are selling your house, you as the seller, pay the estate agent a fee, not the person who buys the house, the buyer will pay the legal fees, surveying costs and such, but in football, where the agent acts in similar ways, the clubs end up footing the bill.

One of the stipulations is qualified and termed as 'impeccable reputation' by FIFA, or the FA's 'test of character'. Managers have done countless interviews, print and radio where the stipulate agents regularly tout their players to other clubs with the current players club unaware. A clear breach of FIFA's transfer rule. In the case of Virgil Van Dijk, neither Liverpool, the player, or the agent, in clear breach of the 'impeccable reputation' by FIFA, or the FA's 'test of character' were sanctioned, which has fans questioning what the point of rules and regulations is if agents can behave how they wish?

Whilst it is important to stress not all agents are bad apples, some do have their players and the games interest at heart when it comes to negotiations. But for the large majority, they do not have the experience of working with an international player, which is why the players interested in brands gravitate towards the more high-profile agents.

Take the World Cup 2022, held in Qatar, a nation like England will have 23 players going to the tournament, with two or three superstars in the team. Meaning, if the FA recognises 2000 agents, assume one player per agent, that leaves 1977 intermediaries active in the UK that do not have an England star on their books. (June 2018 there were 1897 agents registered.)

Another way to look at it is the large majority of agents are still practising on the job as they try to negotiate million-dollar contracts for international superstars. You would not want to have life saving surgery conducted by someone who is still practising and not qualified. Have your next-door neighbour, the IT Technician, do the MOT on your car? This actually is happening with agents, forcing a number of high-profile footballers to the super agents who know how to work the market. So, if you were a young footballer, who only gets one career, would you let someone who is learning manage your million-dollar career?

If England have a few bespoke superstars, the list can quickly dwindle that there are only two or three agents that represent world-class players in the UK. For players who receive little advice in football academies on what would be best for their careers, they can easily be misguided towards an intermediary who is going to use them to build an agent's brand and not the players' career. A theory backed up with Alan Gernon's interview with Clifford Bloxham, Senior Vice President of Octagon, who believes FIFA's deregulation had an adverse effect on the industry. Giving a similar example to the above regarding intermediaries not having the right training or qualifications to manage people.

The argument being that aspiring intermediaries in other industries, film, music are all qualified, some through universities. Which begs the question, if FIFA were to regulate the industry again, should aspiring applicants be made to go through a course sponsored or managed by the local Football Association, with applicants perhaps given contacts with academies and lower league players to sort them off on their journey.

The course would be module based and require applicants to know the ins and out of the football landscape and how contracts can be negotiated. The length and university costs of the courses, licensed by FIFA, would weed out individuals who are in the industry for quick gain, perhaps reducing the amount of money flooding out of the game that could be used in grassroots football.

One way this and regulation could help is if FIFA deregulated the industry. This would allow them to set a % of the transfer fee to be paid to the agent to facilitate the deal. With potential fines imposed if the intermediary is touting their players to other teams without the knowledge of the current club. This could be speeded up by government intervention, possibly following on the back of Tracy Crouch's review on the need for regulation in the football industry.

One further step to avoid money leaving the game is for the player to pay their agents a monthly fee. We discussed earlier how agents are paid by clubs rather than the players to cut a deal, but perhaps if players paid their agents on retainers, or monthly, again at a percentage rate set by a governing body, there would be less money wasted and reinvested within football, possibly helping grow the women's game or youth football.

For example, a Premier League player earning £40,000 a week before tax, (£2,080,000 a year) would pay their agent £2000 a month, or 5%, which equates to £104,000 a year before tax. This represents one player; agents have a number of players on their books. This way the agent or agency would be paid to look after the players personal day-to-day life.

Critics of this method would argue agents would try to force wages up so they could earn more or try to move their players to the Premier League where there is more money. But with the new FFP regulations coming in, accounting for 70% of a club's turnover. Premier League clubs would not have the resources to match these wage demands, and the market would be forced to stabilise.

'Football Leaks' which was a system leak in association in the football world revealing the 'murky' dark side to football's financial side, reported the transfer deal to take Paul Pogba from Juventus to Manchester United netted his agent Mini Raiola a benefit to the tune of £41m. Some can criticise the agent for negotiating a fee of this value for himself, but perhaps the real problem is the industry allows people to make these deals.

It is often said history repeats itself, with Manchester City activating Erling Haaland £67m buy-out clause from Borussia Dortmund, the deal itself was considered cheap for one of Europe's most sought-after players. The deal is also reported to have been concluded with Haaland's agency netting £40m from the deal. The agency, Mini Raiola's, his last transfer deal before his sudden death in 2022. Whilst often painted in the media as a pantomime villain, the former pizza barista, turned tracksuit wearing agent, knew how to work the system to his and his player's favour. A system that has favoured agents in the recent transfer windows, but if the system allows it, is it wrong?

Agents can have several roles to the modern-day footballer and the above would actually re-align football agents with the roles agents play in other industries. Some footballers entrust their agents to look after the following for them during their career. Renewing their passport and visas might seem like second nature for most people, but for footballers, in particular youngsters coming to England, leaving their homeland for the first time, these are things they need guidance over.

The legal sides of the contract, but then comes where does the player stay, initially, some Premier League clubs may let the players stay in houses the football clubs owns, then some players rely on the agent to find them transportation, a car, or an advertisement deal where the player receives a new car in return the player will advertise the brand on social media.

Not all players would know where or what to buy when it comes to cars. As Gianluca Vialli noted before, he only got his first agent before his Chelsea move. Since then, there has been a mammoth shift in what goes into contracts, but it also shows how much certain players need doing for them.

Which perhaps shows another way where academies are failing footballers, with the success rate of academies in the low percentages, education but also basic life skills are needed to be taught to youngsters, with some of the unfortunate ones having the rug pulled from under them at a young age, they need to be ready to stand on their own two feet if they are left behind the fast-moving Premier League juggernauts.

In the summer of 2021, Cristiano Ronaldo, one of the world's greatest ever footballers announced he was going to leave Juventus after three years, despite being under contract, his agent Jorge Mendes set about finding a team that could accommodate the current contract and wages he had with the Turin based club. Mendes focused on Manchester City, a club who were failing to negotiate with Spurs over the transfer of Harry Kane and in need of a striker.

Once City refused to pay a reported £21m to Juventus and began to haggle, Mendes used this to his advantage, using the press to leverage a move to Manchester United. With all news channels questioning whether Manchester United would let one of their greatest ever players join their city rivals who had just won the league title.

United slid into negotiations and tied Ronaldo down to a two-year deal with a club option of a third. Paying Juventus £13.5m to secure his services and ensure he would not end up at their cross-city rivals.

Football clubs can use agents in their own way, Liverpool, in building their best team in thirty years regularly top the table in agents' fees in transfer windows. Using these agents' fees to secure key players in Jürgen Klopp's pressing system. Whilst clubs moan about the rise in agent fees and having to pay them, there are clubs that manipulate this system to their gain.

Looking at agent payment data between 2017 and 2020, has revealed that Liverpool have paid the second highest sum to intermediaries over the three-year period, a sum that stands at £118.7m (€139m). Topping the list in payments to player agents in the Premier League during the same period, Chelsea was second with (£110m) and Manchester City (£103.3m) make up the rest of the top three.

Daniel Geey comments in his book 'Done Deal': "Many agents do earn significant sums, but they are well rewarded partly because of the fragile and unpredictable nature of their job," he writes.

The glamorous signing ceremony is only the tip of the player-management iceberg. The primary role of a player's agent may be to understand when, on the one hand, to aggressively push for a transfer or a new contract with the club and when, on the other hand, to be the diplomat if a player is having trouble settling in, struggling with management, or not performing on the pitch. An agent does their best work when managing and leveraging situations (both positive and negative) to a player's advantage. In some cases, players are paid an 'image right' for the club to use their player, who they have just signed for millions, image on television, marketing promotions.

In one recent high-profile case, Alphonso Davies' agent, Nick Huoseh was reported by Rick Westhead, to have given the Canadian FA an ultimatum, to stop selling Davies' jersey online. He claimed, "National team players have never received royalties from jersey sales, and they should. We only want what is fair and they absolutely can and should do this."

Canada's sponsors were also warned they should not use any of the players images when marketing their products, unless royalties were paid to the player. This was part of the dispute with the current Canadian board, whom the players felt were not redistributing the money that was being made by the players' likeness back into the game or players.

In relation to football transfers, clubs need good agents for selling and buying players, and almost all clubs realise this. They build up relationships with trusted agents so that deals can be pushed through when they need to happen. This means clubs cannot afford to burn bridges with some agents.

The percentage of fees to agents in relation to the total player sales and additions during the three-year period sees Liverpool at the top of the list when it comes to Premier League clubs, with 15 per cent heading to agents. In a market where Liverpool is fishing in the same small pool as all the major clubs, finding a way to secure deals is vital to maintain the foundations built on their good scouting network.

Between 1st February 2017 and January 2018 Premier League clubs paid a net total of £211,011,187m to agents, more than the GDP of some of the world's smallest national economies. Premier League clubs set a precedent for spending these sums on agents to facilitate these transfer deals.

For Gee, he explains that an agent does have a role in football, beyond what we see. The transfer window does not start on January 1st, in fact, clubs and agents are talking all year long. If clubs tell their players they are not needed next year, it gives the players agent months in advance to look for a new club for their players.

In some cases, we see agents talk to owners over Directors of Football and pitch their players to them. When Everton, under the instruction of manager Rafael Benítez, sacked Marcel Brands so he could have more control over transfers. Only to see agent Kia Joorabchian organise a loan deal for his player Anwar El Ghazi, a winger from Aston Villa to Everton, with the Merseyside club in desperate need of centre-backs due to injuries.

Agents on behalf of their clients will do the negotiating between clubs, stopping the awkwardness of players asking for more money between contracts or transfers. This allows the player to play with freedom as the agent negotiates on their behalf. If a player wants £100k for their contract, but the deal is agreed at £60k, there are no hard feelings between the club, the board of directors and player.

This in principle works well, but when the agent does not take the contract offer back to the player and advises them not to sign it, is where the argument of should an agent be forced to show the player the deal and let them decide. With the case of Josh Maja and Sunderland, the player was not aware of several offers the club made to him.

Experienced agents do, however, stop bad contracts being signed. When Harry Kane signed a six-year deal in 2018 organised by his brother, it meant Spurs had all the negotiating powers when it came to any future transfers. So, when Manchester City came calling in the summer of 2021, the player was left frustrated by the mistake as City refused to pay Spurs' asking price. Leading to Kane skipping training to force a move, followed by an embarrassing climb down when the negotiations between his brother met an impasse. An experienced agent like Raiola would not have made this mistake.

Agents also protect the players, but in the odd case, leave the player out in the cold in the negotiation process, here are some examples of good and bad negotiations by agents, as well as an example of a transfer before agents came into the game. When fans read the next headline transfer news, it is easy to forget about the player that is the story of the headline. What goes through a player's mind when he is sold? For their children who are entrenched in schools with their friends who are forced to be uprooted and for their partners, if they are working, do they forgo their careers.

The money they earn, and sacrifice of certain aspects of their personal life, is often banded around as a reason why we should not consider this an issue, but with footballers having a high divorce rate and some of the examples shown in the book so far, some players do not get a say in the transfer, agents and Directors of Football are making the decision for them. So why do fans, managers and DOF's give them a tough time when the player refuses to move. If your family are settled and at an age when another club will not offer you the same terms, why would you move? If you still wanted to give 100% for a club and a new manager has taken away your locker, banned you from using the training ground.

With more and more players retiring and going into the media, we are slowly getting more access to players and stories regarding their moves. Ben Foster, former Watford goalkeeper has lifted the lid on transfer moves and discussed with agents on his podcast. "Fozcast, The Ben Foster Podcast." It provides the insight that fans would never normally see. In one episode, Ben Foster describes his failed move to Newcastle United and how his agent, Richard Lee, who Foster dubs the Goalkeeping Super-Agent, almost brokered the deal on his behalf.

Ben brings us a day which Richard dubs a dark day for Richard, an agent who at midday after the transfer window in the summer of 2022 called up Foster with a proposition. The day started with Lee in the morning due to go to Dublin, allegedly on the runway. He received intel that Karl Darlow, Newcastle's backup goalkeeper had gone down injured and was potentially out for a few months. They were going to need a third-choice goalkeeper. Richard phoned up Ben Foster to see if he could tout him as a free agent to Newcastle, Foster agreed, when Richard was in the air, he knew the domino effect would begin to fall.

Whilst in the air, with no signal, it allowed Richard to plan the move, but also look below at the other targets Newcastle had, Foster could have a move into the Championship. At Newcastle, Foster would have been the number 2, a backup to Newcastle's other new signing, Nick Pope. For Foster, who was a free agent mulling retirement, it becomes a waiting game, the thoughts of relocating a family from his current house in the South, all the way up to the North East. Foster admits that given his age and relocation, he set a wage limit for Newcastle to compensate him and his family on their move up North.

Richard jokes that Foster would not get this but would have been the best paid number 3 goalkeeper, once Darlow regained his fitness. Foster used a wage limit as a line to see if Newcastle really wanted him, for Foster, he was happy 'retired' with the podcast, so he had the power, especially with the transfer window closed.

Richard then began speaking to Newcastle over any deal, the line on the wages which Newcastle described as 'heavy' a bit too high on the wages. At this point, Richard begins the negotiation, at this point in Foster's career, Richard would lay down Foster's principles. For another player, there would have been compromises, and Richard describes how Newcastle, who were interested, came back with 'imaginative' proposals to try and make the deal work. It shows how quick deals for players can be done and almost understand how the frustration of why deals can sometimes take months to push through and go all the way to deadline day.

As the day dragged into the evening, Foster was thankful of Newcastle's fair offer, but given the knowledge they were unable and unwilling to match these demands, he wanted to be honest with the North East club. Richard was now instructed by Foster to explain the deal is likely not going to happen, whilst Richard is in an Irish airport, struggling for signal, Richard then is upfront that this is a red line. It is a fair and honest phone call to the club so they can move onto a new target. With the dial tone ringing off, the phone remained quiet for an hour. Before Newcastle rang back, with a compromise. They would match the salary Foster requested, but there would be no accommodation in the deal and there would be no further add-ons in Foster's contract.

At this point, Richard is juggling flights, trying to get a possible flight to Newcastle, a medical would be at 9, he would land at 5. He calls Foster with the unexpected update. Foster, trying to remain calm, was in the middle of lighting a barbecue, trying to not get a head of himself. At the unexpected call, Foster admits he had an unexpected feeling of dread, his agent, Richard was buzzing, but when Foster said give me half an hour, Richard knew this was not normal for Foster.

Half an hour drifted into an hour, Foster did his due diligence, deciding he would not move his family up North, Aaron Ramsdale of Arsenal explained that current manager, Eddie Howe, only allows players one day off a week, which would make travelling to his family difficult. It was an incredible offer considering Foster's age, after sitting down with his family, Foster knew he could not do it.

Ringing Richard and confirming his family would come first, he had the Fozcast, which is doing well, family was more important over money. The deal was off, and Newcastle moved onto another target, for Richard, he ended up back where his day started, Stansted Airport, deflated that his good and unexpected work had not been successful, but his player was happy overall, a day in the life of an agent.

To give perspective to how transfers have changed over the years, in 1983, Howard Kendall was looking for a striker to finish off his squad overhaul at Everton. When he found out Everton were interested, he was delighted, but recalls the club doctor at his current team Wolves, giving him his medical files to pass onto Everton. Even telling Gray that Everton would see the size of the file (a full ring binder) and would turn him down at the medical. Gray jokes that he went home and looked through the file, allowing some of the documents to go missing in the fireplace.

On arriving at Bellfield, Everton's Club Doctor, who was conducting the medical, remarked to Gray that, "Everton believed he had a chronic knee issue, but there was no paperwork to support it in the file Gray provided." Gray brushed it off as rumours in football, and passed the medical at Everton, he went onto join the club and was an integral part of the club winning the League and European Cup Winners Cup in 1985. Two weeks after the season, and still seething, but motivated to go one better, after Manchester United defeated the Merseyside club one nil in the FA Cup final, stopping them from a historical treble.

The champagne from winning the League and European Cup Winners Cup double with Everton was still flowing as Gray decided to lay down roots in Formby, a small town on the coast in Merseyside. Purchasing a brand-new house, he and his wife were unloading the boxes, Howard Kendall pulls up in his car. Gray mentions he turned to his wife and told her to stop and re-pack the van. Kendall had come to tell Gray that he had an opportunity to sign Gary Lineker and Gray was being sold as part of the deal to fund the move.

With Everton facing restrictions in finances that came with English clubs banned from European football. Gray initially showed resistance, then asked Kendall, "do you want me to go?" Kendall nodded and Gray left Everton. Gray accepted Kendall did not want him anymore and repacked the house. Imagine being that player, after being part of a significant title winning team to be told, we have found a better younger player, and you won't be in the match day squad if he signs. (There was only one substitute at the time allowed in football at the time.)

It is not always the clubs who are cutthroat in terms of transfer deals. Anyone watching Amazon's All or Nothing documentary, discovered the truth behind Pierre-Emerick Aubameyang's ordeal. After benching the player for a disciplinary breach, Arsenal was looking at options to move the player on, find a way for all parties to move on. Barcelona was interested in the player, but due to financial issues, had no money for a transfer fee and were not willing to meet Arsenal's valuation of the player. With a statement reached and no side willing to budge.

The documentary shows a dark side to the window, the players agent and Barcelona asked Aubamayang to fly to Barcelona, a Peter Odemwinge move to force Arsenal's hand to agree a deal. The documentary shows Arsenal when they discovered Aubamayang had not arrived for training on transfer deadline day. When they ask where the player is? They discover, via Sky Sports and Twitter, the player is at Barcelona airport, signing Barcelona shirts, despite no deal being in place.

You can understand why Arsenal in the end let the player leave on a free transfer, choosing to save the millions on wages and get rid of a dressing room distraction, a player on a smaller wage, the club could have let the player hang out to dry. Arsenal waited up until the last moment, to see if they could receive any fee, before agreeing the deal late in the day.

Clubs have also been known to collaborate with agents during transfer windows to get what they both want, money and soaring prices. When the Premier League signed it, the previous record-breaking £8.4bn television deal which would last between 2016–2019, saw European clubs seize an advantage. Putting a premium on all transfers to the Premier League. If the teams' players wanted to leave the European clubs, the clubs instructed agents to tout their clubs' players to the Premier League where a bidding war was likely, the higher the transfer fee, better for the club, but also more commotion for the agent, from the buying club.

UEFA President Aleksander Čeferin stresses that agent fees have become astronomical, with some cases agents demanding 50% of the transfer fee or they will tout their players to another club. Stressing that UEFA were drafting proposals to re-regulate agents and look at ways of fixing the industry where clubs manipulated situations into their Favour.

Fabrizio Romano, a respected transfer insider, tweeted out in March 2022, that Barcelona were in negotiations with Raphinha's agent, discussions had taken place over a five-year deal and the fee was discussed as £25m. Leeds United's relegation release clause, Leeds were in the middle of the Premier League season, and this could be seen as unsettling their key player that would keep them from relegation. If Leeds stayed in the division, the price would be £75m.

Something Barcelona would struggle to afford with their finances currently. They did sign him for £75m once they activated further economic leavers to bypass the La Liga spending reviews. So, their motivation is to unsettle the player, have a pre-agreement in the hope that Leeds are relegated, if they survive, Leeds have an unhappy player on their hands. It is deals like these, outside of transfer windows, that have UEFA balancing finely on a seesaw. These clubs who benefit from these deals are the same clubs who want more money and to break away and form their European Super League. If UEFA or FIFA punish them, it will only fuel their desire to break away further.

It is deals like these that infuriate fans. Mal, a Leeds fan of thirty years, agrees. "It angers you as a fan. This could help relegate a club like Leeds, then Barcelona, breaking all the rules benefit from it. But where is the media? This is corruption in football, but they ignore it. If Leeds broke transfer rules, we would be sanctioned. Transfer bans. But here is a massive story and the media are ignoring it, isn't it their job."

Rob, a Manchester United fan, agrees. "There is bias, if it favours the clubs the media make money off, they will not report these stories. I'm sure United have done it in the past and the media has turned the other way. Currently Rob is seeing the other side of the coin."

"We're struggling at the moment." United will record their worst ever points total in the Premier League and the players have seemingly downed tools against Interim Manager Ralf Rangnick.

"The players are blaming everyone but themselves. The manager, training, owners, leaking private information to former player Paul Scholes so he can air it in public. My football club is a laughingstock, and it does hurt. The owners have made mistakes, transfers have been bad, but the players are not giving a 100%. That is on them. What is worse, when José Mourinho, Louis Van Gaal and Rangnick call out the players and ask for more, they down tools, get the manager sacked, expect the red carpet rolled out for them. Players ask their agents to find them a way out if they fall out of the team due to form rather than fight for their place. It sickens fans, all we ask as a minimum is give 100% in each game."

Mal stresses another key issue with players and their agents. "Players are also guilty of treating clubs like stepping stones." This player... says, "he wants to move clubs, publicly in an interview, no respect to the current club he is in, who scouted him, brought him through the academy, then to publicly tell them he is looking elsewhere mid-season is disrespectful. It is a come and get me." We discussed his statement in the press.

"Even in the words, I want to join a mid-table Premier League club, then in two years move to a top-4 club. He's telling the fans of the club that could pay him £100,000 a week (£5.2m a year), that he will only serve two years of that five-year contract, oh, but he will ask for millions in a loyalty bonus when he demands to be sold. He will probably make business decisions to stop playing if the team is losing to avoid injury."

If agents were paid on a retainer, it would stop them touting their clients to new clubs, agencies could look after the player, their family, and their interests, like other industries. They would still make money, but they would be audited by local authorities in football. It would also help if the national authorities had the same regulations to keep consistent with the rules and eliminate any grey areas.

Agents' contracts are restricted to two years, they can be fewer and extended. But this could be the reason why agents feel they need to move players between clubs, milk the cash cow while they can, or before the player leaves them or decides to not renew their contract, perhaps giving the agent more stability could help take the impetus out of the desire to move their clients.

Taking a deeper dive into the UK's average agent commission which hovers around 5%. Commission is calculated with regards to the player's gross guaranteed remuneration under the deal. For example, 5% of the players salary and any signing on fee under the employment contract. Not 5% of the transfer fee. If you assume a salary of £1m per year, throughout a four-year contract minus 5% = £50,000—generally paid on an annual basis. Depending on agreements and possibly tax, the payment is normally paid for by the clubs on behalf of the player. The exception being if the agent is working on behalf of the club on a transfer, then they are permitted to frame their commission to the transfer fee.

Under the current system, all parties can pay the agent. The buying club, selling club and the player. For example, Liverpool could ask an Agent A to facilitate a transfer away from Liverpool to another club. They could offer the agent 5% of the fee. The buying club could offer and agree with the agent 5% of the players signing on fee and wages. Then the player pays their agent 5% as their retainer.

This creates the huge conflict of interest which has been created by the deregulation of agents and legalisation where the agent benefits three times from one transfer deal. How is this in the players best interest if the agent is always looking for a move every year? Players saying, they struggle to settle, yet don't look to buy houses because they know they are on the move within months.

An argument against agencies is that we would be creating businesses who will be looking at annual turnover and dividends. Accountants will be pushing them to build the foundations of capitalism. Before long agencies could be looking to move players to make more money, but this is where the regulation would stop this and focus agents to look after their clients' basic needs more. It puts the responsibility back on the player. Do they want to make money? Train hard, be patient and become a superstar. It becomes a simple choice for the footballer, focus on building your career, but do not forget to keep playing to your maximum and train to become better.

Agents starting out can be the white knight football needs, for everyone bad agent there are those who are working hard, putting in the hours for their clients. Every year hundreds of players are released up and down the football pyramid, these agents are worth their fees. Building reports, stats, and videos of their clients. Contacting football clubs in the hopes to gain their client a new contract and stay professional, helping them with everyday life, giving them advice on mortgages, helping their children move schools.

Managers do not always help the equation, rather than talk to players and help them understand the situation, they can be known to bomb players out of the squad. Forming 'bomb squads' where unwanted players are forced to train alone. Joe Hart recently described how Spurs Manager Nuno Espírito Santo came up to him before they had trained and told him to find a new club, saying he was not good enough to be a backup at Spurs. The former England number 1 went onto Scotland and Celtic and subsequently won the league.

Former Manchester City player Nedum Onuoha discussed how Roberto Mancini forced him to train alone and took away his first team locker to force him to find a new club on Peter 'Tubes' Dale Golf Life YouTube channel. Detailing how this affected his mental health when he loved the club and had dedicated his career to the club through the academy before the millions flooded through the club.

Then there was Ronald Koeman who took away Oumar Niasse's locker at Everton to force him out of the club. Problem was Niasse, for what he may have lacked in talent, he put on the pitch 100% commitment, passion, and love for the club. When Director of Football Steve Walsh signed multiple number tens and no striker, it was Niasse, who with Everton struggling in the bottom three after a tough start, scored two goals as Everton fought back to beat Bournemouth. Koeman was sacked weeks later after losing the dressing room.

Simon Jordan has been a big advocate for reforming the agent practice within the game to stop a significant proportion of money being lost out of the game. He wants players to pay their agents on a retainer and not have the clubs pay agents to facilitate deals. Or where they do, it is capped at a low percentage depending on the size of the transfer fee. Simon has had direct experiences with agents and whilst some people would argue it is one view, from the owner, whose money it is, his dealings do highlight issues with agents that deregulation has caused.

Recalling a transfer deal in his book where Crystal Palace targeted two players from Skonto Riga from the Latvia league. Palace paid £650,000 for goalkeeper Aleksandrs Kolinko and £1.5m for winger Andrejs Rubins, Simon when dealing with the players agent, Phil Graham, notes the agent wanted a significant fee for the transfer, Simon did not want to pay him a fee for working for the players in negotiating their contracts, but also, paying the fee, Graham said he would lower his players wage demands to meet Palace's wage structure if he agreed to the payment, so much for putting a player's interests first.

Another example Simon gives on agents is why some players actually need them, creating a balance to his arguments, with Palace needing an injection of talent and facing relegation to League 1, he went to Bradford, also facing relegation from the Premier League and wanting to get Palace hero David Hopkin back for a fee of £1.5m, he met Bradford Chairman Geoffrey Richmond, who was desperate to sell the player as the club where facing financial issues relegation could bring, to Simon's surprise, during the meeting between the two chairman, Hopkin was called into the meeting by Richmond and asked how he would feel on the move to Palace.

Hopkin announced he was happy at the club and willing to stay and fight for a place in the team. Only to be met by the following outburst by Richmond, "I don't like you, never have liked you, if you want to stay, by all means stay, but I will make your life a misery."

Hopkin countered with "I've never met you, Chairman."

At which Richmond was forthright with, "I don't care, I don't like you." Hopkin signed for Palace a few minutes later after leaving the room.

Not all agents are bad and to give parity to the discussion, Joel Macadar, an agent, went onto BT Sport to describe the life of an agent and what is their role in the transfer world. He has his own sports agency which looks after sporting clients. Getting into the agency level whilst he was starting out, almost working out as an intermediary, touting clients to other clubs on behalf of their agents if they were looking for a move. Starting to search for players who had been released from clubs or academies to build his client base, previously having a desire to be a footballer, Macadar understands the business of football, but emphasises he wants to be there and manage the career of younger players and be there to guide them. Stating older, established players are more likely to consider football a job, and that some players in the lower league live off a day-to-day lifestyle.

Macadar argues an agent is required and better than a family, is that an agent has the knowledge in how to negotiate, get the best deal, he emphasises the player should always be the priority and the family may make mistakes or be taken advantage off. This book earlier looked at the example of the mistake Harry Kane's brother made not having a release clause in his contract with Daniel Levy.

A good agent can be a mentor to the player, but also discusses with the club's hierarchy deals so the player can focus on football. Macadar explains how if two teams are bidding for a player, how clauses, such as goal bonuses and assist rewards can enter the equation to inflate the weekly wage to compete with bigger clubs.

When questioned why younger players chose to move to clubs for £20,000 a week to sit on a bench, when they could go to a club for £5000 and play every game? Macadar emphasises an agent should have the experience to negotiate deals, as the clubs will have a DOF, a manager, lawyer and accountants looking at and negotiating the deal, the agent is there to get the best deal, not always the best money, the first aim is to get to the first team, or play for the first team, for a young player, it should be about the pathway to the first team and the coaching staff.

He even accepts that some deals should be incentivised, a smaller based salary with bonuses for good performance and that it is down to the player to perform. When pressed by Harry Redknapp if one club offered him a huge agent fee for the player, more than another club, Macadar still maintains that it is about the player and the ambition of the player in the future. The agent would get money from the deal and then more from the next deal with a bigger club.

In this scenario, the agent would be telling the player they must keep performing to get a new deal. Macadar is not sure on regulation, he thinks on certain aspects that can be managed would be ok, he acknowledges that there are some bad agents as much as there is bad owners and DOF who force players out and break promises, but he doesn't think regulation would stop an agent taking a significant agent fee in the millions if the player is coming towards the end of his career and this would be the agents last big pay day.

In fairness to some agents, they are not all bad or looking to take money from the game. Football clubs can ask an agent to find their client a new club if they have fell out of favour with the manager, or, as we seen during the aftershocks of Covid-19, help the club sell the player because they need to balance the books. In the following example, it also shows how clubs can overlook talent when they were not sure they were available.

Recalling his work from the 2022 summer transfer window, football agent Christian Emile sat down, recalling his summer work and the transfer of one of his emerging players in Georgian Khvicha Kvaratskhelia to Napoli to football insider Fabrizio Romano. Kvaratskhelia's talents had outgrown his club Dinamo Batumi of the Georgian League, just one year after joining for £7m from Russian side, Rubin Kazan, Batumi were looking to move Kvaratskhelia on for a small profit and use the proceeds to keep the club afloat following the collapse of football finances following Covid-19. Emile was tasked by the club with finding a new home for Kvaratskhelia and quickly, it was to be harder than he initially expected for the tricky Georgian winger.

Working currently for CAA agency managing their player portfolios, Emile has also worked for football clubs in managing players and therefore has operated on both sides of the fence when it comes to buying and selling players. It therefore explains why Dinamo Batumi enlisted his help in selling their player due to his contacts within the game, something smaller clubs may not be able to have and therefore reduce their market.

Emile explains, "I've been fortunate to know Kvaratskhelia for a while now, another one of my clients, Leonid Slutsky, had returned to Rubin Kazan, following a stint in the English Championship." It was through this working relationship; Emile was instructed that Kvaratskhelia could be one to watch for the future.

Following the games, Kvaratskhelia was 18 years old, Leonid began to build the team around the young Georgian and results began to pick up. Emile had several clients at the club and a young player making waves in the Russian division which has similar physicalities to the English divisions that Leonid had coached in a few years earlier. So why did several clubs miss out on the Georgian? "In general, English clubs are not looking to buy from the Russian leagues."

In the past, a few players who have made the jump have failed to adapt. "They (English clubs) are looking to the established European divisions and the guarantees of the South American League, where they have been able to pick up hidden gems. Countries where players have been able to adapt to the major five leagues. Unfortunately for Rubin Kazan, it was the height of feeling the effects from Covid-19. Clubs were looking to spend money on players. Or, players who may not have been the finished article, they want players to have an impact immediately. Why would Premier League clubs trek all the way to Russia to sign a Georgian player? With all due respect to Georgia, they have not produced many valuable players."

Perhaps it was any scouting they missed a potential bargain when the players market value crashed. Emile discusses clubs that were tentative on Kvaratskhelia. Tottenham Hotspurs made enquiries, "they were interested in sure. Juventus made an enquiry, most of them you heard in the media, were looking, they could see the quality, but they did not put the money down. Rubin were asking for £20m originally."

"Kvaratskhelia was available, here's what happened. I offered Khvicha Kvaratskhelia to many top clubs around Europe. But clubs didn't bid due to his nationality, had he been Croatian, clubs would have spent the money, another player, Mykhailo Mudryk the Ukrainian, Everton had a £35m bid rejected by Shakhtar Donetsk in the same window because they wanted more. Kvaratskhelia had more stats, in a more physical league. Both are good players, but Mudryk before this window was a player who was not a big part of the team."

Everton had stolen a march with their scouting but couldn't get the deal done. "Now, Shakhtar Donetsk wanted £56m for Mudryk, it is so frustrating when clubs do not see the talent, in some leagues Covid-19 has pulled in the transfer fees, in others it has stayed the same. It is unfortunate, but this is the way clubs operate. For sure, clubs will now be scouting Georgia and the Ukrainian divisions." Fabrizio pushes Emile on the price, whether other clubs had put in firm offers and generally, why did Kvaratskhelia only be sold for £9m?

"As for the price, Rubin were correct with their valuation, clubs were not looking to invest in players and pay significant transfer fees." They would have several needs and their budgets were not infinite. "The funny thing is, West Ham spent £30m on Nikola Vlašić in 2021, Rubin had an offer of £10m for Kvaratskhelia, which they rejected, the market and leagues showed no consistency."

"Fair enough, but for a player of Kvaratskhelia talent he is worth more than that. Players are moving for over £100m pounds now, Kvaratskhelia has been doing this for years now. He has hit the ground running at Napoli in the Champions League, for sure, he will be a £100m in two years' time. Many clubs had video conferences with me and Kvaratskhelia, stalling for time, looking for budgets, maybe we will come next year, we must qualify for the European group stages before we bid."

No clubs put firm bids in, Napoli were the only club who tabled an offer. Half of what Rubin Kazan wanted, they may have made a gamble on the player, but they have turned £9m into potentially £100m. "I hope when we as agents propose players from emerging nations, clubs will take us seriously, football is global now and Kvaratskhelia is an example of hard-working players making good of themselves. I was trying to help clubs out, which agents are usually accused of not doing, I am really happy for Kvaratskhelia and what he has achieved."

Emile and his work on the transfer of Kvaratskhelia, is a fine example of how a young emerging talent from a non footballing nation was helped to reach Champions League stardom at age 21. There are several players who may have missed such an opportunity in the past, highlighting how agents can be a force for good for players and football clubs, especially in difficult financial times for the clubs, it is how we regulate the industry to ensure more are like Emile in the future which will be key to footballs ongoing success.

At the turn of the year, FIFA did bring forward some changes into the regulation of agents, and I have summarised the findings here, some have been discussed in the chapter. They have gone back to calling intermediaries, agents. The pantomime baddies of the football world are required to pass a formal set of exams. Under the new proposals, there is a 3% fee set on the players wage when negotiating a renewed contract. Whilst setting a level is seen as an improvement, it does beg the question whether agents will steer their clients towards teams who offer the highest wage, rather than the players best pathway.

There is also a set floor in the inconsistency of the fees set when transferring a player. A buying club would be required to pay 3% to the players agent if they are the active influencers in the deal, but if the selling club ask an agent to find a buyer for one of their players, then the selling club is set at 10%. But this raises more questions if the buying club are offered the player by the agent, and the selling club gives no permission for the agent to tout the player. Who pays the fee? In this instance it should be 0%, if it is the selling club, this would give agents more incentives to actively seek their players without permission from the current club. Any commission or consultancy, as we saw with the Ben Foster deal earlier in the book, would be set at 3%.

Agents representing minors is not going to stop. It is still a rule they cannot represent a player until they are 17 years old and are ready for their first professional contract. This will continue to see more of the best youth players turning their backs on their academies as agents continue to turn their heads away from their current teams.

The rule stating agents can begin to talk to youth players six months before their professional contracts (16 and a half years old). Now considering your player is born in September, players who are born in August would have agents around them, as their teammates negotiate new deals. Leaving parents or guardians to navigate around financial minefields with professional business people and lawyers of the clubs.

Then there is the question of how FIFA police it? Do they want to? We have reviewed stories earlier on how clubs and agents have broken the current rules, and nothing has happened to the degree it should. It may stop teams like Liverpool topping the charts for agents' fees because the percentage fee will cap what agents can earn. Perhaps, a professional regulator is the answer, but this would only work if they were set up as an independent body, if by FIFA or the Football Associations, are they truly independent if they can fine, expel, or have the favoured Premier League teams docked points?

The solution to football's problem with agents is there. Agents are often painted as the pantomime villain, and in some cases, they are with the requests or demands they make. But, like all industries, there are AGENTS who are good at their job and put their client first. Regulation to regain control of the industry seems necessary, for fairness to the players and the clubs. Players deserve to be remunerated, but only with the correct practices.

FIFA needs to get a grip on the industry and allow local federations more power to challenge agents and apply limits to what agents can make from transfer deals to root out the ones who are putting money before player's health. The solution is around the table. The bigger question is, does football want to implement it?

Chapter 12
Is Financial Fair Play Fair?

If Money Does Not Grow on Trees?
Michel Platini: "I just want clubs to spend the money they have."

Introduced in 2009, UEFA's concept of Financial Fair Play (FFP) has helped to drastically reduce club losses over the last decade. The argument from Platini was that certain clubs, owned by billionaires, could just spend beyond their means and rack up huge losses to buy their team's success. A club with no billionaire owner was at the mercy of the other clubs who could buy players with no regard to their losses or impact of the balance sheet. FFP was introduced to create a level playing field financially, ensuring competitive football divisions. In reality, it has had the opposite effect and was met with surprising resistance from the big European Leagues who relied on certain clubs to make them money.

The aim of FFP was to help football clubs make themselves more sustainable and put downward pressure on clubs to fund their transfers on player trading. It had the opposite effect with wages and transfer fees spiralling. Like all businesses following Adam Smith's market is guided by the invisible hand principles they adapted and looked to increase their commercial revenues to allow them to continue to grow their profit levels to continue to spend in vast amounts.

At UEFA, Premier League, and football league this is broken down easier as:

- Clubs playing in UEFA competitions (Champions League and Europa League) can make losses of up to €30m over three seasons (€10m per season).

- Premier League clubs can make losses of up to £105m over three seasons (£35m per season) and can generally spend only £7m more on wages than they did in the previous season. (£134,615 a week more.)
- Football League clubs can make losses of up to £39m over three seasons (£13m per season).

Breaking these rules can lead to sanctions for the football club which can include the following:

- Transfer embargoes.
- Points Deductions.
- Squad size restrictions.
- Expulsion from UEFA competitions.
- Sanctions and spending scrutinised.

UEFA have sanctioned two clubs for breaking FFP rules in the last ten years. In 2015, Dynamo Moscow were the first club to be sanctioned in relation to their significant overspend. Over the three-year period, Dynamo were adjudged to have accrued losses of €257,268,000. At the time, over €200m more than was permitted under FFP rules. UEFA ruled a ban on European competition to be sufficient and the club was barred from that season's Europa League consequently. All punishments and hearings are chaired by UEFA's Club Financial Control Board (CFCB), these can also lead to softer sanctions or spending restrictions.

Galatasaray agreed to a settlement deal as they became the second club to breach FFP. Initially, the club received a range of penalties which included spending requirements to be audited by the panel. This would allow them to compete in UEFA competitions. Galatasaray did not keep up with these spending requirements and had subsequently banned them from the 2016/17 Europa League.

Most fans have been blissfully unaware their clubs transfer spending habits have led to sanctions by the CFCB. Manchester City, PSG, Monaco, and Inter Milan have all been under 'settlement agreements' or plea bargains with the CFCB. These settlements included several sanctions, fines, squad size reductions and future spending usually laid down at the end of the year. Daniel Geey breaks down Manchester City's settlement in his book.

- A maximum loss of €20m for the 2013/14 season and a €10m loss for the 2014/15 season.
- No more than €60m to be spent on transfers in the summer transfer window.
- A freeze on players' wages for at least the next season.
- A limit of 21 players to be registered for the 2014/15 season Champions League season squad.
- A €10m fine based on the 2013/14 Champions League prize money and an additional €10m fine based on their 2014/15 Champions League campaign prize money. An extra €40m fine would have been handed down if City failed to comply with the above conditions.

Delving into UEFA's FFP statistics allows us to evaluate whether their concept of controlling clubs' spending was working. Billionaire owners can no longer lavish millions to buy players for their clubs. If a club wishes to spend money above their allotted budget, they are required to sell players to boost their spending power. Increasingly seeing more transfers amortisation over a period of a player's contract.

An easy example being, Player A is purchased by a club for £25m. The buying club does not pay the £25m upfront, it spreads the payment over five years. (Assuming the player signs a five-year deal)

£25m divided by 5 years = £5m would be paid in July of each year if the transfer were conducted in the summer window. The £5m would affect the budget of the buying club and would see the transfer amortised in their club accounts.

Amortisation is one of the ways football clubs are allowed to spend the vast sums of money they do and stay within the confines of FFP. Football finance expert, Kieran Maguire broke this down for the Daily Mail after Chelsea's recent spending spread over the 6 months covering the summer 2022 transfer window and the January 2023 window. As the signing of Mykhailo Mudryk took Chelsea's transfer spending to a record level in Premier League history, at £445m surpassing the £328m spent by Manchester City in 2017–18, many people have wondered how this can be achieved in the era of Financial Fair Play (FFP).

Under Premier League FFP rules, clubs are allowed to lose £105m over a rolling three-year period, but there are adjustments for virtue spending areas such as infrastructure spend, women's teams, academies and community projects. In addition, further allowances were granted following Covid and the impact it had on clubs playing matches behind closed doors and the increased costs of Covid compliance. UEFA's rules are slightly different, with new financial and sustainability rules introduced in the summer of 2022 that allow clubs to lose up to €60m (£53m) over three years, but the virtue spending allowances are ignored.

Chelsea posted operating losses of £387m in the three years of their most recent published accounts to 30 June 2021. However, the club was able to claim a substantial amount in respect of Covid (Everton, for example, who normally generate around £60m a year less than Chelsea in ticket sales, have claimed £190m of Covid-related costs).

They are, therefore, probably in a relatively strong opening FFP position because player sale profits are deducted from these losses. Chelsea have not however published their 2021–22 accounts at the time of writing, where the club was unable to sell tickets for a period of time or generate money from merchandise and other products and services, following the government sanctions and freezing of the assets of former owner Roman Abramovich. It is uncertain how both the Premier League and UEFA will treat this issue for FFP purposes.

Abramovich lent the club over £1.5billion following his acquisition of the club in 2003, which funded operating losses that averaged £900,000 a week during his period of ownership.

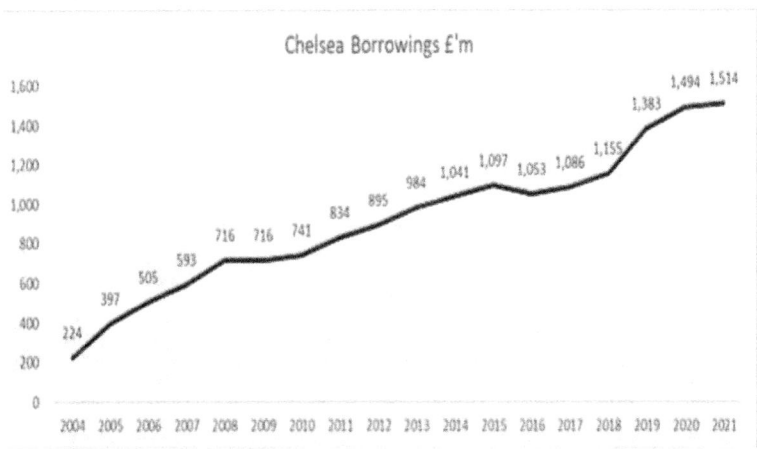

Abramovich's loans came with the benefit of being interest free. This contrasts with the approach taken by Manchester United's owners, who borrowed from the markets and have run up finance costs, dividends, and management fees of over £1 billion, causing resentment from fans who would rather see the money spent on a now dilapidated Old Trafford and the playing squad.

Chelsea benefits significantly from the way the accountants deal with player transactions. If you buy a player the cost is spread, via a process called amortisation, over the contract life. In the case of Mudryk, his £88.6m fee will therefore be divided by the 8½ year contract and gives an annual cost for FFP purposes of just over £10 million a year, and for the season ending 2022–23 it will be half that as he has been signed in January.

Similarly, the club has signed Fofana on a seven-year deal, Badiashile on a six-and-a-half-year contract, Cucurella for six years and Sterling for five. This benefits Chelsea in terms of substantially reducing the annual amortisation cost. An estimated £420m spent on players in 2022–23 to date on an average of a six-year contracts works out as a £70m annual cost in the accounts, plus wages of course.

If the players had signed on four-year contracts, then the annual cost would have been £105m a year (£420m/4 years) and there would have been an increased chance of breaching FFP.

Chelsea's Player sales in £m.

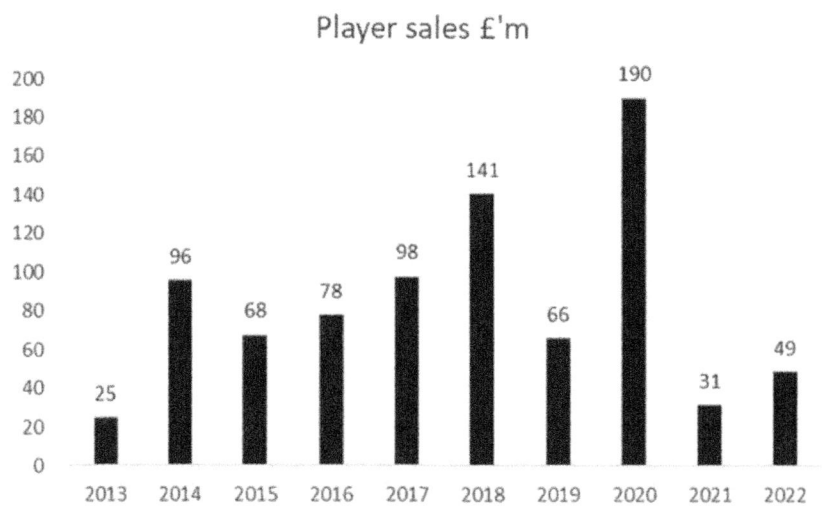

In respect of player sales, under FFP the whole profit is taken immediately into consideration in the calculations. Chelsea have flown under the radar here for many years. Over the course of the last decade Chelsea have made player sale profits of £688m, almost twice the sum of their nearest rivals in the big six, and over half a billion pounds more than Manchester United.

This figure is the accounting profit on player sales, which is the sales proceeds less the book value of players.

The sale of the likes of Eden Hazard, Oscar, David Luiz—perhaps at the top of their market prices—plus the sales of academy-developed players such as Tammy Abraham and Fikayo Tomori have been very lucrative for Chelsea. Chelsea made €120m (£106m) in 2021 from winning the Champions League by beating Manchester City in the final.

When this match took place, they were the two clubs who had incurred the biggest losses in Premier League history, although this was not an issue for either the club owners or their fans. In addition to this, Chelsea have subsequently won the UEFA Super Cup and FIFA Club World Cup, which adds to their revenues. A run to the quarterfinals of the Champions League in 2021–22, in front of fans who were once again able to buy matchday tickets, will also have generated substantial sums. The downside of Chelsea's approach to player recruitment is that if the players do not prove to be successful then the club is stuck with them on expensive contracts for an extended period of time.

This can create bottlenecks for young players coming through the ranks and prevent future signings. This may be because recruited players choose to sit on their contracts, meaning Chelsea are then committed to paying them substantial sums each year for a prolonged period. If the new owners at Chelsea, Todd Boehly and Clearlake Capital, have recruited players who under-perform, and the jury is out at present given the club's 10th place position in the Premier League, then there will be less wiggle room going forwards into the 2023–24 season.

For every £1 generated from qualifying for the Champions League, clubs earn 23 pence in the Europa League and 11 pence in the Europa Conference. Failure to qualify for any of these competitions would mean Chelsea would be hamstrung in the summer 2023 transfer window.

This is because both the UEFA and Premier League cost control rules would be impacted by the lower revenues the club would generate. Players Chelsea might be trying to recruit over the summer may be cautious about joining as many will want to play in the Champions League.

Chelsea would be able to take some solace from the fact that the last time they won the Premier League was 2016–17, when they did not have the distraction of European adventures and therefore could concentrate on the main domestic competition. Whether that will be easy with a resurgent Manchester United, Arsenal worthy present leaders of the Premier League and Manchester City likely to invest heavily following Pep Guardiola extending his contract is uncertain.

Chelsea's spending splurge under new owner Todd Boehly

Raheem Sterling—£45m plus £10m potential add-ons (five-year contract)
Kalidou Koulibaly—£33.8m (four-year contract)
Marc Cucurella—£55m plus £7m potential add-ons (six-year contract)
Wesley Fofana—£70m plus £10m potential add-ons (seven-year contract)
Carney Chukwuemeka—£20m (six-year contract)
Gabriel Slonina—£12m
Cesare Casadei—£12.6m plus £4.2m potential add-ons (six-year contract)
Pierre-Emerick Aubameyang—£10.6m (two-year contract)
Denis Zakaria—loan, £2.6m fee plus £30m option to buy.

Mykhailo Mudryk—£88m (8.5-year contract)
Benoit Badashile—£33.7m (7.5-year contract)
Joao Felix—loan, £9m fee
Andrey Santos—£11m
David Datro Fofana—£10m (7.5-year contract)

From Maguire's analyses, it is not just Chelsea whose accountants have been sharpening their pencils. A byproduct of FFP means most clubs are living in a financial bubble, one which Covid-19 threatened to burst. Prior to Covid-19, FFP seemed to be working, with UEFA boasting clubs spending powers had been curbed and was moving in the right direction. UEFA argued that in 2017, combined club operating profits had risen to €600m in 2017, compared with combined losses of €1.7bn in 2011 before the restraints of FFP kicked in.

In the Premier League before the cost controls took effect for the 2012/13 season, twelve of the 20 Premier League clubs made a loss, overall, the league recorded total losses of £291m. Under the first season of spending restrictions, the loss had been transferred into £198m cumulative profit for the clubs. Deloitte believed this to be the first since 1999, Premier League clubs had boasted a combined profit. Fast forward to the 2016/17 season, 18 of the Premier League clubs made a profit.

Criticisms of FFP levelled by fans and football pundits mostly lie in the matter that the owner cannot invest in a player in the transfer window. With most Premier League clubs now owned by billionaires, they are restricted in the investment in players they can make. Their parent companies (where the owner has made their money) are also restricted in how they can sponsor the club, so the owners cannot sponsor their own club to wash it full of money.

New or aspiring owners cannot challenge the already established clubs in football where the sponsors are attracted to. Successful clubs will earn more revenue, thus giving them the greater margin to sign better players, the cycle is likely to continue as this will mean greater success on and off the pitch, so the margins are wider with each year.

Meaning FFP, whilst the statistics show it has worked, has been bad for competition, widening the gap between clubs as aspiring clubs are restricted on their spending and wage budgets, meaning the competitive balance has shifted. In practice we have seen United go a decade without a league title, spending millions more than the rivals below them in the Premier League and as of the 2021 season, finish with their worst ever Premier League points total.

A significant gap between them and Liverpool and Manchester City having spent similar net transfer spend and wage bills. They still have room to spend in the transfer window due to their commercial pulling power. In comparison, Leicester City's Premier League win, was seen as the start of FFP working, a break in the strangle hold some clubs had on the League title, but it was the opposite, in fact it appears to have been what most side critics claimed as a fluke or outlier.

Leicester winning the league in 2015 under FFP should have meant with the Champions League revenue coming that they should have been able to compete for the title the following year. Attracting more players of a better standard. But the opposite occurred, Leicester's players were poached by more established clubs, offering more wages than Leicester could budget for. Players such as N'Golo Kante departed to Chelsea for £32m in 2016 and in the following year, also to Chelsea, Danny Drinkwater was sold for £30m. Leicester did reinvest the money, but the players moved as there was more wages available at the London club.

Despite a fairytale run in the Champions League, getting through to the knockout stages, Leicester plummeted in the league in 2016 and finished 12th, 35 points less than they had the year before. Quick on the heels of the Chelsea bound pair was Riyad Mahrez, signing for Manchester City in 2018 for £61m in a long-drawn-out affair. The trade-off for fans accepting that some clubs would have more transfer budget and wages is that their club benefits from the sales and can refresh their squads whilst slowly trying to grow commercially.

But where the line seems to be drawn is when the so-called 'top six' start exploring the "International 39th game" or demanding and moaning to have the League Cup scrapped. These are all to give more rest, if the League Cup were scrapped so they could focus more on European competition and the 'top 6' would and have demanded they be given a bigger share of the TV money other the rest of the 14 Premier League teams.

This would just further enable these clubs to grow further and dictate the transfer market in their favour, with other clubs unable to ever build themselves up and deliver on a project. FFP has also fuelled the 'self-proclaimed top 6' English clubs' ambition for a European Super League, delivering more commercial revenue for these clubs than the Champions League. When the fallout from these shady plans were revealed to universal condemnation from fans and pundits alike, the press, who seemingly favour the 'top 6' due to their reader clientele being a large part of their revenue stream, they led with articles on "Don't punish the fans."

The European Super League broke Premier League rules, which could have led to hefty fines, transfer bans, European expulsion and the major one, removal from the Premier League, quickly the clubs realised the extent of the punishment that could come their way, also coupled with the backlash from their own fans, the six clubs slowly backed out, one-by-one. Their punishment means all six English clubs were ordered to pay £22m after the failed breakaway. Manchester United, Liverpool, Arsenal, Chelsea, Manchester City and Spurs.

Reported in the media as "The six Premier League clubs involved in the European Super League (ESL) have agreed to make a combined 'goodwill' payment of £22m. Should they attempt a similar project again, the clubs will be fined £25m each and have 30 points deducted." A fine of £22m for 6 clubs creating a cartel in secret, denying it a year earlier, when called out for it by another Premier League CEO's the fine was a slap on the wrist.

In comparison, the English Football League (EFL) decided that Birmingham were docked 9 points following an investigation into the club's finances, which saw them just breach FFP. Birmingham were found to have breached rules on profitability and sustainability, with the deduction immediately coming into effect for the 2020 season.

Derby, when they entered administration, were deducted 12 points for entering administration. Without the points deduction, Derby would not have been relegated to League One. Both examples of mismanagement of club funds by owners, like that of the 'Big Six', clubs where punished, fans watched helplessly as their teams' faced sanctions.

The media focused on the wrongdoing and reported on the points deductions, no mention of the fans who suffered and were helpless as owners, made the decisions. In both cases the owners left the club, the fans who stayed, where was the media with their 'Don't punish the fans' narrative? FFP was brought in to provide fairness and integrity to the sport, it has maintained its part with the punishment, unfortunately the sport and the media have lagged in consistency which has helped extend the gap between clubs in the Premier League.

The litmus test for the fairness in reporting came to a head in the summer of 2022. With Everton facing a relegation for the first time in 24 years, the Daily

Mail lead with an article which falsely suggested Everton had breached FFP, a claim the club vehemently denied. The Premier League even explained a year earlier that Everton had asked them to independently audit their accounts and sign off on transfers following the effects Covid-19 had on their commercial accounts leading to losses with Covid write offs to be £88m, £17m under the £105m losses allowed over a three-year period. The exact same article was produced in 2023, under the headline, "Send them down!" After Everton were referred to an independent commission.

The fact Everton requested the Premier League to audit themselves and agreed to having the Premier League sign off on their accounts, including transfers, was an example of Everton agreeing to voluntary sanctions to ensure they did not breach FFP regulations. This did not stop the media spinning a narrative and claiming Everton would face a points deduction in their fight for survival.

With Everton's come from behind victory over Crystal Palace securing their top-flight status for another season, the story reappeared, this time Burnley and Leeds United requested the Premier League turnover Everton's accounts. Everton and the Premier League again denied the club had breached FFP. Before secretly opening up another ten-month investigation into the football club.

This did not stop the media from printing the story and pushing for a points deduction. The media compounded their reports with stories and requests for Everton to receive a points deduction for punishment for the pitch invasion at the end of the game in their outpouring of relief from the fans. Pitch invasions are illegal, and wrong for fans to do, but there were no requests for points deductions when there had been pitch invasions at clubs like Manchester United or Liverpool when a few fans had run on the pitch to steal shirts off the players.

By rule, one fan on the pitch is a pitch invasion and interestingly there was no mention of these in the papers. Ironically, Everton were one of the clubs who were most angered by the 'Big Six' European Super League. Interestingly, the media claimed they were aggrieved, but we should not punish the fans. Surprisingly, the narrative changed when it was not a 'Top Six' club under the microscope.

Covid-19 meant a vast number of clubs were going to make losses with some of the losses unable to be written off or claimed back in other circumstances. With games closed behind closed doors match day income was lost for more than a third of the season. TV deals were rewritten and transfer deals with options were no longer affordable. All teams had signed players to transfer fees, amortisation over the players' contracted years meant clubs were paying more than what the players were now worth.

Everton who had gone on a spending spree prior to Covid-19 were impacted by this and took advantage of the write-offs the Premier League agreed was allowed in their accounts alongside expenditure in infrastructure and the new stadium. It would appear Everton's accountants found this clause which other clubs, mainly Burnley and Leeds, seemingly missed leaving them aggrieved.

It was announced in March 2022 that UEFA were looking to revamp their FFP model to make sure clubs are spending within their means. These tweaks will see sweeping changes made to FFP rules in a further bid to make football clubs more sustainable. Proposed new spending rules to replace UEFA's current Financial Fair Play (FFP) regulations would limit club spending on wages, transfers and agents' fees to 70% of their revenue from 2025.

The new model is talked up as 'financial sustainability regulations' a step away from the current FFP guidelines which focuses on minimising losses over the three-year period. These new guidelines are geared towards tying spending towards a club's revenues.

UEFA's president Aleksander Ceferin said: "UEFA's first financial regulations, introduced in 2010, served its primary purpose. They helped pull European football finances back from the brink and revolutionised how European football clubs are run. However, the evolution of the football industry, alongside the inevitable financial effects of the pandemic, has shown the need for wholesale reform and new financial sustainability regulations."

"UEFA has worked together with its stakeholders across European football to develop these new measures to help the clubs to address these new challenges. These regulations will help us protect the game and prepare it for any potential future shock while encouraging rational investments and building a more sustainable future for the game."

What are the new regulations?

Given their name, it is no surprise that the key objective of the new regulations is to achieve financial sustainability. These will be achieved through three key pillars: solvency, stability, and cost control.

For solvency, the new no overdue payables (towards football clubs, employees, social/tax authorities, and UEFA) rule will ensure better protection of creditors. Controls will be performed every quarter and there will be less tolerance towards late payers.

The new football earnings requirements are an evolution of the existing break-even requirements and will bring greater ability to club finances. To ease the implementation for clubs, the calculation of football earnings is similar to the calculation of the break-even result. While the acceptable deviation has increased from €30m over three years to €60m over three years, requirements to ensure the fair value of transactions, to improve the clubs' balance sheet, and to reduce debts have been significantly strengthened.

The biggest innovation in the new regulations will be the introduction of a Squad Cost Rule to bring better cost control in relation to player wages and transfer costs. The regulation limits spending on wages, transfers, and agent fees to 70 per cent of club revenue. Assessments will be performed on a timely basis and breaches will result in pre-defined financial penalties and sporting measures. The new regulations will come into force in June 2022. There will be gradual implementation over three years to allow clubs the necessary time to adapt.

UEFA's executive committee has approved new financial sustainability rules to replace Financial Fair Play from this June. The rules have three pillars—No Overdue Payment Rule, Football Earnings Rule, and Squad Cost Rule. The No Overpayment Rule means clubs' accounts will be checked every quarter to make sure all bills are being paid on time.

The Football Earnings Rule will allow clubs to lose €60m over three years—double what was permitted under Financial Fair Play. Clubs will be allowed to sustain an extra €10m in losses a year if they are deemed to be 'in good financial health'.

As part of The Squad Cost Rule, spending on wages (players and head coaches), transfers and agent fees will be capped at 70 per cent of a club's revenue. This will be assessed over a calendar year and not a season, so spending in the summer transfer window will be included in the calculations.

UEFA will have pre-agreed financial and sporting punishments ready to impose on clubs who break the rules. Clubs could be prohibited from using specific players signed during an assessment year and they could be forced to play with a smaller squad. UEFA will also have the power to deduct points. Relegation as a sanction is also being discussed but it has not been approved as a punishment yet.

This is a potential grey area for the Premier League if they continue to have separate rules to UEFA, as the new rules can still be broken if rich clubs just pay the fines and carry on as normal. The sanctions are progressive so if a club keeps breaking the rules the punishments will become more and more severe. First and second breaches of the rules are likely to result in fines, subsequent and more serious breaches will result in sporting sanctions.

UEFA says it will also closely monitor commercial contracts clubs sign to make sure they are real contracts with third parties who are paying fair value. UEFA will calculate fair value by benchmarking and using external agencies to advise on whether deals are being done at real market prices.

One of the current criticisms of FFP is that it has taken UEFA time, sometimes years, to punish clubs who do break FFP. To counter this, UEFA is hoping the new rules will be more transparent and work much faster than Financial Fair Play. For instance, in 2023 clubs will be assessed from January to December. They will find out in May 2024 whether they have broken any rules. If they have, their punishment will be applied for the start of the season three months later.

The new rules come into force this June, but they will be implemented gradually over three years to give clubs time to adapt to the new regulations. The 70 per cent Squad Cost Rule cap will be phased in over three years. In 2023/24, the cap will be 90 per cent, in 2024/25 it will be 80 per cent and from 2025/26 it will be 70 per cent.

Another drawback to FFP was that it did not bring about competitive balance. It pushed the inequality further and made the gap between clubs wider and reduced competition and it looks like the new rules do not try and address this.

The new rules are about financial stability and not competitive balance. They are designed to make sure clubs are run properly, they are not designed to make competitions fairer or more equal. UEFA decided to drop the name 'Financial Fair Play' because they believe it gave the false impression that they were trying to create a level playing field. They will continue to look at competitive balance, but their key objective has so far been financial stability.

The No Overdue Payment Rule and quarterly audits will start this June. The first assessment period for the Football Earnings Rules will be 2023. Whilst you can understand the need for sustainability and UEFA not wanting to interfere with the competition, the fact that it is weighted towards revenues, which favours the more recent successful clubs and almost creates a trap door for those on smaller incomes or recently promoted teams. With some brands not wanting to sponsor mid-level teams at the current rate, more and more clubs will be forced to branch out into new revenue streams and as we have seen recently with the conflict in the Ukraine, teams are not thinking of the social cost when making the decision to accept the sponsorship money.

We could expect to see more stadiums and stands sponsored and even in Wolves' case, the club has branched out and opened a record label. It may not be too long before clubs are looking at hosting venues, concerts and boxing events to bring more money into their commercial revenue in the race to close the gap.

The global pandemic and the need to refresh Financial Fair Play accelerated the process. UEFA estimates European football lost €7bn in revenues in 2020 and 2021. €4.4bn of revenue was lost from gate receipts, €1.7bn in commercial and sponsorship income, whilst just under €1bn from lost and renegotiated TV deals. At the same time, player wages went up two per cent every year in 2019 and 2020. In 2021, transfer costs were up 18 per cent and transfer profits down 41 per cent.

Ceferin claims he is 'happy and surprised' the new rules have the backing of all stakeholders in European football. The rules were agreed on after a consultation process which included national associations, the European Clubs Association, European Leagues, FIFPro, supporters' groups, the European Commission, the European Parliament and the Council of Europe.

The immediate impact on the summer window of 2022 will be interesting, as teams begin to bring wage bills down the call for wage caps will increase. The first two major deals of the Summer, Erling Haaland from Borussia Dortmund to Manchester City will see the striker earn a reported £375,000 a week. Kylian Mbappé's new contract extension with PSG is a reported £650,000 resetting the market, it seems teams haven't been put off from spending big on contracts and transfers.

It was safe to assume more clubs would look to use the loan market to get unwanted contracts off the books in the similar way NBA or NFL teams do, in football terms, not taking a transfer fee, with the new team taking on the player's wage. Perhaps this may not occur in the first year, but in subsequent years, 2024, 2025, with teams needing to get to 70% of their turnover, we may see teams happy and needing to dump salaries to get to the cutoff point.

When evaluating the new regulations by UEFA, I briefly discussed how some teams have looked at branching out to bring in more revenue to give them more wiggle room in the transfer market. But perhaps clubs are missing a trick with their star players and sponsorship deals for the club. Jack Grealish recently announced he had signed with Italian fashion label Gucci for $1.7m.

With more and more players being approached by brands outside of football is it too long before clubs sign up with more fashion labels for clubs' suits or have fashion brands sponsored inside the club's stadium. Are Everton, whose players Dominic Calvert-Lewin and Tom Davies enjoy fashion, missing out on potential million by not tapping into the market. The same could be said with the gaming, movie and golf industries, with a number of players taking a keen interest in these areas.

As mentioned, Wolves have branched out into music, could clubs start setting up other sporting or live music events at their stadiums to bring in more money? As we have seen with Brentford and Forest Green more and more clubs are looking at methods to raise revenue in the hope of reaching the upper echelons of sport.

For clubs, they have recently been allowed to put sponsors on their shirt sleeve. Training grounds have also been renamed or sponsored, but any gains smaller clubs are quickly negated by the bigger clubs doing the same. Manchester United's sponsorship deal for their Carrington base, which equated to £18m a year, for ten years with AON. In February 2022, United signed a £20m deal a year With Tezos, a company based around crypto currency to further grow their sponsorship portfolio.

Kieran Maguire, a leading expert in football finance and lecturer at the University of Liverpool has reviewed FFP as part of his book 'The Price of Football' and he has looked into whether FFP rules actually match up to what the scheme is promoting to achieve. He writes, FFP rules are split into two broad camps, one of which is profit related, and puts a limit on the maximum losses a club can make, and the other is on wage control. Both controls have some merits, but these approaches ignore a fundamental commercial rule.

Businesses suffer financial difficulty because of an inability to pay their debts as they fall due, which is a cash flow issue and is not always connected to profit, which is an abstract accounting method which can be manipulated. Profit and cash are not the same and so it seems baffling to have profit control methods if the sole aim is to minimise the chances of clubs entering formal insolvency/bankrupt agreements. The nature of these controls reinforces the view that some of them exist for reasons other than simply preventing clubs from going out of business. This would seem to add some fuel to the argument that FFP leans towards the historic bigger clubs like Manchester United and Real Madrid.

Even in UEFA's FFP statement it almost reads as if it is an appeasement for the clubs who want to break away and form a European Super League. Their statement reads, "The aim of Financial Fair Play is not to make all clubs equal in size and wealth, but to encourage clubs to build for success rather than continually seeking a 'quick fix' football clubs need an improved environment where investing in their future is better rewarded so that more clubs can be credible long-term investment prospects [...] By favouring investments in youth and stadium infrastructure and by setting the acceptable deficits in absolute million £ terms and not relative percentage terms, the break-even assessment has been structured to be less restrictive to smaller and medium-sized clubs. In time, more [of the] smaller and medium-sized clubs will have potential to grow."

Essentially admitting they would prefer the status quo in Europe to remain, for clubs like Brighton, they would grow over time, but their growth rate would be outstripped by the likes of Liverpool and Manchester City. An example possibly shown in Brighton signing Marc Cucurella for £16m from Getafe, he was one of the best signings of the window and less than a year later, clubs such as City were preparing bids for the player. An offer due to FFP, it would be hard for Brighton to turn down, Brighton took the chance and scouted the player, gambled he could adjust to the rigours of the Premier League only for another club to come along and can offer Champions League football.

How are Brighton supposed to get to the European places if their players are always poached by clubs already there? FFP has had a negative impact on allowing clubs, like Brighton from competing for the Premier League, or even growing.

"After studying football finances, do you still love football?" Kieran Maguire smiles at the question he has just levelled in our meeting. An interesting point when you consider the explosion of financial power that some clubs have over others and as the cost of living threatens the very nature of our football pyramid in England. As we talk, HMRC have given a winding up petition to Southend United of the National League. More than ever, it feels important to talk about how the transfer market has applied pressure to the hidden spreadsheets of football, the fans on the terraces and the media have yet to get a grasp off.

Taking a minute from giving lectures in the Football Industries MBA at the University of Liverpool Management School and planning his next podcast 'The Price of Football' built on the back of the book he wrote of the same name, Maguire understands the game is changing, we discuss that football is a business, despite the love the fans share for the sport.

"With the transfer window you have to look at the bigger picture, it should not always be considered a bad entity; it is sometimes painted as by external stakeholders. It is a business, businesses pay taxes. The window and the money brought in creates jobs within the industry. Accountants, club secretaries, scouts etc., it becomes its own microcosm, growing and contouring based on several economic factors."

Jobs are created in the media and new ways to discuss the game we love are born as a byproduct of the transfer window. Fabrizio Romano and David Ornstein have built a reputation for breaking reliable transfer news and have online followings bigger than some of Britain's biggest newspapers print circulation. Their contacts and reliability on breaking transfer news as it happens, rather than wait for tomorrow's newspaper have allowed them to carve out a niche market for them to capitalise on. For fans, as we reviewed earlier with Toffee TV, have been able to enjoy and create new jobs for themselves in the game we love, giving new takes on their team often glossed over by mainstream media, but speaking directly for the fans.

Whilst during the cost-of-living crisis the mention of 'trickle-down economics' can be met with a cynical look and a wry smile with the theory yet to be seen to work, in football, the transfer window does allow one way for money to trickle down the pyramid. Maguire notes the current system is not perfect for money distribution but explains that the current transfer windows allow for clubs in the lower leagues to survive and reducing them to one would have significant repercussions on the survival of clubs.

Take Salford City for example, one of their best players Brandon Thomas-Asante was sold on deadline day in the Summer of 2022 to West Brom after they activated his release clause in his contract. The money for Salford is vital in them staying afloat as a club where the growing costs of running a business for some have tripled in recent months.

How they choose to spend it is up to them, the window can be seen as a microcosm for growth, as Hollywood actors Ryan Reynolds and Rob McElhenney have found with their new venture in owning Wrexham AFC. They need as much turnover as they can get, yet current National League rules have prohibited them streaming their games to America, despite America proving to be one of the biggest emerging markets for the UK game of football.

The leagues refusal to take up their streaming proposal reduces the competitiveness of the league to grow stronger, the rejection of the proposal could be linked to the fear that new revenue streams for the National League could be used against them in their current demands for more 'trickle down' parachute payments from the Premier League, leaving the football pyramid stuck in this catch twenty-two scenario where clubs are just as close to going out of business as they are to playing their next game.

Maguire also points out one of the main reasons we have a transfer window, it was born out of the Bosman ruling, a way clubs could see some remuneration for selling players, rather than see them leave on a free transfer following the expiry of their contracts. It also allows players to move clubs, either temporarily on loan, or permanently before their contracts with their parent clubs expire. The transfer or loan fee becomes the compromise for the deal to take place.

For the players, the window allows them to progress their careers, enhances their wages as they are 'sold, transferred' up the pyramid or move to a bigger club. We discuss the explosion in player wages since the Premier League was incarnated in 1992. Whilst the wages are often chastised in the media and in the stands, it is the price we pay for the product we desire to see as fans.

A simple supply and demand curve highlight, limited supply and an increase in demand hands more control to agents when contract negotiations begin. "Fans when a player they love leaves their club take it to heart, it is personal, and it is easy to turn on footballers. But they have one career, once chance, would we not do the same if someone offered us more money to do the same job, is this not what the current labour market is there for?" Yes, the transfer market allows for millions in signing on fees, but it is perhaps a little too easy to pick on footballers for their wages if we would do the same with our careers.

As we have seen with trade unions, the struggle to get their workers a fair wage in line with spiralling inflation is met with disdain from certain aspects of the media and political parties, it is easy to forget that footballers, in the large majority are working class people, some of whom have come from council estates just like the fans who sing their names in the terraces. Maguire explains how agents, 'not all are bad' essentially collectively bargain for their clients to get the best deal, again if they did not receive large percentages from clubs or actively try to sell or unsettle their players when they should not, would we have such a bad feeling towards them?

The window has allowed players to get a pay-rise from the significant influx of cash into the game, this shouldn't be seen as a bad thing when the players pay taxes, give to charity, when much larger corporations do their very best to avoid paying there's. Sadly, some elements of the media feed the narrative that footballers wages are too high and neglect to acknowledge this has stemmed from the money flooding in.

If clubs stopped seeking more and more revenue, vast profits from TV money, profitable pre-season tours, European Super Leagues, then wages would likely stagnate. The Premier League and European giants desire for continued globalisation will continue to cause wage inflation in the top leagues and the disparity among the English football pyramid, yes footballers are paid over the top for the sport, but they should not be painted as the villains here as long as they give 100% every week on the pitch.

This is what fans have expressed to Maguire they want from players at the very least when supporting their club, but, like most things, Maguire is keen to point out the transfer window does have a negative impact on fans, but also on fans and players mental health. Fans become engrossed in football and allow it to consume their lives, their mental wellbeing, weekends are ruined if your club loses or does not get the desired result from a game they have little control of.

Maguire is an advocate for a number of mental health charities and would love fans to remember what is important in life is their happiness, family and mental wellbeing. We can all dive into the minute detail of football accounting, have opinions on wages or agents, but social media can be a cancerous place when people have attacked Maguire after asking him to use his financial analysis on their club.

"It is the Paradox of Football, what makes a successful club and what do clubs fans care about?" When I enquire about controversial money flows entering the game due to new regulations from FFP and the Premier League Profit and Loss rules, Maguire is quick to point to fans' relevancy to success. Some manage it in trophies and wins, some in the Premier League judge it by their status by staying in the division, Maguire is quick to point out fans' discrepancies in the Chelsea and Newcastle case studies.

With the Russian invasion of Ukraine in the Spring of 2022' the UK government sanctioned several individuals and businesses which had ties to the Russian government.

One of the results from this was the number of individuals and sponsors pulled from football clubs leaving a huge hole in their finances, but more importantly, how do fans view their club socially, and does our fascination with the transfer window actually create and encourage a darker side to football we would like to ignore?

Roman Abramovich was one of those Russian Oligarch's sanctioned and have his assets frozen, briefly putting Chelsea at risk of insolvency until it's drawn-out sale to American billionaire Todd Boehly. Under Abramovich, Chelsea had their most successful ever spell in their history, ensuring for a number of years into the future the clubs will be seen as one of Britain's most successful clubs.

Digging into the finances of the club, the business accounts and spreadsheets behind the winning on the pitch, Chelsea, as a business were losing on average £900k a week, having these losses underwritten by Abramovich. "The fans were happy to ignore this major issue, as they had countless successes on the pitch, seventeen major honours across the period that seen Chelsea have countless memories drawn into the history books. For their fans, the losses in the balance sheet were irrelevant and underwritten by the success on the pitch."

When Abramovich was sanctioned and removed from owning Chelsea, there were several fans who were sad to see their owner leave. Chris, a lifelong Chelsea fan, agreed. "He made us relevant again in the English game, there are question marks where his money has come from and whether it is right, but for me, I care about Chelsea FC and its success, not the owner. I find it hard that he has gone but accept the situation."

Maguire then presents the opposite case, Newcastle United. Whilst me and Maguire are not Newcastle fans or close to the club, from a business point of view, Mike Ashley's ownership was textbook how to run a sustainable business, the club never spending outside of its budget and for the ownership, the 'golden ticket' of the Premier League was what he desired. One of his biggest criticisms was his lack of putting his own money into the club for further transfers or to invest in the infrastructure, preferring to use the club's money generated from the Premier League.

No trophies over the period of his ownership, but a much healthier account balance. The appointment of Rafa Benítez saw a relegation and a promotion back to the Premier League and a positive net spend leading to Newcastle competing in the lower echelons of the Premier League.

For Newcastle fans, Ashley is seen as a pariah, checking back in with Becky, who has been a fan for over a decade and makes a regular pilgrimage to St. James's. "It's been hard to go to games under Ashley, the football under Benítez and the politics between the manager creating a us vs. them mentality took away the fun from my club. Ashley promised transfer budgets and investment in the academy we never got. When I ask Becky what she felt Newcastle fans valued the most, success on the pitch or a sustainable club? She quickly jumps on wins. We want trophies and new signings, I understand Ashley cannot buy the players with his money, it is the clubs, but the club is not growing off the pitch either."

The irony came a few months later for Newcastle fans when the drawn-out acquisition of their football club and the sacking of incumbent manager Steve Bruce led to the appointment of Eddie Howe and a new brand of football. But Ashley's frugal nature in the transfer market allowed new owners, Saudi Arabia's Public Investment Fund to spend significantly and as soon as possible, over £120m in January 2022, following with a further £117m, totalling £237m over the 6-month period. Maguire mentioned how Newcastle fans, happy with their new owner's wealth and ambition were initially shocked when the realised that being the richest club in the world did not mean they could buy all the best players.

"I explained they still had to comply with FFP and Profit and Sustainability rules, also Ashley's frugal ownership has allowed them to spend the vast sums now, to save the club from relegation, the fans became quite heated in their responses towards him. I think at the moment, there is a gap in the knowledge of how football finance works and when fans discover this, they take their disappointment out on those explaining it."

Becky is delighted with the turn of events and fortune in the club. "Where the richest club in the world, bought ourselves out of relegation and the media hate us for it. They love when Liverpool or Manchester City spend millions, but when it is Newcastle, the media turn on us, it is brilliant the bias of the national press, this is why fan TV is the future. I put my discussion with Maguire about ownership funding to her and her thoughts regarding Saudi Arabia's human rights record, but for parity the Chelsea situation and other major clubs who have been caught out."

"It's true about sports washing, but as fans, we do care, but the success and power Newcastle have is what we crave, so I am ok with it. We are not the first club to have 'dirty' money in football, and we will not be the last."

Becky is keen to point out a headline from an online publication, "Newcastle Saudi sponsorship to fund spending spree, there is no headline over Liverpool FC having Standard Charter as a sponsor with their money laundering $1.1bn fine hanging over them. We need the media to be consistent and not to protect their top 6 when it comes to highlighting these issues. I am happy with the takeover and the baggage it brings. We're a massive club now and will be competing for trophies for years to come, and this is what fans really want."

"Look at Everton, a massive club compared to us, with a huge social charity side, but they are not competing at the moment and the media do not give them any credit, so we do need parity on what we expect from our clubs, but we cannot jump on certain fans and give others and easier ride in the press."

As light mist rolls over the River Mersey in Liverpool the doom and gloom of getting transfer business wrong looms large over the cranes currently erecting the 'Blue Wall' of Everton's new stadium based at the Bramley Moore Dock. "It is easy spending someone else's money, but with FFP and the Premier League's Profit and Sustainability rules the margins for error are so small. No one can say Everton or Farhad Moshiri lacked ambition with his transfer expenditure at Everton," despite Richarlison's partying comments to Everton throwing shade at the Everton board. Maguire is keen to point out the roar emotion within a fan base and how we judge football board of directors.

It has not worked out for Everton, but take the emotion out of the situation, fans coveted Moshiri and his millions in the transfer market, welcoming the splurge in transfers the club had not seen spending like this since the Sir John Moores "Mersey Millionaire days of the 60s." Moshiri's problem lay in not having the correct people spending his money, or running the commercial operation. The effects of Covid putting a £100m plus hole in their accounts and the ill-judged appointment of Rafa Benítez almost compounded the Merseyside club to an unthinkable relegation in coming years.

Perhaps guilty of association, Moshiri should have employed a new board of directors to run the club, the reason for the recent decline for Everton from regular challenges of the Top-6 to last season's seesaw positioning was down to the initial spending under the Ronald Koeman, Steve Walsh Era hundreds of millions spent on older players with little residual value and huge wages, doubling the wage to turnover ratio to nearly 100%. For every pound of revenue earned, a pound was spent on wages and huge losses followed.

A net spend of £300m and failing to replace Champions League level Stalwarts like John Stones, Romelu Lukaku and Idrissa Gueye, some fans hate if their owners are involved or stop the day-to-day running of the club, in this case, Everton may have needed it sooner that they got it than last year. Behind the failings in the men's team, Maguire is keen to point out that during the last five years, Everton have continued to lead the league in their social charitable arm, Everton In The Community and how they give back to the community and refused to furlough staff, when other more profitable clubs did so for monetary gains.

Re-established their Women's team as a professional outfit and became the first WSL club to have their own purpose-built stadium at Walton Hall Park, then financed the coveted new stadium at Bramley Moore Dock we watch being built among the fog breaking into Autumn sunlight.

"The paradox in football rarely do you get credit for what you do right in football," but stay around long enough to become the villain, certainly not blameless for Everton's current situation, his managerial appointments prove that, but ones that prove failing by even the smallest margins and getting a transfer window wrong can set a football club back years in progress and like all football clubs, fans demand more than anything, results on the pitch above all else, the tribal nature of fans in football.

Just as the media chastise footballers for earning significant wages from playing sport on the back pages, on the front pages, Trade Unions are equally questioned for standing up seeking key workers a fair wage, just like football the narrative that is spun is how finances are assessed by pundits in football, there is a long way to go before they are understood, and even well-run clubs won't be deemed as successful unless they are winning trophies.

The same can be said for how fans perceive players. Alex Iwobi was profiled earlier in this book on how he was signed for Everton by his agent when he was on holiday. Since signing on deadline day in August 2019, Iwobi has had four permanent managers (six if we include two interim appointments of Duncan Ferguson), played in every position at Everton apart from goalkeeper and centre-back. With Everton in dire need of a goal scoring winger to aid their creativity, Farhad Moshiri splashed out the cash and subsequent managers player Iwobi out wide in an unnatural position.

After three middling years where Iwobi struggled to settle, or find form, Frank Lampard was drafted in to save Everton spiralling down the league. Following an abysmal surrender to Crystal Palace in the Quarter Final of the FA Cup, Lampard demanded players step up and be counted. Iwobi who was out the side at the time would have been the least likely of candidates if you would ask the fans who they thought would rise to the occasion. Over the next ten games, Everton went on a run that saw them climb away from relegation and Iwobi seemingly covered every blade of grass.

Top of all the charts for sprints, presses, work rate and creativity. Deployed in every outfield position except centre-back, he answered Lampard's call and then some with his performances. With finances restricting Everton in the transfer market, Lampard deployed Iwobi in his more favourite central position and Iwobi, at the point of writing is second to Kevin De Bruyne in chances created.

With Everton now looking to tie Iwobi down long-term as he is deemed to be one of the main players in Lampard's rebuild at Everton. A thought that 6 months earlier would have been at the bottom of the fans and possibly Iwobi's thoughts, now fans are campaigning for Director of Football Kevin Thelwell to act quicker to get the midfielder locked down on a long-term deal.

"It does highlight the power of a fan base," muses Maguire. "It helped Everton survive last year, rebuild the bond between the fans and the club, in the case of Iwobi, demand a pay-rise for a player six months ago, they would have looked for Everton to move on in the transfer market. More than ever, it is important for clubs to be smart in negotiating contracts with players due to the constraints of FFP. Giving a player a more expensive contract extension protects the players residual value and helps the club making a profit in the future in terms of their balance sheet. Get it wrong, the club could have a player on high wages who will be difficult to shift in a transfer window and hold a depreciating asset. With more and more clubs focusing on younger players, it is tending to see clubs reluctant to give out longer deals to older players."

"To highlight this in easier terms using Alex Iwobi as the example. Signed for an alleged £28m in 2019 to a five-year deal, on the club's balance sheet, as an asset, Iwobi's value depreciates by £5.8 every year. £28m/5 years = £5.8m.

Therefore, as of 2022, Iwobi's value on the balance sheet would have depreciated by £16.8m to £11.2m. If Everton received a transfer offer of £15m for Iwobi in 2022, it would represent a profit of £3.8m. The profit is measured against the player's value on a balance sheet and not a previous transfer fee from 2019.

"With Everton looking to extend Iwobi's contract, his value would again be extrapolated over five years, which means Everton, if they sell Iwobi, would see a possible healthy return on a player who was once deemed a flop and has seen countless incorrect media reports regarding him causing Everton a loss, when the above example of depreciation shows, the media sometimes misunderstanding of accounts can lead to some clubs' transfers and their policies to be misinterpreted."

Maguire also is keen to point out, simple review of the club's balance sheets and quick calculations would highlight how much clubs must spend in the window. We discuss Leicester's current situation and reported losses due to Covid from the 2020/21 season, meaning they would have little wiggle room to spend. This didn't stop the media linking them to several high-profile players.

Leicester needed to sell to buy as their losses pushed them close to breaking FFP with them placed on UEFA's FFP watchlist, Leicester had invested heavily behind the scenes in the academy and structure of the club, Covid took away significant income of the club meaning it left them little wiggle room in the market, as it had with Everton the year before. "Clickbait articles always lead fans to believe their team are in the market for players and can lead to some unfair criticism to the club and their board of directors."

"The transfer window is the ecosystem of football, and it can fascinate how deals can take months to be completed then on deadline day, a mere few hours before a new player is holding up their new team's scarf, but it is important to emphasise how transfer fees are paid."

When we read on Sky Sports News Player X has joined club Y for £20m, it usually means the full £20m is not paid in one instalment. Usually, a quarter of the transfer fee is paid up front, in this case £5m. Negotiations on the instalments usually divide the remaining transfer fee over the period of the player's contract. If we assume a four-year deal, this will leave the remaining £15m paid in £5m instalments usually paid the following June 30th.

In some cases, you may see in the media the transfer fee is also supplemented by 'add-ons' that are not necessarily guaranteed to the selling club. But can be used by the buying club to potentially allow them to afford players currently outside their budget for this year or push the payment further down the line. These can be in relation to:

- Club appearances (50, 100 appearances, a one-minute substitute appearance would be counted)
- Buying club achieving promotion, trophy win, Champions League qualification.
- Avoiding relegation.
- Profit or percentage of a sell on clause.

If the example above was Player X is signed for £20m with £10m pound of add-on, the transfer fee should be reported as £20m as there is no guarantee the add-ons will be achieved. A real-life case study of this is the recent Chelsea interest in Anthony Gordon of Everton. It was widely reported that Chelsea had bid £60m for the young winger, the widespread confusion when Everton rejected the bid for a player who has only recently broken through and given their recent losses due to Covid-19.

It has since been reported the offer was £40m, £10m upfront, given Everton little time or money to find a like for like replacement for £10m this late in the window. The remaining £30m would be split over 5 years (£6m paid on the anniversary each year of the sale). The add-ons were labelled as unachievable by Everton, significant appearances for Chelsea, winning the Premier League, Champions League.

Essentially making the deal £40m. Had Chelsea paid more upfront and guaranteed the add-ons to make it a plausible £60m, Everton would have found it hard to turn down such a fee which would have represented a straight profit to the balance sheet for the sale of an academy graduate. Everton later sold Anthony Gordon to Newcastle United for £45m upfront.

"Transfers are even harder to tie up now with the added implications of image rights and how more players are demanding fees for their images to be used by the club that has just bought them," Maguire explains. In some cases, these can often be around 20% of the players reported value. This can cost the club millions a year, but Maguire explains this can work both ways, as players can be used as media magnates and commercial gains.

Take Ronaldo's transfer back to Manchester United, the fee and wages represent a huge cost to the club yearly, but for United, sponsors will gravitate towards the player and was a positive move for the club who are floated on the stock exchange. As these deals diversify and more and more are added to them Maguire further explains how this impacts the teams outside of the Premier League.

"Clubs face even more burden and financial stress to try and get into the Premier League, they need to take gambles to try and get promoted, more and more clubs need to rely on sales to survive, then free agents to build a team. Parachute payments have almost created a league within a league for the Championship and for League 1 and 2, the dream of the Premier League is that much further away as finances in the game have exploded."

On this point, I question whether the recent changes to FFP and the emphasis on spending around 70% of a club's revenue will bring around more competitiveness in the sport. Again, Maguire is not so sure. "The new guidelines seem to have been watered down and Favour those clubs who threatened to start their European Super League, but it is important to understand UEFA when pressing this new format, stressed this was not to introduce a competitiveness or parity to the game, but more to encourage clubs to be more financial sustainable with their Swiss style rules to be implemented and phased in from 2024."

Maguire, who is a Brighton fan, uses current examples of his club in the previous transfer window which would have happened anyway. "The changes would not have stopped Graham Potter from leaving Brighton to become the new Chelsea manager and nor should it, as frustrating as it can be for a fan. Same can be said for Marc Cucurella, Brighton should be praised for their scouting, turning a player who cost them £16m and selling him for £58m a year later. Same could be said for Yves Bissouma, whose contract was expiring and the player unlikely to sign a new deal was sold for £26m to Spurs, again it could be argued that this is FFP working? Brighton being a well-run sustainable club using their scouting system to make money. The sales from the players highlighted would have paid for three quarters of the Amex Stadium."

Brighton as a case study is intriguing, but one which fans explain the lack of competitiveness in the league, a well-run club, now classed as a Premier League mainstay, a huge emphasis on signing the right player, rather than looking at the price tag for prestige, Brighton still need to sell players in order to move up the league due their lack of revenue the club can achieve, putting an emphasis on the clubs needs to buy low and sell high meaning it is difficult to build a team, just as it looked like Brighton could gatecrash the top 6, they lost their manager and with it the momentum they had built up in the pre-season.

Discussing the impact of Covid-19 and the football finance bubble to the current economic downturn we both predicted there would be more cautiousness around current transfer spending, but the Premier League has fared better than the other European clubs. The golden ticket of the Premier League and guaranteed revenues meant Premier League clubs have had a softer bump in their finances, it has forced some clubs, (Everton and Leicester) to review their spending, but these clubs had heavily invested in infrastructure in the club just prior to Covid-19, both posted losses of over £100m, yet neither club were forced to sell their stars, unlike their European counterparts.

Like the economic theory from Adam Smith 'invisible hand' pulling the market into an equilibrium, those clubs who sold assets to balance their books, those with the deeper pockets, could continue to spend, or sold squad players to upgrade. Digging into the small evidence sample from the past year Maguire found that Premier League wages during the 2021/22 season, the first post Covid-19 with fans back, wages for the league on average increased. The full picture and impact may not be seen until the accounts for the 2022/23 season are audited and the three-year calculations for the Premier League Profit and Sustainability are considered.

Maguire does think outside of the Premier League there is likely to be wage stagnation with the tightening of budgets and softening of wages as the clubs have been forced to understand the financial hole in their accounts. Only clubs with access to parachute payments and those who sold a player where able to spend on transfers in the Summer of 2022, the impact of Covid-19 may still yet to be seen up and down the football pyramid, perhaps emphasising the need for a better payment structure for the EFL outside of the Premier League's current model of 'trickle-down economics' to help support the EFL may not be enough for some EFL clubs.

"Don't forget the Premier League is keen to grow its product, the Newcastle takeover has opened new markets in the Middle East and more and more clubs are turning to Asia and America for lucrative pre-season tours." The new Premier League TV deal is just around the corner and rumoured to be even bigger than the last, factor in streaming giants such as Amazon are producing football highlights to a number of devices straight to your home with a new style of presenting it wouldn't be a miss if the new deal actually meant clubs and the

Premier League came out of the pandemic with the two interrupted seasons merely a blip in the rear-view mirror and soon to be an afterthought.

The potential end to the three o'clock curfew in prohibiting British fans from seeing their team on TV opens more opportunities for the Premier League, fans unable to attend the live matches could now for the first time stream their team and enjoy the game they want to watch.

How the money is distributed will be interesting, will it be even to keep parity to all twenty clubs and upset the six clubs who wish to leave for a European League, or will it give equal opportunity to all twenty clubs who hold one of the Premier Leagues golden tickets?

Just a week after Maguire and I sat down to chat, we discussed future ways the Premier League may look to increase its revenue streams with pre-season tours in America and Asia. Split the division in two, ten teams head West, the other ten head East, where the 39th game would actually be pre-season games in the emerging markets, all twenty clubs could be 'compensated' equally, train in the same facilities and would gravitate other European clubs into these fixtures which could take away the desire for the European Super League and allow for the current leagues to remain the same.

Teams could opt out if they wished, but the benefit would be new fans from these markets can choose which club they wish to follow or support, rather than just the six that are pushed by the Premier League for commercial reasons. The Premier League look to have taken a similar approach, but it may not involve all clubs under current proposals, which is a concern when this year, Nottingham Forest spent £140m on twenty-two players just to be able to compete in the Premier League, their promotion built of loan players and Championship level players, highlighting the ever-growing distance between the Premier League and the leagues below. Without access to these tours, the clubs would potentially face even greater odds just to try and stay in the division, let alone compete in it.

As shown in earlier chapters more clubs have shifted towards data-led scouting to find hidden gems in the transfer market to try and ensure their transfer revenue will see greater returns in the future. We are now seeing more and more higher earners and players in their thirties not having their contracts extended and turning to the MLS for one final pay day rather than drop down the league, highlighting clubs have learnt shorter contracts afford them a get out clause if the older player fails to deliver on the Premier League's inflated wages. We are starting to see the changes to the transfer window and the finances in football and data-led scouting is influencing the current market within football.

Clubs may be getting smarter, but there are also economic and political levers that could well affect the transfer window in the near future. With the effects of Brexit, it made it harder for players to gain work permits following a review from the Home Office building a points system into their application process. For British clubs, this meant players who were not in or around their National Teams or had not played enough international games could still be bought, but to gain a work permit, the transfer fee needed to be higher than the players actual worth.

"It essentially created a Brexit tax," jokes Maguire. "But the Premier League clubs had the money, the TV deals, only those clubs at the bottom were affected by a measure that was implemented." When pushed on whether the FA's decision to remove the points system from the work permit process would now deflate the prices for English clubs, Maguire isn't so sure.

"I don't think it will necessarily lower prices to a more market level. Economic modelling, supply and demand may suggest this, but football is unique. In practice, there are outliers that are confined to push prices up 'a Premier League Tax'."

The supply of money in the Premier League has not stopped. A new TV deal is on the horizon, the Economic Supply Curve reduction is negated by the influx of cash which caused Demand-Push inflation as more Premier League clubs have the money to spend. Case in point being Nottingham Forest above and their spending in the summer of 2022. Clubs who are selling the players to the Premier League clubs also hold significant cards at the negotiating table. They know their players are in demand, from all across Europe they can play clubs off one another.

An example from the 2022 transfer market is the sale of Georgian Winger Khvicha Kvaratskhelia signed for Napoli for £9m from Dinamo Batumi. Kvaratskhelia could have gone to several leagues in the summer.

His value per league could have varied. La Liga: £5m. Serie A: £10m. Premier League: £15m

For La Liga, the value reflects the reduction in La Liga spending power due to Covid-19. His actual price is around the median price Napoli of Serie A paid. Kvaratskhelia was sold for a similar price the year before, had a Premier League club come to the table, if they really wanted Kvaratskhelia, Maguire points out they would have paid more to secure their player.

Which brings us onto another topic around the transfer window and whether the transfer window and the explosion in players prices has encouraged clubs to circumnavigate FFP? "It is a difficult one, on one hand you can make this argument, but on the other hand, a football club cannot control what their sponsor may do in the future."

Chimes Maguire, we discuss Standard Charter history with their fine for money laundering. Liverpool cannot control Standard Charter business actions or principles. Socially, they may draw a line and say, "we cannot associate ourselves socially with this, but if Standard Charter offers Liverpool the best value deal which is much higher than other sponsors, they are going to accept the offer." It is not Liverpool who conducted the malpractice. In a utopian world where there is no race to the bottom, the club may make a social call and turn down the sponsor, but with the margins being so small in terms of FFP and the new spending limits of 70% of a club's turnover, clubs are forced to take on these offers.

More so than ever the recent takeover of Newcastle by Saudi Arabia's Public Investment Fund, RB Sports and Media and PCP Capital Partners brings questions into sports washing a country's political or social history by purchasing Western Sports or investing in them as we have also seen with Liv Golf. The Russian invasion of Ukraine and subsequent sanctions of allies or business associates of Vladimir Putin highlighted how much controversial money was inside world football. The feeling is that there may be a review of where clubs choose to take sponsorship from to a degree, but we also need to be fair when judging football clubs as well.

If we use Everton as an example, their CEO Dr Denise Barrett-Baxendale, made a declaration that she was happy Everton had moved away from their previous sponsor Sportpesa with car supermarket Cazoo. But with the club seeking replacements for sponsors who they dropped in the previous months and the impact from Covid-19, the club sought replacements with the 7th best value in the Premier League.

Everton resorted back to an online crypto casino company Stake, the deal is the best in the club's history, takes them to their new stadium the Bramley Moor, where they would have negotiating power with new and bigger brands. Yet the media and a section of their fans were not happy with the deal, bringing up the past of the club moving on to more socially responsible sponsors.

The issues they raise are fair questions to be asked. But when you consider Everton's board of directors have been accused of underperforming and needing to do better in the commercial sense and decision-making process, had they have not taken the 7th best commercial sponsorship deal offered, the same critics would have openly attacked the board, or pointed to their spreadsheets, whilst hidden behind online social media accounts. "It is fair to ask these questions, but we must judge this based on the realities of the current situation. Would Everton take Stake if alternatives offered the same?"

No, they would not. "Gambling firms are the current sponsorship deals that offer this kind of money and stability for clubs who live on financial bubbles." Looking at their previous sponsor Cazoo, their financial instability has seen them make thousands of employees redundant whilst paying out huge sums in sponsorship to gain market share. Is his socially responsible for a football club to accept? A recent vote by Premier League clubs has seen gambling odds banned from the front of shirts by the 2026/27 season, a few weeks after the Premier League executives met with the UK parliament to discuss future governance.

"Right now, it is legal for gambling and Non-fungible Token (NFT's) to be sponsors in sport. Same with cryptocurrency where we have seen several club initiatives tank causing those fans who have invested to lose their money. Until this is made by government legislation, clubs will continue to use them as a source of funding to allow them to spend in the transfer market. We discuss the impact it has on fans but also why the bigger companies such as Paddy Power and Ladbrokes do not advertise on football shirts."

"We must question the value of the deal. Does being on a Premier League shirt bring in the revenue for the business. Look at Cazoo at Everton and Villa, in the pandemic, more people bought second-hand cars due to the false fear of Covid-19 transmission on public transport, yet Cazoo still needed to lay off thousands of workers. The companies do not see the catchment or value in the sponsorship." The gambling firms do not want to take a punt on raising revenue this way, or they are aware of the negative backlash this could cause.

Paddy Power ran a campaign 'save our football shirt' from ugly sponsors and designs, in 2020 they ran an unsponsored derby between Newport County and Macclesfield Town. Paddy Power has unsponsored almost all the ground's advertising boards, match sponsor, program, and Man of the Match award. The bookmakers have teamed up with several brands to ensure that most of the perimeter boards at Rodney Parade will bear no brand logos. Carrying on their 2019 campaign, the bookmaker was criticised for the campaign on whether they were removing gambling sponsorship from grounds as a marketing campaign, or whether they were taking on board comments from fans and government officials.

An advocate for mental health charities, Maguire explains how when fans reach out to him and colleagues via Twitter to discuss or explain football finances for their teams, when the news is not what they want to hear, they in some cases resorted to abuse. Sharing the same has happened to me we discuss how both mental health and gambling addiction could be resolved and whether the transfer market madness impacts these health problems.

"It plays a part, there still would be mental health issues and gambling addicts without the window, but anything that influences it certainly becomes a factor, but stopping the ads is not the solution to solve the issue. We saw this with Formula 1 and the banning of tobacco advertising from the cars and paddock, it helped and took the issue out of the limelight but did not stop smoking. Gambling like most addictions, is a societal problem. If we stop betting sponsorship in football, it does not stop someone putting a bet on their phone within two seconds. Betting firms will still find ways to advertise around football."

Betting firms have used psychologists themselves in ways to motivate people to bet on football as part of their business model. They found uplifting music such as 'Sweet Caroline' taken on by the England National team during Euros 2020 and 2021 gave a sense of happiness and positivity. It was not long before the song adorned numerous British campaigns, football has a problem, it is not going away, which is more the reason for disappointment with the announcement that government regulation into football and Tracey Crouch's findings.

"Regulation could provide some guidance, but I am sceptical if it can be the answer to all of football's problems. I would say I am marginally in Favour to it. There are varying factors that would define its success, but we must acknowledge a few key points. Who would lead the regulation? Can they be judged, be neutral and act in a fair manner?" A few mere months after me and Kieran sit down for a chat, the Premier League announced they had agreed to ban themselves from having gambling adverts on the front of their shirts from the start of the 2026/27 season.

A start of self-regulation, or a compromise to starve off government regulation by the Premier League appearing to 'want' to be able to regulate itself in the best interests of the public.

As the sun begins to set over the River Mersey on our interview we discuss regulation outside of football, there is regulation in water, but we still have sewage dumped into our rivers and seas, would the six favoured clubs in the Premier League just canvass the regulator to Favour their initiatives, it could work, but it would need serious and strong leadership to enforce real change. Financial inequality distorts competitiveness. It would be great if all the clubs were given similar budgets each season and put the transfer window into the hands of the DOF, let them negotiate the deals and rely on scouting networks to provide the competitiveness and fairness in the game.

Wise men say, only fools rush in, the opening words of Elvis Presley's 'Can't Help Falling In One With You' rings around the racecourse ground. Even as the light rain falls nothing seems to be able to dampen the spirits of the Wrexham fans fresh off their Hollywood takeover by actors Ryan Reynolds and Rob McElhenney. The ink had barely dried on the pairs $2.5m purchase of the world's third oldest club currently plying their trade in the 5th pyramid of English football before people began to question why the pair who had never visited before decided to invest their money into the club.

Given that football club owners can no longer finance player trading in the transfer market and as we have investigated in this book just how hard it is for clubs outside the Premier League to move up the dizzying heights of the football league. They join Chelsea, Manchester United, Arsenal, Liverpool and others who have been purchased by American owners.

UK sports teams are cheaper than the American counterparts in the NFL, NBA and MLB, there are more UK clubs and football is a global game, unlike the NFL, which is currently trying to establish itself worldwide, football already has the audience and the British clubs venture over to America for pre-season tours. There is increasing media and marketing rights in the game which for a club marketed properly would see a return for their investment.

The uniqueness about the takeover is that Wrexham was owned by the fans. Two thousand of them owned shares in the club, Reynolds and McElhenney met them over numerous online video calls to vet the pair's interest in their club. Something that fans of the bigger clubs could only dream of when new owners circle like sharks around their club.

Desperate to ensure their clubs stayed the soul of their town, the fans negotiated a twenty-five-year lease the actors take on if they went ahead with the purchase. The actors agreed and further explained how they would invest in the club's players and the facilities around the club to ensure growth would be the long-term goal of the club.

As soon as the takeover was announced the small town in Wales was all over the worldwide media, a new shirt sponsor was found as TikTok, the fast-rising social media app was announced after agreeing a two-year deal. This was closely followed by Vistaprint and Expedia, companies you would expect to sponsor clubs further up the division.

Understanding the momentum their takeover had had on the club, streaming giants Disney purchased the rights to a documentary following the trials and tribulation of the none league football club.

Assuming they received the average Disney fee for an hour documentary of £375,000, the eight-part series probably netted the club around £3m in revenue. Season ticket sales at the club has tripled in three years from around 2609 to 6820. Wrexham challenged themselves on several fronts and saw their social media accounts soar: Wrexham is now in 2nd place in the National League standings, and their social accounts have exploded: per Joe Pompliano on Twitter.

Twitter: 45k to 209k (+364%)
Instagram: 27k to 208k (+670%)
TikTok: 0 to 459k

A simple football takeover which has captured the imagination of several people and through a creative commercial plan has launched a National League club into the headlines of the back papers of the national media usually reserved for Premier League clubs. The newfound investment allowed the club to purchase players and pay football league wages normally reserved for clubs higher up the divisions. It does highlight however, how clubs outside the Premier League can survive and grow, with a little bit of Hollywood stardust, Wrexham AFC were promoted into the football league following a tense battle with Notts County in the 2022/23 season.

Barcelona economic levers explained: Mortgaging future or calculated bet?

Whilst one set of fans dream of what might be coming soon, another fanbase is deeply concerned and confused about theirs. Dark clouds of uncertainty have been forming over Camp Nou, the very thought of football without Barcelona is one that to the purists is almost unthinkable, their president seemingly gambling the future of their club so they can make a splash in the transfer market to keep chasing European Champions Real Madrid. Before the confetti fell on Real Madrid's Champions League victory over Liverpool in Paris, Barcelona's season was over before a ball had been kicked.

Joan Laporta took over the club Presidency in 2021, the financial situation was a mess. Barcelona had debts of more than €1 billion, Covid-19 losses piled up leaving no wiggle room to improve an ageing squad or give a new contract to arguably the greatest player to play football, Lionel Messi. Messi's tearful goodbye to the club that nurtured him into the generational talent, watched closely by the footballing world, how could Barcelona have let this happen? But more importantly, how would Barcelona survive without him as he had carried the team for the last few years.

The answer, the club struggled, sacking new manager Ronald Koeman and replacing him with club legend Xavi to stem the anger overflowing the terraces to try and keep the club together through the turbulent waters. During which, Laporta requested high-profile first team players take wage reductions, or wage deferrals, which have still yet to be paid, just so Barcelona could meet La Liga's strict salary regulations. Fast forward to the summer transfer window in 2022, with Barcelona still in significant financial difficulty, facing question marks over not paying their players and publicly trying to force midfielder Frenkie De Jong out of the club, despite the player publicly stating he did not want to go, asking for his deferred wages. Barcelona went on an unprecedented spending spree, whilst the rest of European football looked on through their balance sheets and lawyers scoured through FFP regulations.

The Blaugrana have signed Raphinha and Robert Lewandowski. The pair have cost in excess of €100 million. Héctor Bellerín, Marcos Alonso, Eric Garcia, Andreas Christensen, and Franck Kessié signed on free transfers on significant wages, despite other first team players taking the above discussed deferrals. Then came the marquee trio of Jules Koundé, a centre-back for £45m,

Raphinha was finally signed from Leeds after a protracted drawn-out transfer for £54m and splashed a further £40m on 34-year-old Robert Lewandowski, one of the most prolific strikers of the last decade.

There was another major issue for Barcelona, Frenkie De Jong refused to sign for Manchester United for a reported £80m, keeping his wages on the books and no income to offset the transfer expenditure from the summer, but also Barcelona's Winter Spending in January where they sunk €50 million into Ferran Torres and signed Pierre-Emerick Aubameyang from Arsenal on a free transfer agreeing to take on his significant wages, to offset any transfer fee.

The number of transfers and the transfer fees would even make the accountants at Manchester City and PSG raise their eyebrows given UEFA's FFP rules and that Barcelona had previously begged UEFA for an advance on the 2023 and 2024 Champions League payments, even though Barcelona had not qualified for the tournaments yet, UEFA rightly laughed off the arrogance and publicly pointed out to Barcelona they were not entitled to any such funds.

Meaning more drastic measure for Joan Laporta, like a man playing his last chip at a Las Vegas casino at the roulette table, he spun the wheel on Barcelona's future by "activating" his economic levers to allow the club to navigate their way through the hurdles of Barcelona's debts, FFP and competitors, but how, and what does the transfer spending mean for Barcelona's future.

Barcelona's economic levers are partial sales of assets via which the club obtains money immediately, serving to improve and manage Camp Nou's battered accounts. There are two primary levers: those related to merchandising and television rights. The first lever is BLM, a company who manages the club's official merchandise, such as shirts, mugs, pens, and scarves. The sale of 49.9% of BLM was approved at the recent Barcelona club assembly in a deal worth in the region of €200m.

The second economic lever focused on the future television rights. In the assembly, it was agreed that the club would only seek deals worth a maximum of 25% of their overall rights. Barça sold 10% of those rights to Sixth Street in June in a deal worth €267m, on the proviso the US firm will invest €207m back into the club. But the income is not direct and cannot be lavished on new players. This deal was potentially used to service, reduce the debt and interest which was mounting up.

Laporta said at Jules Kounde's unveiling, the club activated a third 'economic lever' by selling a percentage of their Barca Studios production house, whilst admitting that it was unclear whether La Liga would agree they were now able to register their summer signings. Barcelona had agreed to sell 25 per cent of their Barca Studios arm to the controversial blockchain-enabled fan token platform Socios.com, for €100million (£83.7m). However, La Liga stated this was not enough for the club and Laporta moved quickly to find a fourth economic lever.

The Blaugrana announced the sale of yet another part of Barca Studios to a company called Orpheus Media for around €100m. This activation of the fourth lever ensures the registration of their signings of Lewandowski, Raphinha, Kounde, Christensen and Kessie just in time for the start of the La Liga season.

The economic levers, in very simple terms, is the club using its assets to get money, each lever is not direct income, Spanish broadcaster Cadena SER explained, of the money Barcelona generate, 15 percent goes toward increasing the salary limit (player wages accounted for 103% of total income when Laporta took over the reins of the club in March 2021, total debt stood at €1.35bn), 70 percent to improve infrastructure and the remaining 15 percent to further service the club's debt.

Barcelona also signed a €236m sponsorship deal with music streaming service Spotify earlier this year meaning their historic Camp Nou has been renamed Spotify Camp Nou to further bring in sponsorship to bring much needed revenue into the club to help bring the wage bill to turnover down to try and bring some future security to this year's finances. Broken down over four years, the ground can now be used for music concerts, special programs, and even weddings.

These 'levers' were only phase one of Laporta's plan, second was refinancing the club's massive debt through a €500 million loan from Goldman Sachs, including a grace period of five years. Furthermore, Goldman Sachs have also taken on the planned renovation to Spotify Camp Nou over a 35-year plan. Fans of Derby and Birmingham would attest the ownership of a stadium is important for fans, but also key to a club's revenue and several British clubs have seen the football clubs lose their stadiums to owners and banks, it would be unthinkable for this to happen to Barcelona, but it has happened more than you would think.

Barcelona's refusal to pay Frenkie De Jong's €17 million deferred wages and demanding him to find a new club reveals the devil in the detail that finances are tight. The club is not willing to part with any Euro it does not need to. From a player's perspective, it is even more surprising when the players are taking wage cuts, the deferral of wages are potentially going to end with one of the biggest clubs in the world in court.

A review of their last years accounts saw losses amount to €481 million. That was the amount of loss La Liga's strict Financial Fair Play (FFP) rules forbid clubs from going all out on players. Barcelona can only spend 1/3rd of their total income on the purchase of players. By using these 'levers', the club is aiming to get that to 1:1 through these financing methods, bringing short term benefits to the club, but requires and is betting on Barcelona winning silverware this year and regaining the La Liga title.

But with Barcelona dumped out of the Champions' League group stages and trailing Real Madrid, those grey clouds are slowly turning into storm clouds. With key players Lewandowski, Pique, Busquets, Alba, and Ter-Stegen being veterans, their best days behind them and little value to be returned in any transfers, you can be forgiven for worrying about the long-term future of the club.

Barcelona's future has been mortgaged, the bets have been placed, a La Liga championship is a must and even a Europa League victory may force Laporta to activate a fifth economic level, if there is one. A future footballing world without Barcelona would have been unthinkable a few years ago, if the losses on the pitch continue and squad players refusing to leave, there may be a few more searches down the back of sofas in the cobbled streets of Barcelona in search of more "levers" and Euros.

Seeing the changes that FIFA have proposed to FFP and the comments that it is not there to bring parity or increase competition, it is easy to find the short falls within the model. It can be argued the measures are more in line to stop the European Super League from rearing its ugly head again in the near future. Two of the main English teams who tried to orchestrate the move, Manchester United and Liverpool were put up for sale during the World Cup in 2022. A sign that owners believe the value of clubs have peaked in the post Covid-19 bubble, or the reality that football clubs may not be the quick win billionaires seek on return on their investments.

Whether the FFP overhauls will stop these teams seeking a cartel league for themselves time will tell. But reality speaks for itself. The Premier League in the decade of FFP, from 2010–2020, saw five teams win the Premier League, Manchester City, Manchester United, Chelsea, Leicester City and Liverpool. In the last few years, Liverpool and Manchester City have held a stranglehold on the top two positions, but even Liverpool have struggled to keep up with Manchester City. In La Liga, this drops to three teams, Real Madrid, Barcelona and Atletico Madrid.

In the Bundesliga, this tails off to two clubs, Bayern Munich and Borussia Dortmund are the last two clubs to have claimed the title. Of all the clubs listed above, Leicester is the only club which would be deemed as an unexpected win, in a Premier League season where the main players underperformed. Using the baseline facts listed above, FFP was first introduced to improve competitiveness, then it has failed based on this, clubs are now working within the confines of FFP, but Europe's top leagues have become even more uncompetitive.

As we saw in earlier chapters, these clubs can also prey on other clubs when it comes to transfers. If you argue, it was to make clubs sustainable and reduce the number of clubs from making losses, then these statistics seem to back this argument, UEFA explained in their benchmarking reports to support FFP, they argued combined club operating profit had risen from €600m in 2017. When you compare this to 2011, when FFP was introduced, there were combined losses of €1.7bn. Similar parallels were found in the Premier League, before the cost controls in the 2012/13 season, clubs accounted for a total combined loss of £291m, 12 out of the 20 clubs operated at a loss.

The next season, with the cost controls, the losses morphed into a cumulative £198m. In the 2016/17 season, 18 Premier League clubs made a profit. So it has been successful in making clubs think about how their businesses are financed, but what it has not done is level the playing field, if anything, these top clubs have adapted and worked harder to keep the divide even bigger than it was before, and the reforming of FFP to measure clubs against 70% of their revenue predictably will only further this and reduce the competitiveness of the European Leagues in favour of the clubs who tried to start up the European Super League.

One area the media incorrectly report on the transfer window is their understanding of player sales and the actual profit and loss for the selling clubs balance sheet. To explain this, I have used an example from Football Finance expert, Kieran Maguire's book, "The Price of Football". When Andy Carroll was sold by Liverpool after an underwhelming portion of his career, many articles were written about how much Liverpool, as a business, had lost in the transfer, without the knowledge of how football finance works. Maguire breaks down the actual loss for us.

When Andy Carroll joined Liverpool from his hometown club, Newcastle United for a fee of £35m pounds in the January transfer window, he signed a five and a half deal. A football player is an asset for the club, they are shown on the balance sheet by their transfer fee. (Players who come through the club's academy are not accounted for here as their cost is shown in the overall cost of the club's academy.) If they are sold, all the transfer fee is shown as total profit for the football club, even more reason why academy players and youth recruitment is crucial.

The accounting nature of football is like all businesses. Players (assets) decrease in value over time, just as our cars do each year, players value decrease by a value called amortisation, the action of gradually writing off the initial cost of the asset in Layman's terms. For a footballer when they are bought, this is their transfer fee, divided by the length of their contract. For Andy Carroll, £35m, divided by 5.5 years = £6.4m each year.

Carroll was sold two and a half years into his Liverpool career to West Ham for £15m. The media and most fans believed Liverpool had made a significant £20m loss on the player. However, at the point of sale, Carroll's accounting value was £19.1m. (£35m—2.5 years amortisation charge) Equalling an accounting loss of £4.1m for the Merseyside club. This is not to say the deal was a good deal, or to spin the transfer to say Carroll's move or Liverpool's trading was successful, it highlights more how clubs trading of players can show profitable outcomes, or in the case of Andy Carroll, how Liverpool made an accounting loss of £4.1m for the player.

Another misconception fans can misunderstand regarding the transfer window and football finance is how transfer fees are paid between clubs. When a transfer is agreed, the eye watering transfer fees can seem staggering to those outside the game, but also shows why the loss of revenue due to Covid-19 highlighted why several clubs needed to become sellers in the market, they had future transfer instalments hanging over their head.

As with the transfer market, player transfer fees have expanded, when Trevor Francis became the first £1m player when he moved from Birmingham City to join Midlands rivals Nottingham Forest in 1979. At the time, the transfer fee nearly doubled the amount a football club had previously played for a player. Come 1996, Alan Shearer's transfers from Blackburn Rovers to Newcastle United pushed the record fee to £15m and Kieran Maguire's book points out that at the time of writing, Neymar's transfer to PSG from Barcelona for €222m in August 2017 remains the current record fee.

These fees are not paid in full by the buying football club, clubs need their cash flows to be positive so they can pay the bills and balance the books to ensure the football club has enough cash to operate. Therefore, the transfer fee is likely to pay in instalments, if we use the example of Barcelona's protracted transfer for Raphinha from Leeds in the Summer of 2022 for £50m (plus £7.6m in add-ons). With the Catalan club short on cash, the initial fee to Leeds, like most transfer deals, would be between 25–50% of the transfer fee.

In this example, we would say Barcelona transferred Leeds £12.5m upfront to Leeds, the remaining £37.5m would be split evenly over the remaining five years of the Brazilians contract. (£9.4m over the remaining four seasons, paid on the anniversary of the players transfer) Even if Raphinha is sold by Barcelona before these five years, the club would still need to pay the yearly instalments.

How clubs spread the payments for players and their overall club accounts have been under increasing scrutiny following the news of Juventus, the Turin based clubs board of directors, President Andrea Agnelli and vice president Pavel Nedved have resigned from the club alongside entire board of directors; Serie A club have been accused of false accounting and market manipulation in recent months and recorded record losses; the company has denied any wrongdoing.

The club which was one of the instigators of the European Super League now risk demotion if they are found guilty. Juventus president Andrea Agnelli has already courted the ire of fellow Serie A side Atalanta by suggesting they weren't deserving of their place in the Champions League. The Bergamo club have won plaudits from across Europe for their attacking flair and smart recruitment in how quickly the club upset the apple cart in Serie A and moved into a position to challenge the established clubs. But speaking at the FT Business of Football Summit in London, Angelli claimed Atalanta were unworthy of their place at Europe's top table.

Telling attendees, "I have great respect for everything that Atalanta are doing, but without international history and thanks to just one great season, they had direct access into the primary European club competition." Is that right or not? Then I think of Roma, who contributed in recent years to maintaining Italy's ranking. They had one bad season and are out, with all the consequent damage to them financially. The arrogance in the undertone of Angelli's comments show

how clubs at the top operate, but also how they perceive opponents, but also how reliant the clubs are on the European money coming into the club.

To suggest a club like Atalanta should not be in the Champions League despite them finishing within the Champions League places and that Juventus should receive more Champions League money further highlights how tone death some of the European Super League clubs have become. Atalanta have outsmarted several 'established' Serie A clubs, they face an uphill battle with the European football climate to remain there.

*Juventus were found guilty of financial malpractice and falsifying their accounts and have been docked 15 points as a punishment, this was later reinstated in April 2023.

'You cannot buy history' is often a chant heard from the terraces towards clubs who have been accused of 'buying' success, for every trophy Manchester City have won in their dynasty decade, they have been unable to shake off the empty seats, or the taunts from opposition supporters, for the seats left unused during several their home games. The club, before their takeover documented in the earlier chapters, had endured a barren spell and even saw the club drop down into League One for a spell. If their current success has briefly outgrown their fanbase, their long-term success plan will soon see the Etihad filled. Perhaps the signing of Erling Haaland will bring the Manchester club their elusive first European Cup.

But not all new owners chose to follow the established blueprint when purchasing an established club at the top of their game. Red Bull are an energy drinks giant who have grown into a huge sports brand the company own 15 titled sports teams, including five football clubs, but a huge part of their success story has been their focus on their centralised youth setup is threatening to change football practices, but their takeovers and success has not made the majority of fans happy with their sporting juggernaut; from Red Bull Salzburg to New York Red Bulls, FC Liefering, Red Bull Brazil and the crown jewel RB Leipzig, the energy drinks brand continues to grow. They are not the only club who have either purchased or invested in several clubs. The City Group have also in the recent decade built out their portfolio of sports club, but it is Red Bull who have irked football supporters.

In their first takeover, Austria Salzburg in 2005, swiftly renaming the FC Red Bull Salzburg, led to the firing of all members of management and staff, redesigning a new badge, completely changing the club's colours to the white-

and-red kit colour scheme now sported by all Red Bull clubs. Red Bull are also the sole sponsors of the Austrian club. Fans who wore the old team's colours of violet were removed and even ejected from the stadium for wearing it. In response, fans wanted to regain their club, angry that a company had destroyed their history and heritage.

Setting up club, SV Austria Salzburg, are currently languishing in the regional Salzburger Liga, the fourth tier of the national structure. Red Bull Salzburg, meanwhile, have won 13 Austrian Bundesliga titles in that time and spawned stars including Naby Keitam, Erling Haaland, Dominik Szoboszlai, Brenden Aaronson and Sadio Mane and former Leeds Manager Jesse Marsch. With each club takeover, wholesale changes followed, the business model demanding these changes in infrastructure are important for their brand to succeed.

Their MLS franchise New York MetroStars, became New York Red Bulls in March 2006, attracting big names including Thierry Henry and Tim Cahill. But this franchise was to bear the cost of 'win at all costs' mentality, the rebranding of the franchise wore off and despite winning their conference five times in the last decade, no MLS Cup has been secured. Runners-up in 2009 and recently, suffering an agonising defeat in the 2017 US Open Cup final and CONCACAF Champions League semi-final defeat. With the recent changes to the team, they have gone from being an elite franchise into a farm team for some of Red Bull's other franchises.

Head coach Jesse Marsch quit New York to join RB Leipzig in the Bundesliga, as an assistant in 2018 and was later named manager of the Austrian Salzburg outfit in June in a typical example of the organisation's fluidity. Player-wise, American midfielder Tyler Adams, at 20, made the move from New York to Germany with big things expected. In part due to the growth of football operations in Europe, their owner's funding in the MLS franchise has waned as attention turns to bigger challenges.

From the energy drinks brand perspective, Germany was the jewel in the crown for a sports franchise. But given the way the club operated in the past, their previous venture to purchase a Bundesliga club had been vetoed by the DFB (German Football Federation) in 2006, this didn't deter Red Bull who also failed in moves for more prominent clubs including St Pauli and Dusseldorf also fell through because Red Bull felt a team with existing history would be a marketing disadvantage to their brand.

Undeterred, the organisation settled upon fifth tier SSV Markranstadt, located 13km west of Leipzig. Red Bull were only interested in their operating licence for the league. As per the other franchises, the old team was dismantled, officially 'founded' on May 19th, 2009. Title sponsors were banned, the team became RasenBallsport Leipzig. The club used the finances of the brand to climb the leagues quickly.

Promotion from the NOFV-Oberliga Sud to the Bundesliga by 2016. Before a solid start to their life in the Bundesliga, quickly followed by a Champions League place a year later, under the guidance of former Southampton boss Ralph Hasenhuttl.

Despite the criticism on and off the field over the brands disregard for the establishment of the football pyramids, crowds have continued to grow to over 40,000. But not without some fan unrest, claiming they no longer have a say in their football club. RB Leipzig are not the only German club to be owned by a major conglomerate, Bayer Leverkusen owned entirely by pharmaceuticals giant Bayer. Wolfsburg with ties to car manufacturer Volkswagen, yet these clubs target to have strong links to their fan bases and communities.

Ensuring projects tie their clubs to the heart of their communities. Whilst there is a detachment from their clubs' fans, their football prowess has been built on smart scouting and football development.

Using their network of clubs to loan out talent and ensure they get first team football for their progression into the more profile Red Bull clubs. Despite recently suffering a torrid time at Manchester United and a main target of Cristiano's Ronaldo's bruised ego tirade, German coach and director of football, Ralph Rangnick, played a major role in the recruitment and scouting network that brought the club the success and long-term footballing vision.

The Red Bull scouting network was also smarter than half of the Premier League clubs after Erling Haaland had been trialled around by over ten Premier League clubs, RB Salzburg pounced on the Norwegian from Molde, signing the striker for €8m in January 2019. He went onto score 19 goals in sixteen games. He was later sold to Borussia Dortmund the following year for €20m.

Given their success, it is a surprise they haven't been successful in moving into the English game, they have previously tried to Sponsor Leeds United and were rumoured to be looking into Everton and Liverpool in the late 2000s, before all three clubs later were sold to new owners. The DNA of Red Bull's franchises successes are now all over football, from scouting level to the board room with

Directors of Football, Red Bull are not interested in Shirt Sponsorship, maybe not even stadium naming rights, Red Bull want to be part of footballs future and control the influence on the global market.

Football has moved a long way from the cigars and brandy in the boardroom, clubs are businesses and brands, the European Super League proved that fans may have become an afterthought of owners, but the fan protest of the European Super League and our love of the game will mean for now, club owners will still be held accountable and our love for the transfer window is as strong as ever.

Broaching the issue on whether one transfer window would be beneficial to football-to-Football Finance Expert Kieran Maguire is not so sure.

It would reduce competitive balance even more; we have seen this with the move to five substitutes. The ball is in play less, with the Premier League average around 50 minutes and the top Premier League clubs are already hoarding players, the window, yes is hectic, but it does create some boundaries and structure.

Chapter 13
Managing an Ever-Changing Situation

"The most important thing for the manager is certainly their recruitment." Gareth Ainsworth manager of Queens Park Rangers.

The role of the football manager has changed as football transfers and football finance has evolved. Managers such as Nigel Clough were expected to do the deals and boardroom discussions, now more qualified Directors of Football conduct the business side of the deals and the managers are left to the coaching and tactics, one which managers find the hardest as they seem to want to be more DOF themselves and leave the coaching to their first team coaches.

Ask anyone in football and the job of managing a football club is the hardest job in football. Players more than ever are seemingly willing to down tools on a manager, it is easier, quicker and cheaper for a board of directors to sack a manager, than it is to sign new players under FFP.

We hear football analysts say it is the manager's job to control the dressing room, but if players are not giving 100 percent on the pitch or carrying out the managers instruction. Players can seem to get an easier ride than most when it comes to criticism.

When looking for a manager to interview many wanted to talk, but off the record, fearful of how talking about transfers or players not trying would hurt them in future jobs, but one thing was constant, they all discussed how Sam Allardyce has had a major impact on managers and the transfer window, a manager who until recently, was the last of the managers who used to conduct transfer business as well as coach the players. It has not always worked for Allardyce on transfers, but he is a fascinating study for people to review.

Speaking on several podcasts now, Allardyce, known by many Premier League directors as Firefighter Sam, due to his success of parachuting into clubs and saving them from relegation, is a fascinating case study. "I often get asked why we do it, as managers. Football is a drug." He explained to Andy Gray and Richard Keys. "We're only as good as the players we manage." Allardyce was one of the first English managers to use and take advantage of loan to buys, to loans with an obligation to buy into English football which allowed him to take Bolton up the leagues and into European places.

"The game is changing, wingers are no longer wingers, your full backs need to be able to create otherwise your side is unbalanced." Recently, Sam has been criticised for taking jobs in the Premier League then immediately asks the board for money, or funds to dive into the January market, followed by "these are not my players, I need to bring in some players."

It is fair to critique this and argue that when you accept the job of the owner or chairman, you are accepting the job, they are your players, and you are being paid to coach these players to safety. But this is the argument most managers push in the media; they need time and three or four windows to build a team. But time is never given, fans want instant success, but coaching is a dying breed in some corners of the football world and there is an argument on whether panic buys or transfers solve the problem.

Clubs spend millions to climb one or two places to gain (£5m in prize money) Could a good manager with coaching staff lift teams up the league for less? In the 2018/19 season, West Ham United finished 10th, 2 points behind Everton, who finished 12 points behind Manchester United (4 wins). Everton received £4m pounds more for finishing two points ahead of West Ham. Yet, both clubs invested heavily the next summer to try and move up, when the reality is they would likely only receive a few million pounds more in merit payment for finishing a position or two higher.

It also highlights how every game in the Premier League counts. Two points separated two positions, highlighting how good coaching and referee's decision will continue to play a big role in the success of teams.

Football decisions need to be made instantly which puts intense pressure on all parties to get a player signed or sold. It is easy to see why pressure situations can happen. Managers who I spoke to were also keen to point out one issue for use in the book. If a club is operating with a DOF, or the Chairman is doing the deals. Is it always fair to sack the manager? A manager who previously managed in the Premier League discussed, "it is business at the end of the day. They (signings) are not your decisions, you are the coach, not the manager. A manager should be allowed to buy the players. Or at least have a say. If you don't and they are not good, if the team are trained well and tactically well drilled, managers should not always be the fall guy."

It is a fair point made by managers. Both managers and DOF stress that communication between the board, the manager and the transfer committee is key to success. When diagnosing why Allardyce was sacked from Everton after taking them from 13th to 8th, on the surface it appeared to be harsh. But the tactics in the final two months and Everton's inability to catch Burnley for the final Europa League place was to prove both pivotal for the club and Allardyce.

Tactically, Everton found themselves easily beaten at half-time, at both Manchester City and Arsenal, with Allardyce staring down a significant deficit at half-time. A slump in the final month of the season saw Burnley keep Everton at bay. In his only transfer window Allardyce and then DOF Steve Walsh spent £45m and nearly £10m a year in wages to Cenk Tosun and Theo Wallcott believing they could make a difference in their charge for Europe. "We didn't have a goal scorer, and Walcott added pace," this is how Allardyce described the signings, and this is where the criticism came, he had two of Europe's best emerging talents at Everton, who he refused to play, preferring older veteran players.

Ademola Lookman and Nikola Vlašić were jettisoned on loan, both players flopped at Everton and with both young talents leaving Everton in the Summer transfer window as their pathways were blocked, the board sacked both Allardyce and Walsh over the failure. If Allardyce found a young striker, who could score fifteen goals and centre midfielder, who had the work rate and technical ability for the same money, there is an argument to be made Allardyce would still be Everton manager and the club would have been back in Europe, three years after their last appearance. Alas, Allardyce and Walsh went for expensive older players, the sliding door effect, both paid for the mistake for their job.

The role of the manager has changed vastly, but still lower down the football pyramid, managers still do both jobs, usually down to the cost of employing both. But with the new way of conducting business in football has led to many times where a manager ends up with a player you don't want? Or the players you have are not responding to your changes on the pitch. The manager becomes the easy person to blame, but there are other factors that have impacted a manager and their recruitment.

With Spurs struggling in the Premier League, mere months from their fairytale journey to the Champions League final, Manager Mauricio Pochettino coming under increasing pressure with results stalling and Spurs tumbling down the table, blamed Brexit for one of the main reasons why Spurs did not spend any money citing the price inflation caused by Britain leaving the European Union. Social media and right-wing leaning MP's telling the manager to stick to football and leave politics out of football. For Pochettino, the reality was, politics had conspired to dissolve his transfer strategy.

With the new immigration policy, Spurs were seeing a 30% increase in their expected cost of overseas players so they would meet the new points-based work permits needed to register the players. Restricting the supply of European and World footballers meant the price of UK-based players rose significantly. Spurs, despite their recent success, were the only club not to sign any player in the summer transfer window since its incarnation in 2003.

Critics could argue Spurs could have sold unwanted players to increase their transfer budget, but there was some substance to their argument. The value of the pound plummeted versus the Euro, and the need for the transfer fee to be a certain percentage if the player was not a full international, prices did increase. In 2017, Premier League clubs spent £1.4bn in the summer, this dropped to £1.25bn, following Brexit, this rose again to £1.41bn.

With no new players, and a team seemingly running out of ideas, Pochettino was sacked from Spurs, form might be temporary, but managers achievements in football are easily forgotten, management can be the loneliest place in football at times. Pochettino, a manager who was sacked even though he had no say in the transfer dealings, the players 'loved' him, yet it was their performances which got him sacked, they were the ones who made the errors, played poorly, yet it is the manager who is the easy sacking.

In comparison, the director of football and Sporting Directors are given an easy ride. Manchester United are now onto their eighth manager Erik Ten Hag in trying to finally find their successor to Sir Alex Ferguson. Eight years after he retired, the players and the directors were let off repeatedly until the final few months of the season, when it was clear some of the players had given up. Scott McTominey after United's 1V3 loss to Arsenal, "there is a whole load of problems in terms of players, staff, everything higher up…" accused the team of lacking the 'fundamentals of football' including balls and belief.

"There was really no hiding place left for the players, even former United legends had had enough. Gary Neville arguing 'they've got worse,' with Interim Manager Ralf Rangnick not scared of pulling punches, 'It is a total rebuild, ten players need to be moved on, they lack the basics of football and desire,' a damming admission, but one that left the real problem, the players with no way to hide."

talkSPORT ran a segment with Simon Jordan and Jim White debating whether teams can sack their way to success? Looking into the Spurs scenario above it is hard to see why it is always managers who get the sack. Jordan lamented that the directors who make the poor decisions are not held to account. Jordan brings the evidence against the current situation of Manchester United and the players quitting as an example. In Spurs' case, Chairman Daniel Levy was the one hiring the following managers and concluding the transfer dealings off the pitch.

William Still, was the youngest manager in the Belgium First Division, acknowledged the help the game has made on his career so far, explaining how football manager gave him the impetus to want to set up a team, to be able to talk to players and discuss tactics. It gave him a glimpse of what it could be like to manage a team. Something playing the game could not do. The game allows players to understand the game more. With the game evolving, players need to dedicate their time to the simulation to find fresh players, coach and find new tactics to beat a simulation. To be successful players need to invest in the details of the game.

"It opens your eyes to how big of a scale being a manager is. A big part of what happens in the video game is what happens in real life, and when you do it day in day out (being a real manager) you do realise how similar it is."

Still reveals how realistic the transfer part of the game is. "When you make a transfer, there is the initial offer, then a counteroffer, players who do not agree with their wages. The general player conversations, needing to set up training regimes, fitness groups and training programs, collectively as a group and individually for players."

The designers have built the game engine based on real-life scenarios and with hours spent studying the game of football from all areas. For Still, "I think Football Manager has helped me become a better coach." Giving him the pathway into coaching which began with Preston North End's Under 14's when he was attending Myerscough College in Preston, Lancashire, given his current team, Reims, unbeaten run in France's Ligue 1, 30-year-old, Still is one of Europe's hottest prospects as a manager, albeit one whose club would be fined €25,000 per match while he studies for his UEFA Pro Licence, as UEFA rules state any club whose manager does not hold a UEFA Pro Licence would receive such fine.

Still has been recounting his meteoric rise in pre-match and post-match press conferences on Reims current unbeaten run, sitting down with the Coaches Voice, an online website where coaches discuss their careers and tactics for viewers, Still recounts how he became a manager at 30 years old. "At basically any point in my life, if someone had told me I would be the head coach of a Ligue 1 side at 30, I'd have told them to punch me in the face. It would have been a ridiculous suggestion."

"The idea that, at 30, I would be managing a team against Neymar, Kylian Mbappé, Sergio Ramos and Marco Verratti, and in the opposition dugout to Christophe Galtier, was equally mad. Life can be crazy, though. I have never set any boundaries or limits on what I might achieve, but I have also never set any specific goals. When I went into coaching, I did not set out to make it to the top tier in France by a specific age."

"Not at all. I am just not like that as a person. The key thing for me is just to enjoy what I am doing now. I make sure I stay in the present. I guess that means I am never really thinking about what is coming up, so specific moments or achievements can surprise me. I have had pinch-yourself moments over the course of my career. One came when Stade de Reims first phoned me. 'We've just appointed Óscar García as head coach, and we've been tracking you for a while,' the general director told me. 'Do you want to come down for a chat?' 'Just like that, I was assistant head coach in Ligue 1 at 28.'"

"I could barely believe it. It felt surreal that Reims knew who I was, let alone that they had been tracking my progress as a coach. I was not a known name—at least, I did not think I was—outside of Belgium, where I was born and raised, and where my whole career had been spent up until that point. Belgium feels very small and self-contained when you are there."

I went along to Reims, and they offered me the opportunity to be Óscar's assistant. They told me they liked my sessions. They had come to watch several of my sessions without me knowing, and they liked how much energy I put in and how much I got from the players. They said they had other assistants who were good with video analysis and match preparation, and they needed someone to help on the grass.

I did not think twice about taking them up on their offer. Just like that, I was assistant head coach in Ligue 1 at 28, in a league where you get to face some of the best teams in the world. I was going to be on a coaching staff going up against PSG, Marseille, Lyon and so many other teams. Unbelievable teams. I had come a long way from realising I was never going to make it as a player as a teenager in Belgium. I am English—both of my parents are English—but I have spent most of my life in Belgium.

I took up the chance to go to college and spend some time in England at 18. That was when I realised there was so much more to football than just playing. There was coaching, analysis, scouting, physiotherapy, and physical preparation. Coaching seemed like the next best thing. That was the closest I was going to get to the adrenaline buzz of playing.

My first coaching experience was with the Preston North End academy. Being involved in that was fantastic. I had done some coaching before, with my brother back in Belgium, but nothing at this level. "These kids are actually good!" I thought. After that, I knew that coaching was what I wanted to do.

When I got back to Belgium after finishing at college, I set out to get some experience in the professional game. I went knocking on doors. I found the address of anyone I could in Belgian football and went to see them. "I'm young and I'm no one," I would say. "But I have experience at Preston, and I have expertise from college. Can I, in any way, shape or form, be of any help?"

It was no after no after no. Door after door shut in my face. Some people said they would call me in two weeks, but I never heard back from them. I was starting to lose hope. And then, the last coach I tried kept his door open for me. It was Yannick Ferrera, a young Belgian coach who was in charge at Sint-Truiden in the Belgian second tier. I had played for them in the youth academy, and I had made them the last club on my list because I did not really want to go back to somewhere I had already been. But now I wanted a chance anywhere I could get one. "Can you film a game?" Yannick asked me.

"Yeah, I can do that," I replied.

"Can you cut the video?"

"Yeah, I can cut video."

"Our first opponent in the league is playing tomorrow. Go and watch them, film it, clip it, and give me feedback in two days' time." So, off I went. I wanted to prove myself so much. I could not tell you how many times I watched the game back after filming it. I just wanted to show Yannick I could see what was happening on this pitch that I had gone to in the middle of nowhere. I took what I had put together back to Yannick.

"This is ridiculous," he said. "You've done far too much!" He obviously liked what he saw, and he offered me an unpaid apprenticeship at Sint-Truiden. I was doing video analysis at first, but as time went on, I spent more time on the grass. Without anything official being said, I ended up becoming something like an assistant to him. First it was organising set-pieces, then I would be doing a rondo, then suddenly I would be doing a passing practice. I was getting increasingly involved in training.

That is all thanks to Yannick, and it is thanks to him that I got my next opportunity. I moved on to be an assistant at Lierse in the same division, and when I was 24—about three years after getting my first job under Yannick—the manager was sacked. The owner phoned me up almost immediately after sacking the manager. "You're doing it," he said. "What?" I replied.

"As from tomorrow, you are head coach. You are doing it." I told him, with all due respect, that there were a few other coaches there with far more experience than me to whom he should turn. It was: "Thank you, but no thank you."

"No, no," he said. "I do not care about the others. I like you. You have got loads of innovative ideas. You are doing it." I didn't really have a choice in the matter. So, at 24 years of age I was manager—albeit caretaker manager—at a Belgian second division club.

How did I feel? I was absolutely bricking it. But we did really well when I was in charge. We had been second bottom of the league when I took over in October, but we managed to turn things around and get us up the table. What was crazy was how much my world was flipped upside down. I went from being a *complete* nobody to someone who was known—locally, at least. Suddenly, I was getting stopped in the shops and seeing myself in the news and on the telly. Although I was the head coach of a professional team, I was also still trying things out in football manager as well.

I had never considered that football manager had had an influence on my real-life career, but thinking about it now, it did. I got fixated on it as a kid, and playing the game probably ignited the fire in me that I have now as a coach on the touchline. I had been obsessed with it growing up. Me and my brother would play it relentlessly—we were not allowed a PlayStation, so we played football manager on the family computer. We got into building a squad, picking a team, organising training, making sure the team was going in the right direction—all the details.

There was nothing better than that, even if it was virtual! And then here I was, doing it for real. I remember, when I was at Sint-Truiden, I was trying to win the league with them in the game as well! As my career has progressed (back in the real world!), though, I have not had the time to get stuck into the game like I used to. Things started to get really busy for me at Reims.

Being Óscar's assistant was incredible. After half a season, I had to go back to Belgium to complete my coaching badges. Once I had got them out of the way, Reims asked me to come back again. Then, the almost unthinkable happened. My phone rang. It was the owners. "Óscar is leaving," they told me. "These are the terms of your contract, so you cannot leave. We want you to take over."

I did not have much choice or time to mull it over. I had had a brief spell in charge of Beerschot in the Belgian first division in 2021, after three years as assistant there, and I had done pretty well. We finished the season mid-table, but they decided to bring in a new manager during the off-season. I had forged a certain type of relationship with the players, so I decided that going back to being the assistant would not have been a good idea. That is when I decided to leave, and from there I ended up going to Reims.

Just like the bug you get on Football Manager, I wanted to get another opportunity as a head coach. But just like at every other stage in my career, I had not planned it. I had not thought at any point that I would be Stade de Reims' head coach. Especially not yet. This was October 2022, and they initially gave me the job until the World Cup in Qatar. That meant six games to get as many points as possible. Then, they said, we would reassess the situation.

It was another pinch-me moment. But things moved so fast, and there were so many jobs to get on with, that I didn't really have any time to think about it or reflect on the fact that I was now a Ligue 1 head coach—albeit a caretaker at that point.

Three days later, I was stood in the dugout having prepared the Reims squad for their Ligue 1 fixture against Paris Saint-Germain. Pinch-me moments do not get much more dramatic than that: walking past Mbappé, Verratti, Gianluigi Donnarumma, Marquinhos, Ramos, Danilo, and the rest of their players in the tunnel. Simply crazy. Do not get me wrong, though. I was not just in awe. I had a stressful week in the lead-up to the game. My main thought was: "I just hope we don't get smashed 6–0." That was always a possibility against a team like PSG.

Then, the closer we got to the game, I started to become more relaxed. And once the players are out for their warm-up, something just happens to you as a head coach. I do not know how to explain it, but all nerves went out the window and my mind was incredibly focused. It was game time, and I had a job to do. Lionel Messi had picked up an injury in the Champions League in midweek, so he was out, and Galtier was giving Neymar and Achraf Hakimi a rest, so they were on the bench.

Obviously, it was still a ludicrously strong team, but it gave us a bigger glimmer of hope. My players carried out my game plan brilliantly and we got a goalless draw. Neymar and Hakimi came on, but they still could not score. It was the first time in the season that PSG had failed to score. This was October, and nobody had kept a clean sheet against them since March. It was an incredible feeling to do that in my first game in charge. The atmosphere started to change at the club, and we went on a better run of form.

When I took over, we had one win and four defeats from nine games. We had been in the relegation zone. Then, in my six games before the break for the World Cup, we went unbeaten, winning twice and moving up to 11th in the table. The board were so happy with how things had gone and—crucially—how the mood around the club had been lifted, that I was given the job on a permanent basis. So, at 30 years old, here I am, in charge of a Ligue 1 club. I could not be happier.

It is challenging work, there's pressure and there's attention. But I can put that to one side to focus on my job. I am not a fan of the spotlight and attention that comes with being a head coach at all. I am not extremely outgoing. I am open and relaxed with people I know, but I do not feel comfortable getting too much attention. But if I get to spend every day with my boots on, out on the grass with 26 footballers (who are really good!) and three bags of balls, I am happy. I would do it for free, so to do it as a job is genuinely a dream come true.

There are loads of specific moments that stand out already, but the best thing about my job is the feeling of building something together; of working on something as a group, putting it into practice, and producing results. We might not have the best players, but as a group we can create something special together. As I said, I have never planned out my career. Looking forward, I will probably just take whatever is thrown my way.

But the little kid in me who spent all those hours becoming one of the best managers in the world and winning everything on football manager tells me to hold on to the dream of coaching West Ham. I am a massive West Ham fan, and that really would be the dream. Obviously, there is a bit of a way to go before I get there, so I have got plenty of hard work to do and hours in the real world to put in. I am ready for the challenge.

Still is not the only senior professional working in Football to use football manager, Lutz Panenstiel, Hoffenheim's Head of International scouting at the time, recommended to the club that they should sign Roberto Firmino for £3.5m. Making him Hoffenheim's most expensive player. He later moved to Liverpool in July 2015 after sports director Alexander Rosen finalised a deal in the region of £29m.

But after being offered to Hoffenheim and sending their scouts, Lutz used the game to build a profile for Firmino. "I'm not ashamed to say that I discovered Roberto Firmino on football manager. It's not even big news, many clubs need the statistical data provided by this game to find talents. I noticed the stats and parameters and they were remarkably interesting."

One of the hardest jobs for the manager when taking over a new club is how to deal with players who perhaps do not fit their system, or if they want to bring in new players where there is not necessarily a need. But what if the player you wish to sell wants to stay. When Nuno Espirito Santo became the new Tottenham Hotspur manager in 2021, he faced an uphill task from day 1. Spurs Chairman, Daniel Levy, had publicly touted several high-profile managers, failing to attract them, Nuno and his new players he was not originally even on the shortlist of managers Levy wanted.

Not a good start for the manager. He also lost the dressing room quickly with some of his decisions. One of those was Joe Hart, whom he wanted to sell immediately, Hart was the backup goalkeeper. "I was committed," confirms Hart, "I had another year at Spurs, and I wanted to see out my contract, but Nuno came in and wanted control on some aspects of recruitment. He called me in, not to his main office, a side office where no other player could see, with just the sporting director with him. Nuno said he would speak first, I am signing someone, a third-choice goalkeeper, it is absolutely clear, whatever happens you won't kick a ball."

Hart, taken aback by the abruptness, countered, reaching out to Nuno, who himself used to be a goalkeeper. "Out of interest, you were a goalkeeper, why has it come to this? Why can I not even be the backup to first choice goalkeeper and club captain, Hugo Loris?"

To which Nuno was blunt, but clear in his evaluation of Hart as a player. "In my opinion, we all reach a point in our career when the body doesn't allow you to play football. We're at it now, I would not feel comfortable with you playing one minute for me. You're too old, the ball's too quick, you're not moving, you've got no strength."

Hart remembers the moment a manager has essentially "buried me, and I am laughing because whether I am deluded or not, I don't agree with any of that." Hart looked at the sporting director, who shrugged. "Erm... Yeah, pretty awkward, isn't it?"

Joe Hart, despite being told he was finished as a footballer by Nuno, Daniel Levy still "managed" to sell him to Celtic for £1m in the 2021 Summer transfer window. Hart would go onto keep 23 clean sheets in 46 games in all competitions, winning the Scottish Premiership. Nuno was sacked less than three months later.

For every positive transfer story by managers, there is always a sliding doors moment in football, leaving a manager with a 'we almost signed this player'. None more so than Erling Haaland, where ten of the best Premier League and academies missed the chance to sign the striker for £4m. Duncan Ferguson, who was assistant manager under Carlo Ancelotti at Everton, was a first team coach when Everton Director of Football Steve Walsh chose not to sign the Norwegian. Speaking on Footy Accumulator's YouTube channel to hosts, Sam Allardyce and Natalie Pike, Ferguson explains why Everton and the other Premier League clubs missed the signing.

His dad had brought Haaland around select British clubs, Ferguson confirms Everton, like most clubs, had Haaland in for a trial, but his current club, Bryne FK in Norway wanted £3m–£4m pounds. Steve Walsh did not think he was worth the deal and Haaland was eventually sold to RB Salzburg in 2018/19 season for £6.5m. Considering Everton were looking for a striker this season, they and all the other Premier League clubs would have been kicking themselves with this decision. Ferguson, who was a first team coach, thought Haaland was good enough, but unfortunately it was not Ferguson's decision to make.

Perhaps the most significant look into football management and their recruitment is Liverpool FC's recent success and Pep Lijnders, assistant to manager Jürgen Klopp during their recent success, his book 'Intensity' gives readers a look behind the steel curtain of a Premier League club and their operations. It provides us with a view on how one of Britain's most successful clubs in the last few years have operated and his view on coaching players, but also how managers are involved in the recruitment process at the Merseyside club.

Planning and having a vision and one identity flows through the entire book, Pep earlier claims, "logic will get you from A to B, but imagination can take you anywhere." He is also key in pointing out that coaching and training is Liverpool's transfers. The club have spent millions (recent spending has taken this over a billion), but Liverpool has several analysts and scouts reviewing their opponents and their own players even before Klopp and Pep take training sessions. They are given details on where their opponents are weak, and it allows the coaching staff the time and focus to make the players the best version of themselves.

I have been critical of several managers in this book who have taken over clubs and immediately claimed, "these are not my players, I need more players," only to fail later by failing the basics of coaching and several coaches and future Premier League managers could do well to read Pep's book and see how their coaching stacks up against Liverpool's. Coaching and preparations is still the success in football.

Another portion of this book looked into youth academies within clubs and how they play an integral role in the success of clubs, and a lack of a player pathway has seen clubs squander millions just to stand still or move up a few measly places in their respective leagues. One area Liverpool have been keen to stress is their player pathway, and even if this means a player may not succeed at breaking into the first team, they are sold on at significant profit, to fund purchases on quality players.

When Roberto De Zerbi took over the reins at Brighton recently and did not see immediate wins, he did not say the players were not his, or begged for more funds. Brighton had recently lost their Technical Director to Newcastle, scouting team and manager to Chelsea, De Zerbi did not complain or panic, he called out his star players for more and coached the team harder to get his vision across.

All whilst Brighton continually operated on a negative net spend. (Where the club receives more in transfers than they spend.)

With Liverpool in the deep portions of their pre-season, Pep considers their options at centre half, with both Nat Phillips and youngster Rhys Williams seeing extended playing time for the club in 2020/21 due to injuries to Liverpool's three main central defenders, Virgil van Dijk, Joe Gomez and Joël Matip, thus putting Phillips and Williams in the shop window for prospective buyers. With the Summer addition of Ibrahima Konaté for £35m, Pep explains Liverpool need five central defenders for their systems, this would allow one of Williams and Phillips to be moved in the summer window, squad planning is as much as creating a pathway for youngsters, as it is remaining competitive and balanced on the pitch.

Pep discusses not wanting to play, their number 6 pivot, Fabinho 'the Lighthouse' as an emergency defender. Phillips's game time is managed whilst a deal with Bournemouth is struck, a season long loan to the Championship team, the hope is continued game time and a potential future fee for a player who is Liverpool's fifth-choice centre-back.

Looking into Liverpool's pre-season coaching Pep is keen to pass the message onto his players 'the ball will never get tired', a philosophy to move the ball quicker against stagnant opposition, make them move, make them tire and then Liverpool's fresher legs would pounce in the later stages of the match. Reviewing Liverpool's Scoring Rate: percentage of matches where the team scored at least one goal, home and away, Liverpool for this season, home and away, scored a goal 82%, in the second half, but only conceded 24% of goals in the second half.

A statistic which could support the new five substitute rule will Favour teams such as Liverpool and Manchester City more as their squads are vastly better than the rest of the Premier League, this is likely to see more goals scored by Liverpool in the future. A result of their better coaching and transfer business.

Despite the links to a number of players, Pep maintains Liverpool are only seeking quality players, to better the starting 11, or youngsters to boost their academy, but juggling players desires for first team football is always a fine balance, even at a successful club, when Lyon make on offer for backup winger, Xherdan Shaqiri, a player who was entering the final 12 months of his contract and unlikely to sign a new deal.

The offer comes in late on a Sunday evening, after Liverpool have just played two weekend pre-season fixtures at Anfield, with Klopp ringing Pep to discuss, first the offer, but also a workable solution for the club. Transfer negotiations are done by Liverpool's Julian Ward—sporting director, taking over from Michael Edwards, who was stepping down and looking for a new challenge. They acknowledge the player has desire to leave for more game time, but discuss the fee needs to be higher, the bargaining chips with the players contract running down are in the player and Lyon's corner, but Liverpool can still demand or set a price.

The offer has come in late in the window, but also late in the day, Sunday evening. It is true with the window; the transfer window truly is twenty-four hours. With no time to unwind from the pre-season game and focus on Norwich in the Premier League opener in seven days, Liverpool are discussing selling one of their squad players. Shaqiri would be sold to Lyon a few days later for €6.00m.

It highlights how the sporting director (director of football) system works in football, the coaches and managers can still coach and allow a qualified director to deal with the negotiation, so there are no distractions for the team or manager. Another manager whose team does not employ a sporting director, would be forced to negotiate a deal and not be preparing for the next Premier League game, negotiating against a professional whose job it is to get the best deal, whilst the manager is employed, to get the tactics right. It further emphasises how both roles need to work together, in tandem and agreement.

If Klopp and Pep did not understand the player and situation, or had a different philosophy on transfers, Liverpool could lose out on €6.00m, and a player on their short list could be purchased by another rival before they get to act. It is a small part of the transfer ecosystem, but indicates Liverpool had a plan for it, by not offering Shaqiri, a player who wanted to move to clubs, it allowed them to have some barging when it came to a fee, if they had offered him out, teams would have bid significantly less money.

Even for clubs like Liverpool, unexpected bids for players can come in, they must be accessed by managers and Directors alike. Southampton registered an interest in loaning Alex Oxlade-Chamberlain for the season. Despite him being a squad player, Pep and Klopp have been impressed by the way he has played, trained and fits in with the club. Liverpool will not entertain it and Oxlade-Chamberlain came through Southampton's academy and is from the area, is not tempted by the link.

Pep reaffirms that he is integral to Liverpool's plans, allowing them to switch between their 433 and a 442 Diamond formation, he can play in three central positions and at this moment, only permanent deals could tempt Liverpool, because Liverpool have a transfer policy that any replacement must be 'Plan A' improve the team, we have reviewed Liverpool's pursuit of Virgil van Dijk earlier in the book and Pep reaffirms, Van Dijk, was Liverpool's only option, they had him rated above all centre-backs.

Even admitting they held personal conversations with the player. "I remember sitting in Jürgen's kitchen just before we had a personal conversation with Virgil (when Van Dijk was set to sign for the club.) I have never seen Jürgen so determined: We must get him, Pep—it's him and nobody else. We only had plan A. Jürgen did not want a plan B. We were convinced we could take the next steps as a team, but for a long time it did not work in trying to get him."

Another aspect this book has highlighted to fans is the use of data has been employed in football, both in scouting new players, but Lijnders lets us see how coaches are using data in their coaching to make their teams better. If managers are reluctant to use data, they risk becoming the dinosaurs of coaching. Their analyst had drawn up how they attacked and defended corners, where it is best for players to be stationed at set pieces like corners. It is the reason why Liverpool for this season are ranked highly for goals scored and have few goals conceded at corners.

But their analyst, Mark, has drawn up where their 'Lighthouse' Fabinho could be coached to be more central, "Lighthouse because he guides and controls us." They have run the data and seen when Fabinho is more central in transition, he breaks up attacks more and Liverpool have attacking oppositions off the counter press.

Focusing on a youth pathway to maintain their next crop of footballers coming through the academy is also a key role, not just for a football club, but for the coaching staff, Pep joined Liverpool from Porto, initially as a youth coach and has coached a number of their players coming through. Leighton Clarkson joined Blackburn Rovers in the Summer transfer window on loan, a move that is discussed in the book as being in the works for several weeks. In Austria, Pep was discussing with Julian Ward.

At the end of last season, the coaching staff highlighted Leighton as a player who was ready to step up and go on loan to taste first team football to continue his possible development towards the first team. Player progress is difficult, for any team, trying to get their younger players game time and not impacting results is a fine balance, teams in Europe have a benefit, as they have more games where they can deploy their youth players, but Liverpool ensure their under-21's are training almost twice a week with the first team. This is not a new or imaginative idea, most teams do it, but it allows the players to interact with the first team players and learn from them.

When discussing Ben Woodburn's loan in the same window, Pep admits it can be difficult to let a player go, because you care about him and worry about the coaching they receive. "Jürgen had called me into the office, he had just finished talking to Ben, and he wanted to let him go out on loan, I must admit, I became a little emotional because I believe in him so much and he had enjoyed a good pre-season with us… In the past, a loan process sometimes was a bit like flipping a coin: sometimes it worked, sometimes it didn't. It depended on too many processes which we didn't have control over at the loan club. But now, as a club, I believe we are one of the best around at managing this."

Pep continues to explain how you must motivate these younger players and encourage them that the pathway is there, they can play in your system, "I prefer talents without many games over players with many games but with not a lot of talent."

The opposite of sending a player on loan is to integrate them the youth player into the first team, whereas described above, managers cannot always attend every youth game to review players, so every week, the first team can come into the first team dressing room at the training ground, experience their coaching, their facilities, make them feel like a first team player years before they actually are good enough to be one. It shows the clubs identity to be a 'one club mentality' a proven pathway for younger players but allows the clubs first team analysts to scout their own youth set ups to find their strengths and weaknesses.

This 'one club mentality' flows into Liverpool's transfer strategy, "keeping a group together plus talent and training is, for me, the three main ingredients in a successful formula. Training, improving players, improving the team. One thing for sure: when we sign (a player) we should sign for the first 11 and nothing else."

Not panic buys, a clear plan, recruitment strategy and vision, when several Premier League clubs have recently spent significant money on players, only to see them be expensive squad players, not good enough to challenge the first team, then seeing them sit on a bench, perhaps taking up a position a younger player could use. Liverpool have spent significantly, as we have detailed in this book, the 2022 summer Window took Klopp's spending north of £1bn, but crucially, it has been spent on players who have made them better, whilst other teams have spent similar amounts chasing them, yet stood still.

Another interesting insight is how transfer deadline day affects the management team. Again, Pep tells us how Deadline Day is less stressful as they have been planning since February, almost seven months prior. In this February meeting, they discussed the importance of signing players early, it allows new signings to be integrated, avoids expensive panic buys, and be prepared for any late moves. With Ibrahima Konaté signing for £35m early in the window, it gives Liverpool the marquee signing fans crave, the player gets a full pre-season in a new system, and gives coaches like Pep, the chance to focus on getting their youth the best loan deals.

Pep being an assistant manager is new to press conferences, both before and after games, he has stepped up in a few recently, some due to Covid, where he has actually taken over the team on match day but understands they can be used to probe managers for transfer snippets. He also understands how players listen to them, key to use them to motivate his players and provide an insight into his coaching methods, but why as a former youth coach, he is keen to maximise the players in Liverpool's Under 21's.

With Liverpool progressing into the League Cup with a game against Norwich, Liverpool and Pep saw an opportunity to rotate and give first team debuts to several academy graduates. Sometimes a team needs luck in the cup draw, playing against Manchester United and Manchester City, Liverpool may not have had the fortune to make these calls. But Norwich, in a relegation fight, Liverpool gave full debuts to Conor Bradley and Kaide Gordon, as well as Tyler Morton, who came on for Naby Keita.

In the press conference after the game, Pep was key to indicate, young players never let you down, always offer 100% effort, "we need to create a new generation of Liverpool players who can continue our project. In five years, Mo (Salah) would be 34 and Kaide 21, Fabinho 32 and Tyler 23. Curtis Jones, another academy graduate, played his 50th game for the club." The encouragement for Liverpool does not stop on the playing field or press conferences. Pep is a believer that competition breeds success, training should be harder than actual games, if a team is 'shocked or under cooked' during a game, then the coaches have failed to prepare them properly. "There is no substitute for competition in training, it drives all athletes to levels they couldn't even dream of."

Behind the scenes, planning for January recruitment began in earnest, in a cold damp room in Liverpool's training complex in Kirkby. Julien Ward, Klopp, Pep, and an assistant, meet in November to discuss January targets, discussing four key targets they have been reviewing. One target is lucky to still be on the market. Heralded as a game changer, Luis Díaz of Porto, whom Liverpool had seen up close and personal in the Champions' League Group Stages. The irony as we have seen earlier in this book is Díaz should have signed for Liverpool's cross-city rivals Everton in the summer.

Only then manager Rafael Benítez's power struggle with then DOF Marcel Brands over transfers, players and strategy, an example of how managers wish to overrule or run other departments, leading to a clouded strategy, meant the already agreed deal between Porto and Everton came off the table. Another missed opportunity for the Merseyside club riddled with boardroom issues and a lack of vision. Everton's loss became Liverpool's gain. With the January transfer window opening, the discussion to sign gained pace.

With Díaz almost joining Everton in the Summer of 2021, several clubs were circling, with this in mind and more European clubs having the financial muscle the following summer, Liverpool chose to explore the possibility of signing Díaz in January 2022. Pep explains how Jürgen Klopp, himself and Victor Matos, their Elite Development Coach, settled down to run through the possibility of exploring their positive relationship with the Portuguese club due to their recent loan move for Marko Grujic from Liverpool, and the understanding Porto may need to raise funds as a consequence of Covid-19.

Liverpool had already sounded out the player who had expressed interest in coming to the Premier League, Pep was reassured Julian Ward and his scouting team had the details from their reports confirming what Klopp and Pep believed Díaz would be a game changer for Liverpool. Pep even highlights how Liverpool's management team is aligned with the thoughts of their owner, board of directors and scouting team, a direct contrast to that at their city rivals who passed up on Díaz.

"Luis was a fighter, a winner and someone who could play immediately for us. We needed players with energy." Pep is also letting any reader into the knowledge that Liverpool have noticed successful Premier League players need pace, energy, work rate and technical ability to perform at the highest level.

Perhaps a sign to other Premier League clubs, if your new signings are not fitting this mould, you may be looking at the wrong type of player.

"It would be a statement if we did it then, a message to the team, Luis is a threat from everywhere, connects well with the ones around him, which is a huge plus for such a quick, intelligent, skilful winger, we needed to be smart, the player wanted to come." As Julien Ward began negotiation, it did not stop Pep from continually scouting the player, complimenting his scouting team for drawing up videos of highlights of specific moments of the player at certain moments, counter press, movement off the ball.

Steering clear of the fan videos of goals and assists on YouTube. Focusing on the phases of the game and ensuring he is watching the 90 minutes to see how Díaz reacts to certain moments, adversity, how he performs under pressure. But it is also here where Pep seemingly takes a cheeky jab at the media and their transfer rumours, Liverpool's move for Díaz came out of the blue, not predicted by the media, we know the ones we really like a long time before it is in the media.

As the transfer window drips on day by day, you can see the nervousness in Peps words, a true belief in the player, a stark contrast to Rafael Benítez who felt the player would not adapt to the Premier League, Pep describes his feelings as "we needed the boy as much as the desert needs water, he would come here and play, we needed this boost. He was the best player in Portugal at that moment and all top players from Portugal came to England and made an immediate impact at new clubs."

The hope is that it would have a similar impact to the Virgil van Dijk signing in January 2018, which took Liverpool onto the next level. Perhaps if Benítez had the same philosophy of Pep, "players can achieve so much more when they feel wanted. Triggered and inspired." He may still be in a managerial role.

During a break, Pep details how on holiday, he receives a phone call from Julian Ward, Spurs have bid for Díaz, it is a good offer, and he has asked could Klopp and Pep be ready in five minutes to convince the player to sign for Liverpool. At a dinner with his partner, a coach's job and transfers never stop. Within minutes, Pep and Klopp are Face Timing Díaz, Liverpool have matched Spurs' offer of €47.00m, more than they could have paid for him in the previous Summer, but the bidding war with Spurs had worked against them, as had Díaz's form in the Champions League.

Pep offers us the insight in how Klopp talks to Díaz, offering his vision and passion to sign the player, where he fits in with the Liverpool project, how current players will provide for him, (Andy Robertson, Trent Alexander-Arnold, but also Mo Salah and Jota.) Pep even jokes how he knew of the player from his days as a Youth Coach in Portugal. It seals the deal and days later, Díaz signs for Liverpool, catching fans and media by surprise, behind the headlines of "Díaz signs for Liverpool" none of us where the wiser to how Liverpool managed to get the deal done, the struggle late on with Spurs, how they tracked him for months, nearly signing for Everton.

More twists than a Hollywood film, now brought to life by an assistant manager, now we can see why this is a drama fans would love to see more of. Liverpool got their player, Spurs would need to move onto a new target, signing winger, Dejan Kulusevski, on deadline day on loan for a Loan fee of €10m, as one domino falls, another needs to be picked up, in the transfer market, you hope you are not the club at the bottom who lost a player they cannot replace. For Porto, they moved on from Díaz, signing his replacement, Galeno for €10m from SC Braga on transfer deadline day, who had no time to sign a replacement, their season and team weakened for the rest of the year, influenced by Díaz's move to Liverpool.

The Díaz signing is an example of Liverpool's strategy, as Pep explained earlier, only signings for the first team, players who can lift titles, for Liverpool, keeping in line with their academy pathway. "Academy and game-changers, that's where we need to invest, not second line players who take the space for our talents. We must buy premium and use the academy." A model all clubs should really strive for, money makes it easier, but even in the lower leagues of the football pyramid, if you have money to buy a player, you need to be sure they can take your club to the next level but use your academy and the loan system to build around your team.

Moving towards Summer transfer window of 2022, Liverpool were on the hunt for a new striker, rumours of Sadio Mané, whose contract was entering the final 12 months could be leaving the club, Liverpool were on the scouting search for a new player. Pep highlights his admiration for Darwin Núñez. (Liverpool would go onto sign the player for a deal that could reach up to €100m.)

After Liverpool had played Benfica in the Champions League knock out stages, Pep detailed notes on the striker, "I thought to myself we had watched one of Europe's purest and most powerful strikers fighting against our centre-halves. Not many make them work that hard, but he did. He is, for sure, one to keep an eye on; he has lots of potential."

Another target for Liverpool was Erling Haaland, who Manchester City were able to beat Liverpool in the race to sign him for €60.00m from German club Borussia Dortmund. "Lijnders, despite the disappointment in missing out on a player, explains how the transfer window, and their fees are perceived in different countries." It is a busy day in the football world as Manchester City announced a deal for Erling Haaland. It's a proper culture shock between Holland and England, where people believe the more you spend the better. But the game is so much bigger than that. Fans will always be at the heart of the club's success, they should identify with the values, the characters and leadership of the club.

Pep Lijnders gave us a chance to look behind the scenes at Liverpool, in a season where they won both domestic cups, just missed out on the Premier League and losing a Champions League Final to Real Madrid, for any aspiring coach or manager, his standards should be the bare minimum coaches and managers strive to. Owners should be asking managers in interviews how they prepare teams for matches and contrast it to Pep's ideas. It is a start, Liverpool's budget helps with the prep, but the training and tactics are the basis principles of a manager, similar to Robert De Zerbi at Brighton, currently flying in the league after beating Pep's Liverpool 3–0 in January 2023.

Coaching is the bottom line, good coaching by De Zerbi, despite losing all his scouts, players to other clubs has kept the club marching up the leagues, as others squander millions, only to go from European contenders to relegation scraps. Lijnders and De Zerbi make a mockery of managers who claim, "I need new players, these are not my players." Lijnders and De Zerbi would shrug their shoulders and say, make them yours. Transferring players for millions of pounds is not the be all and end all, it doesn't always lead to success either.

Chapter 14
Transfer Story and Quotes

Whilst researching for this book, I came across the following transfer stories and quotes that did not quite fit within the chapters I had drawn up. But I thought I would share them here to show the uniqueness and sometimes the funny unique side of the operation of the transfer window.

1) Mainz 05 Managing Director used German Magazine Sport Bild to put his players up for sale following the Covid-19 pandemic with the club needing cash to secure the business. Telling them, "Everything is cooking in the transfer market. If there is a request, we'll gauge every opportunity."

The subsequent story was followed by player names and prices for the football world to see.

- ST Robin Quaison €10m
- ST Jean-Philippe Mateta €12–€15m
- CB Moussa Niakhate €11m
- AM Jean-Paul Boetitus €4m
- Ridle Baku €5–7m

There was no guarantee he would get these prices, but to stop the haggling and speed up the process he put European clubs on notice that the club was open for business in the hope to stimulate a slow transfer market following the Covid affected seasons.

2) Jamille Matt—Journeyman/Lone Ranger

2010/11—Joins Kidderminster from Sutton Coldfield Town—free transfer
2012/13—Joins Fleetwood Town—£216k.
2015/16—Joins Stevenage—Loan
2015/16—Joins Plymouth—Loan
2016/17—Joins Blackpool—Loan
2017/18—Joins Grimsby—Loan
2018/19—Joins Notts County—Free
2020/21—Joins Forest Green Rovers—Free

Jamille has represented nine different clubs across his career. Meaning he has had to change and uproot on a near continual basis. The hidden cost of following his dream and the constant change to his lifestyle up and down the country.

March 2022, Jamille scored 17 goals for Forest Green in their bid to take their green sustainable club up the football league.

3) Malcolm

In the summer of 2018, Malcolm was chased by several clubs across Europe. Roma looked to have won the race when they reached an agreement with his club Bordeaux and agreed personal terms. Roma fans were waiting for his arrival at the airport on the plane he was scheduled to be on. Covering the airport with shirts, welcoming placards and club scarves, they were disappointed when the winger had failed to turn up.

Barcelona had intervened at the 11th hour and made Bordeaux a better offer as Malcolm was on his way to the airport. No one at Bordeaux had let Roma know they were no longer the preferred choice. Their sporting director Monchi threatened legal action against Bordeaux, claiming the deal had been concluded and paperwork had been sent to the Italian FA. Malcolm's agent said the U-turn was 'revenge' after the Italian club used a different agent to sign one of his other clients, goalkeeper Daniel Fuzcato.

4) Paul Gascoigne—1988—Manchester United were very keen on signing him. Sir Alex Ferguson recalls the conversation. "We spoke to him the night before I went on holiday." Gascoigne is alleged to have said, "go enjoy yourself, Mr. Ferguson, I will be signing for Manchester United." Ferguson went on holiday and received a phone call by then United Chairman Martin Edwards with the shocking news. "Gascoigne has signed for Tottenham Hotspur for £4.68m. It's rumoured Spurs chairman Irving Scholor had managed to change Gascoigne's mind by offering to buy a £120,000 house for Gascoigne's parents and crucially his sister a sunbed."
5) John Obi Mikel—2005—When Manchester United signed John Obi Mikel for £4m in late April 2005. Even pictured in a Manchester United shirt at a press conference unveiling him as a United player. and staged a press conference to announce the exciting prospect's arrival, not many could have predicted what would happen next. Chelsea claimed they had already had an agreement with the players agent.

United asked the Premier League to launch an investigation which caused a 12-month legal battle between the two clubs. Spring 2005, Mikel was playing for Lyn in Norway, his performance at international level at the under-17 World Cup had several clubs chasing the 18-year-olds signature.

When United brought Mikel to Carrington on trial, he was still at school and had no agent, relying on the Nigerian FA's secretary to set up meetings for him. Despite shining at his trial and Sir Alex Ferguson telling Mikel he wanted to sign him, the offer didn't follow. This created a window of opportunity for an agent, John Shittu, who told Mikel Chelsea were interested in signing him.

He spent some time on trial at Chelsea and Jose Mourinho before Shittu found Mikel a professional contact in Norway with Lyn Oslo. After six appearances, Ferguson travelled to Norway to sign the player who he had already lost once. United even took a photograph of the contract and happily shared it with the Manchester Evening News a few years later.

So, we come to Mikel, posing in a United shirt at a press conference. But behind the scenes, Chelsea were furious. Unbeknown to Mikel, Chelsea had an agreement with Lyn Oslo that the club would not sell Mikel to any other team but Chelsea. After being flown to London, Mikel claims he was accommodated and hidden away by Chelsea's owner Roman Abramovich, whilst Ferguson, agents, secretaries all tried to contact him.

Finally, after being stuck in purgatory where he couldn't play at club level, Premier League chief Sir Dave Richards intervened, engaging with Mikel to organise a meeting to decide the conflict between the clubs and find a resolution to the transfer.

The following transcript is from the Manchester Evening News. "He [Richards] offered to help me. Told me it was making enemies between the two big clubs. I told him I wanted to play for Chelsea, and he said he would help resolve it. Then I had a secret meeting with Mourinho at his house."

"Roman Abramovich organised six cars to get me there. It was like a military operation. I started in one car, then the drivers would talk to each other. Suddenly I was dropped off and then picked up by another car. Once there, Jose told me: "The boss really wants you. I will play you and make you what you want to be." That really helped as there were times when I thought: *'Have I made the right decision?'*"

"For Mikel, his decision for Chelsea was easy, they came for him after United initially didn't offer him a deal, and Chelsea had four Nigerian players on trial at the time and housed them all together to help them acclimatise. Mikel states these were the deciding factors in wanting the move to Chelsea."

"They were staying with me at the house in London to keep me company. Those guys, their lives depended on the decision I was making. If I went to United, they would be gone. If I went to Chelsea, they were going to have a career. No matter how long it lasted, that was important to me. Just to give them a chance, you know? I chose Chelsea, and four lives changed that day."

The legal saga was settled when Chelsea agreed to pay £4m to Lyn Oslo. Then £12m to United as the contract Mikel had signed for United was legal and binding. For perspective, Mikel cost Mourinho's side £3m less than the Reds had paid PSV Eindhoven for Ruud van Nistelrooy's signature just a few years earlier.

Mikel went on to enjoy an outstanding career, winning the Champions League and Europa League, two Premier League titles, four FA Cups and two League Cups across his 11 years spent at Chelsea, making 249 appearances at Stamford Bridge before leaving in 2017.

6) Emmanuel Petit—1997—travelled to North London to meet then Tottenham Hotspur Chairman Alan Sugar. Spurs even paid for the taxi to drive Petit back to the hotel. The midfielder asked the driver to take a detour once he had heard Arsenal were interested in signing him. The cab driver is alleged to have taken him straight to Arsene Wenger's house to meet David Dein, were a deal and contract were thrashed out. Spurs ended up paying for all the travel none the wiser they were about to lose out on the player.

7) Roy Keane—1993—Keane announced that he would leave Nottingham Forest after their relegation in 1993, agreeing personal terms with Blackburn Rovers. Manager Kenny Dalglish tried to get the paperwork through late on Friday afternoon, but the offices at Ewood Park had closed for the weekend. They agreed to finish the paperwork on Monday when the deal can be finalised. Hearing there was a delay, Alex Ferguson jumped in and called Keane, convinced him to renegade on his gentleman's agreement with Kenny Dalglish and they signed the paperwork over the weekend.

8) Moussa Sissoko—2016—Everton had looked set to sign Sissoko after meeting Newcastle's £30m valuation of the box-to-box midfielder. They lined up a private jet to bring him to Merseyside to sign his contract. Tottenham, learning the deal was agreed and personal terms had been finalised, swooped in and lured the player away from Goodison with a sensational last-minute bid on deadline day. With a plane waiting in Newcastle airport for Sissoko, he turned his phone off to avoid calls from Everton manager Ronald Koeman whilst he was completing his medical and move to Spurs.

9) Robinho—2008—Chelsea had begun selling replica shirts with his name on the back. Manchester City wanted and needed to make a marquee signing following Sheik Mansour's 2008 takeover of the club, signing Robinho for £32.5m. The bid came out of the blue, even confusing Robinho at his introductory press conference. "On deadline day, Chelsea and Real Madrid made offers, they were accepted." Before a reporter pointed out his error. "Chelsea? No. Manchester. Sorry."

10) Wayne Rooney—2004—Rooney had burst onto the scene at Everton, breaking through their academy at Bellfield and forcing his ways into David Moyes' plans. Moyes, reluctant to play two strikers, even played

him as a winger, or as an impact substitution off the bench. Rooney had become a hot commodity for the Merseyside club, who had unearthed a world-class player even for his tender age, the clubs' finances, despite being in the Premier League, Owner Bill Kenwright was unable to support the club from his own personal fortune, had touted him to Chelsea in the bid to raise funds. Something Rooney, or his agent were aware about, Rooney discussed on Toffee TV's podcast on Patreon, how this moment felt like a betrayal to him and one that left his agent looking for a new club during the next season.

Starting at the Euro's that year for England, Rooney started to be influenced from players and clubs. Gary Neville recently admitted on his overlap podcast (February 2022), that he had tapped Rooney up and had conversations Sir Alex Ferguson knew about.

On his return, rehabbing from a broken metatarsal, Rooney strutted into David Moyes's office and asked to leave the club. Moyes, knowing he had a world-class generational talent on his hands, said no. "If you want to leave, you'll have to submit a written transfer request."

Rooney walked into the canteen, picked up a napkin, wrote, "I want a transfer" on it and walked back into Moyes's office and said, "Here you go."

Rooney was sold to Manchester United for £27m, rising to £30m. Scoring a hat-trick on his debut, in the Champions League against Galatasaray.

11) Harry Redknapp—2022—Speaking proudly to talkSPORT radio in January, days after the January window shut, Redknapp declared he had told new Everton Manager Frank Lampard (his nephew) to sign Spurs' midfielder Dele Alli to help boost Everton's survival bid.
12) Harry Redknapp—2022—Speaking to talkSPORT radio in March Redknapp denies he advised Frank Lampard to sign Dele Alli.
13) Jürgen Klopp—2016—On criticising other British clubs and in particular Manchester United for their purchase of Paul Pogba for over €100m. "The day that this is football, I'm not in a job anymore, because the game is about playing together. I will leave football. Other clubs can go out and spend more money and collect top players. I want to do it differently. I would even do it differently if I could spend that money. Klopp would go onto having a net spend a billion pounds, helping

Liverpool win the Premier League, Champions League, FA and League Cup and the Club World Cup. Seems even Klopp enjoyed spending a penny or two to build his successful Liverpool team."

14) Jürgen Klopp—2022—Splashed out on Benfica striker Darwin Núñez for €100m. Klopp did not resign.

Chapter 15
Fergie Time

We've all been there in the stands when the Fourth Official holds up the electronic board, used for indicating to those in the stadium who is being substituted on and off and how much injury time the referee has allocated. It either brings anger if your team is protecting a one goal lead and is hanging on, or hope, if you're a fan of the other team, chasing the game, with your team on the chasing the equaliser, and it is with this either side of the fence analogy where I will look to bring this book to a close, and to provide an answer to the question. Can we have a fair transfer window model for all clubs?

When I set out to write this book, I wanted to see if we could have a fairer way for football clubs to conduct business, one that would suit all clubs, asking each person I interviewed the question on whether the two-window system we have in Europe is best and whether it should be changed. Discussing both windows, initially thinking one window for permanent (with transfer fees) and a loan window in January, for youth development, or for teams to give players six months to impress teams before a permanent move in the summer window would offer parity and competitive balance to football.

Whilst this would stop the likes of Manchester City and the rest of the 'Big Six' being able to separate themselves from the rest of the Premier League, it would also stop clubs from the lower leagues from being able to trade financially. Now more than ever, lower league clubs face a mountain to climb and need the transfer windows to sell players to stay afloat.

Denying a team from the Championship, the National Leagues and across the football leagues across the league would be wrong and could cause football clubs to go out of business. Yes, it favours the bigger, more financially secure teams, but any change to the system must not be at the detriment to the other teams in the football pyramids.

That is not to say the system cannot be improved. The current trolley dash on deadline day saw prices inflated and after interviewing several people whose jobs are affected by the system, they are all frustrated how it always comes down to the final moments. For fans, it does provide the entertainment of Deadline Day, but if the European transfer window started a day after European football's curtain raiser, the Champions League final, this would provide clubs around an extra month to trade.

Hopefully reducing the last-minute trolley dash that clubs face when the transfer dominos begin to fall late in the window. Another suggestion is to marry up the European football calendar, so the leagues start at similar times, this would allow the window to close, and no team would be selling key players three or four games into the season. The hope is this will allow for a competitive balance to be restored for all clubs across Europe.

By giving all clubs the same start and end date, whilst initially, there would likely be an economic shock to the window which would cause inflationary prices, there would be a theory that after a year or two, the 'invisible hand' would pull prices back into line with what we have seen pre-2020. New television deals and overseas tours are likely to ensure the Premier League will still be awash with funds to spend on players, scouting is improving and more Premier League clubs are catching up to their European counterparts so the need to pay a 'Premier League Tax' may also be reduced providing players choose the Premier League earlier.

But as we have looked at in this book, the stalling of the European Super League is likely to be a short lived one. With changes to the Champions League coming in 2024 and changes to the coefficient meaning it favours the teams who have been in the competition the longest, the gap between clubs desiring to improve or grow is to widen.

Discussed earlier in this book and already being tempered by the media is the prospect of the Premier League going on pre-season tours. With the rumours of a '39th' Premier League game not going away, this is one way the Premier League can expand its horizons for all 38 clubs without compromising the season or following the NFL route where a team plays a home game abroad. If the Premier League focused on its two emerging markets, North America and South Asia.

It could take ten teams to both locations in the pre-season and play their '39th' games in the pre-season. It would spread the game to new markets and allow fans to choose their own clubs, as fans who I interviewed for this book pointed out the current media coverage in America favours the 'big six' thus creating a bigger gap to the rest. Clubs could opt out of the tours, but this would provide a fairer way clubs could each earn the same fair amount and fans can choose which team they would like to follow and give them access to the players.

Scouting is another intriguing aspect of football transfers that will continue to evolve as the game and those analysts inside it begin to understand the data and how it breaks down what players contribute onto the field of play. It could and should be used to help develop young players by identifying what they are good at and areas to improve. This would help coaches develop players further rather than needing the manager or director of football to continually dip into the transfer market to find more expensive replacements.

With managers spending an average of 537 days, or 1 Year, 5 Months, 2 Weeks, 5 Days, 19 Hours, 13 Minutes and 20 Seconds to be precise, you understand why managers dip into the transfer market to buy quick wins. (Figure for the 92 clubs in the English Football League) If owners and clubs could be more patient, perhaps the data can be used to help coaches further develop themselves, who can then use it to coach the players themselves.

The future of Financial Fair Play is likely to play a significant role in the future influencing of the transfer window and club financing in the future. How its new form, working in relation to allowing a club to spend up to 70% of its turnover should favour the more financial developed clubs, the model should make clubs more sustainable and if that is the aim, then it will work, but can we get a system where all clubs have some sort of competitive advantage? I am not sure, does football even want this, with clubs putting pressure on FIFA and UEFA, some clubs have become like global conglomerates where they have the power to influence government policy in such a way any changes will continue to favour them.

This is not to say football cannot change. Look at Wrexham in the National League with Hollywood owners Ryan Reynolds and Rob McElhenney creating waves and growing the National League games stature abroad. Dale Vince and Forest Green Rovers changing the game in the football league and proving a team focused on being green and renewable can also be competitive.

Given how some owners have treated clubs in the football league and the apparent failure of the Leagues ownership test on several occasions, I wonder how long it will be until we see an ownership model in the same vein of the

NFL's Green Bay Packers? The Packers are the only publicly owned major professional sports franchise in the United States. Rather than being the property of an individual, partnership, or corporate entity, they are held as of 2022 by 537,460 stockholders.

The issue here, again, is that the number of owners, or shareholders will all have different opinions on how the club should go forward. Also, with how quick fans can turn on their clubs or over analyse defeats in the immediate aftermath of the game could lead to the club being unstable, it would need a stable board of directors to manage the club on a day-to-day basis, with a clear vision and proper governance on voting right to allow the club to operate.

One area that has been recently championed is the theory of regulation and independent commissions set up to regulate football operations. We would need to address this across the areas of football, as it may help certain areas rather than others. For example, as we reviewed in the chapter regarding football intermediaries. (Agents) Not all are bad, but the large majority have seen this as a way of making themselves vast sums of money or stature within the game.

Again, payment or remuneration for succeeding in a line of work should not be frowned upon, but there should be tighter rules or regulation that stops agents from crossing the lines of transparency when we are dealing with millions of pounds worth of transfers. Considering how tight both UK and European laws are on money laundering, any transaction over €10,000 or more would require the business to declare themselves as a high value dealer, some footballers are valued at millions of pounds as assets. If agents are as open to moving their clients nearly every transfer window by exploiting or exploring the grey area between UEFA and FIFA's rules then surely, it is an industry that needs regulation to stop any foul play.

An agent failing the exam in the UK should not be able to go to another country or Football Association to gain it there. As I explored earlier in the chapter, it has been made easier to become and agent, and whilst there are courses that are bringing through the next batch of agents and teaching them the right side of the lines, it is the powerful ones, who are building agencies and empires and openly flouting the rules, declaring their asset, sorry, I mean player will be on the move in the next window are the ones, the regulation would need to review.

Agents play a key role in football, they make it easier for these deals to happen, but they should be paid on a retainer by the player. The only time a club should pay an agent fee is if they ask the agent to find a buyer for the player. I believe a set commission fee, based off the total transfer fee, should be set for all transfers. For example, 5% of the transfer fee, so if a player is sold for £5m, the agent is potentially paid £250,000 for their service. If the player receives a loyalty bonus of the new club, I think this is where the cost should be split from the player and then the buying club. If agents are found to be flouting the rules or touting their players without the club's permission, I do believe the licence should be rescinded and they should be banned from working in football.

An argument could be made that the money that would be saved by these rules could be ring fenced into grassroots levels or filtered down the football pyramids. Critics will argue that by setting a low percentage, agents would use this to haggle up the transfer fee for their clients and again, this could happen, but when transfers begin to fall through, how long before the players turn on their agents for not acting in their best interest.

As my conversation with Kieran Maguire digging into football finance dug into the benefits of regulation, Kieran's view that regulation could be limited unless they are separate from the industry, their goals and motivations need to be to grow the game fairly and not to take away or stop the industry, but to steer it in the correct direction. But what about the governance and power to act? If there is no direct power to influence the game and make change, then it could end up like several government committees, where the findings are buried or ignored when it comes to policy.

The committees and regulation must also avoid conflicts of interests and be a separate entity from football. As the documentary, Gate Money: Inside the Non-League Football's Funding Fiasco by Fred Atkins, which can be watched on YouTube, found that the lottery funding grant of £10m, which was supposed to be split fairly between the National Leagues to cover the lost revenues during the pandemic, was potentially decided by owners of ten National League clubs. Despite government and the National League Chief Financial Promises that the revenue would be split fairly by a formula that worked off gate receipts, some clubs were better off and somewhere even not paid enough.

Those who did come out better, the large majority were in support of the National League board. This fresh example in football highlights why the regulation is needed at all levels in football, the lower leagues cannot always point to the 'greedy' Premier League clubs keeping all the money at the top when funds are funnelled to certain teams at this level.

This is where the independent regulators would work, they could and would work to find fair solutions, but we need them to be transparent in their work. Critics of the FA, UEFA and FIFA have argued that they have not always acted in football's best interests, and this is why Kieran's view is important to listen and understand, the commission in the wrong hands could do as much harm as they could do good.

Where regulation could provide instant relief is avoiding the next Bury FC incident, or Derby County, where an owner takes money from the football club and strips it of its assets. Stopping owners sell the stadiums to themselves in another one of their companies to circumnavigate Financial Fair Play for their clubs in a high stakes gamble to get their clubs promoted. As Tracey Crouch MP has discussed in Parliament, football clubs are the beating hearts of communities, if they are poorly managed and fail, it can mean jobs are lost and communities can lose millions in revenue from visiting fans.

Former Prime Minister Gordon Brown is the latest, but also the highest political figure to put his weight behind regulation in football after Premier League owners rejected claims the Premier League needed to be regulated. Speaking exclusively in a column in The Mail on Sunday, Brown believes the Premier League risks being destroyed by 'runaway GREED' if sweeping reforms are not imposed on English football. The former Prime Minister said professional football needs an independent regulator to scrutinise its club owners and prevent teams being 'destroyed' by the unscrupulous among them.

He also lent his support for a transfer tax in the Premier League and the ownership model that grants fans a 'golden share' in their club. Brown reviews Crouch's findings, highlighting his continuing concerns after owners of several Premier League clubs, notably Leeds United and Aston Villa, opposed key tenets of Tracey Crouch's review of the sport. Clubs outside the so-called 'top 6', these rejections included the following: the proposal for an independent regulator and a 10 per cent transfer levy, with clubs understood to prefer an oversight body that would remain within football's administrative structure.

Richard Masters, the Premier League chief executive, has also suggested that aspects of Crouch's review were too radical. 'The Premier League's implacable opposition to sensible reforms that will, for once, put the aspirations of the fans and grassroots football ahead of the greed of billionaire owners is yet another reason why it is time to seize an unparalleled opportunity to force through change,' writes Brown.

'Runaway greed, made possible by what often seems like a free-for-all in club ownership and poor overall supervision, is in danger of destroying the best football league in the world and all that is good about the game.' The government commissioned Crouch, the former sports minister, to chair the fan-led report in response to the flood of opposition to the European Super League proposals last spring. Six Premier League clubs signed up to plans that included no provision for relegation. Published in November, Crouch's review laid out 47 recommendations designed to safeguard the football pyramid and prevent the elite from attempting to distance themselves from the lower echelons again.

In this column, Brown says he agrees with most of the proposals. On the proposed levy on Premier League transfers, he explains that even a five per cent tax could generate £80 million for the grassroots game. He says fans should be granted a golden share in clubs, to prevent owners from imposing unwelcome decisions such as changing the team's name or leaving a stadium.

He also proposes a legislative change of his own, suggesting that the tax on gambling companies is increased from 15 per cent to 20 per cent, with the extra tens of millions generated from betting on football being reinvested in the game outside the Premier League. Crouch, the Conservative MP for Chatham and Aylesford, welcomed Brown's intervention and said her review had earned the widespread backing of politicians because mismanagement in elite football stretched back decades.

"There has been cross-party support for the report's recommendations and their urgent implementation, in part because there is universal recognition that politicians over the years have been let down by the football authorities who promised to reform themselves but then failed," she told The Mail on Sunday.

"This happened throughout the Blair/Brown era and continued post 2010. The former PM's support is a welcome recognition that the report recommends positive change that will continue to enable growth at the top of English football while supporting the rest of the pyramid and grassroots football." Nadine Dorries, the Culture Secretary, said the government endorsed the independent regulator 'in principle' and it is expected to pass into law.

Her office is working through the other conclusions in Crouch's report and is hoping to publish a substantive response in the spring. The government is also planning to publish a white paper based on a review of the gambling laws. It will address the betting industry's relationship with sport but whether it will set out a legislative change as radical as the one Brown has suggested remains to be seen.

For the former Prime Minister, however, only root-and-branch reform will ensure that the game's grassroots are not perilously cut adrift from the rich elite.

"Small clubs," he writes, "must not be neglected or starved. It is time to bring an end to the greed that has been disfiguring football. The profiteer owners have had it their own way for too long and they have ridden their gravy train for as far as they can, milking the fans at every single stop along the way. The proposals in the Crouch review will put the brakes on."

At the time of the review's publication, the Premier League said they would study its recommendations and work with stakeholders including the government, the FA, and fans on the issues it addressed. In response to Mail on Sunday's publication, they also highlighted their pledge to fund the wider football pyramid to the tune of £1.6billion over the next three years and the £3.6bn in tax which they and their clubs contributed to the economy in 2019–20.

We all await the Premier Leagues comment and action, failure and it would be down to Westminster and their desire to include it in legislation. But perhaps the real answer could lie in regulating the fans game, be a vote winning come election time.

One final thing I hope this book highlights is our love for the game and the transfer window can have a negative effect via online hate and people's mental health. More so than ever when England lost the Euro 2020 final to Italy on penalties. Jadon Sancho, Marcus Rashford and Bukayo Saka were racially abused for missing penalties in the shootout. Football is not doing enough to remove racism from its game, both from within, from online, and from the terraces.

False transfer rumours have also seen an increase in online hate. With club fans arguing over whether a player moving from X club to Y club is a step up. It is a side to the game which regularly rears its ugly head and one that football, and social media platforms don't do enough to tackle. Both players and fans should be able to enjoy the game of football without being abused for plying their trade. It would be my hope that any sort of regulation would have the power to enforce punishment of clubs and fans who hide behind social media profiles to inflict abuse. It should not be needed, but one where fans can call it out, block accounts, but sadly football is not able to escape this hatred.

We all need to do more to stop this kind of hatred. Here is hoping any sort of commission could do more than the current window dressing of tackling racism is doing. Football can be a healer, an escape for many, but it should be for everyone, for us to love and laugh, not used as a vehicle to spread hate, social media can be influenced to be a vehicle for hate, the transfer window and false rumours fuel this, but we as fans can stop this from further influencing the game we love.

From a transfer window point of view, it is unlikely that these potential positive moves would change clubs enduring a mad trolley dash on deadline day replicant of Christmas Eve or the January sales? But it could lead to a fairer, more transparent business. The transfer window is a living and breathing entity. Itself is a million-pound business even before a player is bought or sold. It provides hope for fans even before a ball is kicked, intrigues us and adapts over time. Long may it continue in the right way. A fair way. It would be a start, but certainly would not be the end of the improvements we could make.

Acknowledgements

Firstly, thank you for reading what has been a passion project of mine for a long time and a journey around the football leagues and into Europe. I would just like to thank you for reaching the end of the long journey that is writing the book and I would like to take the next few paragraphs thanking several individuals who have contributed and taken the time to be interviewed for this book.

To my publisher, Austin Macauley, for their support and guidance in bringing this passion project to life and maximising its potential. The everyday nature of the transfer window and ever-changing landscape has meant a number of chapters have been rewritten and updated as players have been bought and sold. Clubs have found new ways to offload costs, with Chelsea using the emerging Saudi Arabian football market to ensure the club starved off the FFP ticking clock their 2022 summer spending placed them under. I appreciate their support and acceptance of allowing chapters to be written during the production and editing process, including their ambition to have the book meet the potential market within football.

To my family, for their help, always being there and growing support to push me every step of the way in my screenwriting and career as an author. As one of my family attain, the first step is always the hardest one, just make sure you make it and if life keeps throwing you curves, lean into them and come out better on the other side.

To the fans who I have met out on the road, camped out on deadline day, or on the terraces in the stands. Thank you for providing an honest and raw view to how fans view the transfer window and what football really means to you.

To Tosh Farrell, for taking the time out from your coaching and your grass roots dedication to give opportunities to the next Wayne Rooney or Leah Williamson. Revealing to us what it is like to be part one of England's most successful academies and explain to readers how the system is changing over the years due to the transfer window.

I would also like to thank Alan Myers, for his time talking about the incarnation of the transfer window. Revealing what it is like for a Sky Sports reporter on transfer deadline day as the news and chaos begins to break, whilst we are sat at home in the warmth, watching on our televisions. Remember your scarf and thick coat if you are back out in the January transfer window in the North of England.

Mick Rathbone, for his enthusiasm to football, love of the game and taking time out from being a physio, to sit down and discuss how the transfer window affects the medical side of the football teams during the transfer window and how it's fast-paced nature adds stress to the medical teams racing to get the deals done, but most importantly, safely. As he said in his excellent book *The Smell of Football 2*, "it is nice to be important, but it is more important to be nice."

Kieran Maguire, thank you for sitting down for a chat on football finance in between lecturing students on football finance. Discussing transfers and breaking down the real financial cost to teams, what it means to the football clubs balance sheet, how transfers are paid for and an honest chat on what the future of football of football could behold as we come out of the Covid-19 pandemic.

Grace and her data analysis for providing significant information for the book and discussing her role in football and how data has transformed club recruitment in recent years. How it has now become a regular tool used for most clubs in their transfer strategy, but also how it will be used to analyse games in the future by football pundits when they analyse games.

Pep Lijnders, whilst I have used extracts from his book, the insight he has given football into how managers work behind the scenes, both in relation to tactics and transfers, has allowed fans to see how a football club is run daily. It has also allowed me to compare how a number of managers have recruited, but also coached in the past, it certainly should give an owner something to consider on who their next manager is and accept nothing less in the day-to-day preparation for their club. It allowed me to show you, as fans, insight on how players are scouted and dealt in the transfer market, and we could compare this to the hundreds of transfer rumours fans see in the press. Don't always believe what you see in the media is gospel truth. I don't think it will be long before Pep Lijnders is a manager himself, building his own team.

To the club secretary who gave us a glimpse into her life and the stressful nature of deadline day for the people who work in football. Giving us a peek behind the curtain of a day in the life of someone who a million-pound transfer hinges on and what last-minute changes to a transfer can have to the everyday person working in football clubs.

Lastly, thank you reader for purchasing and reading this passion project of mine. I hope it gave you an insight into the hidden nature of the transfer window, opened your eyes to how transfers are financed and why for some clubs, navigating the transfer window can bring as much heartache as it can bring success. I hope it has provided ways to see past the false stories and rumours that are likely to continue to plague certain aspects of the media as it has become entwined in their business model as Print media has rapidly declined and finally has given you fuel to continue the debates on football, the sport we all love to have as fans, because football is nothing without the fans. Football is like music, just when you think you have heard every note and melody there is to offer in every possible format, another classic anthem pops up. Here's to you, the fans, the ones who will always live and breathe the beautiful game.

Printed in Great Britain
by Amazon